Warrior to I

David K Brown

WARRIOR to DREADNOUGHT

WARSHIP DESIGN AND DEVELOPMENT 1860–1905

Seaforth PUBLISHING

Frontisepiece:
HMS *Caesar*, of the pre-dreadnought eight-ship *Majestic* class. (US Navy)

Copyright © David K Brown 1997

This edition first published in Great Britain in 2010 by
Seaforth Publishing,
Pen & Sword Books Ltd,
47 Church Street,
Barnsley S70 2AS

Reprinted 2014

www.seaforthpublishing.com

British Library Cataloguing in Publication Data
A catalogue record for this book is available from the British Library

ISBN 978 1 84832 086 4

First published by Chatham Publishing 1997

Typeset and designed by Tony Hart, Isle of Wight
Printed in China

Contents

Foreword and Acknowledgements

WARRIOR REPRESENTED the ultimate technology of 1860 but, in the next 45 years, her single screw, iron hull and thin, soft armour and her inefficient machinery were superseded by steel hulls, shaped by scientific experiment and driven by turbines, hardened steel armour and guns which could reach to the horizon. The theory of naval architecture had advanced to the point where every part was shaped and sized with understanding and usually by calculation rather than by judgement.

This book follows my earlier work *Before the Ironclad* and deals with developments in the design of the ship, including its protection and its engines, though it is not a full history of marine engineering; guns, their projectiles, and other weapons will be discussed only briefly in the light of their effect on the ship. The emphasis is on the development and application of innovative technology rather than on describing each and every ship in detail. A few tables of data are included for comparison but for full information the reader must turn to reference books such as *Conway's All the World's Fighting Ships 1860-1905*. The text will concentrate on the battleships which were usually the most advanced ships, although there was much of interest in the smaller classes where, sometimes, a new idea or a new type of engine would be tried first. In photograph captions, the date given for a ship is that of its launch, unless otherwise specified.

The text is, of course, the view of someone who has designed real ships and had experience in reconciling the conflicting views of individuals and of departments. I hope that, in consequence, my comments on the great designers will be sympathetic, understanding and only critical in the most proper sense. The most complete definition of 'Design' is that given by Fielden in 1963:

Engineering design is the use of scientific principles, technical information and imagination in the definition of a structure, machine or system to perform specified functions with the maximum economy and efficiency.

Creative ship design is the art of putting together many specialist technologies, of keeping many balls in the air at the same time. A designer will usually work with three parameters simultaneously whilst keeping some five or six more in mind. It is a team sport:

The Irregular Verb – 'To Design'.
I create,
You interfere,
He gets in the way,
We co-operate,
You obstruct,
They conspire – (written by the author whilst head of preliminary design)

A book can only give an imperfect description of design since each topic is dealt with in turn and hence the text must jump frequently from one subject to another. The treatment is roughly chronological but it will often be necessary to follow some particular topic to its end. Where appropriate, subtitles contain dates for the section.

The main issue for much of the period was stability, still not well understood today, which I have tried to explain painlessly using generalisations in the text and a slightly more detailed treatment in an appendix. The Royal Navy was not involved in a major war during the period of this book and there were few elsewhere involving large, modern fleets. The actions which did take place were studied carefully and these studies were supplemented by full-scale trials. Such studies and trials had a major influence on design and will be described in detail.

Good designs develop at the same time as the statement of the role – as the chicken and the egg – but a clear idea of the role of the ship was sadly lacking for much of the period, whilst funds were usually very scanty. As Admiral Fisher was to write:

Strategy should govern the types of ships to be designed. Ship design, as dictated by strategy, should govern tactics. Tactics should govern the details of armaments.

The Naval Defence Act provided the funds from 1897 and White, probably the greatest designer of all time and a superb manager, provided the ships and the organisation to build and support them. His first battleship design, *Royal Sovereign*, was a major advance and further refined in *Renown*. The similarity in style of his later ships concealed major advances in armour, guns and structure and the success of his ideas was demonstrated in the battles of the Russo-Japanese war. The loss

THE CHIEF NAVAL CONSTRUCTORS FROM 1544

SURVEYORS OF THE NAVY		
WILLIAM BROOKE 1544-1545	JOHN HOLLOND 1649-1652	
BENJAMIN GONSON 1545-1549	GEORGE PAYLER 1654-1660	
WILLIAM WYNTER 1549-1589	WILLIAM BATTEN 1660-1667	
HENRY PALMER 1589-1598	THOMAS MIDDLETON 1667-1672	
JOHN TREVOR 1598-1611	JOHN TIPPETTS 1667-1686	
RICHARD BINGLEY 1611-1618	ANTHONY DEANE 1686-1688	
THOMAS NORREY 1618-1625	JOHN TIPPETTS 1688-1692	
JOSHUA DOWNING 1625-1628	EDMUND DUMMER 1692-1699	
THOMAS AYLESBURY 1628-1632	DANIEL FURZER 1699-1715	
KENRICK EDISBURY 1632-1638	WILLIAM LEE 1706-1713	
WILLIAM BATTEN 1638-1648	JACOB E. ACWORTH 1715-1749	
WILLIAM WILLOUGHBY 1648-1649	JOSHUA ALLIN 1716-1755	

SURVEYORS OF THE NAVY	CHIEF CONSTRUCTORS
WILLIAM BATELY 1755-1765	ISAAC WATTS 1860-1863
THOMAS SLADE 1755-1771	EDWARD J. REED 1863-1870
JOHN WILLIAMS 1765-1784	**DIRECTORS OF NAVAL CONSTRUCTION**
EDWARD HUNT 1778-1784	NATHANIEL BARNABY 1870-1885 *
JOHN HENSLOW 1784-1806	WILLIAM H. WHITE 1885-1902
WILLIAM RULE 1793-1813	PHILIP WATTS 1902-1912
HENRY PEAKE 1806-1822	E.H.T. d'EYNCOURT 1912-1923
JOSEPH TUCKER 1813-1831	WILLIAM J. BERRY 1924-1930
ROBERT SEPPINGS 1813-1832	ARTHUR W. JOHNS 1930-1936
WILLIAM SYMONDS 1832-1848	STANLEY V. GOODALL 1936-1944
BALDWIN W. WALKER 1848-1860	CHARLES S. LILLICRAP 1944-1951
	VICTOR G. SHEPHEARD 1951-

of the *Victoria* led to improvements in watertight integrity.

The title of the chief designer changed several times: they were all great men.

Unless the title is important, I will generalise as the 'Director'. In most cases they made their reputation before reaching the top, in their mid-40s, credit for their contribution going to the then Director. However, the Director was responsible, shown very formally when he signed the building drawings. These great designers owed much to their staff and frequently failed to acknowledge such help. Where possible, I have tried to rescue these men from obscurity and show their contribution. I have also tried to record the achievements of engineers of other specialisations.

The naval officer of the period, and the Board of Admiralty in particular, are usually portrayed as reactionary, opposed to all new technology. This impression is discussed in the last chapter where it is suggested that it is only true, if at all, to a very limited extent. The enthusiast will always see any opposition or even a pause for thought as reaction and obstruction, as the author well knows from his own experience pushing the case for hovercraft and hydrofoils.

Comments based on the author's experience, with hindsight, will be found, mainly as footnotes. Ship design is fun; I have included a few incidents to justify that statement.

Acknowledgements

I am grateful to the following individuals for advice, material, helpful advice or criticism. Messrs J Brooks, J D Brown, J Campbell, A Holbrook, W J Jurens, Dr A Lambert, S A Lilliman, Dr A R J M Lloyd, D Lyon, G Maby, I McCallum, G Moore, Rear-Admiral R Morris, Dr J R Reckoner, J Roberts, A Smith, Professor J Sumida. I am grateful to the Bath Public Library, the Royal Institution of Naval Architects (Secretary J Rosewarn) and the libraries of Bath University, Washington Navy Yard and the Ministry of Defence and their staffs for tracing material. The late David Topliss, Guy Robbins and Graham Slatter of the Ships' Plans Department of the National Maritime Museum have made available the Ships' Covers which are such an important source and provided the plans.

The photographs were almost entirely selected from the author's own collection. That this is so comprehensive owes much to successive secretaries of the Naval Photograph Club, of which the author is Vice-President. The original source is acknowledged individually; in some cases, the original source is unknown and I apologise for any unwitting use of someone's material.

Introduction

THE POPULAR view of the latter half of the nineteenth century is of a peaceful world, dominated by an all-powerful Royal Navy, leaders in technology and supported by an increasingly prosperous nation. Whilst there is much truth in this view, each phrase needs some qualification. Until the Naval Defence Act of 1897 the Royal Navy was barely superior to that of France. It is usually thought that 1860 marked the high-water mark of British industrial supremacy and, from that date, this country was matched or even passed as, for example, in the French lead on many aspects of steel technology. This high-water mark was tragically emphasised by the deaths of three of the greatest engineers in 1859-60; Isambard Kingdom Brunel, Robert Stephenson and Joseph Locke. Though the wealth of the country was increasing rapidly, this was paralleled by an increase in the number of its inhabitants so that wealth per head was rising much less rapidly and few were disposed to pay for a large navy to defend against a distant and ill-defined threat. This chapter will outline the background to the naval technology which fills the rest of the book.

Comparison

In the first half of the century, differences between ships of different navies were small and a count of hulls and guns was sufficient for a comparison of material strength, though neglecting the all-important aspects of training and skill. By the late nineteenth century, developing and rapidly changing technologies made it difficult to compare the fighting capability of new ships whilst it was virtually impossible to value the capability of older ships, sliding rapidly into obsolescence. A few tables of comparison are included, more to show what was believed at the time, than with any belief in their absolute truth. Armour is usually compared on a basis of its maximum thickness with little mention of its extent in relation to the vitals of the ship (and what was vital?) or of its quality. Exercises were held in the sum-

Warrior entering Portsmouth Harbour on 16 June 1987, after 8 years' restoration work by the Maritime Trust in Hartlepool. She is the only surviving British warship of her era. (Author's collection)

9

National income and population 1861-1901

Date	GNP, £m current price	GNP £m const. price	Population million	GNP per head
1861	668	565	23.1	24.4
1871	917	782	26.1	29.9
1881	1051	1079	29.7	36.2
1891	1288	1608	33.0	48.5
1901	1643	1948	37.1	52.5

mer months and the importance of seakeeping was greatly underestimated, whilst reports from sea were often expressed in imprecise terms which made comparison difficult. The lengthy building times, particularly in France, and the frequent cancellations, made it hard to forecast the magnitude of tomorrow's threat.

Wealth and budgets

There is a widespread impression that Victorian governments funded the Royal Navy very generously. Expenditure on the Navy and its ships in particular can only be judged against a background of the wealth of the nation. The figures in the table above show that though the total wealth of the nation (Gross National Product or GNP) was growing rapidly over the whole period covered by this book, the increase in population meant that only in the later years did income per head increase rapidly, partly due to a fall in average prices of about 25 per cent.

The view that naval funding was generous is quite incorrect in the early years and only true to a limited extent in the final years, as is made clear in the following lengthy extract from a paper by White.[1]

1. Sir William H White, RCNC, 'Presidential Address', *Proc ICE*, Vol CLV (London 1904). (A key reference – See Review of Sources.)

Parliamentary returns, which few people consult, give the expenditure on new construction, for each financial year, from 1869-70 onwards. From this record it can be seen that, from 1870-85, the average annual expenditure on new ships was under 1¾ millions sterling. From 1885 to 1 April 1902 (17 years), the total expenditure on new ships was about 88½ millions sterling, the annual average being nearly 5¼ millions. For the last seven years during which I held office, the total expenditure on new ships exceeded 50 millions; the average was £7,200,000 annually, and the maximum (1900-01) nearly 9 millions.

This large expenditure, of course, involved the extensive employment of the great private firms, while the Royal Dockyards contributed no small share. For the Dockyards the real measure of expenditure is the cost of labour expended on new construction; since private firms furnish the materials, machinery, armour and other items which are combined into the ships. On this basis it is probably near the truth to say that out of the 88½ millions spent between 1885 and 1902 the dockyards expended about one-sixth, and the balance – say 74 millions – fell to the share of the great private establishments of steel and armour plate manufacturers, shipbuilders, marine and mechanical engineers, timber merchants and other industries. Out of the whole sum expended probably more than 60 millions was spent on labour.

The capital value of the Fleet has been enormously increased by recent additions, not merely by the number of ships built but by the great growth in the cost of individual ships consequent upon increase in size, speed and fighting capability. Taking the combatant ships of the British Navy, their total first costs have been represented about the following at the respective periods: – 1813, ten millions sterling; 1860, seventeen to eighteen millions; 1868, a somewhat higher figure; 1878, about twenty-eight millions; 1887, thirty-seven millions; 1902, one hundred millions. Guns and ammunition are not included. The value of the French national Fleet in 1870 was put at about 18½ millions sterling, and in 1898 at 47¼ millions; a great increase but a slower rate of growth than that of the Royal Navy.

White went on to show that this larger fleet implied further expenditure on dockyards and other infrastructure, discussed later. Detailed figures, supporting White's view, are given in Appendix 1 and summarised in the diagram opposite. It should be noted that there was little inflation or deflation over this long period and hence money values did not change appreciably.

It was generally believed that size and cost of warships were directly linked – true only in part – and hence economy-minded politicians frequently imposed a limit on the size of individual ships. They also looked for the cheap 'wonder ship' solution, reaching a tragic conclusion in the *Captain*.

Distribution of the Fleet 1860

In 1860 the Royal Navy was undergoing two transformations; on the one hand, the first four iron-hulled

Distribution of the Fleet 1860 (sailing ships omitted)

Area	Battleships	Frigates	Paddle Frigates	Corvettes	Others
Mediterranean	13	3	1	2	18
Channel	10	3	-	-	1
Cape & W Africa	-	2	1	2	-
North America	1	-	1	2	12
S America	-	1	1	-	3
Pacific	-	4	-	3	8
E Indies, China	-	2	4	-	47
Australia	-	-	-	1	3

armoured ships were under construction, whilst on the other there were still a large number of sailing ships in service. Indeed, the flagships of both the Cape and Pacific stations were sailing line of battle ships.

In reserve there were some twenty-five screw battleships, eleven block ships etc, eleven screw frigates and a very large number of smaller craft, mainly gun vessels and gunboats of the Crimean War.

The main fleet was in the Mediterranean where the French had ten screw battleships, three screw and two paddle frigates and many smaller vessels. Note the size and composition of the China squadron with a large number of gunboats for riverine operations. Though there were a number of 68pdr guns in service, the majority were 32pdrs of various sizes. In all the Channel Fleet mounted 1055 guns and the Mediterranean Fleet 1597 guns (these totals include guns on sailing ships).

Technical developments

Wood construction was nearing its end for big ships in 1860 but was to be retained for many years in unarmoured ships because of the uncertain behaviour of wrought iron against gunshot and because of the difficulty in preventing fouling on iron hulls. Eventually, both wood and iron gave way to steel when reliable material became available, by which date the loading on a ship in a seaway was understood and applied in calculating the scantlings. For nearly 20 years, the fuel consumption of simple expansion engines was so high that sails were essential for ocean passages and, even later, when the compound engine had made sail unnecessary in major ships, coaling stations were so few in distant seas that sail was retained in many cruising ships. Copper sheathing, for all its difficulties and cost, was essential to maintain the performance of ships serving in tropical waters until the end of the century when effective anti-fouling paints became available.

The battle between guns and armour was a central problem. In the earlier years, this was simply the contest between ever-bigger guns and ever-thicker armour but from the mid-1870s there were new materials for both armour and guns – and for their projectiles. The arrangement and mounting of guns on the broadside, in turrets or in barbettes was debated with great acrimony. The thickest armour could only be applied to a limited area of the battleship and, in the remainder of the ship, the emphasis had to be on damage limitation. Many cruisers and smaller ships had no belt armour at all but were given a very sophisticated protective deck system. Wars were infrequent, though what lessons there were, were studied carefully, and the effectiveness of weapons and protection was tested in many full-scale trials. Before the Official Secrets Act, many trial results were published and openly discussed. Comparisons between ships of different navies are difficult because there is no easy measure of the effectiveness of their protection but

this difficulty was recognised and the Admiralty did the best they could.

The detail phase of ship design changed from being an art to a science with most of the major advances occurring in a very short period around 1870. Rules of thumb and guesswork were superseded by calculation and model testing, so that ships would float at their design draft and reach their design speed without costly excess. Much of the credit must go to Edward Reed, the Chief Constructor, who himself made important contributions but who also encouraged his staff and both accepted and sponsored work from outside the Admiralty, notably from William Froude on rolling, resistance, hull form and propeller design. New theories of stability were proved correct by the tragic loss of *Captain*, though still misunderstood today by many writers – and readers. In particular, a 'stable ship' may mean one which heels only slightly under an off-centre load, one which is unlikely to capsize – which may be different – or a ship with an easy roll; different again. These advances in the design process itself were linked to the high standard of education provided by the Admiralty for their naval architects and marine engineers. The latter were among the leaders in adopting compound engines, triple-expansion engines, water tube boilers and the turbine. In later years, metallurgy became of increasing importance in armour, machinery and many other components – and naval architecture students studied the subject for twice as long as other engineers.

Progress from *Warrior* to *Dreadnought* was steady, despite a few setbacks, and rapid – even adventurous – and with rare exceptions, ahead of all other navies.

The upper curve shows the total figure for Navy Estimates in millions of pounds. The lower curve shows money for new shipbuilding; the sum of Vote 6 and Vote 10 up to 1887, Vote 8 in later years. (There was a change in definition of Vote 6 in 1865 which makes the earlier not quite comparable.) Actual figures are given in Appendix 1 together with some qualifications.

Navy Estimates 1860 – 1905
Total and Shipbuilding (Vote 6 and 10, later Vote 6)

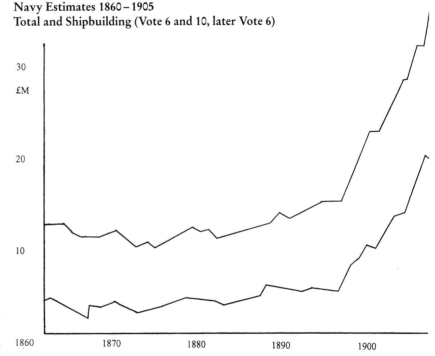

One | Broadside Batteries

IN ALMOST all aspects of technology, the *Warrior* was evolutionary rather than revolutionary,[1] her hull shape and structure were typical of good practice of the day, her engines were the well-proven Penn trunk design, while the majority of her numerous guns were smoothbore muzzle-loaders, arranged in a long battery extending over much of her length. Only in her armour was there a major advance over previous ships. What made her truly novel was the way in which these individual aspects were blended together, making her the biggest and most powerful warship in the world and, in this sense, one may even feel that her major advance was psychological; for the first time naval officers, naval architects, politicians and gunners realised that new ships did not have to be similar to their predecessors with only slight improvements. Change would now be rapid.

The design team

Warrior was a success, despite a few shortcomings which will be discussed, and that success was largely due to four men. Sir Baldwin Wake Walker had been appointed Surveyor in early 1848, changing his title to Controller in 1859. He had been a fine seaman and was trusted by the Service, whilst his tact and understanding did much to heal the feud with naval architects caused by his predecessor, Symonds. He seems to have been a capable and conspicuously honest administrator, liked and trusted by politicians, with the exception of the Prime Minister, Lord Derby, and the Chancellor, Disraeli, with whom he had clashed in a previous administration. His role differed considerably from that of a modern Controller as he was largely responsible for setting the requirements for new ships such as speed, number and type of guns etc, a task now carried out by the naval staff. In technical matters he was a progressive conservative who could see – and act – when the time for change had come. He had led the Navy through one major technical revolution, the introduction of the steam, screw-propelled, wooden battleship and the many technical developments of the Crimean War.

The design of the *Warrior* was the responsibility of Isaac Watts, a shadowy figure. He was born in Plymouth in 1797[2] and became a student at the School of Naval Architecture in 1814. He seems to have been a foreman at Portsmouth for many years (probably 1833-47), becoming Master Shipwright at Sheerness on 12 May 1847 before being brought to the Admiralty as Assistant Surveyor (senior naval architect) on 4 May

Warrior arriving at Portsmouth in 1987 after restoration. (HMS *Warrior* (1860) Trust)

1848, overlapping for some time with his distinguished predecessor, John Edye. As part of the 1859 re-organisation he became Chief Constructor of the Navy. It is clear that he was an autocrat[3] and had little use for consultation. Technically, he was not a true innovator but in his big wooden frigates, in *Warrior* and, later, in his early turret ships (Chapter 3) he was willing and able to press contemporary technology beyond its accepted limits. He did acknowledge the contribution of Baldwin Walker, of Thomas Lloyd (Chief Engineer) and, unusually, of his own assistant, Joseph Large, in the design of *Warrior*. Lloyd's outstanding contribution to the machinery and propulsion systems of the Navy has already been discussed in an earlier book[4] and his later work appears in following chapters.

The building drawings for *Warrior* were signed by Large. Then, as now, the signing of these drawings was a significant event, marking the formal acceptance by the Director of responsibility for the design. It may be that Large had to sign because Watts was ill but this signature together with Watts' unusual tribute, mentioned above, may imply that Large's contribution to *Warrior* was greater than has been recognised.[5] One should not forget the importance of the political backing for *Warrior* from the First Lord, Packington and the Political Secretary, Corry.[6]

Warrior's machinery

The Committee on Marine Engines examined, in 1860, the contractual and technical activities of the Engineer-in-Chief and found it satisfactory. There had been complaints that engine building for the Navy had been restricted to a small number of Thames works but the Committee accepted the evidence of the Controller and of Lloyd that engine builders were selected on a basis of their record of cost and reliability and of the skill and experience of their current staff. They reported that naval machinery had to satisfy different requirements from those of merchant ships and set out these requirements as;

The machinery should be arranged entirely below the waterline.

Engines should be simple in construction as far as was consistent with efficiency.

All parts of the engine must be readily and easily accessible so as to be easily removed and replaced when required.

The Committee recognised the value of using steam at higher pressure and temperature but thought that there was then no way of using these conditions reliably. They recommended the Penn trunk engine for higher powers, whilst for lower powers they suggested the return piston rod engine introduced by Humphrys[7] and later made by Penn and Maudslay as well.

Warrior's machinery was typical of the best engineering practice of the day.[8] She had ten smoke tube, box boilers built of wrought iron with brass tubes, experience having shown that the problems from galvanic action were less than those due to the corrosion of iron tubes. The boilers were water tested to 40lbs/sq in and the safety valves were set at 22lbs/sq in though in service they were normally[9] operated at 15lbs/sq in. Each boiler contained 17 tons of sea water at working level.

Steam was delivered to the twin-cylinder, double-acting, single-expansion trunk engine through a condensate separator and this engine drove a single shaft and propeller. Steam cut-off to the cylinder could be varied over a wide range by a link mechanism on the valve gear. All valves needed for the operation of the engine and its condenser could be worked from the starting platform over the condenser. There was a small 'donkey' engine which could work a bilge pump, the firemain and hoist ash buckets to the upper deck for ditching. This engine also worked ventilation fans which kept the gun deck at a slightly increased pressure so that smoke would be blown out through the gunports, one of many ingenious novelties in this ship.

Particulars of the engine

Cylinder bore	112in	
Trunk dia	41in	
Stroke	48in	
Total weight	898 tons	ihp /ton 5.67
Floor area sq ft/ihp	0.78	Cost £/ihp 13.6

Warrior's engine-room complement was ninety-five officers and men. Once a few teething troubles had been overcome, her machinery proved very reliable. During her service with the Channel Fleet she covered 51,000 miles and a further 36,000 whilst in First Reserve. While in the Channel Fleet she spent 36 per cent of her time at sea under steam alone, a further 42 per cent with both sail and steam and only 22 per cent under sail alone. During normal cruising she would run at 25-30 rev/min with either four or six boilers working, giving roughly half full speed.

All fuel consumption figures for this era varied considerably with the quality of coal, accuracy of measurement, fouling, sea state and, most important, the experience of the engineers and the figures in the table are good average values.

Warrior's coal consumption

No. Boilers	Speed (kts)	Coal (tons/hr)
4	11	3.5
6	12	4.5
10	14.5	9.0

1. D K Brown, *Before the Ironclad* (London 1990).

2. I am indebted to Mr A R Henwood, whose grandfather, a Master Shipwright, married Isaac Watts' daughter, Emmeline, in 1862, for new material on the life of Isaac Watts. He was probably the Isaac Watts baptised on 31 July 1797 at How Street Baptist Church. Watts died at Broadstairs on 12 October 1876.

3. Some examples are given in *Before the Ironclad*.

4. Brown, *Before the Ironclad*.

5. Joseph Large entered the School of Naval Architecture in 1822, graduating seven years later. By 1834 he was acting Foreman at Sheerness showing that promotion of graduates from the School could be quite rapid, for the position of Foreman in a Royal Dockyard was greatly superior to that of men styled foreman in a commercial yard. By 1849 he was Assistant Master Shipwright at Sheerness and later at Woolwich, moving to the Admiralty in 1858 as Assistant Surveyor, changing title to Constructor in 1859, retiring in 1864. In 1861 he became a Vice-President of the newly formed Institution of Naval Architects. He died on 21 May 1875

6. A Lambert, *Warrior* (London 1987).

7. Like most Thames engine-builders, he was trained at the Admiralty's Woolwich Steam Factory still visible near Woolwich Dockyard Station.

8. Rear-Admiral J C Warsop and R J Tomlin, 'HMS *Warrior* 1860 – A Study of Machinery Installation, Operation and Performance', *Trans I Mar E*, (London 1991). This paper contains a great deal of information on *Warrior's* machinery which was not previously available.

9. It should be recognised that most reference books quote boiler pressure as the safety valve setting and that the working pressure was usually considerably less.

The boiler room of *Warrior* as restored. (HMS *Warrior* (1860) Trust)

10. J Scott Russell, comments on A Holt, 'A review of the progress of steam shipping during the last quarter of a century', *Trans ICE* (London 1877). A classic on merchant shipping.

11. This passage and later sections on machinery are based on a series of articles: D K Brown, 'Marine Engineering in the RN, 1860-1905', *Journal of Naval Engineering* (1993-4). Though classified, most issues of the *Journal* may be obtained through the British Library or the Science Museum Library.

12. D K Brown and A R J M Lloyd, 'Seakeeping and Added Weight', *Warship 1993* (London 1993).

13. Evidence to the 1871 Committee on Design.

14. Probably about 23-28kts wind speed and 6½-7½ft wave height

15. Roll angles were usually quoted out to out rather than one way only as now.

16. Committee on the Design of Ships of War. Parliamentary papers 1871. (hereafter referenced as '1871 Committee'), evidence of Vice-Admiral Sir Thomas Symonds, C-in-C Channel fleet, December 1868–June 1870.

17. Submission to Board of 27 July 1858, quoted Lambert, *Warrior*, p16.

18. J Scott Russell, *The Fleet of the Future in 1862* (London 1862).

19. D K Brown, *A Century of Naval Construction* (London 1983).

20. Naval Estimates 1867.

It should be appreciated that fuel consumption was not seen as very important since coal only cost £0.8 per ton in home waters and £1.5 in the Mediterranean. As Scott Russell said (of merchant ships), 'The fuel cost is so little that I do not care so long as one man is enough to put it in. If I required two men to put it in, I should have to economise.'[10] With fuel consumption at this level, sails were essential for ocean passages.

Several changes were made during her 1874 refit, as well as making good some defects. The valves were modified to give an earlier cut-off, making more use of the expansion of the steam, and new boilers were installed with superheaters to reduce the carry-over of water. Such superheaters were in common use until about 1870, more to reduce the amount of water carried over, which could cause priming, than to improve efficiency.[11]

Shortcomings

Though Watts and Lloyd had got most things right in the design of *Warrior*, it is hardly surprising that, in such a novel concept, there was room for improvement. The heavy knee bow was there purely for appearance and added 40 tons right forward; particularly surprising since the armour had been stopped short of bow and stern as it was believed that weights near the end

increased pitching. This seems to have been a long-standing belief, reinforced by Froude's theory of motion in waves, but it was not until big computers became available that such effects could be quantified. In fact, practical changes in weight distribution have virtually no effect on pitching.[12]

Accounts differ concerning *Warrior*'s seakeeping but that of her first captain, the Hon A A Cochrane, may be reliable. He said[13] that she could make 10-10.5kts against a gale Force 8 and sea equivalent to 'strong double reefed topsail' wind[14] and 3.25-4kts against very heavy seas. Against a Force 8 she took in no seas at all but the sea was not proportional to the wind and there was a fair amount of spray. Cochrane said that she had carried out target practice rolling 23° with water coming into the ports.[15] Admiral F Warden in his report on the 1866 manoeuvres said that *Warrior* broached frequently when running at 8kts with the screw down with a strong breeze on the quarter.

The lack of armour at the ends was less serious than many contemporaries believed, since the ends were well subdivided and even if both ends were flooded the draught would only increase by 26in. The lack of protection to the steering gear was more serious, although it was a small target and not likely to be hit. However, the unprotected broadside guns outside the armoured battery were a bad feature.

Warrior was considered to be good under sail when she first went to sea but experience seems to have shown problems. Admiral Symonds[16] said in 1871 that *Warrior* and *Black Prince* could make a passage under sail by themselves but could not keep in company, 'they cannot put the helm up with effect; if they do, they do not go off for two to three minutes, they go from one line to another . . . they are not under command'. The sailing of early armoured ships is considered a little later but Symonds' views apply generally to *Warrior* and later ships.

Cheaper ships, 1859

To the Government, *Warrior*'s biggest shortcoming was her cost of £264,664 contract price, £377,292 as completed, compared with £135-176,000 for a *Duncan* class wooden steam two-decker and this was exacerbated by Walker's suggestion that the new ships were additional to the battlefleet rather than replacing it.[17] Shortly after *Warrior* was ordered, in June 1859, the Duke of Somerset became First Lord with Lord Clarence Paget as his Political Secretary and they decided to build smaller armoured ships, laid down in December 1859 (see table opposite).

Defence and her sister *Resistance* were armoured in similar style to *Warrior*, with the ends of both the battery and waterline unprotected. They introduced the ram bow and, for some time, were known as steam rams. They were also given double topsails, then common on merchant ships to reduce the number of men needed to work aloft but adding 6 tons of weight high up. Further ease in handling was intended by fitting Cunningham roller reefing but it was found that this was unsatisfactory on heavy, wet canvas and they were soon converted to conventional single topsails. *Resistance* was to make an important contribution to naval development as a trials ship (Chapter 6) but otherwise they achieved little.

The most serious fault with the *Defence* was her speed, inferior to many wooden battleships, and this was increased in *Hector* and *Valiant* of 1861 which were also given full-length armour at battery level though the ends of the waterline were still unprotected.

These four ships were unsatisfactory but it should be possible to sympathise with a Board of Admiralty who were trying to make their limited budget stretch as far as possible; the argument between quantity and quality remains unsolved today and certainly they hardly deserve the ridicule poured on them by Scott Russell[18] and others. They could easily deal with an unarmoured wooden battleship, although the slow first pair might have difficulty in forcing action, but they were not capable of dealing with a *Gloire*. The cost per gun is a crude measure but it does show that their limited effectiveness was expensive. Can anyone doubt that two *Warriors* could defeat three *Defences*? The active life of these early broadside ships ended about 1872 by which time the 12in, 35-ton gun was in service which could pierce 14in of iron at 1000yds.

Achilles, problems solved (ld 1861)

The *Achilles* was laid down before *Warrior* went to sea but most of the latter's shortcomings had already been recognised and corrected. Her battery was entirely protected by 4½in armour and the waterline belt, 13ft deep, was extended to the ends though only at 2½in thickness. She mounted four of the unsatisfactory 110pdr BL on the upper deck and sixteen of the new 100pdr SB Somerset guns (muzzle-loaders) in the battery to which six 68pdrs were added in 1865. She had a blunt ram bow and a rounded stern intended to protect the steering gear.

Achilles was the first iron ship built in a Royal Dockyard. The Master Shipwright at Chatham was Oliver Lang, son of the Oliver Lang who designed so many early steam warships, and he hired a number of North Country boilermakers to help in the unfamiliar task. They saw themselves as irreplaceable and went on strike for more pay. Lang sacked them all and gave the job to the shipwrights who, in the Dockyards, to this day, carry out the metal work which commercial yards entrusted to boilermakers. *Achilles* was built in dry dock and this, too, was a success for Lang.[19] She took about three years to build which compared very favourably with the more experienced private yards.

Initially, she was fully rigged on four masts but the

foremast and bowsprit were removed in 1865 which still left her unsatisfactory. The foremast was then moved forward 25ft and the bowsprit replaced, giving a total sail area of 30,133sq ft. She became a barque in 1877. *Achilles* was highly regarded and only retired from seagoing service in 1885, long after *Warrior* had been put to rest. Admiral Warden's report of August 1867 on recent exercises praised *Achilles* highly and, in forwarding this report to Parliament,[20] Spencer Robinson noted that *Achilles* was praised 'for qualities of which I am so largely responsible'.

Diminutives

Ship	Cost (£)	Speed (kts)	Disp (tons)	Guns	Cost £/gun
Warrior	377,292	14	9137	26-68pdr, 10-110pdr	10.5
Defence	252,422	10.75	6070	10-68pdr, 8-110pdr	14
Hector	294,000	12.6	6710	16-110pdr, 2-8in RML	16

Top: Defence 1861. An unsuccessful diminutive of Warrior. (Imperial War Museum: Q40591)

Lower: Valiant 1863, a little faster than Defence but still not value for money. (Imperial War Museum: Q40602)

Above: Achilles building at Chatham c1862. Working for the first time on an iron ship, the shipwrights did a good job – and quickly too. (Author's collection)

Above right: Achilles, 1863, under sail. (Author's collection)

British and French building programmes to 1868

Ironclads launched or converted (cumulative)

Year	Britain	France
1859	-	1
1860	1	1
1861	4	5
1862	9	5
1863	12	8
1864	15	12
1865	17	15
1866	18	15
1867	18	15
1868	19	15[21]

The French ships were steady developments from *Gloire* and did not differ greatly in technical aspects, except for *Magenta* and *Solferino* which were the only two-decker, broadside ships.[22] The great majority had wooden hulls with a limited life and making it impossible to provide effective watertight subdivision. *Courronne*, designed by M. Audenet, was ordered at the same time as *Gloire*

giving her some claim to be the first iron-hulled battleship but she took a long while to build, completing in 1862, well after *Warrior*.

The last British new construction ships of this style were the *Minotaur*s which were overgrown versions of *Achilles*. There were designed as 50-gun ships with 5½in armour over the battery and 4½in ends. The fore end of the battery had a 5½in bulkhead which was extended to bulwark level to protect the chase guns. At 400ft they were the longest single-screw battleships and handled badly even when *Northumberland* was completed with the first steam steering gear in 1868. *Minotaur* spent her first 18 months trying various rigs, all with five masts, and none was very satisfactory.

Northumberland[23] was modified by Reed, the new Chief Constructor, whilst building and completed with a shorter battery mounting fewer, heavier guns (four 9in, twenty-two 8in, two 7in MLR), foreshadowing the centre battery ships described in the next chapter. These three ships were quite successful but it is not unfair to suggest that their design was a blind alley.

The wooden ships were mainly conversions of uncompleted hulls of the *Duncan*s and were the equal of the French ships. When designs were invited for *Warrior* it was recognised that a wooden hull had to be armoured for the whole length, as it was impossible to give such a flexible structure efficient subdivision by bulkheads and hence even *Royal Oak*, the first British wooden ironclad, was so armoured.[24] The last four conversions were delayed and completed as centre battery ships as were the two new construction ships (see Chapter 2). These conversions were cheaper than new construction ships and could be produced quickly using Dockyard resources not then available for iron construction. They were capable fighting ships but their service life was short, of the order of seven years.[25] The concentrated weights and the vibration from engines

21. Britain: 1860 *Warrior**, 1861 *Black Prince**, *Defence**, *Resistance**, 1862 *Hector**, *Prince Consort*, *Caledonia*, *Ocean*, *Royal Oak*, 1863 *Valiant**, *Achilles**, *Minotaur**, 1864 *Royal Alfred*, *Zealous*, *Lord Clyde*, 1865 *Lord Warden*, *Agincourt**, 1866 *Northumberland**, 1868 *Repulse*. France: 1859 *Gloire*, 1860 *Normandie*, 1861 *Invincible*, *Couronne**, *Magenta*, *Solferino*, 1863 *Provence*, *Savoie*, *Heroine**, 1864 *Flandre*, *Valeureuse*, *Magnanime*, *Surveillance*, 1865 *Gauloise*, *Guyenne*, *Revanche*.*

Iron hull. Omitted – *Research*, *Enterprise*, *Favourite*, *Rochambeau* as not battleships.

22. These ships had unarmoured ends at battery level and are sometimes said to be centre battery ships. However, their large number of guns show that they are properly seen as of the earlier style while the lack of armoured bulkheads made them very vulnerable to raking fire.

23. She was said to be the first ship in which the armour was made entirely by rolling. That for earlier ships had been formed by a mixture

of rolling and hammering: C E Ellis, 'Armour for Ships', *Trans INA* (London 1911). There was considerable discussion on this point but the note above seems the most likely.

24. The purist will argue that 'ironclad' should only refer to wooden hulls clad with iron.

25. In a time of rapid change, the Controller was to argue that short life was an advantage!

26. G A Ballard, *The Black Battlefleet* (London 1980).

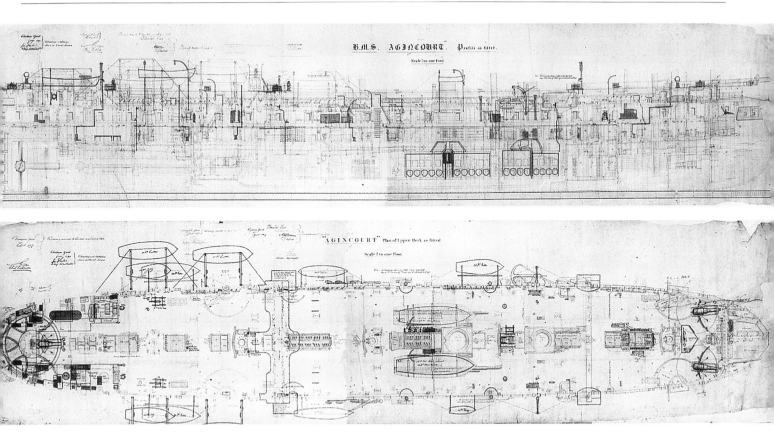

Agincourt 1865. These plans clearly show the great length – 407ft – of this ship and her sisters. This length was necessary to arrange the long broadside battery with four 9in and twenty-four 7in MLR. Since virtually the whole of the side was armoured, it had to be relatively thin (5½in, 4½in ends). The complicated racers for the bow and stern chasers are clearly shown, but it was difficult to use them in a seaway. The large number of boats may be seen as part of the armament since landing operations were quite frequent in the mid-nineteenth century and boarding was still contemplated. (National Maritime Museum, London: 7386, 7387)

and from a propeller behind a bluff hull soon loosened every joint. Martin's shell, a hollow iron sphere filled with molten iron, would have been very effective against the unarmoured upperworks of all wooden-hulled ironclads.

On completion, *Prince Consort* was sheathed with copper in normal fashion for a wooden hull but it was found that galvanic action was causing very rapid corrosion of the lower strake of armour. The copper was removed and replaced with Muntz metal,[26] with much inferior anti-fouling properties and this was used on all wooden-hulled armoured ships.

Trade protection and lessons of the American Civil War, 1861-65

The war on trade, the blockade of the Confederacy by the Union Navy, had a major, perhaps decisive, effect on the result of the American Civil War. During the war the Union Navy captured 1149 blockade runners (210 steamers) and destroyed another 335 (85 steamers). Clearly, the success of the blockade discouraged a much larger number of shippers from even trying to trade.

The blockade was not totally effective but the highly-publicised success of a few blockade runners did little to help the economy of the South.

Royal Oak 1862, a wooden battleship armoured while building. (Imperial War Museum: Q41002)

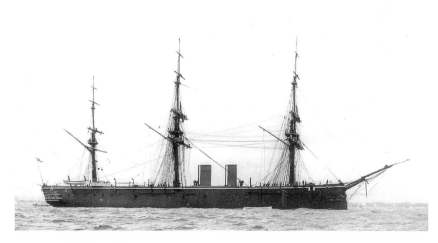

Inconstant 1868. A very big and very expensive frigate, she was probably the fastest ship in the world at the time. (Imperial War Museum: Q21380)

Commerce raiding by the Confederacy using a small number of warships and a larger number of privateers caused a considerable number of losses and led to a large number of transfers to other flags. This campaign is worthy of study as an indication of what might have happened to the British merchant marine under a similar attack. Overall, the Confederates captured 261 ships of which only two were steamships.[27] The effect on Union shipping was much greater as many ships were laid up, others were taken up by the Union Navy and many were sold or transferred to other flags. Transfers to the British flag were:

Transfers to British flag

Year	No. ships	Tonnage
1861	126	71,673
1862	135	74,578
1863	348	252,579
1864	106	92,052

Total 715 ships of nearly half a million tons.

These figures were a major factor in the decline of the seagoing US merchant fleet from 2.4 million tons in 1860 to 1.3 million in 1870 with corresponding benefit

Successes of Confederate cruisers[28]

Ship	Built	Captures etc	Fate
Sumter	Philadelphia	18	Sold to avoid capture
Florida	Liverpool	37 + 21*	Seized, 'accidentally' sunk by USN
Alabama	Birkenhead	64	Sunk
Georgia	Bordeaux	Nil	Captured
Rappahanock	London	Nil	Ex RN *Victor*
Tallahassee	London	39	Seized in UK, handed to USN
Shenandoah	Glasgow	30	Seized after war

* Captured by tenders – earlier prizes. The activities of privateers are not fully documented.[29]

to the British merchant navy. There were other factors; US building before the war was mainly of sailing ships constructed from soft wood. After the war it was found more profitable to deploy the output of iron mills and engine builders into the development of the West whilst there was a diminishing demand for sailing ships.

There were a number of lessons to be learnt from the activities of the Confederate cruisers. Their activities were worldwide; *Alabama* cruised the Atlantic and Indian Oceans whilst *Florida* covered the Pacific. Coal supplies presented few problems, as it could be taken from prizes or purchased at acquiescent 'neutral' ports. Few countries were prepared to enforce the rules on neutrality, particularly that limiting a belligerent ship to a 24-hour stop. At the end of the war, the UK had to pay $15 million damages, mainly as a result of the *Alabama*, built in England during the war.

Raiders were very difficult to find before there were many overseas cables; it is said that from 1 January 1863 the Union Navy employed seventy-seven warships and twenty-three chartered vessels searching for these raiders.[30] It should be noted that the USA had not signed the Treaty of Paris, 1856, which attempted to set rules for war on trade (Appendix 2).

Inconstant and trade protection (ld 1866)

In 1863 the US Navy ordered a class of six[31] high-speed cruisers which the Secretary of the Navy said were to 'sweep the ocean, and chase and hunt down the ships of an enemy'.[32] Since the United Kingdom was the most likely enemy, the potential threat was taken very seriously – perhaps too seriously. The *Wampanoag* and her sisters entirely failed to live up to expectations. *Wampanoag* herself and a sister engined by Isherwood were very fast making over 17kts on trial.[33] However, it is claimed that there was ⅝in wear on the wooden gear wheels during the first voyage, coal[34] was only enough for three days at speed and the lines were so fine that a chase gun could not be mounted, a serious flaw in a ship designed as a commerce raider.

The British response was planned by the Controller (1861-71), Vice-Admiral Robert Spencer Robinson KCB, FRS[35] who had one of the best brains of any Victorian admiral. In particular, he was one of the few who realised the need for proper strategic and tactical thinking from which the role and hence the characteristics of ships would derive. In his lengthy evidence to the 1871 Design Committee he said, 'Before I come to any absolute opinion I like to make calculations and experiments and then derive the best conclusion I can'. This broad thinking was alien to the Admiralty of the day and his views would not have been easy to put across but his personality made this even more difficult as he did not suffer fools gladly and, with the exception of Reed[36] (Chief Constructor), he saw most of his colleagues and staff as fools.

Spencer Robinson gave his views on trade protection and the need for big, fast frigates in evidence to the 1871 Committee on Design. He saw that the threat to trade came from two classes of raider, warships which would drive off our cruisers and privateers which would pick up everything which came their way. Fast and heavily armed warships (*Inconstant*) could not be armoured but must be excellent seaboats. However, the cost would be great and not all powers could afford such ships (France built two) and most navies built slower, cheaper ships such as *Volage*. Sloops such as *Druid* were fast enough to catch any privateer. This statement from Spencer Robinson is amongst the clearest on trade protection but he leaves it unclear how these three classes of ship should operate. He appears to be thinking of a convoy with the frigate driving off warship raiders and sloops taking on the privateers but he then goes on to oppose convoys as impractical for steam merchant ships.

The design of the *Inconstant*, which was approved on 26 April 1866, presented a number of difficult problems to the new Chief Constructor, Edward Reed.[37] She was to be fast; Reed told the Committee, 'The promised speed of *Inconstant* was 15kts, the realised speed was 16.5kts and the expected speed lay between the two,'[38] but there was then no way of estimating the power required for this speed except the Admiralty Coefficient[39] which it was already suspected became increasingly unreliable as speed increased. Reed wrote that 'I was unwilling to propose that she be built of wood . . . the strains which such large engines and guns must necessarily exert upon a ship in a seaway', the heavy vibration from a heavily loaded, single propeller being a particular problem made worse by the need for a long, fine hull which ruled out the use of wood. However, a light hull would be needed for the speed and there was no weight to spare for armour but the 1850 trials[40] had shown all too clearly the suspect performance of unarmoured iron hulls against solid shot. The main problem was with a shot which would lose much of its velocity in penetrating the engaged side and then hit the far side at relatively low speed. Under these conditions the shot would tear rather than pierce, breaking seams and pulling plates away from the framing. Reed decided to sheath the outside of the hull with a double layer of oak each layer about 3in thick, the first layer worked vertically and the second horizontally. The 1850 trials had shown that this was not very effective but it was the best which could be done with an unarmoured iron hull.

Reed was undoubtedly aware that the problem of fouling on iron ships had not been solved and the use of a wood sheath permitted an outer copper sheath which would be effective in stopping fouling. If iron and copper are in contact, they act as an electric battery, the iron corroding very rapidly. He told the 1871 Committee that though he was aware of merchant ship experience with sheathed iron hulls, he used his own method, *agreed with his assistants*.[41] 'I propose to screw the first

layer of sheathing worked vertically direct to the joint straps of a new form designed for the purpose, the screws in this case being of galvanised iron and to screw the second layer, worked horizontally, to the first by means of metal screws [brass].' The copper was nailed into the outer layer of wood, care being taken that these nails did not touch the bolts holding the inner layer to the hull. Care was also needed where pipes passed though the skin. Barnaby told the 1871 Committee that when *Inconstant* was docked, a small portion of the sheathing was removed and the iron found to be in good

The elaborate sheathing fitted to *Inconstant*. Two layers of oak were arranged, partly to minimise the effect of shot on the iron hull and partly to insulate the copper anti-fouling sheathing from the hull.

Vertical section of side

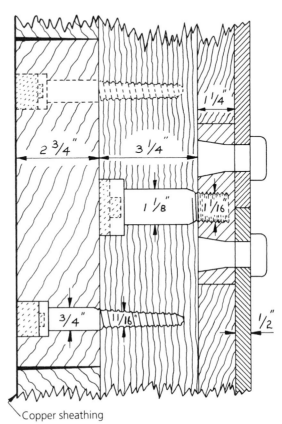

Copper sheathing

Fast, unarmoured frigates

Name	Wampaoag	Inconstant	Duquesne	Raleigh
Disp (tons)	4215	5780	5905	5200
Speed (kts)	17 (?)	16	16.8	15
Armament	3-5.3in RML, 10-9in SB	10-9in MLR, 6-7in MLR	7-7.6in, 14-5.5in	2-9in MLR, 14-7in MLR

27. H W Wilson, *Ironclads in Action* (London 1896).

28. Tony Gibbons, *Warships and Naval Battles of the US Civil War* (Limpsfield 1989).

29. H P Nash, *A Naval History of the Civil War* (New Jersey 1972). He lists only eight but admits this is incomplete.

30. Gibbons, *Warships and Naval Battles of the US Civil War*.

31. One was never started, one was not launched and another not completed.

32. N A M Rodger, 'The Design of the *Inconstant*', *The Mariner's Mirror* Vol 61 (1975). An important account of the origins of *Wampanoag*, *Inconstant* and the characters involved.

33. Reports of these trials are suspect. It is said that she made a maximum of 17.75kts and could sustain over 16kts but these figures were recorded out of sight of land and may have been assisted by current. See Rodger, 'Design of the *Inconstant*'. Isherwood was a controversial figure and attacks on his engines may have been politically motivated. See also J C Bradford, *Captains of the Old Steam Navy* (Annapolis 1986).

34. The design figure was 700 tons but drawings do not appear to show room for this amount. *Madawaska* after being refitted with smaller engines only carried 380 tons.

35. N A M Rodger 'The Design of the *Inconstant*' and The Admiralty, (Lavenham 1979) .

36. It is remarkable that two such irascible characters as Robinson and Reed got on so well.

37. An outline of the background and career of this brilliant man is given in Chapter 2.

38. The difference in power between 15kts and 16½kts would be at least 33 per cent showing how inaccurate power estimates were before Froude's work (Chapter 4).

39. For a full description of the Admiralty Coefficient see Appendix 2.

40. Brown, *Before the Ironclad*.

41. The words in italics are among a number of indications that Reed consulted his assistants to a considerable extent and that there was mutual respect. See Chapter 2.

GZ Curve for INCONSTANT

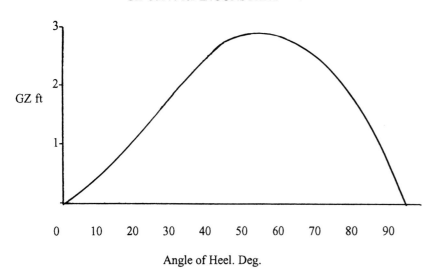

The curve of righting levers (GZ) for *Inconstant seems* very good (gunports closed).

condition.[42] Worries over the life of *Inconstant* were unjustified, she was scrapped nearly a century later in 1956.[43] Narbeth refers[44] to working steel into *Inconstant* at Pembroke.

Inconstant in service

Inconstant was started at Pembroke on 27 November 1866 and made 16.5kts (mean of 6 runs) on trial in Stokes Bay on 26 July 1869,[45] and 13.7kts with half power and could sustain high speed for long periods; bringing home the news of the disaster to the *Captain* she maintained 15.75kts for 24 hours.[46] However, her coal supply was adequate only for 1170 miles at full speed, 2700 miles at 10kts and, at best, 3020 miles at 6.4kts, making sails essential for the long ocean passages even though full rig cost about 1.5kts when under steam alone. She sailed quite well with 26,655sq ft of canvas

reaching 13-13.5kts with an average heel of 10-11° and a maximum of 15° but the combination of a single hoisting propeller and a balanced rudder, worked by two manual treble-handed wheels, made her difficult to handle under sail[47] – 'very slack in stays'. She trimmed by the stern even when deep and as the stores, which were forward, were used, this trim increased.

Inconstant was given a very powerful armament (see table above) so that she could destroy her enemies at long range where her own lack of armour might be less critical and when she completed only two armoured ships in the RN mounted a heavier battery. This intention was never conveyed to the operators and even her own captain, Waddilove, told the 1871 Design Committee that he did not know what she was for and proposed to fight at close range.[48] The committee was also told that she could not use both bow ports together. On one occasion, whilst rolling 5-6°, her 12-ton gun fired eight rounds in 8 minutes 48 seconds. She had ten bulkheads, watertight to the main deck.

Technically, she was almost a complete success but there was soon concern over her stability. In June 1870 Admiral Sir Thomas Symonds[49] ordered her to use steam when tacking in succession with the squadron saying 'I believe her crankiness had a great deal to do with it'. Ninety tons of ballast were added but an inclining experiment[50] showed the metacentric height (GM) was 2.48ft deep and 1.29ft light and a further 90 tons of ballast was added. This gave GMs of 2.8ft deep, 1.66ft light. The light figure was thought too low and she was ordered to keep boilers and condensers full when sailing giving a minimum GM of 2.05ft. The GZ curve (see Appendix 4) seems excellent due to her high freeboard[51] but it is that for the deep condition and it assumes the gunports are closed and watertight.[52]

Barnaby thought the ballast unnecessary, writing of her behaviour at sea,[53] 'It appeared to me to be as near perfection as possible. The Atlantic waves as they rolled across her beam, lifted her up vertically, and she remained steadily upright when some of the other ships of the squadron were showing the whole of their decks to the ships in the other line. To my extreme regret 180 tons of ballast . . . [were added]'.[54] Her sister *Shah* (ex-*Blonde*) was designed with a beam of 50ft 8in and 90 tons ballast but this was changed to 52ft and no ballast. *Shah* had a different armament with two 9in and two 64pdrs on the upper deck and sixteen 7in and two 64pdrs on the main deck. The greater beam allowed normal slides.

The real problem with *Inconstant* was her cost which Reed gave[55] as hull £160,000, machinery £68,000[56] – but 'this excludes the extraordinary charges amounting to 35 per cent with which our ships are now being burthened in the Parliamentary returns under the head of incidental expenses'. Her running costs, with a crew of 550-600, were also high and, in consequence, *Shah* was the only similar ship. Reed suggested that the size of

42. This was a risky procedure; removing and replacing part of the sheath is likely to end up with a leak path, creating the very problem the inspection was to prevent!

43. The author remembers walking across her during his diving course in 1950 when she was part of the *Defiance* establishment.

44. J H Narbeth, 'Fifty Years of Naval Progress', *Shipbuilder* (London, October 1927).

45. Displacement 5328 tons, area of midship section 900sq ft. Stokes Bay is on the shallow side for a ship of this size and speed and she may have lost ¼kt.

46. E C Smith, *A Short History of Marine Engineering* (Cambridge 1937). She maintained this speed using only nine boilers.

47. See Chapter 2 on balanced rudders. Reed had considered a

twin-screw design with hoisting propellers but, luckily, decided to wait for *Penelope* trials before repeating what proved to be a very bad feature (1871 Committee, Constructor's evidence).

48. See Rodger for other examples of ignorance over the design concept of *Inconstant*.

49. 1871 Committee.

50. Inclined 22 February 1870.

51. A point made in the Constructor's dept report to the 1871 Committee on *Inconstant*.

52. Maximum GZ 2.8ft at 50° and a range of over 90° at 5782 tons.

53. 1871 Committee.

54. For many years the author was involved in approving the stability characteristics of modern RN ships. There seems little doubt that *Inconstant*, even without ballast,

was safe in seagoing condition even under sail (provided that the ports were kept tight). However, the angle of heel reported and quoted above would make work on deck very difficult and the seamen may well have been correct in asking for greater stiffness.

55. 1871 Committee.

56. W H White, Presidential Address ICE 1903, gives £213,324 total.

57. *Shah* 32-9in (2 common, 19 Palliser shot, 11 Palliser shell), 149-7in (4 common, 145 Palliser shot) and 56-64pdr. *Amethyst* 190-64pdr common. Details from an unpublished article by Andrew Smith. The best readily available account is by G Woodand and P Somervell, 'The Iron Turret Ship *Huascar*', *Warship* 38 (London 1986).

58. *Brassey's Naval Annual*, 1886.

Raleigh 1873, a smaller, cheaper and much inferior derivative of *Inconstant*. (Imperial War Museum: Q39909)

Inconstant in terms of her builder's measurement tonnage was exaggerated because of her fine lines. Whilst there may have been some truth in this, it was the cost which was the real concern. He also said that he preferred *Inconstant* to more *Volages* because of the morale effect – *Hercules* or *Monarch* could catch *Volage*. A third ship had been approved in the 1867-68 programme, with more to follow, but the First Lord decided, despite extremely forceful protests from Spencer Robinson, to build a smaller, cheaper ship, *Raleigh*. Spencer Robinson pointed out that the savings were small and *Raleigh* was of little more capability than the much cheaper *Volage*.

Shah and *Huascar*

Shah was one of the few RN ships of the period to fire her guns in anger. On 29 May 1877 she fought the rebel Peruvian turret ship *Huascar* which carried two 10in MLR in a Coles turret and had a 4½in belt. *Shah* fired 237 rounds[57] at ranges between 1500 and 2500yds; in tests a 9in could pierce *Huascar*'s 5½in turret at 3000yds and a 7in at 1200yds whilst her 64pdr and those of *Amethyst* would be ineffective, firing only common shell. There are two damage reports on *Huascar*, one by *Shah*'s gunnery officer and a more detailed one by a Peruvian officer. There seem to have been at least fifty hits and the figure of seventy to eighty, often quoted, is quite possible.

Most of the damage was superficial, though one 9in common shell hit near the starboard waterline, 50ft from the stern, piercing a 3½in plate and bursting in the backing, killing one man and injuring three. There were

problems in moving the 9in from one broadside to the other and four carriages of the 7in broke pivot bolts, forcing the use of 'full' rather than 'battering' charges. A 7in shot fired at about 1700-1800yds penetrated 3in into the 5½in turret face. Towards the end of the action, the crews of *Huascar*'s exposed 40pdrs were driven away by Gatling fire. *Huascar* scored no hits though near misses cut some rigging. She probably fired only some six or seven rounds from her turret which needed sixteen men to turn it, taking 15 minutes for a complete revolution. *Shah* also fired a torpedo (see Chapter 5).[58] This inconclusive action illustrates one of the great dilemmas of colonial and trade protection; a fast, unarmoured ship could not deal with even small armoured ships yet the latter were not suitable for protection duties.

The wooden corvette *Volage* in c1894 under sail. Although smaller and slower than *Inconstant* she was still expensive. (Imperial War Museum: Q38030)

Volage, the Second Class cruiser (ld 1867)

As mentioned earlier, Spencer Robinson always realised that it would not be possible to afford sufficient numbers of *Inconstant*s and Reed was asked to design a cheaper ship, *Volage* and her sister, *Active*.[59] They were of 3080 tons, had a speed of 15kts and cost £130,000, still a considerable sum. Several changes were made to their armament reflecting different thoughts on the way cruisers might operate as well as the effects of improving gun technology.

Armament

Initial;	6-7in MLR (6½ ton), 4-64pdr MLR
1873:	18-64pdr MLR
1880:	10-6in BL, 2-64pdr.

Like *Inconstant* the initial armament seems to have envisaged opening fire at long range though, lacking any fire control, it must be doubted whether the effective range of the 7in was any greater than that of the 64pdr.

They were handsome ships of the old style but the third ship, *Rover*, adopted the vertical stem. They had very fine lines forward and aft which may have accounted for their reported severe pitching and they rolled heavily until deep bilge keels were fitted. In 1890, Reed[60] said '. . . I made the mistake of making them vessels with forecastles – low-waisted vessels without a covered deck; and I think those vessels had not been long in service before it was ascertained that they would have been much better if they had been covered deck

corvettes.' The stability of the first two seems to have been inadequate as *Rover* was given an extra 18in of beam whilst the others were ballasted after the loss of the *Captain*. They were iron-hulled with a single layer of oak sheathing. Captain Waddilove of *Inconstant* said they were nearly as fast as his ship under sail. At full speed they burnt 200 tons of coal a day, giving 2½ days steaming (70 tons/day at 9kts).

It is interesting that attempts at Second Class battleships were always seen as a failure but Second Class cruisers such as *Volage* were successful and many Second Class cruisers were built; the balance between quality and quantity is always a fine one and in cruisers numbers were essential.

Ramming

The introduction of the iron, armoured ship led to a renewed interest in ramming, partly because the strength of the hull and the power of the engines appeared to make such attacks possible and partly because it seemed impossible to sink such ships by gunfire. The interest in sinking is a little strange since sailing battleships very rarely sank their opponents. Views on the value of ramming were reinforced by the sinking of the *Cumberland* by the *Virginia* (*Merrimac*) at Hampton Roads and, even more by the confused battle of Lissa (1866) in which there were eight ramming contacts, leading to the sinking of the *Re d'Italia* (*Palestro* also sank after ramming but her damage was mainly from fire following gunfire). Numerous accidental collisions with several ships sunk also seemed to show the power of the ram.

It is now clear that these views were mistaken[61] but they were held strongly at the time and had a major influence on both tactical thinking and on ship design. In particular, the number of collisions showed the difficulty of controlling these ships and should have been seen as demonstrating the difficulty in achieving a deliberate collision. A detailed list[62] of ramming attempts showed hardly any successes unless the victim was stationary and serious damage to the attacker was common. The seventy-four incidents considered are summarised in the table opposite.

In most of the serious incidents, the damage itself was not very extensive and losses were due to inadequate subdivision (including leaving doors open). The rammer was as likely to be damaged as the intended victim. As a result of the importance attached to ramming, considerable emphasis was placed on end-on fire.

Damage in ramming

Prior state of victim	Incidents	Effect On Victim			
		Nil	Slight	Serious	Disabled
Under steam with searoom	32	26	5	1	-
Under steam, narrow water	32	9	9	3	2
Unmanageable	4	1	-	1	-
At anchor	6	-	4	-	-
Effect on rammer	74	56	13	3	1

Early Rams

	Hotspur	Rupert	Conqueror	Cerbere
Displacement (tons)	4331	5440	6200	3532
Length pp (ft)	245	250	270	215
Speed (kts)	12.6	13.6	14.0	12.5
Turning circle (yds)	400			310-360
Main armament	1-12in MLR	2-10in MLR	2-12in BL	2-9.4in

Rams, *Hotspur* and *Rupert*

All armoured steam ships were seen as capable of ramming, even *Warrior*, and *Defence* was often described as a 'steam ram'. Dupuy de Lôme's *Taureau*, laid down in 1863, before the battle of Lissa, was the first ship designed primarily as a ram. She was intended for coastal work, had a speed of 12.5kts and was a poor seaboat. She was followed in 1865 by four larger ships of the *Cerbere* class. All five had wooden hulls and would have suffered severe damage in ramming.

Encouraged by enthusiastic reports of the value of the ram in the American Civil War and at Lissa, the Admiralty decided in 1868 to build a ship as a specialist ram. Unlike the French ships, *Hotspur* was intended to accompany the fleet at sea.

Hotspur had an 11in belt (8in ends) with a Reed[63] breastwork 8in thick protecting the base of the turret and the machinery uptakes. Unprotected structure outside the breastwork gave her flush sides with a freeboard of about 12½ft. The gun was mounted inside a fixed armour box since it was thought that a true turret would not resist the impact of ramming. There were four ports which gave the gun a theoretical arc of about 135° either side of the bow,[64] though obstructed forward by latrines.

Her low freeboard meant that she was slowed in head seas and her coal stowage was too small for ocean work. She had only some two years active service before her modernisation in 1881-83 which cost £116,600. After that her active service may be measured in months. The breastwork was abolished in favour of an upper belt at the side.

Rupert was designed in 1870, before *Hotspur* was completed. Confidence in the turret was greater and she had a conventional Coles twin 10in turret. Her belt was 11in thick (9in ends) with a 12in breastwork. She suffered from unreliable machinery (unusually, her engines were built in Portsmouth Dockyard) and rolled heavily. Her seagoing life was limited and she had a major reconstruction in 1891-93. Though, with hindsight, it is clear that these two ships were useless, there were many at the time who believed in the concept of seagoing rams with a heavy forward firing armament. Amongst these was the captain of *Rupert* in February 1878 who suggested a list of improvements to her.

Stability

The theory of stability is central to the discussion of warship design in the 1860s and 1870s but presents some difficulty to many readers, particularly in its interaction with rolling. It is intended to split the subject into sections spread over several chapters, related to specific incidents, with the more detailed material in Appendices 4 and 5.

The theory of stability, at least for small angles of heel, was well understood by the end of the eighteenth century but it was not directly used in ship design. Stability was linked to 'power to carry sail'[65] and if a ship was seen as crank, it could be improved by ballasting which would lower the centre of gravity or by girdling, in which the restoring force would be increased by providing more beam.

A new impetus to the application of stability theory

The unsuccessful ram *Hotspur*, 1870. (Author's collection)

was given in 1855 when the troopship *Perseverance* capsized while completing at Mare's shipyard on the Thames.[66] After she was salvaged, Isaac Watts had an inclining experiment carried out by one of his assistants, Barnes, which showed her stability was quite inadequate. The inclining experiment is described in Appendix 4 but, in brief, it involves moving weights a known distance across the deck and measuring the angle of heel. From this can be determined the stability as measured by the metacentric height, the distance between the centre of gravity and the metacentre through which the buoyancy force acts when the ship is heeled.

The problem which Watts and Barnes appreciated was that theory gave little indication as to what value of metacentric height (GM) was acceptable. They set out to incline a considerable number of warships, hoping that it would be possible to distinguish between satisfactory and poor ships (and even those with excessive stability). This approach is still the starting point for most modern stability criteria though modern naval architects have many more samples – including disasters – than were available to Watts. (See Appendix 4 for some typical values of metacentric height.)

The position of the metacentre could be obtained during the design stage by a simple but tedious calculation but this was of little value unless the position of the centre of gravity was also known. Surprisingly, as late as 1865, Barnaby, who made a great contribution to the practical application of stability theory, told the Institution of Naval Architects that direct calculation of weights and the centre of gravity was so laborious as to be virtually impossible. In discussion, William Froude pointed out that William Bell had calculated weights and centre of gravity for the *Great Eastern* and there was no reason why such calculations could not have been carried out a century earlier. It is clear that the Admiralty were making such calculations by about 1870 and likely that Barnaby's reluctance was due to shortage of design staff as three assistant constructors were added to the Controller's department at about this time.[67] Design was to be a team effort and no longer would the designer work by himself.

59. Famous to naval architects as the towing ship in Froude's *Greyhound* trial (Chapter 4).

60. E J Reed in discussion of W H White, 'Notes on Recent Naval Manoeuvres', *Trans INA* (London 1890).

61. D K Brown and P Pugh, 'Ramming', *Warship 1990* (London 1990).

62. Sir William Laird Clowes,. 'The ram in action and in accident', *RUSI Journal* No 193 (London, March 1894).

63. Reed seems to have been enthusiastic for the concept of *Hotspur* judging from his remarks in *Our Ironclad Ships* (pace Parkes).

64. Parkes and others state that the gun could not fire directly forward. Drawings show that it could be trained right forward from either of the bow ports. It would be difficult to work the gun in this extreme position and blast on the forecastle would be severe so it is likely that firing in this position was forbidden in peacetime.

65. Power to carry sail is defined as W.GM/A.h where A is sail area, h the height of their centre of effort (Appendix 4).

66. *Perseverance*, ex-Russian *Sobraon*, purchased May 1854. Launched 13 July 1854. 273ft x 68ft.

67. Naval Estimates 1866.

Barnes was one of many little-known men who made an immense contribution to warship design. He started as an apprentice at Pembroke in 1842 and was one of the first students selected for the Central School of Mathematics and Naval Architecture at Portsmouth in 1848 where Reed was a fellow student. Though he is best known for his work on the theory of stability and its application to design, he was responsible for the design of the *Nile* and, from 1872 to 1886 when he retired, he was head of the Dockyard department.

The Institution of Naval Architects (INA), 1860

In the autumn of 1859, John Scott Russell invited Wooley, Reed and Barnaby to his house to discuss the formation of a learned body to promote the subject of naval architecture. Reed offered to act as (unpaid) secretary and a formal meeting was called for 16 January 1860.[68] Of the eighteen attending, eleven were, or had been, Admiralty employees and several others were Admiralty contractors. Sir John Packington became the first President. It is interesting to note the enthusiasm for the Institution from the Admiralty officers compared with the comparative lack of support for the earlier Society for the Improvement of Naval Architecture.[69]

The new Institution got off to a good start with a classic paper on rolling by William Froude which was to have a major influence on ship design. In the early years a considerable number of naval officers joined the Institution as Associates discussing tactics as well as technology, providing useful experience from sea and, often, less useful thoughts on design. The INA pressed the Admiralty hard to open a new School of Naval Architecture, proposed by Scott Russell in a paper of 1863, and, with Parliamentary support, the school opened in 1864.[70] Since there was then no Official Secrets Act, new designs were often described in great detail.

The Royal School of Naval Architecture and Marine Engineering, 1864

The Director of Studies was Dr Wooley, with the strange title of Inspector General, and C W Merrifield, a mathematician, became Principal.[71] Studies were concentrated into long hours during the winter with the six summer months spent on practical studies in the Dockyards. There were six other full-time instructors together with considerable use of very distinguished outside lecturers. Like previous Admiralty schools – and the current course at University College (London) – much of the teaching was by experienced designers on short-term secondment ensuring that the teaching was up to date and relevant.

The school produced many distinguished naval architects – William White, Phillip Watts etc – and marine engineers – Durston – while others made their names

outside the Admiralty. There were also a number of outstanding overseas students, particularly from Russia. The school in South Kensington was small and cramped and living conditions poor so that all were pleased when it moved to the newly opened Royal Naval College at Greenwich in 1873.

Guns and armour

Warrior's protection was a success; even at ranges as short as 200yds it could not be penetrated by any gun then in service. The development of this protection is covered fully in *Before the Ironclad*[72] but, to summarise, a target 20ft x 10ft was hit by twenty-nine projectiles with individual weights up to 200lbs and totalling 3229lbs, none of which penetrated. This protection was designed under Isaac Watts and his successor, Edward Reed was to write;

> I must also express my strong conviction that the *Warrior* target was not, as some have supposed, a lucky hap-hazard combination of parts, or a mere attempt to imitate a wooden ship's side in connection with an iron hull; but, on the contrary, a highly skilful and scientific construction, carefully designed in view of the objects which had to be accomplished.

There were three criticisms of *Warrior*'s scheme of protection. The plates were united by tongue and groove joints which could transmit the shock of impact to adjoining plates and which made the replacement of damaged plates very difficult and was soon abandoned. The risk that the through bolts securing the armour would fail under the tensile shock wave following impact on the exposed head was dimly perceived and largely overcome by the thick backing and, by the use of rubber grommets on the bolts which damped the shock wave.[73] This problem was only finally overcome when the use of a hard steel face meant that bolts had to be tapped into the back of the plate.[74]

The *Minotaur* was the next design of First Class battleship having both waterline and battery protected from end to end. The armour thickness was increased to 5½in whilst the backing was reduced to a single layer of 9in teak. Tests were carried out on a replica target by the same 'Committee on Iron' which had carried out the tests on the *Warrior* target. There was initial concern when it was penetrated by a 150lb cast iron spherical shot but it was discovered that a more powerful '2A' powder had been used in the trial which increased the striking velocity from 1620 to 1744ft/sec making the comparison with the *Warrior* trial more difficult.[75]

Projectiles and rifling[76]

Weapon designers soon realised that spherical shot, fired from a smoothbore gun, was ineffective against armour of even moderate thickness. The first major advance

68. K C Barnaby, *The Institution of Naval Architects 1860-1960* (London 1960).

69. Brown, *Before the Ironclad*.

70. An interesting point; the Council was overwhelmingly drawn from 'Admiralty' officers but they were able to tell the Admiralty from outside what, presumably, they could not achieve from within.

71. Brown, *A Century of Naval Construction*.

72. Brown, *Before the Ironclad*.

73. Palliser, 'Armour Fastenings', *Trans INA* (London 1867).

74. Parkes says that a replica of the *Flandres* protection had only about half the resistance of the *Warrior*.

75. E J Reed, 'The *Bellerophon*, *Lord Warden* and *Hercules* Targets', *Trans INA* (London 1866).

76. John Campbell, 'Naval Armaments and Armour', *Steam, Steel and Shellfire* (London 1992).

77. W Hovgaard, *Modern History of Warships* (reprint London 1971); H Garbett, *Naval Gunnery* (first published 1897, reprint Wakefield 1971).

78. Lambert, *Warrior*.

79. Ballard, *The Black Battlefleet*.

80. E J Reed, *Our Ironclad Ships* (London 1869). An invaluable source.

came with General Sir William Palliser's invention of the chilled iron shot, tested successfully at Shoeburyness in 1863. It was an elongated projectile with thick walls of cast iron, hardened on the outside by being cast in a cooled metal mould. Initially the whole body was so chilled but it was found later that the shell was less liable to break if only the head was so treated. It was designed with a cavity which could take a small bag of gunpowder which would be compressed against the back of the cavity by the impulse of firing and, on hitting the target, would be flung forward violently, causing it to detonate. The explosion would usually take place before the shell had passed through the armour, causing only minor damage, so Palliser projectiles were normally used against armoured ships without the charge as 'shot'. These were quite effective against wrought iron armour but would break up on impact with a hardened steel face. They were very cheap (£3-10-0) and were retained by the RN until the early years of the twentieth century, long past their 'best before' date.[77]

Rifled guns had been tried during the 'War with Russia' but the Lancaster muzzle-loader with a twisted elliptical bore was not a success. During building, ten of *Warrior*'s 68pdrs were replaced with Armstrong 7in, 110pdr breech-loaders which were not a success either since their muzzle velocity of 1175ft/sec was much inferior to the muzzle-loader's 1580ft/sec. The Armstrong breech design was unreliable, the barrel was often cracked when delivered, and during the bombardment of Kagoshima (Japan) in 1863 there were 28 accidents in the 365 rounds fired from 21 guns. The gun was also inaccurate. This initial over-enthusiasm for the breech-loader was to lead, with the swing of the pendulum, to over-conservatism in later years.

As a result of extensive trials between 1863 and 1865 a series of rifled muzzle-loaders (RML) was developed by Fraser at Woolwich Arsenal with a steel inner tube, reinforced by hoops and tubes of wrought iron. There were six to nine grooves with increasing pitch which engaged with bronze studs on the shell. These guns were cheap and effective but the shell was not centred correctly in the bore and the considerable windage allowed hot and corrosive gasses to erode the bore quite quickly.[78] Such guns, firing Palliser, could penetrate a thickness of wrought iron (unbacked) roughly equivalent to their own calibre at 1000yds range, the maximum range at which hits were likely. Rates of fire are rarely quoted but *Hercules*, with a well-trained crew, is said to have been able to fire her 10in at 70-second intervals.[79]

Penetration was later increased by about 10 per cent with improved powder. MV without gas check except 12½in and 16in. The designation of guns was uncertain at this date, sometimes being given as weight of gun, sometimes bore and, less often, weight of projectile. This book will generally give both bore and weight of the gun the first time mentioned, bore only after that. The earlier guns were mounted on wooden carriages,

A replica (GRP) Armstrong 110pdr aboard the restored *Warrior*. (HMS *Warrior* (1860) Trust)

little changed since Nelson's day, although Sir Thomas Hardy had replaced the rear wheels with an iron plate, reducing the force of recoil somewhat though the breeching rope was still the only limit of recoil. This was further developed into a slide mounting in which the carriage itself slid on a wooden base. These were linked by compressors which could take up much of the recoil. By 1864 this was developed into the RCD (Royal Carriage Department) iron mounting which incorporated a much more elaborate, Elswick compressor which was later further developed by Admiral Scott. The USN, briefly, tried an alternative method of attacking armour, using very large – up to 15in – smoothbores, relying on sheer mass to batter in the framing rather than penetrating with a smaller shot. One of these guns was tried at Shoeburyness using cast steel shot (the US used cast iron) weighing 484lbs with 50lbs powder (equivalent to 60lbs US powder).[80] It failed to penetrate the *Lord Warden* target which could be penetrated by the British 9in. It was estimated that *Warrior* could not be penetrated at over 500yds. Isaac Watts had made a fine start to the ironclad programme but the revolution he had triggered with *Warrior* was gathering pace. Competition between guns and armour would soon force a change of style.

Penetration of wrought iron at 1000yds by Palliser shot

Date introduced	Bore (ins)	Wt (tons)	Wt shot (lbs)	Burster (lbs)	MV (ft/sec)	Penetration (ins)
1865	7	6.5	115	2.5	1525	2.6
1866	8	9	180	4.5	1413	8.8
1866	9	12	256	5.5	1420	9.9
1868	10	18	410	6.8	1364	11.7
1875	11	25	536	6.5	1315	12.5
1869	12	25	614	14.0	1297	12.7
1871	12	35	820	9.8	1300	13.9
1874	12.5	38	820	11.75	1415	15.7
1879	16	80	1684	17.5	1604	22.5

Two

Edward Reed and the Centre Battery Ships

Sir Edward Reed, Chief Constructor of the Navy 1863-70. (RCNC History Archive)

1. Edward James Reed, born at Sheerness 20 September 1830, died 30 November 1906.

2. Career development for graduates was the major problem for graduates of this school and its successor, The Royal School (see Brown, *A Century of Naval Construction*). On the other hand, 'supernumerary draughtsman' was by no means as derogatory a title as it sounds today. One story has it that the last straw for Reed was compulsory military service in the Militia.

3. See, for example, his correspondence with White on the Royal Society paper.

4. Naval Estimates 1868-69.

5. The Duke of Somerset.

6. O Parkes, *British Battleships* (London 1956)

7. It is suggested by Parkes, Rodger and others that Reed was resented within the Admiralty as an outsider. There does not seem to be much evidence either way but it is possible that his contemporaries within the Admiralty still saw him as 'one of us' and his attacks on the Admiralty in *Mechanics Magazine* as what they would, themselves have liked to have said. Indeed, it is clear from the evidence to the 1871 Committee that he was respected and, probably, liked.

8. 1871 Committee, Evidence of Spencer Robinson 10 March 1871.

THE RAPID increase in the weight and power of guns meant that fewer guns could be carried and these would need thicker armour for their protection. Viewed in this light, the centre battery, a heavily-armoured box containing a fairly small number of guns, was inevitable, although Reed deserves every credit for introducing this style well before his contemporaries. The battery was carried above a shallow waterline belt, extending from bow to stern and, other than in a few early ships, arrangements were made to permit some degree of end-on fire.

Sir Edward J Reed KCB, FRS, Chief Constructor 1863-70[1]

Reed's early career followed the conventional pattern for a mid-nineteenth century naval constructor. His ability was recognised soon after he became a shipwright apprentice at Sheerness and, in 1849, he was selected for the three-year course at the Central School of Mathematics and Naval Construction under Dr Wooley at Portsmouth. He was to meet as fellow students many of those who were to become his assistants later – Crossland, Barnaby, Barnes and others. On graduating he returned to Sheerness as a supernumerary draughtsman, working in the mould loft, but finding the work uninspiring he resigned in 1853.[2] He released his creative instincts in writing poetry and a book of his verse was published in 1857. In 1853 he became editor of *Mechanics Magazine*, a most influential paper amongst the increasing number of engineers and technicians, using his position to attack what he saw as the over-conservative policies of the Admiralty. This experience enabled him to develop a clear and popular style of writing which helped him to advance his technical ideas. In 1854 he submitted to the Admiralty his idea for an armoured frigate but the time was not ripe and it was shelved.

He was one of the small group whose efforts led to the formation of the Institution of Naval Architects and in 1860 he became its first secretary which gave him direct contact with many influential men, inside and outside the Admiralty, including Sir John Packington, the former First Lord. In 1861 he submitted a design for an armoured corvette of 2250 tons, acknowledging the help of his brother-in-law, Nathaniel Barnaby, then working in the Chief Constructor's office. He also said that some features of the design derived from the work

he had done as Lungley's assistant in developing his patent for unsinkable iron ships. Reed was far more willing to acknowledge the help of others than were most of his contemporaries.[3]

In 1862 he proposed a scheme for converting wooden sloops into armoured vessels and was given a contract to develop these ideas within the Admiralty. This was extended to enable him to develop ideas for bigger ships, which developed into *Pallas* and *Bellerophon* and for which he was to receive an *ex gratia* payment of £5000[4] in 1868. When Isaac Watts retired, the First Lord[5] invited Reed to become Chief Constructor, which he accepted, taking up his duties on 9 July 1863. Though he had to resign as Secretary of the INA, he became a Member of Council where he served until his death. There was some opposition in Parliament to the appointment of a young and relatively inexperienced man, a charge against which Reed defended himself with so much vigour that he was summoned to the Bar of the House, charged with breach of privilege.[6]

He was an inspired and creative designer introducing first the centre battery ship and then the breastwork monitor style, both widely copied. His work on developing the theory of naval architecture is less well known but in the long term may have been even more important. He encouraged Barnes and others in their work on stability which had been started under Watts; he then initiated a new approach to structural design, acknowledging the value of the young William White's contribution. He adopted Froude's theory of rolling in waves and sponsored Froude's later work on model testing to improve hull form and for power estimation. In the last few years of Reed's directorship ship design became a true science. He was assisted greatly by his brilliant assistants – Barnaby, Barnes, Crossland, White and others, most of whom had been at the Central School with him.[7] Reed wrote a number of technical books and papers, quoted extensively in this chapter, as well as a novel and a second book of poems.

The Controller, Spencer Robinson, had a clear idea of the type of ships needed by the Navy and then delegated almost total authority in technical matters to Reed. Robinson, who had the highest impression of his Chief Constructor, said to the 1871 Committee[8] of Reed after his resignation – '. . . the greatest naval architect in England – a man whose absence is a positive national loss – and without the means of communicating with him and taking his advice, I should not like to come to any conclusion upon any specific design'. Praise indeed from a man not noted for speaking well of others. Reed was skilled in the presentation of his views, aided by the clarity of his writing.

After his departure from the Admiralty, particularly as an MP from 1874 until 1905 (with a brief interruption), he was a bitter critic of the Admiralty, objecting particularly to unarmoured ends, until his views were demolished by White in the debate at the INA on the design of the *Royal Sovereigns* (Chapter 7). Rodger is probably correct in suggesting[9] that Reed's genius flourished best when kept under tight rein as by Spencer Robinson.[10]

The small ironclads

When *Gloire* and *Warrior* were conceived, there were many who thought that even the smallest warships should be armoured. Reed's proposals of 1861 led to three conversions from ships under construction; *Research*[11] and *Enterprise*[12] from sloops and *Favourite* from a corvette to which may be added the slightly later, new construction corvette *Pallas*.

Research completed in April 1864 and was inspected by Admiral Fremantle the following month who made a number of intelligent criticisms.[13] The funnel had been run up through the battery for protection but, with eighty men, four guns, the wheel and a hatch in a small space it was over-congested and over-heated. The funnel was moved forward of the battery. Recessed ports were fitted to give some degree of end-on fire but the arrangements were unsatisfactory. It was thought that it would be impossible to move the heavy guns (100pdrs) in any seaway and the arcs of fire were very limited. It was said that the arcs from the end ports was only 10-12° with a blind arc of 34° before the arcs covered by the broadside ports. The sights were impossible to reach in some positions of the guns.

Admiral Fremantle then asked for blank charges to be fired with the guns as close as possible to the axis. The damage caused by muzzle blast was much exaggerated in the press – repairs cost about £20 – but it could be expected to be much worse with live rounds and bigger guns, a subject to be considered later.

Enterprise had a section of the bulwark hinged to permit firing from the end ports of her battery; no records of the effect of blast have been found though Reed was later to advise the 1871 Committee against moveable bulwarks.[14] She had the unique combination of a wooden hull below water (to permit copper sheathing) and iron upperworks. The real problem was the role of these four ships. Three of them mounted two heavy guns on the broadside (*Favourite* four) which was insufficient to engage a battle ship and, against an unarmoured ship, the original lighter but more numerous armament would have been more effective. Parkes says that the Constructors' Department claimed that it was impossi-

ble to build an effective ironclad of less than 4000 tons and goes on to suggest Reed was clever to get below this 'limit'. Since all four were ineffective, and *Research* was such a bad seaboat that she was not supposed to go more than 100 miles from land, it seems that the Constructors were right.

Armoured gunboats, *Waterwitch* (ld 1864) and jet propulsion[15]

In 1864 three small armoured gunboats were ordered in another attempt to explore the lower limit of size for ironclads. They were of about 1230 tons and 160ft in length with a complete waterline belt, 4½in thick. The belt was raised amidships to form a casemate and they carried two 7in MLR and two 20pdr BL. *Viper* and *Vixen* had twin screws, then a novel feature, but with each screw behind a deadwood, the hull form was bad and performance was poor. *Vixen* was amongst the first ships of composite construction, planked over iron frames.

Research was a small ironclad converted from a sloop, completed in 1864. (Imperial War Museum: Q39964)

Waterwitch 1866, an unsuccessful waterjet-propelled armoured gunboat. (Author's collection)

9. N A M Rodger, 'The Design of the *Inconstant*', *The Mariner's Mirror*, Vol 61 No 1 (February 1975).

10. Reed was Vice-President of the INA from 1865-1905; he became FRS in 1876 and was awarded the CB in 1868 and the KCB in 1880.

11. Ex-*Trent*, *Perseus* class.

12. Ex-*Circasssian*.

13. Navy Estimates 1884

14. See Chapter 3, evidence to 1866 Committee on the Scullard design.

15. See detailed articles in the *Engineer*, 26 October and 2 November 1866.

Waterwitch was much more novel, having Ruthven jet propulsion which used a centrifugal pump, mounted internally, to drive the ship. J & N W Ruthven took out their patent in 1839 and many found it attractive as it did away with the external propeller, seen as vulnerable in grounding, improved sailing performance and offered high manoeuvrability. The steam engine of 760hp was a three-cylinder radial mounted horizontally with a single crank.[16] At the bottom of the crankshaft was a large centrifugal pump working in a chamber 5ft deep and 19ft in diameter. The impeller was 14ft diameter, had twelve vanes and weighed 5 tons. Water was admitted through an inlet 6ft in diameter and discharged through outlets 24in x 19in.[17] Valves could direct the flow to ahead or astern nozzles, just above the waterline amidships and *Waterwitch* was double-ended. On trials she made 9.3kts with 760ihp, apparently only slightly less than her twin screw sisters. At full speed, *Waterwitch* could turn in 3 minutes 17 seconds whilst at rest she took 6½ minutes to turn in her own length. The figures for *Viper* were 3 minutes 17 seconds and 3 minutes 6 seconds respectively.[18]

It is possible to deduce that the efficiency of the jet itself was about 0.5 compared with about 0.65 for a comparable propeller. Her overall propulsive efficiency was about 0.16. In 1865 Rankine developed a theory of propeller action in which the propulsor – paddle, screw, jet etc – was replaced by a mathematical abstraction which he called an actuator disk. In its early form this theory could not be used to design a propeller but it did give an understanding of propeller action showing what factors affected efficiency and that 100 per cent efficiency could only be achieved at zero speed and zero thrust!

For real ships a slow-turning propeller, moving a large mass of water slowly was the best. It is very surprising that the 1871 Committee, which numbered Rankine and William Froude amongst its members, still saw hydraulic (jet) propulsion as worthy of further trial.

To complete the story of jet propulsion up to 1905 one must note *TB 98* completed in 1883.[19] She was designed by Barnaby, chief naval architect of Thornycroft (Sir Nathaniel's son) and achieved a speed of 12.6kts on trial compared with 17.3kts for similar propeller-driven boats. Her overall efficiency was about 0.25, better than *Waterwitch* but not encouraging. At the end of the First World War, two trawlers were built with jet propulsion as it was thought they would be quiet and could use hydrophones for hunting submarines whilst moving, and a few landing craft had jets between the wars. The design of a jet unit is not easy and modern hydrodynamics has improved considerably over these early units so that in very fast craft they have an overall performance similar to that of a propeller.[20]

Pallas (ld 1863) and *Penelope* (ld 1865)

Pallas was designed by Reed before he joined the Admiralty as a ram with a speed which he hoped would be 14kts but proved to be about 12.5kts. Her central battery mounted two 7in MLR on either side which could be moved to end ports, recessed into the hull, so that they could fire at 15° to the centre line and there was a 7in BL swivel at each end. The waterline belt and the battery were protected by 4½in iron plating. She had Woolf compound engines made by Humphrys and Tennant in which there were two pairs of cylinders with

Pallas was designed by Reed before he joined the Admiralty and was laid down in 1863. (Imperial War Museum: Q40608)

the high and low pressure of each pair in line, sharing a common piston rod and crank. This machinery was efficient and reliable. *Pallas* was not a success but remained active until 1879.

The design of the *Penelope* was dominated by the requirement for shallow draught – a maximum of 17ft 6in compared with 24ft 4in in the smaller *Pallas*. It was not then thought possible to design a single propeller to fit within this draught and transmit 4700ihp at low rpm so she had to have twin screws. In a vain attempt to give her better sailing performance it was decided to give her hoisting propellers which led to a strange double after hull with a skeg each side. This led to a considerable form drag, probably due to cross flow over the skegs, and she was poor under both steam and sail. This poor performance contributed to a long lasting prejudice against twin screw ships.

She had very little active service other than occasional manoeuvres until 1882 when she had a moment of glory in the bombardment of Alexandria (Chapter 4) for which her shallow draught suited her. She then operated in the Suez Canal until the war ended. She had a reputation for being a very steady gun platform which suggests poor stability though her GM is given as 3ft which, in conjunction with a high freeboard, should have been adequate.

Bellerophon (ld 1863)

The *Bellerophon* was a much better test of Reed's ideas and marked a major advance in battleship design. She had been conceived by Reed and the main features selected before he joined the Admiralty but it would seem that the development of the design was in the hands of his successor and brother in law, Nathaniel Barnaby.[21] The main armament of 9in MLR was mounted five on either side of a short (90ft) battery protected by 6in armour. Two 7in MLR were mounted on the main deck at the bow protected by 3in armour and there were a further three 7in, unprotected, aft. *Bellerophon*'s bluff form generated such a high bow wave that it was difficult to use the bow guns at speed, even in calm weather.

Iron weighs 480lbs/cu ft or 40lbs/sq ft for every inch of thickness – and there are many square feet on the side of a battleship – while the teak backing weighs 48-60lbs/cu ft, depending on source and seasoning. The weight involved in thick armour was so great that the whole side could no longer be protected and armour was confined to the waterline and a short battery containing a few heavy guns. There was a complete waterline belt from 6ft below the water to the main deck, 6in amidships, then 5in with 4½in aft and 3in right forward. Against contemporary shot the resistance of the armour varied as the square of the thickness making *Bellerophon* invulnerable to the guns of earlier ships.

The length of these single-deck ships was governed

Penelope 1867, had twin skegs aft supporting her two shafts which greatly added to the hydrodynamic drag. (Maritime Photo Library)

by the number of guns and their separation so that *Bellerophon* could be much shorter than earlier ships (300ft *cf Achilles* 380ft). Reduction of length will reduce the loading on the structure of a ship so that saving in weight is greater than *pro rata* to reduction in length.[22] This reduction in length was a brave policy by Reed as contemporary thinking held that length was essential for high speed. He thought that the extra cost of more powerful machinery would be offset by the savings on a shorter ship and he was probably right in this case.

Using the Admiralty Coefficient (Appendix 3) as a basis of comparison the penalty on power was some 36 per cent. There was a somewhat greater penalty in head seas. The shorter ship also had a much smaller turning circle.

Long and short

Ship	Dispt (tons)	ihp	Speed (kts)	Turning circle (yds)
Achilles	9280	5722	14.3	618
Bellerophon	7550	6521	14.1	401

16. Bore 38in, stroke 3ft 6in.

17. The pump could also take suction from inboard if the ship was flooded.

18. D K Brown, 'Jet Propulsion in the RN' *Marine Propulsion* (March 1980).

19. K C Barnaby, *100 Years of Specialised Shipbuilding*.

20. The author remembers, with delight, carrying out trials in the jet-propelled hydrofoil HMS *Speedy* off Seattle at some 45kts.

21. The division of responsibility and of credit between the Director and the head of the design section is a complex subject discussed a little later. There is no doubt that Reed was responsible for the main features of *Bellerophon*.

22. The structural weight of modern frigates varies as about L^1.3 and it is likely that *Bellerophon* followed a similar rule.

These two sections show the difference between the structure of *Warrior* and that of *Bellerophon* described in the text. The greater longitudinal stiffening of the bottom of the latter is clear.

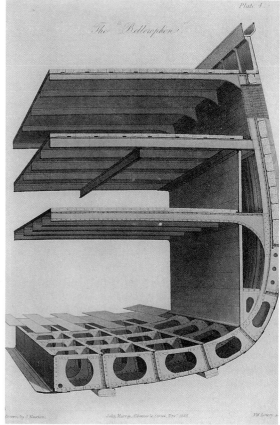

23. Hovgaard says that the bracket frame structure was due to Barnaby but quotes no evidence. (Parkes says the same but he is probably quoting Hovgaard.) Perhaps the strongest point in favour of Barnaby is that Reed, who was not reticent over his own achievements, does not claim credit for it!

24. E J Reed, 'The Structure of Iron Ships', *Naval Science* (London 1871).

25. E J Reed, 'On the value of Science to Shipbuilders', *Naval Science* (London 1871).

The structure of *Bellerophon* was on the bracket frame system.[23] There was a double bottom with continuous plate longitudinals between the inner and outer bottoms. The transverse frames were light 'brackets' arranged intercostal between the longitudinals. Victorian battleships ran aground quite often and the

Bellerophon 1865, Reed's first battleship, under sail. (R Perkins)

double bottom was a useful precaution against minor leaks. The structure was more efficient in terms of weight and cost than in older ships. There was some use of steel, presumably made by the Bessemer process, probably as in the *Audacious* (*qv*) which would have saved a little more weight. Reed[24] suggests that the designers of the *Warrior* adapted Scott Russell's system of longitudinal framing for the bottom but from the lower edge of the armour up to the upper deck they used transverse framing as the best way to support armour under the impact of shot. Below the armour, *Warrior* had deep longitudinal framing but, instead of the widely-spaced partial bulkheads used in longitudinally-framed merchant ships, she had deep plate frames spaced at about 4ft. This transverse framing gave far more strength than was needed at the expense of an unduly heavy hull. Reed then describes the advantages of the bracket frame system and other features of the *Bellerophon*.

This system derives its name from the fact that light brackets are substituted for the transverse plate frames used in *Warrior*; and by this means all necessary transverse strength and support for the skin plating are combined in a weight of transverse strengthenings, not much, if anything, greater than would be required if Mr Russell's partial bulkheads were fitted. But this does not exhaust the improvements made in recent ironclads. The depth and strength of the longitudinal frames have been increased; a complete inner skin and watertight double bottom have been adopted; and very considerable weights of iron have been added in the form of inner plating and longitudinal girders behind the armour, in order to increase the defensive powers of ships. Yet in spite of these additions and improvements – adding as they have done to the strength and safety of the structure – the weight of hull has actually been *decreased* as compared with the *Warrior* and earlier vessels.

The individual changes in *Bellerophon* are evolutionary but one gets the impression of the ship being conceived as a whole with a new outlook and this is greatly to Reed's credit. She was the starting point for a number of similar ships, always the hallmark of a good design. Reed's own view of this and other developments in structure is of interest:[25] 'I will not disclaim all credit for myself in this matter, for it is one to which I have given much anxious attention; but much more is due to the fact that my staff of colleagues and assistants embraced such highly educated officers as Mr Barnaby, Mr Barnes and Mr Crossland, all of whom are masters of the art of getting the maximum strength in a ship out of the minimum of material.'

The strength of ships (see Appendix 6)

Though, overall, the weight of a floating body must equal its buoyancy, there may be considerable differences between the weight and buoyancy at any one transverse section. These differences in loading will lead to vertical forces in the side – known as shearing force – and their sum will try to bend the ship – bending moment. These forces will exist even when the ship is stopped in still water but are much increased when she is moving through waves. The worst cases occur when she is head on to waves of her own length; if there is a crest amidships the ends will tend to droop (Hogging) whilst if there is a crest at bow and stern and a trough amidships, the middle will drop (Sagging).

White's description of the loading on the *Devastation* may make this clear.

When the *Devastation* floats on a wave of her own length (300ft long, 20ft high), the weight and buoyancy are distributed as follows; first 37ft from the bow, weight 130 tons in excess; next 34ft buoyancy 90 tons in excess; next 35ft (under fore turret) weight 580 tons in excess; next 84ft (in way of wave crest), buoyancy 940 tons in excess; next 22ft (under after turret) weight 160 tons in excess; next 37ft, buoyancy 260 tons in excess; and thence to the stern, weight 420 tons in excess.

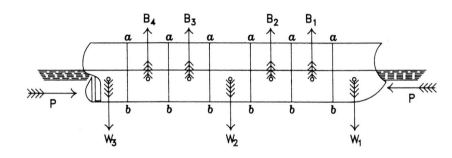

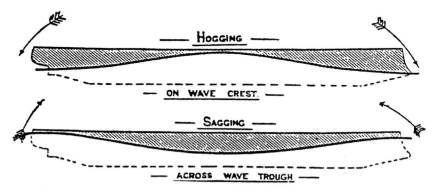

Top: For some sections of a ship weight will exceed buoyancy, at other sections the converse. The vertical force attempting to slide one section relative to its neighbour is known as the shearing force (SF) and the combined effect along the length is the bending moment.

Above: A ship is hogging when the wave crest is amidships reducing the support to the ends which tend to droop. With a crest at each end the ship is sagging with the midships relatively unsupported.

Below: For some sections of the *Devastation* weight exceeds buoyancy, in other sections this is reversed. This diagram illustrates White's description given in the text.

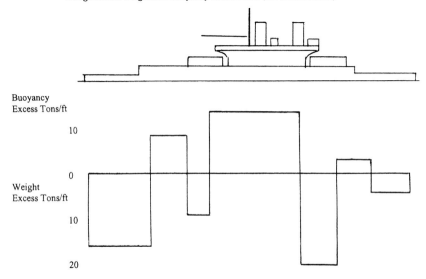

Longitudinal Weight and Buoyancy Distribution (DEVASTATION)

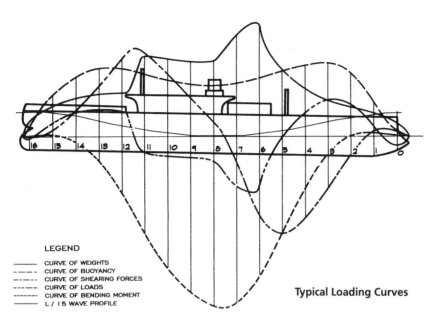

LEGEND

———	CURVE OF WEIGHTS
– – –	CURVE OF BUOYANCY
–·–·–	CURVE OF SHEARING FORCES
–··–··–	CURVE OF LOADS
–···–···–	CURVE OF BENDING MOMENT
———	L / 15 WAVE PROFILE

Typical Loading Curves

For a turret ram, these curves show wave profile (sagging), weight, buoyancy, load, shearing force and bending moment.

The nature of this loading was understood in very general terms by the middle of the eighteenth century and it was such thinking that led Seppings to his system of diagonal framing for wooden ships,[26] which was very effective in resisting the shearing forces. Fairbairn's work on the Britannia bridge added to the understanding of the behaviour of big tubes, like a ship, and, in particular, the problems of buckling, but the first comprehensive theory of structural loading is due to Rankine (1866).[27] He showed that a curve could be drawn showing how the load varied along the length of the ship. This curve could then be integrated (summing the area along the length) to give the shear force distribution and this curve could then itself be integrated to give the bending moment.

Reed realised the importance of Rankine's work and initiated action within his department to apply it to ship design. The work was carried out by White and John and led to a paper by Reed to the Royal Society.[28]

White, then a very new graduate, was dissatisfied with the acknowledgement of his work in Reed's draft of the paper and after discussion, they agreed on a phrase which credited Reed with initiating and directing the work and White with its execution.[29] At that date it was very rare for a Director to acknowledge any help at all[30] and it was a brave act for White to protest;[31] that he did shows his confidence in Reed's generosity.

The implications of this work were enormous. Firstly, accurate weight calculations were needed, together with the distribution of that weight along the length. As recently as 1865 Barnaby told the INA that weight calculations and those for the position of the centre of gravity were 'so laborious as to be virtually impossible'.[32] In the discussion, W Froude pointed out that William Bell had carried out such calculations for the *Great Eastern* (and the much more difficult moment of inertia in roll, for good measure). By 1869 such calculations were be carried out in the Admiralty for all new ships.[33] Once the weight distribution was obtained, the waterline at which the ship was balanced on a wave in both the hogging and sagging condition had to be found and hence the distribution of buoyancy; another tedious calculation. With experience, short cuts were developed but, even so, it was a laborious task for the next century. The calculation of the shearing force and bending moment curves was simple in comparison.

Once the loading on the hull was known, it was possible to design a structure which was just adequate, without the excessive factors of safety (or ignorance) which were necessary when the designer had to rely on judgement alone. In turn, this led to significant weight saving which could be used for guns and armour. In *Bellerophon*, Reed had designed a light and efficient structure. In comparing the hull weights[34] of different styles of ship it is convenient to consider the ratio of the weight to the product of the dimensions – LxBxD.

Comparison of hull weights between *Warrior* and *Bellerophon*

Ship	Hull Wt (tons)	LxBxD/ 1000	W/LBD	Cost (£x1000)
Warrior	4969	908	5.47	380
Bellerophon	3652	714	5.11	356

Using the ratio of 5.11 from *Bellerophon* on *Warrior*'s dimensions gives a structural weight of 4640 from which it can be deduced that Reed saved about 330 tons by improved structure and the rest from his shorter hull. It was time to advance from Watts' fine start.

Who was the designer?

The design of a warship is always attributed to the Director of the day as he was finally responsible. He

26. Brown, *Before the Ironclad*.

27. W J M Rankine (with contributions from Watts, Barnes and Napier), *Shipbuilding – Theoretical and Practical* (London 1866). One of the first books to distinguish between stress – the load per unit area of structure – and strain – the extension per unit length.

28. E J Reed, 'On the Unequal Distribution of Weight and Support in Ships and its effect in Still Water, in Waves and in exceptional positions', *Phil Trans. Royal Society* (London 1866) (reprinted in *Naval Science*).

29. F Manning, *The Life of Sir William White* (London 1923).

30. When White became Director himself, he hardly ever acknowledged the work of his staff.

31. This incident adds to the impression that Reed was liked and trusted by his staff.

32. Sir N Barnaby, 'An Investigation into the Stability of HMS *Achilles*', *Trans INA* (London 1865).

33. The difficulty lay in the mind; prior to 1865 the designer would carry out all calculations himself and there was no time for one man to do weight calculations. Once it was realised that an assistant could be used in lengthy analysis the way was clear. The increase in staff of the Chief Constructor's office by three assistants in 1866 probably marks the realisation of this fact.

34. Note that the 'hull weight group' contains many items which are not part of the structure. See Chapter 8.

35. I was often asked about my own contribution relative to that of my deputy on one task. Our agreed answer was that we had each contributed a quarter individually and the remaining half grew in discussion between us.

36. After the First World War, Joffre was asked if the victory of the Marne should be attributed to him. He said that he was not sure how much he had to do with the victory but was quite certain he would have been blamed for a defeat.

37. Hence the significance of Large's signature on the *Warrior* drawings.

38. Benevolence is optional.

39. Presumably made by the Bessemer process.

would, however, be responsible for several concurrent designs, run by different sections and those section heads would have an important, sometimes a dominant, role in the design. Though there is no doubt that *Bellerophon* was Reed's concept, it is clear that even before he joined the Admiralty, he had a lot of assistance from Barnaby who was to play a major role in later Reed designs.[35] Though Reed got the credit for these ships, Barnaby's reward came in promotion to the top post when Reed resigned – and Barnaby's own reputation is due to ships designed whilst he was Director and White his principal assistant. White's renown, in turn, owes much to his able assistants; Whiting, Deadman, Smith etc.

Design is – or should be – a team effort and it is not wrong to credit the Director with success; he would certainly be blamed for failure.[36] The departmental tradition was that the Director took formal responsibility (and credit) when he signed the building drawings.[37] However, a strong assistant could frequently impose his stamp on a family of ships. Section heads were – are – generally in their early forties and were titled as constructor in the 1870s (even assistant constructor) but inflation of titles made them chief constructor in later years.

Outsiders never realise the extent of differences in opinion within a design team. This conflict is usually beneficial and good-tempered but can sometimes get out of hand; the head needs to be a benevolent dictator.[38]

Later centre battery ships – *Hercules* (ld1866)

Hercules was an improved *Bellerophon*, laid down in 1866 in the dock at Chatham nearly a year after the former was floated out. There were four 10in, 18-ton guns either side of her battery with alternative ports for the end guns, giving some degree of end-on fire through recesses in the ship's side. There was also a 9in forward and aft on the upper deck; ammunition supply to these guns was very difficult. Improvements to the lines and to the machinery made her slightly faster and more economical. Her cost was about the same as *Warrior*. *Sultan*, laid down in 1868, was a further development with a bigger upper deck battery providing end-on fire. Reed refers to the fracture of a steel plate[39] in the upper deck during a cold night, a few days after it had been riveted in place. Test pieces were cut from this plate and it was found to be very variable in its properties. It was thought that it had been exposed to a cold draught dur-

Sultan 1870 was typical of Reed's larger centre battery ships. The main battery mounted four 10in MLR each side and an upper battery carried one 9in MLR each side with ports giving nominal end-on fire, although it was virtually impossible to move the guns in a seaway. The racers for two more 9in MLR can be seen at the bows, protected by an armour bulkhead. (National Maritime Museum, London: 18626, 18630)

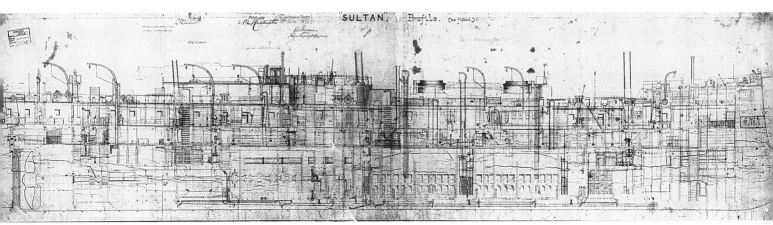

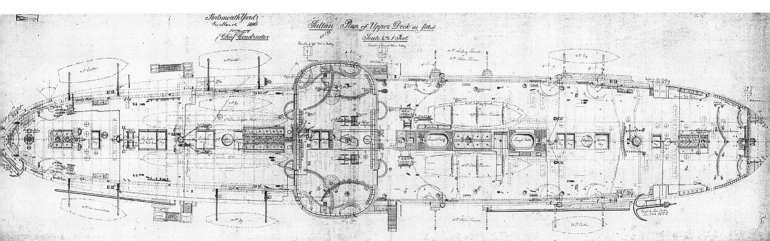

The structure of *Hercules* was generally similar to that of *Bellerophon* but the longitudinal stiffening in the backing to the armour should be noted.

ing rolling which had hardened parts of the plate making it brittle.

Thicker and thicker armour over less and less

The designer's response to more powerful guns firing improved shot was, initially, to increase the thickness of the wrought iron plate used for protection, though there were significant improvements in the design of supporting structure. The early conversions of wooden-hulled ships to ironclads call for little comment[40] but *Lord Warden* (ld 1863) had some features of interest. She was conceived as an enormous wooden frigate with 4½in plate bolted on for protection but Reed made two improvements. First he filled in the space between frames with teak so that the minimum thickness of backing was 31in instead of 9in. He then found that there was weight available for an extra 1½in of iron over a 10ft depth. The armour was already being manufactured and could not be made thicker so, after considering the options, Reed decided to put a 1½in plate between the wooden frames and the planking to protect against shells penetrating the armour and bursting in the backing.[41] Parkes[42] misunderstood this passage in Reed's paper and wrote that *Lord Warden* and her sister had a complete iron skin, an error copied by most later writers.[43] Though *Lord Warden* did have a considerable amount of iron in her structure which would take some

Lord Warden 1865, the second new construction wooden ironclad. (Imperial War Museum: Q39449)

40. The first ones were lengthened to accommodate a long battery and were weak. The later ones were of the central battery style and did not need lengthening.

41. E J Reed, 'The *Bellerophon*, *Lord Warden* and *Hercules* Targets', *Trans INA* (London 1866).

42. Parkes, *British Battleships* .

43. Me too!

44. Admiral H S Robinson, 'Armour Plating Ships of War', *Trans INA* (London 1879).

45. Ibid.

of the shearing forces, her claim to be the largest 'wooden' ship may be more correct than has been believed in recent years.

Protecting the centre battery

Bellerophon's protection incorporated two small but worthwhile improvements. The skin of the ship was formed from two thicknesses of ¾in plate riveted together and horizontal iron stiffeners were fitted within the teak backing. Following trials, these stiffeners were stopped short of the armour plate, so that if the armour was deflected on impact, it would not be forced directly onto the stiffener which might then cut into the plate.

A replica target was made and hit by fourteen shot and shell, spherical and cylindrical, cast iron and steel. None of these penetrated the complete protection though a few dented the inner skin. In particular, a 150lb shell penetrated the armour and exploded in the backing, bulging the skin plating. The striking velocity varied considerably[44] but in most cases was between 1300-1500ft/sec, although one 165lb steel shot hit at 2000ft/sec, penetrated the armour and dented the skin. Following the success of these trials, the improvements were used in later ships.

Hercules had a similar arrangement of armour and framing with a 9in waterline belt amidships and 8in over the battery. However, Reed much increased the depth of the timber backing, effectively filling in the passageway arranged behind the belt in earlier ships. The protection was made up of 9in wrought iron, 12in teak backing into which iron longitudinals were incorporated, this was followed by the skin of two layers of ¾in plate with 10in frames filled in solid with teak. Behind this came the new layer of 18in teak in two layers followed by an inner skin of ¾in plate, supported by 7in frames. A replica target was made with one 8in and one 9in plate and was hit by thirteen steel shot up to 600lbs in weight and striking at between 1300-1500 ft/sec. One 600lb shot penetrated the whole system, hitting the 8in plate where it had already been penetrated by an earlier round. The Committee concluded that the protection could not be penetrated in a sound place by any gun then existing.[45] It should be realised that the shot always struck the target perpendicularly in these test firings whereas, in action, impact would often be more oblique.

End-on fire

The manoeuvrability of the steam ship, independent of the wind, together with the increasing power of chase guns, made end-on fire seem more important. The strength and watertight integrity of the iron hull made ramming appear as a feasible tactic; and even *Warrior* was supposed to have the capability to ram.

Reed's early designs, such as that for *Research* (1861)

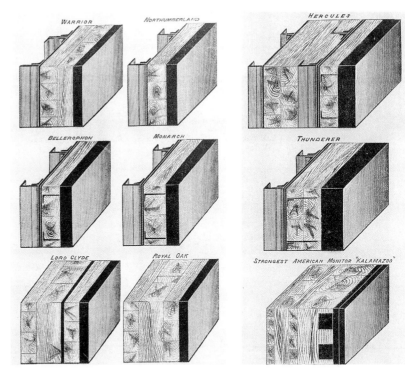

were intended to combine the advantages of the centre battery with enhanced axial fire by providing alternate ports at the fore and aft ends of the battery to which guns could be traversed, combined with recesses in the hull sides to permit the gun to point along the axis. This scheme was developed and applied to many of Reed's later ships and, in impressive style, to Barnaby's later *Alexandra*. It was also copied in many other navies. Books of the day, which are still copied, make great play of the number of guns which could train fore and aft. *Hercules* had ports on the four corners of her battery

These sketches, by Reed, show the armour arrangements of the early armoured ships.

Hercules 1868, a much improved *Bellerophon*. Note the recessed end ports of the battery which gave her some arc of fire towards the axis. (Imperial War Museum: Q40610)

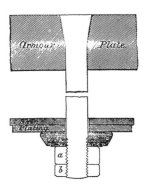

The type of armour bolt used in early ships. Impact on the exposed head could cause failure.

Iron Duke (below) and *Vanguard (bottom),* both 1870. The latter was rammed and sunk by the former. (Author's collection)

which were intended to give her 10in, 18-ton guns some degree of end-on fire. In evidence, Vice-Admiral Sir T Symonds said[46] that these could not be used and that her end-on fire was confined to two 12-ton guns. There is mention[47] of her firing the 10in, with battering charges, from the corner ports but the angle to the hull is not reported.

There were a number of practical problems which suggest that these claimed arcs of fire were geometrical curiosities rather than usable capabilities. For a start, traversing the gun to the alternate ports was difficult, and virtually impossible in a seaway. The lower end ports, such as those on *Alexandra's* main deck, could not be opened in a seaway[48] and their recesses through up vast sheets of spray. Finally, and most important, there was the effect of muzzle blast on adjoining structure. It is not easy to quantify this effect and it is certain that some damage, unacceptable in peace time, would be accepted in action, as with the severe self-inflicted wound endured by *Rodney* in action with *Bismarck.* However, it is very hard to believe that arrangements

such as the hinged bulwarks in *Enterprise* and *Favourite* would have survived undamaged. No records of trials have been found and the fact that this curious attempt to achieve end-on fire was not repeated suggests that may not have been any. Damage there was; see the later section on *Temeraire* and the blast damage at the bombardment of Alexandria, even though most firing was close to broadside. Peacetime firing practice was confined to arcs close to the broadside and it is likely that damage would have been unacceptable if guns were fired within 30° of fore and aft structure.[49]

The manufacture of armour plates *c*1870

The manufacture of and the fitting of a big armour plate was always a major technical feat and this short note, based on Reed,[50] is needed to appreciate the achievement. In 1870, a big plate would be some 15ft long, 4ft wide, 6in thick and weigh about 6½ tons, then about the largest piece of iron which could be made. It would have to be shaped to fit the sides of the ship, curved in all directions, and also bevelled to butt precisely against adjoining plates.

The edges and butts of the armour plate would be drawn on the half block model so that they were clear of joints in both thicknesses of the shell plating and avoided frames. The small sketches of each plate so obtained were then expanded at full size on the mould loft floor. Wooden moulds were then made and sent to the manufacturer showing the curvature and twist but, even so, ¾in extra was allowed on the edges of difficult plates.

As the shell plating was built onto the ship, the position of the big armour bolts was marked, clear of other fastenings, and more wooden moulds made. The position of the bolts had also to be clear of any supporting girders within the backing. The diagram above shows some of the difficulties in arranging these bolts. The timber backing was installed with both sides protected by red lead or, more often, waterproof glue.

In order to bend a plate, it was first put in a furnace and slowly raised to a bright red heat and kept there for 3-5 hours. The plate would then be bent to shape either using a hydraulic press or a heavy cradle in which the plate could be forced to shape using wedges. Reed says that both methods were satisfactory and were selected on the basis of cost and experience – though he hints that pressure from the work force to save jobs sometimes led to uneconomic use of the cradle. The press needed eight men working for about 10 hours whilst the cradle used seventeen men for about 25 minutes followed by a further 6 hours adjustment in a press. The plate would then be drilled and countersunk to take the bolts and the edges planed to the correct bevel to fit against the neighbouring plates.

The bolts used in British ships were conical headed, countersunk into the outer side of the plate and secured by nuts inside the shell plating. In the case of *Hercules,*

the 6in plates were secured with 2¾in bolts with 3½in heads and the 8in and 9in plates with 3in bolts with 4¼in heads. Holes in the backing were smaller than the bolt which was forced through to give a tight fit. There were two nuts on the inner end with a rubber washer to reduce the effect of the shock wave should the bolt be hit by a shot. In *Hercules* the bolts were spaced about every 2ft round the edges and the centre of the plate was unpierced. Very considerable thought was given to bolting arrangements and many variations were tried – even the threads for the nuts were of a special shallow form to avoid weakening the bolt.

The French used wood screws passing through the plate, securing it to the timber backing which absorbed the shock wave. A test of this system was carried out at Shoeburyness in 1864 on two plates, each 5ft 9in x 2ft 6in, approximately 4.75in and 5.9in thick.[51] Though the trial showed that this method was very effective, it was not adopted as it was thought that it would be very difficult to remove the screws later when they had rusted into place. It was also thought desirable that the armour should be attached to the iron structure and screws could be torn out of the wood with less force than that needed to break them. Reed's full account is worth studying as the care taken over the details which have been omitted in this short summary is most impressive. The Admiralty took immense care to get every detail right in the protection.

Audacious and *Iron Duke*

These ships are exceptionally well-documented, mainly in evidence to the 1871 Committee and hence this section is, perhaps, a little longer than justified by their importance. It does, however, bring out much of the thinking of admirals and naval architects at that date.

The *Audacious* class were to be second-rate ships, dictated by economy but, in part, justified by their role which was for use on foreign station where it was expected that they would fight only armoured cruisers. The original requirement was for a 3000-ton (bm) ship with 6in armour and only 8in RML but Spencer Robinson 'begged as if for my dear life' for 8in armour and 9in, 12-ton guns[52] and the final design was submitted on 2 February 1867 at an estimated cost of £220,000 and approved on 8 February 1867. Reed told the 1871 Committee[53] that the requirement was to produce a 'better' *Defence* on the same dimensions bearing the same relation to *Hercules* as did *Defence* to *Warrior*. This involved many sacrifices to get the cost down. There was also a requirement for maximum sail power and an upper deck battery with bow and stern fire from behind armour. Spencer Robinson said that they were 'the only broadside ships in existence which could fire their heaviest guns in line with the keel'.

The requirement for shallow draught led to twin screws which were hard to combine with good sailing;

though it was originally intended that they should be lifting, no satisfactory solution could be found. A balanced rudder was fitted in three ships giving them a turning circle of 318 to 423yds with 40° rudder angle while *Iron Duke* with an ordinary rudder took 505yds. In 1871 Reed maintained that this design was better for foreign service than a turret ship.

In earlier classes the only structural drawing sent out by the Admiralty was the midship section and the Dockyard used this as guidance in developing the rest of the structure. Reed thought the Admiralty would need six times as many draughtsmen as at present (sixty instead of ten) to produce full drawings.[54] On a visit to Chatham, Reed noticed, with horror, that the details needed amidships had been 'worked at the ends at great weight and cost' and great efforts were made in *Audacious* to reduce weight where possible, including a considerable use of steel in the structure. Unfortunately most of the saving was in the bottom structure so that the centre of gravity rose. On completion they were 6–11in light (170-320 tons).[55]

Reed claims to have been influenced in the design of this class by Froude's theory of rolling (1861, discussed later) and had intended them to have a fairly low metacentric height and the further reduction as a result of the weight saving low down was serious. It was said[56] that *Invincible* arrived at Plymouth on one occasion with 16° loll due to negative metacentric height. She was also said[57] to heel 10° under helm. *Iron Duke* was inclined at Devonport and needed some 300 tons of water in the double bottoms. The *Invincible* was inclined with 300 tons of water in the double bottom.[58] With 312 tons of ballast she had a GM of 3.43ft, *Iron Duke* 3in more.[59] As a result they were given 340 tons of ballast in the form of concrete in the double bottom.[60]

Reed claims that he always realised ballast might be necessary but this sounds unlikely. The navigating officer of *Vanguard* said that she had been tender before ballasting but was so no longer; she was a 'most comfortable ship in bad weather'.[61] The ballast increased the draught by 15in and reduced speed from 14.8kts to 14kts. She carried coal for three days at full power. She was almost unmanageable under canvas alone and he would like the balanced rudder replaced. The best speed under sail was 6.5kts. The mizzen was thought to be of little value and rarely used.

The double-deck battery was based on Reed's design for the *Fatikh*[62] and seems to have been successful; on trials the guns were fired in the end ports causing only trivial damage, most of which could be prevented in future by minor changes. The forward gun could fire at 3° abaft the beam. The main damage was to the wooden hammock stowages which were replaced by iron.[63] A dummy man on the forecastle was destroyed. Captain Lambert (*Vanguard*) said he never tried firing ahead as it would destroy the skylights and said that great caution was needed in moving the guns in a seaway. He also said

46. 1871 Committee

47. 1870 Naval Estimates.

48. Ballard, *The Black Battlefleet*.

49. At the end of the century it was reported that USS *Olympia* could fire her 8in at ± 10° to the keel.

50. E J Reed, *Shipbuilding in Iron and Steel* (London 1869).

51. Admiral H S Robinson, 'Armour Plating Ships of War', *Trans INA* (London 1879).

52. 1871 Committee.

53. 1871 Committee evidence of Reed, 17 April 1871

54. He did not mention that there would have been a corresponding saving at each building yard.

55. 1871 – Constructor's report.

56. 1871 Committee, evidence of W Pearce. This figure seems dubious in the light of the stability found on inclining.

57. Staff Captain W W Kiddle, 1871.

58. It is almost impossible to get an accurate inclining with any liquid in a double bottom.

59. The report attributed the difference to differences in form or difference between actual and calculated weights of ballast. It is much more likely to have been movement of liquid ballast.

60. After ballasting, they exceeded the design draught by; *Vanguard* 6in, *Invincible* 5in, *Iron Duke* 1in and *Audacious* 6in. This amount of ballast would increase GM by about 1ft.

61. 1871 Committee, evidence of Lieutenant D Farrat. The fact that she was comfortable in bad weather may suggest that GM was still on the low side.

62. Designed by Reed for Turkey, built by Thames Iron Works, sold to Germany as *König Wilhelm*.

63. 1871 Committee, evidence of Rear-Admiral W H Stewart 6 May 1871.

that the arcs of fire forward were very limited and one could only get off a 'snap shot' whilst the ship was yawing. The main deck port sills were 8ft and the upper ones 16ft 6in above the waterline. There was some concern that a shell exploding in the lower level would also cause casualties in the upper battery but others thought that the thick deck would give protection. The overhanging underside of the upper battery had strong iron flash plates to take the blast of the main deck guns. The box amidships was cramped and it was difficult to work the ship from it. Lambert would prefer the battery further forward where he thought it could fire at 30° across the bow.

The Design Committee seems to have been obsessed with the need for these ships to ground without damage; the requirement for shallow draught seems only a partial explanation. Two of the class suffered damage to the bottom during building, *Audacious* because the launch ways were positioned over an unsupported plate instead of a frame and *Invincible* was allowed to ground at low tide on a boulder. Neither of these incidents reflect on Reed's design and there is no evidence of weakness in service though he did say that in a future similar ship he would bring the longitudinals closer. The report of damage to *Audacious* mentions that several steel longitudinals had fractured,[64] one of the earliest mentions of steel in warship structure.

The first two ships were ordered from Napier on 29 April 1867. Before ordering repeats, the Admiralty invited alternative design which could be turret ships or broadside. The displacement was to be between 3500 and 3800 tons with a draught not exceeding 22ft 6in. The belt was to be 8in and the turret 10in. Turret guns should be 18- or 23-ton, a broadside ship should have ten 9in, with two lighter end guns; six of the 9in should be on the main deck, four on the upper deck. Ports should be 8ft wide, spaced at 17ft. They were to be capa-

ble of 13.5kts and carry 4.4sq ft of sail per ton. They were to be of iron (with some steel) and a balanced rudder would be accepted. Seven designs were submitted, mostly for turret ships, but none showed any great advantage over Reed's design. Some of the detailed criticisms are of interest:[65]

London Engineering Co. The recessed ports were disliked as Brazilian experience showed that these could guide splinters into the port. The design was too narrow.
Millwall. Weight estimates at least 400 tons out.
Palmers. Their proposal for a moveable battery was thought impractical.
Napier. Belt too low.
Thames Iron Works. (Broadside) Doubts on weights.
Samuda. The draught was exceeded by 6in – and, even then, the weights were suspect.
Laird. Virtually a copy of *Monarch*. It was claimed that the after turret could fire forward through the tripod mast. 7ft 6in freeboard.

There was also an Admiralty turret ship design whose details have not been found but the original *Audacious* was preferred. One was ordered from Pembroke on 26 September 1867 and the fourth from Laird's on 21 October. The average contract price was £220,190 (*cf Resistance* £223,055).

Name	Hull wt (tons)	Armour wt (tons)	Protection
Resistance	3750	697	4½in, 18in back, ½in shell
Audacious	2600	924	8-6in, 10in back, 1½in shell

Swiftsure 1870, a single-screw version of *Iron Duke*. (Author's collection)

The Constructors' report to the Committee concluded: 'We have, however, no reason as naval architects for wishing to keep large sail power in steam ships of war; we are aware of all the disadvantages of all the disadvantages that a large rig entails on the steaming and fighting powers of such a ship and as we are informed that the complements of these ships are small for the satisfactory working of the sails in ships of such peculiar construction, we should on the whole consider it an improvement to reduce the sail power.' Later, *Vanguard*'s topmasts were reduced by 10ft and the rest by 6ft; in common with other rigged armoured ships, the yards were removed from the mizzen. Admiral Houston Stewart summed them up as 'very clever ships – so many good qualities in a small, handy hull'.

A modified design with deeper draught and a single screw was submitted on 7 April 1868 and approved a week later. The draught was increased from 22ft to 24ft

9in, displacement from 5900 tons to 6504 tons. There was some loss of speed due to extra 600 tons, largely offset by the greater efficiency of single-screw propulsion.

The new ship was to be sheathed with copper over wood which increased tonnage from 3774 tons to 3892 tons due to effect of sheathing on beam. Freedom from fouling made them faster at sea after they had been at sea 'for a few weeks'. *Audacious* had been given a zinc sheath which was not very effective in stopping fouling though it was easy to clean. Spencer Robinson said of fouling 'I scarcely know anything more variable', sometimes one would be better than another solution whilst at other times the order would be reversed. Fouling was very severe in tropical waters with a loss of speed of about 3kts after 4 months (equivalent to doubling the power required).

On 28 July 1868 the Controller wrote suggesting a look at a turret ship with a moderately high freeboard, safe, and well-adapted for a cruiser – four 25-ton guns in two turrets capable of all-round fire. Robinson commented: 'I believe that this concession to the opinions of a great number of the members of the House of Commons and of a large portion of the public could be made without much prejudice to the wants of the service; for if a vessel certainly less able to cruise with comfort, would be produced, it is equally certain that the turret ship would turn out a more powerful fighting ship than the *Swiftsure* and considering all the circumstances it would appear unobjectionable to make some sacrifice of the cruisers qualities for the sake of greater powers of offence and defence in at least one of these two ships.' It was decided on 30 July that there should be no alteration. The calculation for the height of the centre of gravity was as for twin screw with 360 tons of ballast.

Balanced rudders

It is interesting that there was universal hostility to the use of balanced rudders in sailing ships even though its merits under steam were appreciated. Attention was mainly focused on the *Vanguard* with a balanced rudder and her sister *Iron Duke* with a traditional hinged rudder. The word 'unmanageable' is used by several officers describing the former under sail.[66] Both were twin-screw ships (the propellers were not lifted for sailing), *Vanguard* having Mangin propellers – twin, two-bladed propellers set in tandem with the blades behind each other, intended to reduce drag when sailing – whilst *Iron Duke* had two-bladed Griffith screws.

Monarch had a balanced rudder and was also said to be 'unmanageable' when wearing, which took some 20 minutes, though as a one-off there was no comparison to be made.[67] The Controller, Spencer Robinson, a very perceptive officer, thought that these ships had rudders which were over-balanced and instanced *Hercules* with less balance as being better, though still not good. This matches with Rev Dr Corlett's comments on *Great Britain*[68] where overbalance is also described as a problem under sail.

No explanation was offered at the time and, even today, it is not clear what was happening. Discussion with Corlett suggests the following tentative approach. Under sail, the ship would be yawed and, with the bluff forms of the day, flow round the stern would tend to separate. The problem was worse in shallow water; Ballard says that in the Suez Canal they either required a tug ahead or dragged a chain astern.[69] The balanced rudder is an isolated lifting surface which works well in the slipstream behind a propeller. The traditional hinged rudder was a trimming tab on a lifting surface formed by the whole ship which would be yawed slightly into the wind when sailing. The sails would usually be trimmed so that the ship carried a small amount of weather helm and any movement of the rudder would cause considerable pressure changes on the quarters. Under sail, a balanced rudder, isolated from the hull by the aperture, would have much less effect.

The forts of the 1859 Commission

By 1859 there was a belief that the steamship made it possible for the French to land a large body of troops whilst the fleet was engaged elsewhere. In particular, the Royal Dockyards were vulnerable to long-range bombardment.

The work of the Royal Commission 'to consider the defences of the United Kingdom (1859)' will be outlined only very briefly since it is fully described by Saunders[70] and Hogg.[71] In the light of developments in artillery, they were asked to '. . . examine the present state, condition and sufficiency of the fortifications existing for the defence of the United Kingdom, examine works in progress' and consider any additional work needed. They were directed to start their work at Portsmouth (including the Isle of Wight and Spithead), then, Plymouth, Portland, Pembroke, Dover, Chatham and the Medway, Woolwich and (later) Haulbowline at Queenstown (Cork).

The membership of the Committee was well balanced;[72] the most influential were Lieutenant Colonel Lefroy, a distinguished gunner and founder of the RA Institution, Captain Cooper Key, a technically informed naval officer and James Ferguson, a 'civilian'[73] who had written an essay on fortification rejecting conventional views and proposing massive earthworks. Their report was presented on 7 February 1860. They began with some general remarks which may be seen as outside their terms of reference and will be discussed in the following section. They concluded that the fleet alone was insufficient for the defence of the kingdom as the introduction of steamships, the vastly increased power of artillery and shell-firing guns would enable an enemy to concentrate superior naval power and a large

64. *Audacious* was launched in February and there must be a suspicion that the temperature was low leading to brittle fracture in poor steel.

65. Naval Estimates 1867. Parkes is scornful of the Admiralty's choice of their own design but their reasons seem sound and were exposed to Parliamentary scrutiny.

66. Captain E H G Lambert, Lieutenant D Forrest, Vice-Admiral Spencer Robinson (Controller), Rear-Admiral W H Stewart and E J Reed.

67. Captain E Price, Commander E C Curtis.

68. Dr E C B Corlett, *The Iron Ship* (Moonraker Press 1974), p64.

69. Ballard, *The Black Battlefleet*.

70. A Saunders, *Fortress Britain* (Beaufort, Liphook 1989).

71. I V Hogg, *Coast Defences of England and Wales* (Newton Abbott 1974).

72. Membership: Major Generals, Sir H D Jones, D A Cameron and Sir F Hallett, Rear-Admiral G Elliot, Captain A Cooper Key, Lieutenant-Colonel J H Lefroy and James Ferguson.

73. Ferguson is often described as representing the Treasury but according to Moore, there is no direct evidence of this.

body of troops at any point on the coasts. At the same time they recognised the importance of the sea as a barrier and most strongly urged the Government to ensure the efficiency of the fleet. Protection of naval arsenals and dockyards was of prime importance. They also concluded that 'neither our fleet, our standing army, nor our volunteer force, nor even the three combined can be relied on as sufficient in themselves for the security of the Kingdom against foreign invasion'. Given that the fleet was the first line of defence, fortifications should protect dockyards, harbours and, hence, indirectly, London. In the light of the new rifled guns, such as the Armstrong, the Commission saw 8000yds as a likely range for an enemy to use for bombardment and the defences must command sea and land within that range of vital targets. A limited programme of fortifications had been in hand for some years and this range was largely an endorsement of the earlier work. The forts and batteries were to be designed to be defended by the smallest possible number of men and, even within that number, the quota of skilled gunners should be small, the balance being local volunteers. The design was to permit rapid construction and it was envisaged that the main ramparts and ditch should be defensible within 3 – 4 months of commencement. The scale of the proposed works was vast. There were to be forts on shoals in Spithead (five, later reduced to three), a number of forts and batteries were to prevent a landing on the Isle of Wight and to control the Needles passage. The whole 7-mile length of Portsdown Hill was to be fortified and there were various minor works. The sea defences of Plymouth needed some strengthening but a considerable number of new forts were needed to protect the land side. Some plans had already been made for strengthening the defences of Pembroke (Milford Haven) which were endorsed, together with increased land defences. Some forts were in hand at Portland and two more were added; nothing was to be done about land defences. The defence of the Thames and Medway was seen as very difficult but a considerable number of works were proposed which would also protect Woolwich and, to some extent, London. The cost of these works was enormous by the standards of the day. It was estimated that the works would cost just over £7 million, armament another £500,000 which together with work already approved (£1,460,000) totalled £11,850,000 – note, for comparison, the cost of *Warrior* was £380,000. The report was debated in Parliament in July 1860 by which time fear of a French attack had somewhat abated. Those most vociferous in demanding forts were among the most reluctant to pay for them, a not unusual phenomenon. However, the Bill was approved in August for £9 million of works, the armament and floating batteries to be provided from normal

votes. It was suggested that this was not a great sum as the French had spent £8 million on Cherbourg alone. By 1867 seventy-six forts and batteries were under construction even though some reductions had been made from the original proposals. There were a considerable number of changes made during the construction of these forts, mainly as a result of more powerful guns. The Commission had envisaged the 68pdr and the 7in BLR as the principal gun for the land forts with larger guns for the sea forts. During construction many of the latter were altered to mount much larger guns, which meant larger casemates and fewer guns. There was a reserve of guns from which they would be armed in times of tension but there is evidence that there was a considerable shortfall. The lessons of the American Civil War suggested further use of earthworks while rising living standards meant that the space per man was increased from 400 to 600cu ft per man – since the forts were well advanced, this meant a reduction in the number of men which could be accommodated, at least in peacetime. All this meant substantial extra cost, only partly offset by further reductions in the work planned. It is not easy to find actual costs; nineteenth century official accounting was complex and often muddled (for ships as well as forts). Figures for those completed to something near the original plan suggest that the commission's estimates were of the right order though rather low. For example. Fort Wallington's actual cost according to the 1868 Committee was £103,195 compared with an original estimate of £75,000. The sea forts were greatly altered, completing as almost all iron instead of stone but it would seem that the difficulty of building them had been greatly underestimated. The progress of the works was examined by Parliamentary committees in 1867 and in 1869. Their overall report was favourable though they found much to criticise in the detail. There is general agreement that the French had no plan for an attack on the British Isles but they, too, had built many coast attack vessels during the Crimean War and there was a real, potential threat.[74] The response, in terms of land forts, may have been excessive but a considerable amount of building was wise. The biggest problem would have been manning them quickly in an emergency. As planned in 1860 the works required 72,000 trained men supported by 108,000 militia and it was thought at the time that the numbers available fell short by at least 63,000 men. The sea forts, in particular, had living quarters for a small garrison only and the extra needed in wartime would have to sleep round the guns with very few primitive toilets. In considering the defences of the UK it should be remembered that coastal attack was an important role for the Royal Navy and Cherbourg was very vulnerable.[75]

74. See for example the papers of the 'Ships v Forts' conference, RN Museum, Portsmouth, November 1995.

75. Various papers by Dr Andrew Lambert. See also the section on Flat Iron gunboats in Chapter 7.

Turrets and Capsize | *Three*

AFTER WARTIME experience in the Black Sea, Captain Coles, a brilliant gunnery officer, became convinced that heavy guns should be mounted on an armoured turntable, a turret or cupola,[1] as the mounting was originally known, and he patented his design in March 1859.[2] His sound and well-publicised arguments had already won support and within 6 months the Admiralty ordered[3] a prototype cupola of Coles' design, mounting a single 40pdr BL, from Scott Russell. Progress was slow, suggesting changes were made, and it may have been completed at Woolwich Dockyard. It was installed for trial on the armoured battery *Trusty* in September 1861.[4]

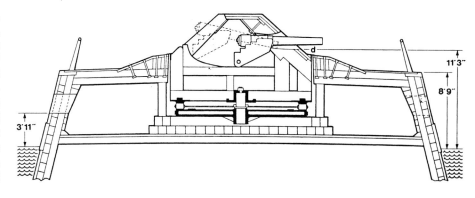

The Coles cupola built by Scott Russell and tried in *Trusty* in 1861. Note the sloping sides, abandoned in later turrets.

Trusty trials, 1861

The detailed report of the trials by Captain A Powell was published in 1866.[5] Overall, the trials, which covered many aspects, were very successful; the turret-mounted gun could fire faster and more accurately than one on the broadside, whilst the turret withstood thirty-five hits without significant damage. Powell said that the gun, a 40pdr BL, ran out after firing without the need for tackle, even when the ship was heeled 2°. The space inside the turret was sufficient and, though the recoil was severe, the crew were well out of the way. There was less trouble with smoke than on a gun deck and the temperature rose only 2° F. The concussion was severe and the men should use cotton wool in their ears even when it was reduced by enlarging the hole in the roof.

The cupola gun achieved a better rate of fire than the broadside mount in all conditions but particularly when the target or the firing ship was moving. Twelve rounds were fired more quickly than ever achieved before and the arrangements for supplying ammunition were sufficient. The gun could be pointed using the sight on the gun, which was difficult since the aperture was small and the gun could not be fired until the aimer was clear. There was also a sight on the turret roof which was exposed and it was difficult to pass the elevation to the gun. It was clear that these minor problems were specific to the prototype mounting and could easily be remedied in later versions. The turret mount needed a smaller crew: a 40pdr in a 'cupola' needed nine men, while on the broadside eleven were required.[6]

Altogether eighty-eight rounds were fired with no mechanical problems. Training was smooth, whether rapid or slow and there was no difficult in tracking a small target moving through 8 points in 1½ minutes. With four men at the winch and the ship heeled 2° the following rates of training were achieved with two winches:

180° in 55½ seconds
90° in 22 seconds
45° in 12½ seconds

A third winch was added and these times were roughly halved. Maximum elevation was 10° and depression 6°.

Most of the rounds fired at the turret were from an Armstrong 100pdr but Coles pointed out that the turret was designed only to resist 40lb shot[7] so to begin with five of these were fired with 5lb charges, with little or no effect. Thirty-four 100lb shot were fired with 12lb charges of which twenty-six hit – eight missed in calm water against a stationary target! – causing very slight physical damage, one cracked plate, and the gun was still operational. Two rounds broke in the port and would have caused numerous casualties. Finally four 68lb shot were fired with 16lb charges and the turret withstood this very severe test.

Captain Powell summed up the trial as follows:

Advantages

Accuracy – ease of getting sights on target.
Rapidity – faster at moving target.
Quicker – Smoke clears from sights.
Large angle of training – 10-11 points.
Perfect system of concentration.
Cupola needs fewer men and, with three exceptions, these need less training.
Casualties less.

1. Coles' first design, as fitted in *Trusty*, had sloping sides and all later ones had vertical sides. For a time the convention was that cupolas had sloping sides; turret was used for those whose sides were vertical.

2. J P Baxter, *The Introduction of the Ironclad Warship* (Harvard 1933, reprint Archon 1968).

3. The *Engineer* (2 Aug 1861) says the order was originally placed by the War Office and later taken over by the Admiralty. This could have referred to the Ordnance Board.

4. 'Iron Cased Shield Ships', *Engineering* (2 August 1861).

5. Navy Estimates 1866-67; Parliamentary Papers.

6. For a 100pdr the cupola needed eleven men and the broadside nineteen.

7. The cupola was protected with 4½in iron, doubled round the port over timber backing, so it is not surprising that it stood up well.

Disadvantages
Amount of structure below cupola but connected to it.
Concussion great.
Difficult to move gun if disabled.
Elevation complicated.

Powell's report then gives some very detailed records of the time taken to fire under various conditions. Some of the published figures seem to be in error but the summary which follows compares the best intervals in seconds between rounds achieved by turret and broadside mounts.

	Turret	*Broadside*
Quick fire – horizontal	31½	41
Independent fire at 600 – 800yds.	34	44
Independent firing at different targets, 600, 800 and 1000yds, 9° off, 20° apart.	45	73

The turret appears to show to greater advantage as range and difficulty increases – as one would expect.

As a result of this trial, the Admiralty ordered the iron-hulled, armoured coastal defence ship, *Prince Albert*, designed by Isaac Watts, in February 1862 and in April 1862 ordered the wooden three-decker, *Royal Sovereign* to be converted into a low-freeboard turret ship, also for coastal defence. These were the first major

Top: A model of *Prince Albert* showing the arrangement of the turrets. (Author's collection, courtesy of the Science Museum Reserve Collection)

Above: *Prince Albert* 1864, a new design, coast defence turret ship. (Imperial War Museum: Q21640)

Right: The Coles turret of *Royal Sovereign*. Note the wood packing under the rollers to match the 'tween decks height of the ship. Though generally very good, there was a leak path between the side of the turret and the deck. It originally carried a 10½in SB. (Courtesy John Roberts)

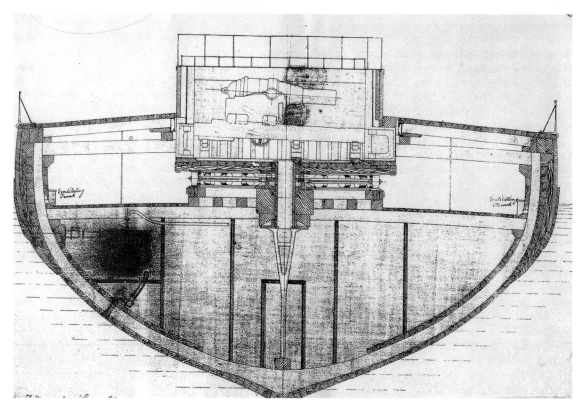

British warships without sails.[8] *Prince Albert* of 3880 tons cost £208,345 whilst the conversion of the 5080-ton *Royal Sovereign* cost £180,572.

At first sight, it might be thought that some of Captain Powell's points are trivial, mere nit-picking. However, the object of this trial as with many later ones was to correct all errors, however trivial, before the turret or other device went into service.

The 'First'

'Firsts' in technology are rarely significant as there are usually parallel developments elsewhere and it is almost chance which completes first and, not necessarily the same thing, which wins fame and fortune; *eg* Petit Smith and Ericsson for the screw, and for the turret, Coles and the same Ericsson.[9] However, this is an important exception; the nineteenth century Admiralty has too often been accused of being technologically reactionary and its 'failure' to adopt the turret until after the battle of Hampton Roads is often quoted as 'evidence'. In fact, the experimental turret was ordered a few months after Coles' patent, it was tried before Ericsson's plans were known and *Prince Albert* and possibly *Royal Sovereign* were on order before news of the fight between *Monitor* and *CSS Virginia* reached London. Ericsson had been working on plans for a turret since about 1854 but the first public exposure was at the end of August 1861 (just before the *Trusty* trial) in response to the Union Navy's invitation for ironclad designs.

In no way does this discredit Ericsson's work; it is clear that he and Coles worked independently and their eventual designs were significantly different, The Coles turret revolved on a roller path on the lower deck and projected only some 4ft above the main deck. This did mean that there was a leak path between deck and turret and, though this could be sealed with canvas for passage it remained a problem, albeit minor. The Ericsson turret stood entirely above the deck and the armoured side was 8-9ft high. It was pivoted on a spindle which carried the whole weight of the turret guns and mountings and turned in a bearing in the hold. When not in use the turret rested on the deck and in order for it to be able to turn the spindle had to be wedged up. This made it possible for the turret to be jammed by projectiles hitting at the base as happened at Charleston and it was not ready for action at all times as was the Coles turret.[10] Other early turret ships were *Rolf Krake* (Denmark, l 1863), *Affondatore* (Italy, ld 1863), and *Huascar* (Peru, ld 1865), all built in the UK with Coles turrets.

Royal Sovereign

The gunnery trials of the *Royal Sovereign* were described[11] in detail by her Captain, Sherard Osborne, famous for his exploits in the Sea of Azov during the late war. The trials began cautiously on 26 July 1864 when

Royal Sovereign, a wooden three-decker converted to a coast-defence turret ship, completing in 1864. (Author's collection)

the crew was exercised in clearing for action and a single gun fired with blank across 18ft of deck. Another round of blank was fired from the second turret at 20° abaft the beam. Crockery and glasses had been placed on the mess tables below and these were undisturbed, as were full buckets of water placed on the turret roof. Concussion below was barely perceptible and there was no sign of fire on the upper deck which had deliberately been left unwetted.

The next day reduced charges were fired at 66½° forward of the beam followed by full 35lb charges and solid shot. Twenty-two rounds were fired with up to 3° depression. There was no damage and the machinery, with steam up, was undisturbed. On 27 July firing with 20 and 35lb charges was carried out against a target at 1000yds, showing the need for a rangefinder.[12] The only damage was the loosening of the nails in the hen coop – the hens were unhurt! – altogether fifty-seven rounds were fired of which forty-two were full charge. The ship was at sea the next day, rolling slightly in a swell and fired another 103 rounds. The turrets were fired towards each other, just missing, with no problem. The usable arcs of training were found as:

Forward (Twin)	78°F – 52° Right gun, 57° Aft Left gun (Angles from the beam)
2nd	47°F – 40°A
3rd	50°F – 40°A
4th	40°F – 75°A

The aft turret was fired 5° from aft and blew the officers' heads away.

In his letter of 15 October, Osborne noted that the ship behaved well, rolling to a maximum of 10°, ten times a minute (probably half rolls, see Appendix 5). By this date 177 rounds had been fired with only the most minor defects. The seal where the turret passed through the deck was the only remaining problem. He thought his ship could destroy any ironclad afloat due to her handiness, speed, weight of broadside and she was a small target. He believed he could see his way to firing at night with similar accuracy.

8. *Prince Albert* did have two small fore-and-aft sails to steady her rather than for propulsion.

9. One might add Ericsson yet again and Robert Stephenson for the practical railway engine.

10. Hovgaard, *Modern History of Warships*.

11. Letters of 1 August 1864 and 15 October 1864, reprinted in Navy Estimates 1866-67; Parliamentary Papers.

12. Osborne notes that he bought with his own money an Adie 'telemomete'.

An Ericsson turret as mounted in the Swedish *John Ericsson* class monitors. It originally mounted two 15in SB. The conning tower was carried above the turret and the spindle had to bear the whole weight. (Courtesy John Roberts)

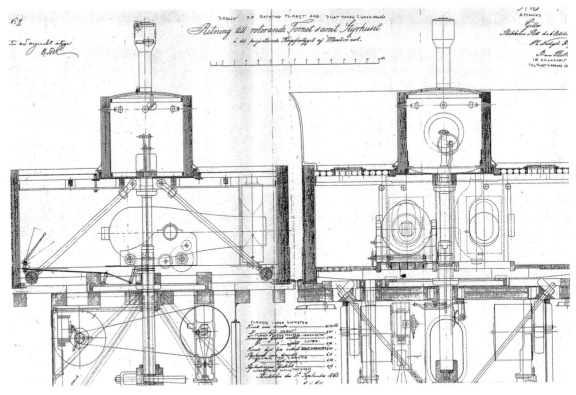

The first French turret was designed by Napier on the Coles' style and fitted in *Cerbere* of 1865.

Next steps

In Britain, the next step was an elaborate mock-up of a turret with two 100pdr guns which was fitted to the hulk *Hazard* to check loading arrangements in a twin turret. There were delays in completing the two coast defence ships due to changes in the design of the turret, mainly so as to carry bigger guns. *Prince Albert* completed with four single turrets, each mounting a 9in, 12-ton gun and with a hull coated with 4½in plate from end to end. *Royal Sovereign* had five 10.5in, 12½-ton guns in one twin and three single turrets with 5½in armour. The turrets in both ships were open at the top, presumably to get rid of gun smoke. Tests were carried out with 100lb shot fired against the turrets in both ships.[13] These two ships carried only jury rig and were flush-decked so that the end turrets had wide arcs of fire; as coastal defence ships they were very satisfactory.

Ocean-going turret ships posed many difficult problem ignored by Coles. Fuel consumption was too heavy for a battleship to cross the Atlantic under steam alone, whilst Reed was surely right in saying that the upper deck of a fully-rigged ship was no place for a turret. Coles was pressing hard for a fully-rigged turret ship. In 1859 he proposed a ship with ten turrets which was so ridiculous, though praised by the credulous, that considerable ill feeling was generated with Controller and his department. In 1862 Coles proposed a more sensible ship to the RUSI and early in 1863 the Admiralty agreed to allow Barnaby to work with Coles in the development of a practical ship. This design, completed in 1863, carried two twin turrets and a full rig on three tripod masts.[14] Work continued until June when the Admiralty decided to wait until the trials of the *Royal Sovereign* was complete making it clear[15] that '. . . their Lordships were not abandoning plans for the turret'. That spring there was a furious debate between Coles and Reed at the Institution of Naval Architects in which it may now be thought that both parties overstated their case.

The 1865 Committee

In 1864 Coles tried again, suggesting a ship to be based on the *Pallas* and again asking for assistance. The Admiralty agreed, lending Joseph Scullard, Chief Draughtsman of Portsmouth Dockyard. The design with a single turret carrying a pair of 600pdr guns (12in, 25-ton) was submitted in early 1865. The Admiralty decided to set up a committee[16] to 'obtain the unbiased opinion of practical naval officers'; Coles' demand to nominate half the members was, understandably, ignored. Coles was invited to give evidence or, when he declined in the light of his serious illness, to nominate a representative but in a letter of June he declined either to attend or to answer questions.

The Committee was asked 'To examine the design of the seagoing turret ship submitted by Coles' with a long list of specific questions whose nature is clear in the light of the report which may be summarised as follows.

Advantages. The turret was the most efficient way of carrying and working very heavy guns in a seaway. The turret ship would be steadier in a seaway and because the gun mounted in a turret was higher and on the centreline it could be fought longer and more effectively than one on the broadside. Training was limited only by obstructions (three tripod masts). The turret could be trained away from the enemy during loading to protect the crew against musketry aimed at the port. Fire would be more rapid as the layer always had the enemy in view, the gun would have greater elevation and there was better protection for the men – 6in armour was invulnerable to guns smaller than the 12-ton.[17]

A ship with *two* turrets could direct all her guns over a greater arc and with greater weight than any alternative scheme. The turret ship had greater ability to keep head to sea in action.[18] If the ship was dismasted and the screw disabled one turret probably and two turrets certainly would continue in action better than other styles. Similarly, turret ships could keep their guns on a target whilst navigating a winding channel.

Disadvantages. There was a risk of a shot entering the hole in the roof of the turret either when the ship was rolling or from plunging fire from a shore battery mounted high up. In the case of the proposed design, the belt and turret could be penetrated by the 12-ton gun and even shots not penetrating could send splinters into the base of the turret, jamming the machinery. There was also the possibility of boarders jamming the turret with wedges.[19] There was some concern over the blast damage to the deck and hatches. In action, the bulwarks would be folded down leaving men working the sails unprotected.

They also saw difficulty in constructing a seagoing turret ship with sufficient freeboard to make her a good seaboat, particularly in head seas. The need to hinge the bulwarks and other moveable items such as the anchors was also a problem. The Committee fully recognised the great advantage for floating batteries and coastal defence ships but these were reduced in the case of a seagoing ship. They saw that all seagoing ships needed the same freeboard; the *Monitor* was not a seagoing cruiser.

To conclude, they thought it most desirable that a 'conclusive trial should be given to the (turret) system in a seagoing ship armed with two turrets, capable of carrying two 12-ton guns in each turret or, if necessary, one 22-ton gun in each'. There were many disadvantages to more than two turrets and a single turret was most objectionable and if more guns were needed they could be arranged in a battery between the turrets. Almost the sole reason for rejecting Coles' proposal was because it had but a single turret which could not fight on both sides at once and could be jammed by accident or in action. They noted that they did not condemn a single turret for coast defence ships. There were a number of details specific to the proposal which they objected to and which could easily have been corrected, though much was praised.

This Committee has been criticised by some writers, notably Parkes, but it seems that they did their work well and quickly came up with a sensible recommendation. They were given a rational list of questions, the witnesses all had relevant experience (most of the naval officers had taken part in firing trials from turrets) and were unbiased.

Evidence to the Committee

To a considerable extent the questions asked of the witnesses were the same and it is unnecessary to repeat these answers in detail but there were points worth bringing out. Joseph Scullard was questioned in detail over the design and his replies were impressive. There was some disbelief over the weight of the turret, said to be lighter and smaller than *Royal Sovereign*'s twin mount but this was explained as mainly due the weight of a timber bed needed in the older ship to match her existing deck heights to the turret. Thomas Lloyd assured the Committee that some lack of protection to the uptakes was unimportant but was worried over the tortuous routing of the uptakes. Like Reed, he thought that the speed had been slightly over-estimated. Spencer Robinson and Reed both objected to the hinged bulwarks, Reed pointing out that if they were strong enough to resist heavy seas, they would be too heavy to move. Interestingly, Reed admitted his own small ironclads had this problem. He was somewhat more concerned over the structure of the double bottom. All in all, the witnesses did not find any problem which could not have been overcome in the normal development of a design.

Many of the witnesses had experience of firing turret guns in the *Royal Sovereign* and several referred to the difficulty in firing muzzle-loaders alternately from a twin turret. The loading number would be holding some 40-60lbs of gunpowder 6ft from the muzzle of the other gun when firing, a problem which could be overcome by firing simultaneously or by drill. Most agreed that the turret was the only way of using guns larger than the 12-ton but Scott, the designer of guncarriages, and Reed dissented, both seeing it quite possible to design a mechanically worked broadside mount. Reed pointed out the need for an Admiralty department to design gun-mounts.

There was some interesting evidence on rates of fire. Cooper Key referred to a trial in which twenty-five rounds were fired from a 9in RML with an average interval of 75 seconds. He thought that 12-ton guns should be 20ft apart on the broadside. The normal crew was twenty-four which could be reduced to six – Scott thought his carriage would need nine. Donohue, gunner

13. Ballard, *The Black Battlefleet.*

14. Parkes, *British Battleships.*

15. Admiralty letter to Coles of 30 June 1863.

16. Vice-Admiral Earl of Lauderdale (Chairman), Rear-Admiral Yelverton, Captain Caldwell, Captain Kennedy, Captain Phillimore, Secretary A Price.

17. This is a most interesting conclusion; the table in Chapter 1 gives the penetration at 1000yds for a 12-ton gun as 11.7in. It is likely that the Committee were aware of the view that armour did better in action than on the test range.

18. It is unclear what the Committee meant by this. Presumably they thought that turret ships were less limited to firing close to the beam.

19. This threat was taken very seriously, particularly in the light of a night boat attack and the low freeboard.

Reed's moderately successful fully-rigged turret ship Monarch 1868. The fastest battleship of her day under steam (14kts), she was difficult to control under sail. (Imperial War Museum: Q21535)

Monarch was the most successful of the rigged turret ships but the arcs of fire of her big guns were limited by the forecastle and the midships deckhouses. She had sufficient freeboard for seaworthiness. Note the balanced rudder which did not function well when the propeller was not in use. (National Maritime Museum, London: 7426)

of the *Royal Sovereign*, thought a well-trained crew could fire three times in 5 minutes against a target 1000yds off from a single turret when the ship was rolling 5° either way. Scott also pointed out that no fuse could be relied on in a common shell fired with a heavy propelling charge.

Spencer Robinson pointed out that a turret ship needed as much armour as a broadside vessel. He objected strongly to a single turret and pointed out[20] that Dupuy de Lôme 'who is, without doubt, the greatest naval constructor in the world, disapproves of a seagoing ship with moveable turrets'. Reed doubted if 10ft freeboard was sufficient to steam against a head sea but he said he was not referring to safety – 'nothing but the greatest carelessness could make a ship of that sort unsafe from the wash of the sea over her'. He was quite willing to design a seagoing turret ship provided that the demarcation of authority between himself and Coles was clearly spelt out. He was concerned that Coles appeared to be trying to make Scullard responsible for the overall concept of the proposal and not just for the details. These two points, safety and design authority bear directly on the later tragedy.

Monarch (ld 1866)

The Board decided to build a ship more or less in accordance with the Committee's recommendations. They were persuaded by Spencer Robinson to increase the armament to two twin 25-ton turrets and the armour thickness to 7in. They decided that she should have a forecastle and, because this would block the bow arcs of the forward turret, it should be armoured and carry two 6½-ton guns, later changed to two 9-ton. Spencer Robinson also decided that the freeboard amidships should be 14ft, increased by hinged bulwarks.

The *Monarch*, designed by Reed, was seen as a very successful ship and remained in service for many years.[21] Under steam, she was the fastest battleship yet built; under sail she was fast but uncontrollable. The turrets were trained by a steam engine but control of the training was not satisfactory and, at the bombardment of Alexandria, the turrets had to be kept rotating continuously and fired as the guns came to bear on the target.

Reed, himself, was not impressed; he wrote[22] '. . . no satisfactorily designed turret ship with rigging has yet been built, or even laid down.' Reed continued:

. . . the middle of the deck of a fully-rigged ship is not a very eligible position for fighting large guns. Anyone who has stood on the upper deck of a frigate, amidst the maze of ropes of all kinds and sizes that surrounds him, must feel that to bring even guns of moderate size away from the port-holes, to place them in the midst of these ropes, and discharge them there is utterly out of the question.

Reed did his best 'by many devices' to alleviate the problem, such as a flying deck to carry the hammock stowage. In clearing for action, the topmasts and yards would be lowered and, since this reduced the forces on the lower masts due both to wind and to rolling, the shrouds could be reduced to one each side per mast, increasing the arcs of fire.[23] Further consideration will be given to *Monarch* in comparison with *Captain*.

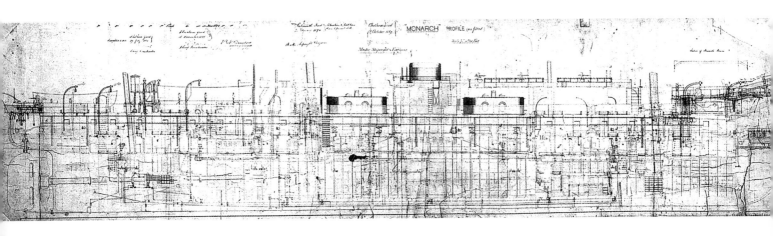

Reed's views were surely correct at the time in the context of fully-rigged ships.

Not surprisingly, Coles was unhappy with the design of the *Monarch*. He wanted the height of the belt to be reduced by 2ft (presumably reducing the depth of the ship), the turrets lowered by 2ft and the forecastle with its guns and armour removed. He put his views so strongly in public that in January his contract as consultant to the Admiralty was cancelled because of 'repeated attacks on officers of Controller's Department which could no longer be permitted without injury to public service'. On 30 January Coles replied claiming he had been misunderstood and he was re-employed from 1 March 1866. By 24 April the Board was tired of the argument and told Coles that the features he objected to were there at the request of the Board and there was no advantage to further discussion of the *Monarch*. There was tremendous public pressure to adopt Coles' system in its entirety and this was backed by politicians. There was also a press campaign supporting Coles, perhaps the first time such influence had been applied in a technical matter.

Captain

During the design and building of the *Captain* there were several changes in the position of First Lord, the political head of the Admiralty, which may have contributed to the lack of understanding of the problems and of control over the work.

First Lord	Took Office	Action re Captain
Duke of Somerset	28 Jun 1859	Approved Coles communicating with shipbuilder
Packington	13 Jul 1866	Approved Laird's design
Corry	8 Mar 1867	
Childers	18 Dec 1868	*Captain* launched Mar 1869, complete Mar 1870. Sacked Spencer Robinson

As a result of these pressures, Packington wrote to Coles: 'My Lords will give you the opportunity of reducing to practice your own views of what a sea-going turret ship should be, and they will authorise you to put yourself in communication with any of the firms named in the accompanying list[24] and submit a design for a sea going ship to carry not less than two turrets; should my Lords be able to approve the design and should they receive from the firm concerned such a tender as they would feel themselves justified in accepting they would then propose to Parliament that provision should be made in next years Estimates for building such a vessel by contract.' The letter added (summarised) 'indispensable provision for the protection of vitals from heavy shot, for the health and comfort of a crew sufficient to

Captain, designed by Laird to Coles' specification. She capsized on her third voyage, Coles himself being lost with her. (National Maritime Museum, London: B33)

work the guns and hull and to manoeuvre her, sufficient beam and the seagoing qualities of a good cruiser'.

Coles decided to use Laird's and so informed the Admiralty on 8 May 1866. Laird's submitted two designs on 14 July, one with twin screws which they preferred and the other with a single screw. Reed commented on the proposals on 20 July;[25] the crucial points from his minute are:

I see no reason to doubt, from the preliminary examination I have made, that this is in the main a well considered and well contrived design for carrying large guns in turrets upon Captain Coles' system *if we take it for granted that the deck is high enough*,[26] . . . if this Department is to undertake responsibility of ensuring satisfactory construction and equipment of such a ship it will be necessary to subject the drawings and specification to a fuller and more minute examination.

and

I am satisfied that the ship is well designed and proportioned, and that her dimensions are not unduly large, for the weights to be carried and the speed to be attained. I do not think she differs very materially in these respects from what would have been proposed in this department, had Their Lordships seen fit to sanction in our design an upper deck 8ft[27] above the water.

On stability, Reed said 'I have no doubt that both designs are satisfactory[28] in this respect.' The Controller, Spencer Robinson, forwarded Reed's report doubting if 8ft freeboard was adequate and called for a more careful examination before any decision was made. However, on 23 July the First Lord (Packington) wrote to Coles approving the building of such a ship 'on the entire responsibility of yourself and Messrs Laird, but the work will be carried on under the usual Admiralty inspection as to workmanship and materials'.

20. It is interesting to compare this statement of 1865 with Spencer Robinson's evidence 6 years later in which he saw Reed as now the greatest naval architect. Both statements are probably correct; in 1865 Reed still needed more experience.

21. Nominally till 1902 though her service after 1885 was mainly in harbour.

22. Reed, *Our Ironclad Ships*.

23. Evidence of Captain H May, formerly of *Monarch*, to the 1871 Committee. It is strange that this has not been brought out in previous books, particularly as NMM photo HBR/1, published in *The Black Battlefleet* (reproduced here) shows her cleared for action with no shrouds to the foremast, two to the main and two to the mizzen.

24. Thames Iron Works, Samuda, Millwall, Wigram, Laird, Palmer and Napier.

25. Proceedings of the Court Martial. Summarised in D K Brown, 'The design and loss of HMS *Captain*', *Warship Technology* (London 1989). I failed to do justice to Reed in this article.

26. Author's italics.

27. Reed justified this statement to the Court Martial by saying that he had repeatedly objected to freeboards less than 12ft.

28. Reed meant metacentric height; the importance of large angle stability and the work of Barnaby and Barnes was not yet fully available.

A similar letter went to Laird's on 9 August and their reply on 15 August together with Coles' reply of 24 July appeared to accept their joint responsibility. The formal contract when prepared in November placed on Coles the responsibility for supervising the building but, due to his illness, the words 'Controller of the Navy' were inserted wherever the name Coles had appeared. Reed was clear that Laird's alone were responsible for the design and his staff were instructed that drawings sent to the Admiralty for inspection were not to be 'approved' but, if appropriate, returned marked 'No objection is seen'. This was the first mistake (the second if the basic error in accepting a low-freeboard, fully-rigged ship is counted); Spencer Robinson should have seen that the demarcation of responsibility between Laird's and his department was clear. It is almost impossible for the ministry to devolve total responsibility for the design of an artefact as complicated as a warship. In the case of a tank or an aircraft there is a prototype and the production contract, after testing, is 'build 100 like that' but for a warship there is no prototype.

Reed had already had serious doubts over the technical quality of the design. As early as 24 July 1866 he wrote to Controller saying that '. . . on investigating the matter I find that the centre of gravity of ships armed and plated in the proposed manner is situated higher than would appear probable at first sight, and I would advise that Messrs Laird be requested to satisfy themselves thoroughly on this point, especially as it is proposed to spread a large surface of canvas on the *Captain*.' The substance of this note was passed to Laird's on 10 August and they replied on 15 August saying they had considered the matter carefully and were satisfied. From the evidence given by William Laird to the court martial it is clear that any consideration was superficial[29] – 'an approximate estimate was made in 1866 and a more complete estimate made after the ship was completed in January or February of this year' (1870). The actual figures were:

Date	Height of centre of gravity (ft) (Load condition)
1866 Estimate	21.5
1870 Calculation	22.24
Inclining expt.	22.2

The agreement between the 1870 calculation and the measured value is excellent and shows that had Laird's taken proper note of Reed's warning, the tragedy might have been avoided. This was the second major error and the effect on stability and safety will be considered later. By 2 August Reed was concerned whether the estimated weights were sufficient for the construction proposed and feared that she might float more deeply than intended. Barnaby visited the yard several times while she was building and in September 1867 warned that excessive weights were being worked into her. A list of items accounting for some 860 tons was published (reproduced in Parkes) but there is no way of telling whether the difference between estimate and reality was due to errors in the estimate or to overweight components; the former is much the more likely and, in either case, the blame lies squarely with Laird's as designer and builder; the third major error. She was built in dry dock and floated out on 27 March 1869 when a check on her condition and draughts showed she was already floating deep. It was then estimated that she would complete at least 427 tons overweight and float 13in deeper than intended. In fact, when she completed, she was 735 tons heavy and floated 22in deeper. Her already inadequate freeboard of 8ft would have been reduced by this 22ins but careless construction meant that she completed with a depth of hull 5ins greater than shown on the drawings giving an eventual freeboard of 6ft 7in in the load condition. The extra 5in of depth itself must have contributed appreciably to overweight!

Though overweight components certainly accounted for some of the weight increase it is certain that Reed was correct in suggesting that the original estimates were wrong.[30] On 24 February 1870 Laird's wrote to the Admiralty proposing an inclining experiment. There seems to have been no sense of alarm either at Laird's or the Admiralty at this stage; she was a novel design and the experiment was to provide data for future similar ships.

Resignation of Edward Reed, 1870

By this time, Reed had resigned, tired of ill-informed criticism – a national disaster as Spencer Robinson described it. While at the Admiralty he had designed twenty-five ironclads, two armoured gunboats, twenty cruisers, twenty-eight gunboats and twenty coastal gunboats, costing in total some £10 million. As described earlier, he had instigated, directed and encouraged major improvements in every aspect of design procedures. He worked briefly for Whitworth before becoming chairman of Earle's shipyard in Hull, acting as a design consultant as well. He designed a number of ships for Germany, Brazil, Chile and others but, while generally successful, they lacked his earlier genius. Rodger is probably correct in suggesting that Reed worked best in harness. He became a Member of Parliament which he used as a platform to attack his successors at the Admiralty. He was active in the Institution of Naval Architects, becoming Vice-President in 1865 until his death on 30 November 1906.

Comparison of *Captain* and *Monarch*

All design is compromise; there are good points and bad points in most ships but, in this case, it must be appreciated that, in making a comparison, like is not compared

29. This remark may seem a little hard on Laird's as the calculation of the height of the centre of gravity had only been introduced in the Admiralty a year or so earlier. However, the Admiralty letter of 10 August had asked for special consideration and warned that the solution was not obvious. The blame lies squarely with Laird.

30. Parkes is quite wrong in suggesting that the designer was let down by the builders. It was and is the responsibility of the naval architect, Laird in this case, to ensure that the estimates are realistic and that the building conforms.

with like; *Captain* was not seaworthy. When *Captain* joined the fleet Lieutenant Rice was ordered to make a detailed report on the advantages and disadvantages of *Monarch* and *Captain*. His lengthy report was given in evidence to the 1871 design committee and seems to have been accepted as impartial by everyone; the short section which follows is largely based on his report.

Armament. Both ships carried four 12in guns in twin turrets. The turret design was not identical and it was thought that *Monarch*'s were easier to work. The table below compares their firing arcs.

These small differences would probably have had little significance in battle but showed a slight advantage to *Captain*. It was generally agreed that the turrets were too close together, particularly in *Monarch*. Shifting from maximum elevation to maximum depression took about 5½ minutes in *Monarch*, 4 minutes in *Captain*. Neither ship could fire its main armament anywhere near the fore-and-aft line. *Monarch* had two 7in forward and one aft, both protected by 5in plate forward, 4½in aft. *Captain* had an unprotected 7in at either end. Both ships could clear for action in 5 minutes but this did not include lowering topmasts and yards and the time needed for this would also permit *Monarch* to cast loose her shrouds.

Protection is not easy to compare. Both had a 7in belt over much of the length with 4½ at the ends but *Captain* had two 40ft lengths of 8in under the turrets. The side between the turrets and the top of the belt was 8in thick in *Captain*, 7in in *Monarch*. The latter had 4½in bulkheads fore and aft of the turrets (supplemented by the bow and stern battery armour) whilst *Captain* had no end-on protection. It was generally agreed that *Monarch* had the better protection to the uptakes. The table which follows compares the penetration of 10in and 12in guns and, it is clear that under test conditions, neither ship could withstand hits from guns similar to those which she mounted.

Speed – Steam and Sail. Monarch reached 14.9kts under steam, versus 14.25kts for her rival in a 10-hour trial. At 5.25kts both burnt about 17½ tons of coal. Both were fast under sail – *Monarch* consistently faster – but neither handled well. *Captain*'s flying deck was very congested and not an ideal place from which to work ropes. Under steam and sail together *Monarch* was so

Monarch cleared for action about 1880. The upper masts have been struck, which has permitted most of the shrouds to be removed. Note that the remaining shrouds are not quite the same as described to the Design Committee (see text). In this condition her arcs of fire were virtually the same as those of *Captain* with tripod masts and no shrouds. (National Maritime Museum, London: HBR1)

Arcs of fire for *Monarch* and *Captain*

	Arcs of fire (Deg)			Sills above WL (ft-in)	Elevation (deg)	Depression (deg)
	Aft turret	Fore turret	Both turrets			
Monarch	122	127	108	16-2	15	7
Captain	138	131	129	8-0	13.5	5.5

31. See Introduction on overheads; it is probable that *Monarch* was charged at 45 per cent.

32. Captain H May. Evidence to Committee on Designs, 1871.

33. It is unclear why the turrets should be slower, contrary to the results in *Trusty*. It may be that *Captain* had muzzle-loaders, *Trusty* had breech-loaders.

34. E J Reed, 'The Stability of Monitors under Canvas', *Trans INA* (London 1868).

35. To obtain a useful result from an inclining experiment it is essential to obtain a complete record of all consumable and moveable weights on board and of those to go on (fuel, stores etc). It is also essential to check all tanks and void spaces to ensure that they do not contain liquid which can slop from one side to another. The author has carried out many such experiments – and checked many more – and would expect to take about two days on the preparatory work for a ship the size of *Captain*. Barnes' figures must be seen as no more than a good approximation.

36. Wind speed *c*20-23kts as then defined.

37. The basic source is the Report of the Court Martial which should be consulted by any serious student. Other accounts are selective, depending on the author's point of view. The most accurate general account is in K C Barnaby (a grandson of Sir Nathaniel Barnaby), *Ship Disasters and their Causes* (London 1968).

38. One is reminded of the current Ministry of Defence note:– The Stages of a Project.

Enthusiasm,
Disillusionment,
Panic,
The Search for the Guilty,
The Punishment of the Innocent
Praise and Honour for the Non-Participants.

39. The curves reproduced are those obtained from a modern computer program in 1989. While they agree almost precisely with Barnes' values for *Monarch*, those for *Captain* are significantly worse, the maximum occurring at 18°.

40. *Captain* 2.8ft, *Monarch* 2.8ft. These figures have been deduced as the measured values have not been found.

considerably better that Lieutenant Rice said he went back to check for errors.

Turning Circles. Monarch 639yds with 35° rudder (579yds with 43°), *Captain* 7-800yds with 30°.

Accommodation. Monarch's extra deck clearly gave her a great advantage. There were complaints that the doors to *Captain*'s forecastle and casing had to be kept closed in any sea, the latrines were smelly and accommodation for both officers and men was dark and dingy.

Cost. Monarch cost £371,274 – £72-8 per ton (bm); *Captain* £345,515 – £86 per ton, but these figures are not truly comparable due to the way in which overheads were treated.[31] It is probable that there was not much difference in the cost per ton and *Captain* was cheaper because she was smaller.

Comparison with centre battery ship

Reed and others claimed that it was possible to carry twice as many guns on the broadside as in turrets with the advantage of being able to fight enemies on both sides and leaving the upper deck clear for sailing. No centre battery ship was built with 12in guns but those who were informed on the subject saw no great difficulty in working such guns on the broadside. Comparison has to be made with *Hercules* carrying 10in guns.

Rigged turret ships compared with centre battery

	Hercules	Monarch	Captain
Displacement (tons, load)	8677	8322	7767
Main armament,	8-10in	4-12in	4-12in
Main armament, one broadside	4-10in	4-12in	4-12in
Penetration at 1000yds (ins)	11.7	12.7	12.7
Armour, max thickness (ins)	9	7	8
Complement	638	575	500

The table compares a centre battery ship, *Hercules*, with the turret ship, *Monarch*, of about the same size. *Monarch* had a broadside of four 12in, 25-ton guns in turrets whilst *Hercules* could fire four of her eight 10in, 18-ton guns on each broadside, giving her some advantage in the unlikely event of engaging an enemy on both sides. On the other hand, *Monarch*'s 600lb shot were far more damaging than were the 410lb of *Hercules*.

The Commander-in-Chief decided to test the accuracy and rate of fire of these three ships against a rock off Vigo which was 200yds long and 60ft high. The range was about 1000yds and they fired filled Palliser shell with battering charges. Each ship fired the four main armament guns for 5 minutes, starting with the guns loaded and very carefully trained. Speed was about 4-5kts (some accounts say stationary), visibility was perfect and the sea was calm. The results were:

Ship	Rounds fired	Hits	Wt of shell hitting (lbs)
Hercules	17	10	4000
Monarch	12	5	3000
Captain	11	4	2400

It was noted that a large proportion of hits came from the first, carefully-aimed salvo (*Captain* three out of four). The first salvo caused the ships to roll heavily, *Captain* ± 20°, and thick smoke made aiming difficult. The indirect sights of the turret guns were not as good as *Hercules*'s simple sights. 'A large proportion of Palliser shells burst and no granite fort could have survived.'[32] Captain May exaggerated the effect of shells on granite but his clear evidence shows the difficulty of hitting even a stationary target from a moving ship. *Monarch* and *Captain* were new ships, with the novel turret, and could probably have improved with more practise and development.[33] *Hercules*' seventeen rounds in 5 minutes (starting loaded) from four guns is probably as good a figure as ships would achieve before power loading. All three hit with about half the rounds fired against a large, stationary target.

A warning

Henwood, a supporter of Coles, proposed that some of the old wooden battleships of the *Duncan* class should be cut down and converted to rigged turret ships with a freeboard of about 3½ft. This proposal was examined by Reed's staff and led to a paper which he read at the Institution of Naval Architects.[34] This was the first public demonstration of the significance of the GZ curve, showing that the maximum righting lever could occur at only 6½° and that the vanishing angle was less than 20°. The debate was very bad tempered, Henwood 'feeling' that the maximum stability was at about 20° which was safe since they would only heel 5° under sail! It is probable that no one changed their mind as a result of this discussion but tragic justification for Reed's team was soon to follow.

The loss of the *Captain*

Captain won high praise when she entered service, particularly from the press. At the end of her second voyage she came into Portsmouth on 29 July 1870 and Barnes carried out the inclining experiment the same day.[35] Barnes reported his results in the form of a curve of stability (GZ curve) on 23 August, after *Captain* had sailed. Some writers have unjustly criticised him for the time taken, but such critics have never used Barnes' method by hand. I have. The results and their significance will be discussed in the next section. *Captain* sailed on 4 August.

The fleet, including *Captain*, was exercising in heavy

weather off Cape Finisterre on 6 September 1870. Rear-Admiral Milne visited her that afternoon when she was under sail, in a fresh breeze, at a speed of 9.5kts increasing to 11kts as the wind rose. Even then, the sea was washing over the lee side of the upper deck, and the deck edge went under at about 14°. During the evening the wind rose further and the fleet was ordered to send down royal yards and proceed under double reefed topsails, fore topmast staysail and foresail. The wind increased again to an estimated Beaufort Force 6-7.[36] As the new watch came on deck at midnight the wind strengthened and *Captain* heeled to 18°. Captain Burgoyne ordered the topsail halliards to be cut but before this could be done the ship heeled over and sank. There were 17 survivors out of 490 men on board and Captain Coles was one of those who died.[37]

Enquiry – the court martial – stability

In accordance with the custom of the day, the enquiry into the loss of *Captain* took the form of a court martial at which the survivors were charged with losing their ship. It was, of course, recognised that the real trial was of much more highly-placed individuals. The defendants were duly acquitted but, in giving their verdict, the court said that it was '. . . their duty to record the conviction they entertain that the *Captain* was built in deference to public opinion expressed in Parliament, and through other channels, and in opposition to the views and opinions of the Controller and his department, and that the evidence all tends to show that they generally disapproved of her construction'. They went on to criticise Laird's for completing the ship with nearly 2ft less freeboard than the inadequate figure of the original design.

The First Lord, Childers, issued a paper justifying his own actions and attacking everyone else, forcing Spencer Robinson to resign. Nathanial Barnaby was put in charge of the Constructor's Department on a temporary basis as Childers wanted Laird, the man responsible for the errors in *Captain,* to be given the post.[38]

The damning evidence came in the form of the stability curves (GZ) for *Monarch* and *Captain*, reproduced above. The maximum righting moment for *Monarch* was at 38° whilst that for *Captain* was at 20°.[39] The *Captain* had a marginally greater metacentric height than *Monarch*[40] but the righting moment fell away once the deck edge was immersed and capsize was inevitable once she reached 20°.

The mistakes

1. The concept of a fully-rigged, low-freeboard turret ship was wrong. Spencer Robinson and Reed had pointed this out on numerous occasion. Coles' bad-tempered and unreasonable utterances confused the mind of the public and ministers making rational debate impossible.

2. Failure to define responsibility between Laird's and the Controller, particularly when Coles' illness prevented him from taking any part.

3. Laird's failure to take heed of Reed's clear warning that the centre of gravity was higher than they thought.

4. Laird's errors in weight estimation which led to her floating deeper than intended.

For over 100 years the authority of the naval architect in matters of safety was unquestioned.

Modified *Monarch* and corrected *Captain*

During the hearings of the 1871 Committee, it was clear that many witnesses thought highly of the *Monarch* and there were a number of proposals for altering her and for designing an improved version. Indeed, the Constructors' Department had already begun such a study which was suspended when *Captain* was lost. This would have had thicker armour, including deck, and would have had 'self-supporting masts'. There would have been no gun aft, with the turret guns firing astern. Forward, there would either have been an 18-ton gun in the forecastle behind 9in armour or a divided forecastle with the turret firing forward through the gap! This would have put the beam up to 60ft and slightly increased the cost.

It is surprising that, although most saw *Monarch*'s great virtue was as a rigged turret ship, several wanted masts removed from *Monarch* herself. Spencer Robinson, the Controller, said '*Monarch* is the first seagoing turret ship that we built and I consider her for the year 1866, as in the first class of ironclad ships-of-war. If your question goes further than that; and if I now considered in 1871 that the first class ships of the Navy should be of the same pattern as the *Monarch* I should say "No" . . . In 1871 I consider her as no longer the representation of a 1st class ironclad . . .'

In designing an improved version he would first consider thicker armour which, in association with the

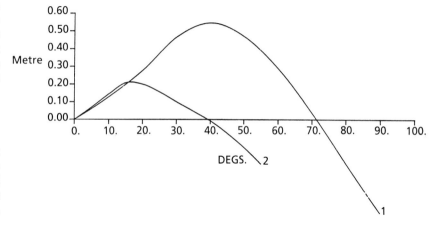

The curves of righting levers (GZ) for *Monarch* (1) and *Captain* (2). These curves were produced by a modern computer programme and, while that for *Monarch* is almost identical to the contemporary curve, that for *Captain* is slightly worse. There is some doubt as to the form and dimensions of *Captain* as completed which may account for this difference – she was certainly 5in deeper than intended.

The Danish *Rolfe Krake*, the first Coles turret ship, launched by Napier in 1863. The two turrets originally each mounted a pair of 68pdr SB. (National Maritime Museum, London: PAD 6236)

progress in artillery in 5 years, would lead to a much larger ship. As cruiser, some sacrifice in armour would be possible. He would want iron lower masts without rigging, also an armour deck. *Monarch*'s turrets were close together at Coles' wish. He would fit a light, jury rig: 'I consider that any advantage which might be gained by being able to manoeuvre the ship in light winds is more than counterbalanced by the tremendous risk incurred of fouling the screw, or injuring or destroying the ship in every way, both in gales of wind or in action, through carrying large masts and spars.' Admiral Sir Sydney Colpoys Dacres thought that *Monarch* should have masts removed while Vice-Admiral Sir Thomas Symonds (C-in-C Channel) suggested removing the mizzen and cutting the fore and main masts. He also wanted to do away with the unarmoured forecastle. He would not fire the turret guns over the bow guns as shot and shell frequently broke up on firing! There was certainly no reactionary support for sail *per se*.

Reed doubted if the type should be repeated in the light of developments in guns. He reiterated his view that if full sail was a requirement, the centre battery configuration was to be preferred. However, if an improved *Monarch* was needed he would propose 12in armour, extending 5ft below the waterline and reduce the free-

board slightly to about 12ft. He would not have a forecastle so that the fore turret could fire forward, and similarly aft. He thought that a sailing ironclad could be designed to handle well to windward, probably with a single lifting screw. He would design the structure with more longitudinals and fewer transverse frames.

A study of *Captain* by the Constructors' Department showed that for her maximum righting lever to be at what they saw as a safe angle of 29.5°, her metacentric height should be increased to 5ft 3in. This would have meant increasing the beam by 5ft to 60ft; a measure of the size of Laird's design errors.

Sailing of the ironclads

By the time the 1871 Design Committee assembled, it was recognised that none of the ironclads sailed well. They could make quite good passages by themselves[41] but as Admiral Sir Sydney Colpoys Dacre put it[42] 'they cannot sail in company at less than 4 cables [1 cable =100 fathoms, almost 200 metres], which is too great for poor visibility' – and other witnesses made similar comments, *eg* Vice-Admiral Wellesley: 'Would not handle a squadron under sail'. Their main problem was that they took a long while to wear; typical times to wear[43] were given as:

Captain	10 min
Volage	13
Monarch	33

'Unmanageable' is a word used by several witnesses, particularly referring to ships with balanced rudders. Part of the problem was flow round a locked propeller and the Controller was asked if was it possible to fit an auxiliary engine to turn the screw under sail. He replied that the hydraulic engine being fitted to *Monarch* would turn the screw and water would be pumped out by donkey engine – the motive power would be the static head of water.

They were poor at beating to windward; the dissenting report looked for an ability to make good one mile per hour to windward compared with an old frigate's three. There need be no surprise over this problem as their sail area with respect to their size was about half that of the old-style sailing ship.

Ship	Sail areas square ft per sq ft/mid sec	ton/dspt
Queen (As 3 dk)	26.29	5.94
Queen (2 dk steam)	26.66	6.03
Vanguard (Sail)	30.99	7.47
Mars	27.68	6.67
Leander (Sail)	38.01	9.99
Shannon (Screw)	33.22	6.82
Niobe (Old sail)	44.38	15.42
Niobe (Screw)	28.52	8.06

The Constructors' Department report suggested that, except for *Hercules*, the sail area per ton should be doubled for good sailing (per sq ft of mid sec area somewhat less). They preferred to use displacement to the power $\frac{2}{3}$ as the base which would suggest the old *Vanguard* should have 49,740sq ft in place of 28,882sq ft. If this was arranged on three masts the centre of effort would go up 50 per cent and, since the area is doubled, the righting moment should be trebled – implying an increase of beam from 59ft to 66ft making them heavy rollers. A sketch was supplied showing that it would be virtually impossible to carry such a rig and a very large crew would be needed.

Many witnesses agreed with Vice-Admiral Sir Thomas Symonds who wanted to remove the mizzen – 'mizzen is only a thing to play with' – and move fore and main '. . . to steady ship in seaway, to enable bow to go free and to save coal when wind is fair; but on a wind it is utterly absurd to think of these ships sailing'. Two short masts as ventilators and topmast thrown away in action.[44] Others thought that the mizzen mast should be retained (without spars) to handle boat hoisting.

The Controller, Spencer Robinson, said: 'I consider that any advantage which might be gained by being able to manoeuvre the ship under sail in light winds is more than counterbalanced by the tremendous risk incurred of fouling the screw, or injuring or destroying the ship in every way, both in gales of wind and in action, through carrying large masts and spars.' Asked if it was necessary to work to windward under plain sail in still water, he said 'No'. He disagreed with the suggestion that the cost of a sailing ship was much greater due to a bigger complement as complement was set by the armament. The figures in the table below suggest that he was badly wrong in this.

The table shows that there was little difference in complement between centre battery and turret ships but the abolition of sails in *Devastation* made possible a dramatic reduction.

There was considerable support for a 'Jury Rig'[45] as suggested by Symonds. Some suggested labour-saving devices, *eg* combined top and topgallant mast, double topsails, mechanical handling etc. There was no support for trying to make them into sailing ships; sail was an auxiliary. A very few years later, the economy of the compound engine made sail unnecessary except, perhaps, for small ships on isolated stations.

Committee on Designs for Ships of War – general topics

Following the loss of the *Captain* and the inquiry into that loss, the Admiralty set up a Committee to enquire into a number of current designs[46] considering both their safety and their effectiveness. Their comments on these designs appear in the relevant sections of this book but the Committee also made some more general points which are given here together with some views as to the value of their work. In the letter setting up the Committee the Admiralty wrote: 'All my Lords seek on the present occasion is a professional and scientific opinion from persons competent to give it on such designs as are or may be referred to them for that purpose.' They were also directed to advise on '. . . the present state of the science of Naval Architecture and the requirements of naval warfare' and whether these principles are fully satisfied by the design examined (modified if necessary) or whether any further changes are needed'.

The members of the Committee were an outstanding

41. Captain Lord Giffard (*Hercules*): 'Not as good at sailing as old but not bad. Beat from St Katherine's Point to 5 miles off Eddystone from 5pm to 7am against fresh SW gale – 116 miles – benefit of tide. All rig which could foul screw removed in 21-22 minutes, has been done in 18. Can clear much more quickly than *Monarch*'.

42. Evidence to 1871 Committee.

43. Wearing is changing tack, keeping the wind astern. See J Harland, *Seamanship in the Age of Sail* (London 1984).

44. Was this the origin of brig rig for *Temeraire*?

45. Full rig implies ability to beat to windward under plain sail at 1mph (old frigate 3mph). Limited rig would assist in passage and keep station – 20sq ft/ section. Jury rig merely allowed the ship to heave too and wear in gale. Area of close reefed tops and reefed courses 11sq ft/section.

46. The designs to be examined were *Captain, Monarch, Invincible, Devastation, Cyclops, Glatton* and *Inconstant*.

Comparison of sailing ships and *Devastation*

	Hercules	Monarch	Captain	Devastation
Date laid down	1866	1866	1867	1869
Displacement (tons, load)	8677	8322	7767	9300
Main armament,	8-10in	4-12in	4-12in	4-12in
Main armament, one broadside	4-10in	4-12in	4-12in	4-12in
Complement	638	575	500	358

selection of admirals, engineers and scientists.[47] In particular, the engineers covered the whole range from the most theoretical skills to those of the practical shipbuilder. In a few cases, members of the Committee were examined as expert witnesses on topics where they had special skills, notably Froude on hydrodynamics. A very large number of witnesses were examined and these, too, were impressive in their professional competence. In particular, it is interesting to note how often a seaman officer would respond to a question with an answer such as 'We have tried it'.[48]

After the preamble, the Committee turned to some generalisations of the nature of compromise in design. 'A perfect ship of war is a desideratum which has never yet been attained, and is now further than ever removed from our reach. Any near approach to perfection in one direction inevitably brings with it disadvantages in another.' They continued that before guns had reached their current power '. . . the question how to unite in one ship the power of sailing, steaming, and carrying both heavy guns and armour, although difficult, did not appear to be insoluble, and was met with remarkable ability, and a very large measure of success, by the Constructive Department of the Navy'. The Committee drew attention to the total omission of sails in *Devastation* and of armour in *Inconstant* and appeared to recommend this extreme form of compromise for future ships. It is strange that they did not at least examine the cost of providing all features in a bigger ship, particularly in the light of Spencer Robinson's evidence that in 1866 Reed had produced a study for a battleship of 22,000 tons carrying guns both in turrets and on the broadside and 10,000 tons of coal. 'I think everyone would admit that was going rather far and fast'!

They then drew attention to the evidence from gun makers[49] that guns would soon appear which could penetrate up to 24in of armour at 1000yds. Wisely, they saw that this would not be the end and that even 24in plate would not be invulnerable for long. They drew attention to the value of thinner armour in keeping out common shell with its large bursting charge but also sought other forms of protection such as cellular decks.

They strongly recommended the introduction of compound engines but do not seem to have fully realised that their economy and lighter weight would permit the abolition of sails. They also drew attention to the importance of Froude's work on rolling which had such a deleterious effect on the accuracy of gunfire. In particular, they supported the use of large bilge keels.[50] The Committee made a number of minor but important recommendations, most of which were already being implemented to the greater effectiveness of the Navy. These can only be summarised.

(a) The need for fire resistant materials.
(b) Give up the use of tonnage (bm) and replace by displacement and to replace nhp by ihp.

(c) The need to insulate copper sheathing from iron parts.
(d) The need for a remote indicator which would read draughts fore and aft.[51]
(e) The need for a trial of hydraulic (jet) propulsion.
(f) The importance of good stability at large angles of heel and the need for inclining experiments on new ships.

The Committee concluded by thanking Barnaby and his staff for their assistance. Froude wrote[52] '. . . we were a large and somewhat miscellaneous committee, and a great many questions were asked by members of the committee which had to be answered by the Constructors' Department, and that department was worried out of its life almost by constant demands on its time in preparing reports on various questions, and many of the questions, I am satisfied, were questions which need not have been answered . . .'. It was a large committee with a great deal of relevant experience and generally a good committee but such a committee 'is very likely to wear out the department by demands on its time, when in many cases they might be better employed'. The problem with such committees was that they took so long to understand the problem and the background or as Froude put it 'the dream and the interpretation'. Henry Brunel made similar comments but doubted Froude's wisdom in making them public. The bulk of the work fell on the two Assistant Constructors, White and John, who carried out the majority of the calculations. The minority report by the two admirals has too often been dismissed as reactionary. Their main points were as follows; they favoured protection with an armour deck and a cellular layer. This was not a silly suggestion; it was adopted in the *Italia*, for the ends of the *Inflexible* and for protected cruisers. They were in favour of limited sail power which they justified by a map showing the distance between coaling stations in the Pacific. They suggested that the guns should be mounted on turntables inside fixed armour rather than in turrets. This was not reactionary; the Coles' turret was soon superseded by the barbette, quite similar to the admirals' proposal. They supported the use of the stability (GZ) curve but wondered how closely it represented behaviour in a heavy and confused sea (120 years later, naval architects still argue on this!) and pointed out that the vanishing angle was not important, what mattered was the angle at which big openings such as ventilators became submerged. It is clear that they felt the chairman had been dominating and over-hasty in drawing up the majority report. It does not seem that it would have been difficult to incorporate most of their points in the main report. Altogether it was a most thorough investigation with many useful conclusions – and any other navy could buy this review of the Royal Navy's forward thinking for a few shillings!

47. Lord Dufferin and Clandeboye (Chairman), William Thompson, G Phipps Hornby, W Houston Stewart, J Wooley, W J M Rankine, W Froude, A W A Hood, J G Goodenough, G W Rendel, P Denny, G P Bidder, T Lloyd, C Pasley, G Elliot and A P Ryder. The two last named refused to sign the report and issued their own views separately – discussed later.

48. In particular, one may note the evidence of Lieutenant McNeile, gunnery officer of *Monarch*. Asked if it was possible to stand at the muzzle of one gun, run back for loading, while the other was fired, he replied that he'd done it and it wasn't very pleasant!

49. Armstrong and Whitworth.

50. It should be noted that Froude did not feel that his work on the need for adequate bilge keels had been properly implemented – a fault repeated until well after the Second World War.

51. Surprisingly difficult to achieve and still needed in 1995.

52. Evidence to the Duke of Devonshire's Royal Commission on the Advancement of Science 29 May 1872.

'The Ship is a Steam Being' | *Four*

IN A letter to *The Times* of 1 January 1877, Edward Reed described the *Inflexible* as '. . . a huge engine of war, animated and put into activity in every part by steam and steam alone. The main propelling engines are worked by steam, a separate steam engine starts and stops them; steam ventilates the monster, steam weighs the anchors, steam steers her, steam pumps her out if she leaks, steam loads the gun, steam trains it, steam elevates or depresses it. The Ship is a steam being . . .'

This chapter tells the story of the abolition of sails in major warships and of the growth of auxiliary power.

Monitor

The full story of the design, construction and brief life of the *Monitor* is given by Baxter;[1] this section will concentrate on her influence on British warship design. *Monitor* was designed for the Union Navy by Ericsson in 1861 as a rapid response to the ironclads building or converting in the Confederacy. The upper part of the hull was a heavily armoured raft with four layers of 1in plate on the side[2] and two of ½in plates on the deck. There was a very thick wood backing to the plating so

that the side projected 3ft 9in beyond the lower hull, a shallow iron box. The freeboard was intended to be 2ft but, fully loaded, seems to have been about 14in. This overhang gave protection to the lower hull against ramming and also provided resistance to rolling.

There was a single turret mounting two 11in Dahlgren SB and protected by layers of 1in plate, up to nine layers on the face. The only other projections above the deck were a small conning tower forward and a funnel and a pair of ventilators aft so that the turret had nearly a 360° arc of training, though experience was to show that it could not fire within 30° of the bow or 50° of the stern due to blast on the conning tower and boilers respectively. Her nominal speed was 8kts but was about 6kts in service.

In the battle with *CSS Virginia* (ex-*Merrimac*) her guns were unable to penetrate the latter's 4in laminated armour as they were using cast iron shot with reduced charges. *Virginia* fired only shells, ineffective against armour though the concussion was distressing.

On a displacement of 1200 tons, *Monitor* mounted a powerful armament and good protection[3] while her low cost also made her seem attractive to politicians and tax-

USS *Monitor* engaging CSS *Virginia* (formerly *Merrimac*) on 9 March 1862. Although the RN's first turret ships were already ordered, Reed was impressed by *Monitor* and adopted several of her features in later ships. (National Maritime Museum, London: 1037)

1. Baxter, *The Introduction of the Ironclad Warship* .

2. At close range, this protection could probably be penetrated by *Warrior's* guns.

3. Built-up armour of layers was much less effective than a single thickness.

payers. Her design was a great success for the intended role but she was not suitable for work in the open sea. On her first passage from New York to Hampton Roads she took in water through most openings and was saved with difficulty. Later that year, in December 1862, she foundered off Cape Hatteras, probably due to splits between the upper and lower hull.[4] Her ventilation was inadequate and the turret could not be used in anything other than a calm. Most British enthusiasts for the *Monitor* type ignored these problems. Reed saw much virtue in the concept but he was aware of the problems and came up with solutions.

Miantonomoh and the Atlantic crossing

In 1866 the US wooden-hulled monitor, *Miantonomoh*, crossed the Atlantic partly under her own power but towed for 1100 miles by the side-wheeler *Augusta*. This crossing and that of her sister, *Monadnock* via the straits of Magellan to San Francisco, created considerable interest as their freeboard of about 2ft 7in had been thought too low for ocean passage. Captain John Bythesea VC RN was on board *Miantonomoh* during the passage from Newfoundland to Queenstown and described the voyage to the 1871 Design Committee in a report summarised below.

The hatches were kept closed at sea and had a 2ft coaming. Ventilation was quite good while the engines were running but became very stuffy within 10 minutes if the engines stopped. The roof of the turrets were in the form of a grating to allow smoke to escape in action and this was covered with canvas on passage. The

Ericsson turret had to be lifted 1in before it could be rotated and Bythesea suggested that a two-man boarding party with hammers and wedges could put it out of action. It took about 5 minutes to raise or lower and it was claimed that it could turn through 90° in one minute, a claim which he saw as dubious. The turrets could always fire astern or to leeward but were limited to windward because the port lid mechanism was defective. He thought there was no need for guns to fire at depression from low-freeboard ships. *Miantonomoh's* wooden hull had a short life and she was scrapped in 1874.

Miantonomoh had a metacentric height of 15ft and an angle of vanishing stability of 73°. This led to a full roll period of 5 seconds and the Constructors' Department report to the 1871 Committee says that crossing the Atlantic she was only rolling 4° while ships in company rolled 20°. Ships with an exceptional metacentric height behave like rafts with the deck parallel to the surface of the waves but accelerations and lateral forces are severe (see Appendix 5).

Cerberus (ld 1867) and the breastwork monitors

The State of Victoria, through a Mr Verdon, approached the Admiralty for the design of a low-cost monitor with Coles turrets for the defence of Port Phillip Bay. Reed realised that the Coles' design of turret, which pierced the deck, would expose a low-freeboard ship to even more flooding than that of an Ericsson design which may have contributed to the loss of the *Monitor* herself. The loss of the *Weehawken* while at anchor by flooding through an open hatch was another warning of the danger of low freeboard.

Reed's solution to the hazards of the low-freeboard ship whilst retaining most of its advantages was the breastwork monitor, which he described[5] as follows: 'These ships resemble American monitors in having their upper decks at a comparatively small height above water; but instead of having those decks flush, except where the turrets, funnels, air-shafts, and casings to hatchways rise above the deck height, they have a space amidships, enclosed by an armoured breastwork, which rises several feet above the deck, in which space the turrets, funnels, air shafts and principal hatchways are situated.' Reed's solution, *Cerberus*, is compared with *Miantonomoh* in the table opposite.

Cerberus' 10in MLR were more effective in attacking armour than *Miantonomoh's* smoothbores and she had thicker armour as well as being considerably more seaworthy. There were two remaining problems with the breastwork design; the freeboard forward was so low that they could make little progress against a head sea and the armoured breastwork made little contribution to stability at large angles of heel. The breastwork concept was important as it led to a number of highly-

Cerberus 1868. Built for the State of Victoria in Australia as a coast defence ship, she was Reed's first 'breastwork' monitor. (Nautical Photo Agency)

Comparison of Monitor types

	Miantonomoh	*Cerberus*	*Cyclops*	*Glatton*
Displacement (tons)	3400	3344	3480	4910
Length (ft-in)	258–6	225	225	245
Armament	4-15in SB	4-10in MLR	4-10in MLR	2-12.5in MLR
Armour side (in)	5	8	8	12
turret	10	10	10	14

regarded First Class battleships. It is interesting that *Miantonomoh* was very highly rated by the public and many seamen whilst the greatly superior *Cerberus* was seen as second rate.

In July 1866 the India Office asked for two 'floating batteries' for the defence of Bombay. The Controller suggested monitors of 'the most perfect type' with a 12in belt, 15in on the turret with the largest possible guns and which would cost £220,000. The India office preferred a cheaper design and *Magdala* was almost a duplicate of *Cerberus*, while a similar but slightly smaller and cheaper ship, *Abyssinia*, was built by Dudgeon to their own design.

Cyclops class (ld 1870)

In 1870 there was the threat of war with Russia and it was decided to build four coastal defence ships. Reed states that a design prepared in 1866 was used and this was very similar to *Cerberus*. The Controller, Spencer Robinson, told the Committee that the design 'is a very good one for the purposes for which it was intended, and that was to aid in the defences of the roadsteads and estuaries of our rivers and commercial ports in conjunction with other ships of war.' Asked if they were purely defensive, he said '. . . you might use these ships in conjunction with your other ships of war to attack an enemy's port in shallow water where large vessels could not get into . . . very often the best defence is a vigorous attack.' He said that they could be taken to the Baltic in convoy.

In shallow water, where the First Class battleships could not enter, they were formidable opponents and their armament could defeat local fortifications. Like all the breastwork ships there were stability problems, though the Committee were unduly specific in saying that there was danger only in waves with a period exceeding 10.5 seconds.[6] It was proposed to increase the size of their bilge keels which were 15-22in deep, con-

fined to the parallel body 'to avoid added resistance . . . and cause no effect on turning'.[7] Later, they were given light superstructures, extending the breastwork. The Committee was very concerned about the strength of their bottoms as they suggested that ships intended to work in shallow water would frequently ground (possibly an exaggerated fear).

Glatton

Her design was put in hand early in 1868 and submitted in April that year, a single turret design being chosen in preference to a twin turret design with lighter guns.[8] There has been confusion over the intended role of this strange vessel; Reed's statement '. . . there is no vessel with the objects of which I am less acquainted than the *Glatton*' is often quoted but it is likely that he was deliberately concealing the truth. Spencer Robinson was much more forthright: '. . . the *Glatton* was an engine of war for breaking into first class fortified harbours where there was plenty of water.' Almost certainly, he had Brest and Cherbourg[9] in mind – he said she was 'capable of deadly use in attacking Cherbourg or other French

Hydra shown after her 1885-89 modifications. As built, she was very similar to *Cerberus*. Note that the breastwork has been brought out to the side to improve her stability. However, this light structure would soon have been destroyed in action. (Author's collection)

4. The remains of *Monitor* have been found and a photo of the remains appears in *Warship International* 3/90.

5. Reed, *Our Ironclad Ships*.

6. This figure was based on William Froude's paper 'On the Practical Limits of the Rolling of Ships in a Seaway', *Trans INA* (London 1865). Though this paper was a step forward, the values given for excessive rolls were too high.

7. Abbreviated from Barnaby's evidence to the 1871 Committee.

8. This may be seen as indirect evidence supporting her coast attack role.

9. Reed pointed out in evidence that she was too deep draught for the Baltic. Her fuel stowage was also insufficient.

Glatton, 1871, seems to have been designed as a coastal attack vessel, for the particular purpose of attacking the French fleet in Cherbourg. Her low freeboard, however, made her barely seaworthy. (Imperial War Museum: Q21289)

military ports' – with two of the heaviest guns in the world and very thick armour she would have been a formidable opponent. In particular, her 12in-thick armoured bulkhead forward would have been most valuable in steaming up to a powerful fort.[10]

However, her freeboard was so low that she was barely seaworthy; Reed gives an imaginative forecast of her fate in bad weather (summarised): Her problem was the inability to face head seas rather than that of capsize. In heavy seas no one could remain anywhere above deck in *Glatton* – even the flying deck would be swept – water would come down the vents and accumulate, the fires would go out, she would become unnavigable and would be overwhelmed in the trough. Her design shows that coast attack was never far from the minds of the mid-nineteenth century navy.

The Glatton *trial*

In 1872, the turret of the coastal defence ship, *Glatton*, was fired on by the 12in, 25-ton gun of *Hotspur*. The two ships were at anchor, 200yds apart and the first of four shots missed.[11] The next 600lb shot (charge 85lb pebble powder) hit 28in from the point of aim. The impact was on a 14in plate near to its joint with a 12in plate at an angle of 41° to the normal. and penetrated the armour coming to rest in the 15in oak backing within 2in of the skin of two thicknesses of ⅝in iron which was pushed in and split. The other hit the glacis plate before hitting a 14in plate and coming to rest within it. The turret protection weighed 726lbs/sq ft.[12] There was no damage to the turning gear, guns or 'live objects' inside. The 'live objects' may have been lucky as other reports say that many rivets were dislodged and flew around inside. During the long life of the armoured ship there was a belief that armour performed better on a ship than on a test range. Though evidence supporting this view will be given in later chapters, this particular trial was close to test performance.

The Suez Canal

The Suez Canal was opened in November 1869 and brought about major changes in the routes and economics of trade to the East and, in consequence, to warship design. Initially, the canal was narrow, shallow and unlighted. Movement was restricted to daylight hours and passage took 54 hours on average. Gradually it was deepened and widened. Lighting was installed in 1885 and by the following year the *Carthage* was able to transit in 18 hours, partly in the dark. In 1887 portable searchlights were available for night use.

Date	Permitted draught (ft-in)
1870	24-4
1890	25-4
1902	26-4
1906	27-0

The cost of coal was much less at the Mediterranean end than at the southern outlet but, though ships would wish to complete their bunkers before transit, the draught limits sometimes prevented this. Traffic steadily increased as the savings in distance were very considerable and tolls were roughly halved. The route to Bombay was reduced by 4500 miles and that to Yokohama by 3000 miles.

Year	No of ships	Net Suez tonnage
1870	486	654,914
1875	1494	2,940,08
1880	2026	4,344,520
1885	3264	8,985,412
1890	3389	9,749,129
1895	3434	11,833,637
1900	3441	13,699,328

During this period the percentage of British ships varied from 80 per cent in 1880 down to 63 per cent at the end. British earnings were boosted in 1875 by Disraeli's purchase of shares in the company.

Devastation (ld 1871)

Early in 1869 Reed was asked by the First Lord (Childers) to consider a monitor which could steam at moderate speed from Queenstown (Cobh) to Halifax, mount two very large guns (40-45 ton), with thick armour, limited sail – and all on 3000 tons (presumably tons builder's measurement) . Reed did his best but said '. . . limitation to 3000 tons precludes the possibility of it being a war vessel'. In February 1869 he wrote to the Controller[13] suggesting a study at 4400 tons giving details of his proposal which are recognisably those of *Devastation*.

The next important development was a meeting of the full Board, chaired by the First Lord, together with Reed and some other distinguished naval officers and civilian engineers.[14] The Controller outlined Reed's design, pointing out that the 600pdr, 12in, 25-ton gun had been under development for 4 years and was not yet entirely satisfactory; it would not be sensible to expect a bigger gun to be available quickly and it was agreed that two twin turrets mounting this gun should be mounted. It was also decided that there should be a 12in belt and 14in armour on the turret. She was primarily for home and Mediterranean service but should carry enough coal to reach Halifax or Bermuda. The First Lord asked all present to give their views 'without reserve' on four contentious items. All agreed that low freeboard was necessary and that there was sufficient as proposed - 4ft 6in (Coles thought this was too much!). Twin screws were desirable for security[15] as there was a 'strong concurrence of opinion' to do away with masts and sail.

10. A Lambert, 'The Royal Navy and the Cherbourg Strategy, 1840-1890', *Ships v Forts Conference* (Portsmouth 1995).

11. Accounts differ; this is based on the *Gunnery Manual 1892* and that in *Naval Science*, Vol II, p35

12. Sir R S Robinson, 'On Armour Plating Ships of War', *Trans INA* (London 1879).

13. This section is based on evidence to the 1871 Design Committee in which much original correspondence was reproduced.

14. Admirals Earl of Lauderdale, Yelverton, A G Key together with W Fairbairn, J Whitworth, Dr Wooley, Captain Cowper Coles.

15. It is interesting that in 1869 twin screws were seen as essential in ships without an alternative means of propulsion; modern tanker owners please note.

16. As discussed elsewhere, the division of responsibility between the Director and his assistant is never clear. In 1873 Barnaby told the INA 'Whoever else may, or may not, be responsible for them [*Devastation* and *Thunderer*], there can be no doubt as to my responsibility. I was an Assistant-Constructor of the Navy, intimately connected with the design in its earliest stages, and I am the chief professional adviser of the Board of Admiralty today'.

17. A rule of thumb in use in the Second World War suggests 19ft minimum at the bow.

18. Member of the 1871 Committee, President of the Institute of Civil Engineers, a brilliant mathematician.

Reed applied his breastwork concept to a battleship in *Devastation*, 1871. (Imperial War Museum: Q21155)

One or two thought a light fore-and-aft rig desirable to steady her in a seaway.

Today, *Devastation* is seen as Reed's masterpiece[16] but his evidence to the Committee makes it clear that she was far from his ideas of a 'perfect type of vessel'. He was very much influenced by the limits imposed and said that the 'first design was for a much larger ship, intended to be much faster, fast enough to bring any and every vessel that an enemy could send out within her power as regards her steaming properties'. High speed and a higher freeboard would be improvements. The freeboard was kept down to reduce the size of the target and, in so doing, reduce the weight and cost of armour and to get depression firing. More freeboard was not needed for safety but for comfort. He suggested 6ft minimum, pointing out that the ship would be wet.[17] Later, Spencer Robinson was asked if he would agree with Reed that more freeboard was desirable and replied: 'I would certainly agree with anything Mr Reed said, as I consider his opinion about matters of naval architecture is the first in the world. Nobody has the same experience or knowledge, or has taken the same pains, and has the same talent.' From a man described as the most intelligent naval officer of the day and who rarely agreed with anyone, this is a true compliment.

Bidder[18] took up Reed's point on limits and asked the Controller: ' When you order a *Devastation* to be con-structed, would it not be as well if the constructors were left entirely to themselves to determine the dimensions of the ship – that they should simply be called on to design a ship for a certain purpose?' Spencer Robinson replied 'I think so. I think it a very great mistake that the Board of Admiralty has always made, in limiting the naval architect to tonnage and dimensions. I can assure you that I have had to fight the matter over and over again in this room. I have always contended that the naval architect should not be limited in the tonnage or rather the displacement. I hardly know of a case in which we have built a ship in the manner we should have liked to have built it.'

Reed continued to make some other interesting points about the design. The low freeboard of the hull did nothing to reduce the visual target in the light of the tall superstructure. He thought it would be better if the breastwork were brought out to the side, provided that the turrets could be raised to maintain depression; this is interesting in the light of Reed's later objection to the similar change made in changing his *Fury* into *Dreadnought*. The armour was reduced at the bow to save weight and hence reduce pitching. The discontinu-ity of the decks was so that the top of the side armour would always land on a deck. He did not think this would prove a weakness in ramming. Subdivision was difficult; she was designed to be safe with any one compartment flooded which he thought inadequate against a torpedo.[19] He was worried about the effect of flooding on a low-freeboard ship. Reed did not have the opportunity to check the subdivision of the final design which was completed by Barnaby. Reed thought that longitudinal bulkheads were useful if the compartment was small but not amidships where the beam is great and asymmetric flooding would cause a heavy list. Reed was making a very important point here, as centreline bulkheads in the machinery spaces were to lead to many losses in later British and foreign designs (Chapter 10).

A replica of the *Devastation* turret was fired on by a 25-ton gun with Palliser shot and shell with a charge of 85lbs of pebble powder at Shoeburyness in May 1872[20] (Target 34). The protection consisted of a solid 11in plate, 15in teak backing and 1¼in skin. The range was 200yds with a muzzle velocity of about 1270ft/sec. None of the projectiles penetrated, shot causing more damage than shell. One shot hit on a joint and forced the plates apart by some 7in. Though the protection had resisted the 25-ton gun, the largest at sea, the 35-ton was

coming which would penetrate at 1000yds as well as the 25-ton did at the muzzle.

The ventilation was always intended to be artificial but Reed admitted that some experiments might be needed to get it right. (See Henry Brunel's comments on the smell in a later section!) He expected her to exceed her design speed since no allowance had been made for the elimination of the aerodynamic drag from masts and rig. With later (1871) knowledge, she should have had compound engines.

Power operation, 1877

As guns and their ammunition grew in size and weight, manual operation became increasingly difficult. The first fully power-worked turret to go to sea was designed by Rendel, of Armstrong, and was fitted in the forward position of *Thunderer* in 1877, mounting two 12in, 38-ton guns. Their recoil was absorbed in a hydraulic ram with a spring-loaded return valve and the same ram was used to return the gun to its firing posi-

Thunderer 1872. The plan shows that the breastwork armour was set in from the side and there was a light superstructure outboard. This would soon be rendered non-watertight in action which would seriously reduce her stability at large angles of heel. The number of fittings arranged in the *cul-de-sac* aft – accommodation ladders, skylight, etc – suggests that it was designed to keep quarterdeck fittings clear of the turret guns. (National Maritime Museum, London: 7472A, 7474A)

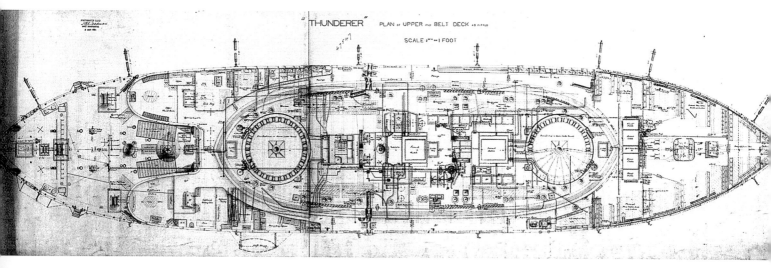

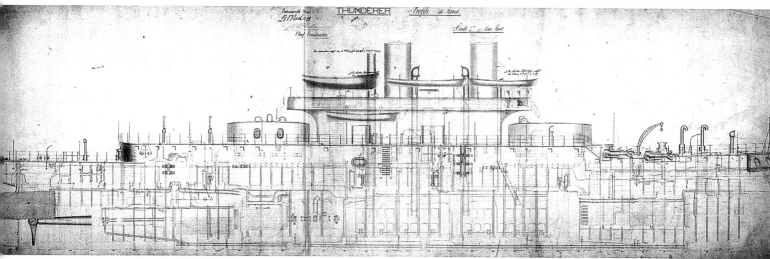

tion. A hydraulic jack was used to elevate the gun, the effective pivoting point being arranged near the muzzle so as to permit a smaller gun port. The turret, which was 31¼ft in diameter and weighed 406 tons, was carried on rollers. A steam engine below the turret drove a pinion which engaged a rack on the turret for training.

To load, the muzzles were run in and depressed below the deck where the charge and shell were lifted and rammed hydraulically. In case of accident, the muzzles pointed well above the waterline during loading. The crew consisted of one officer in the turret and one operator below, together with eight others wheeling shells and charges to the loading position, a total of ten compared with twenty-two for the after turret. It was claimed that a prototype mounting on shore could fire a round every 45 seconds.

In 1879 one of *Thunderer*'s guns exploded during firing practice and the enquiry concluded that it had been double-loaded. This particular accident could not have happened with a breech-loader and was the last nail in the coffin of the muzzle-loader. She seems to have been an unlucky ship as in 1876 a boiler exploded killing forty men. The cause was primarily maloperation as the stop valves had not been opened whilst, for different reasons, the pressure gauge and the safety valves were inoperative. The inquiry noted, with some surprise, that boilers were not built under Admiralty oversight, though this had no bearing on the accident. There had been some reluctance to adopt higher steam pressure for fear of the consequences of an accident but, since this explosion showed that even low pressure steam could be lethal, it seems to have been argued that high pressure steam would be no worse.

Freeboard, stability, rolling and seaworthiness

Much of this section deals with the stability of ships at large angles of heel – the GZ curve (Appendix 4). The first such curve was produced while *Captain* was building. The author has been responsible for many years for recommending to the Chief Naval Architect acceptance (or otherwise) of such data. Understanding the desirable features of large-angle stability depends on comparison between good and bad ships in service. The many comments in this section to the effect that Reed and his staff did not understand something are purely factual and in no way critical. Reed, Barnaby and Barnes are deserving of all credit for introducing a method of appraising stability which has lasted so well.

The loss of the *Captain* led to ill-founded fears over the safety of all low-freeboard ships, fears which were the main reason for setting up the 1871 Committee on Design. They responded very quickly and issued an interim report of a 'scientific' subcommittee on the safety of *Devastation*. This subcommittee was chaired by Rankine but their report was clearly based on Froude's

Thunderer seen after her 1890-92 modernisation when she was fitted with breech-loading guns and triple-expansion engines. (Imperial War Museum: Q40330)

studies of rolling. They suggested that the danger of excessive rolling which might lead to capsize was greatest when the ship was lying in the trough exposed to waves on the beam. If these waves arrived at her at an interval equal to the ship's natural period of roll, the impulses would build up, increasing the roll each time until she capsized (Resonance). They then pointed out that the natural period of roll would change considerably when the deck edge went under and that waves which caused her to roll the deck under would no longer be resonant. This is an ingenious explanation and true as far as it goes but, like many modern 'scientific' theories, fails to recognise the part played in capsize of real ships by slow leakage through hatches, doors and ventilators.

The main problem with Reed's monitors was that the breastwork did not extend to the ship's side and hence made little contribution to righting moment at large angles of heel. The original stability curves of the *Devastation* are poor at large angles, hardly acceptable for an undamaged ship in good weather and there is no margin for flooding due to leakage or action damage.

The Constructor's Department report to the Committee recommended that the breastwork be extended to the side with light structure which would also be carried aft. They said this structure was not necessary for safety but was to improve living conditions, in particular, better latrines. These structures greatly improved the large angle stability of *Devastation* and *Cyclops* but they would soon have been riddled in action. It is not clear whether the constructors were trying to deceive the Committee in saying that the structure was not needed for safety or whether they believed it themselves.[21] The Committee recommended that one ship only be altered but it was decided to modify both.

The after extension contained rows of cabins down the side with an open space – often referred to as the *cul*

19. There was probably about 25 per cent chance of an early torpedo or a major collision rupturing a bulkhead and flooding two compartments.

20. Based on evidence to the 1871 Committee by Captain W A Hood (DNO) and Captain Noble, RA.

21. The fact that *Fury* was redesigned with the original breastwork armour brought out to the side suggests that it was recognised as essential for safety.

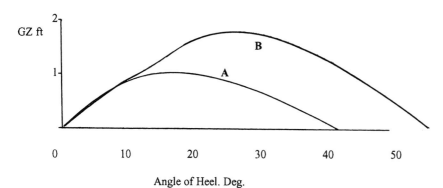

GZ ft

Angle of Heel. Deg.

These curves of righting levers (GZ) for *Devastation* show (A) as designed with a breastwork and (B) with the breastwork brought out to the side and extended by light structure. In the original condition she was barely safe and, in action, the light structure would soon be damaged and her stability would revert to condition A. Similar remarks apply to the coast defence ships of the *Cyclops* class whilst *Glatton* was much worse.

de sac – on the centre line. Barnaby's evidence was unclear but implies that this recess was to keep quarter-deck equipment low and out of the way. It is often said that this was to enable the after turret to fire aft at depression and this may also be true, as great importance was attached to depression firing. However, the blast would have seriously damaged the structure and it is possible that the open space was a light well for the cabins.

Rolling and trials

William Froude's appointment to the 1871 Committee was due to his work on rolling during the previous decade and he was to carry a number of further studies for the Committee. In the first of these the *Glatton* was rolled by men running across the deck to build up a roll of up to 12°. His long series of model tests and ship trials[22] on the rolling of *Devastation* was more important.

In the spring of 1871 Froude tested a 9ft model of the *Devastation* in still water and then in waves off Portsmouth. Different depths of bilge keel were tried, ranging from nothing to that corresponding to 6ft on the ship. In the still water tests the model was pulled over until the edge of the breastwork was in the water and then released. Without keels she rolled thirty times before coming to rest but only four times with the 6ft keels.[23] The tests in the sea were even more dramatic, with trains of waves 15-18in crest to trough (45-54ft full scale, and exceptional ones 70ft). Without bilge keels, the average roll was about 20° with occasional capsizes, reduced to 1-2° by the 6ft keels. The tests were repeated with an 18ft model, large enough to carry an automatic roll recorder. Reed said he wanted 6ft keels but these would have interfered with docking arrangements. Records are incomplete but drawings of the ship show keels 21in deep, probably fitted during her refit in 1880. Froude then carried out further trials with the sloops *Greyhound* (with keels) and *Perseus* (without) off Portsmouth which led to a deeper understanding of the action of the keels and an elegant method of analysis.

The first trials on the *Devastation* herself were carried out in April 1872 when she was rolled by men running across the deck. A roll of 7° was built up by 400 men

running 18 times across the deck.[24] Later that month, Froude and Henry Brunel went to sea for trials which led to some interesting comments from Henry.[25] Froude had the captain's spare cabin which was behind armour and very gloomy. Brunel and Phillip Watts[26] shared a cabin in the light superstructure under the after turret. The ships' officers were described as 'kind, agreeable, cordial and wondering' and co-operated well with this unusual investigation. There was little bad weather during the trial and they tried again in August and September.[27] In one trial they met waves some 450-600ft in length and 20-26ft high. *Devastation* pitched 5-8° (maximum 11.75°) and with the sea on the quarter she rolled about 14° either way. Brunel wrote 'Grand pitching and plunging yesterday, taking in green seas' while another account said :

> A wall of water would appear to rise in front of the vessel, and dashing on board in the most threatening style as though it would carry all before it, rushed aft against the fore turret with great violence, and after throwing a cloud of heavy spray off the turret into the air, divided in two, to pass overboard on either side.

Froude and Brunel went out again in November – this time Brunel thought his cabin was comfortable but very cold and 'the "bogs" stank again'. They were due to go to the Bay of Biscay to find bad weather but the First Naval Lord, Milne, was still concerned over the safety of *Devastation* and the trial was postponed until April 1875 and, even then, she was thought to need a safety attendant. As so often with seakeeping trials, the sea was calm but just enough swell was found to get the readings needed to confirm Froude's estimates. Arriving at Lisbon the ship was visited by the King of Portugal and a Portuguese admiral both of whom had read Froude's works and wanted to see his ingenious roll recorder.[28] The crew were turned out to roll the ship so that the King could see the recorder working.[29]

Devastation had a long active life and there is no doubt that she was safe, at least with her superstructures intact, but she would have been very vulnerable to battle damage in rough weather. One of Reed's objects in giving her low freeboard was to provide additional roll damping from water flooding over the low deck, an advantage which was forfeited when the breastwork was extended. He also arranged the armour proud of the hull so that the bottom edge would form an addition bilge keel (copied from Ericsson's *Monitor*) but its impact with the sea was so noisy that it was faired in.

Fury into *Dreadnought* (ld 1870)

A modified *Devastation*, to be called *Fury*, was laid down in September 1870 under that year's estimates to Reed's design. She was to be 35ft longer with more power as designed, giving an extra ½kt of speed. The armour was generally similar but rather more extensive at the bow. She was in frame and partly plated up to the bottom of the belt when *Captain* capsized and work was stopped while the design was reconsidered.

In evidence to the Committee, Barnaby outlined several possible changes and after they reported, work began on a complete redesign. It was clear that the central breastwork failed to contribute to stability at large angles of heel and that the light structure added to *Devastation* was an unsatisfactory cure. Barnaby decided to move the armour of the breastwork out to the side of the ship, at the same time increasing its thickness. His initial intention seems to have had very low freeboard at the ends[30] (4ft 6in) but as completed it was 10ft aft and slightly greater forward, protected by armour. New compound engines were fitted, discussed later; she introduced a centreline bulkhead in the engine-room.

This new design, for such it was, was renamed *Dreadnought* and the ship was much admired for many years, particularly for her end-to-end belt, even though it reduced in thickness and depth at the ends. Her success led several to claim the credit. However, there is no doubt that Barnaby set out the basic characteristics of the new design and White then developed those ideas. White himself, who was not prone to give credit to others, stated positively[31] in later years that Barnaby was the designer. Reed often maintained that he designed *Dreadnought* but this is clearly incorrect though there is considerable evidence that, if allowed a little more size and cost, *Cerberus* and *Devastation* would have been more like *Dreadnought*.

The new *Fury* – *Inflexible* (ld 1873)

The 1873 Estimates envisaged the building of a single, improved '*Fury*' (in fact, this meant *Fury*, not yet renamed, with the modifications which made her *Dreadnought*). The problem facing Barnaby was stark; the 12.5in, 38-ton gun fitted in recent ships could fire an 820lb projectile through 15.7in of iron armour at 1000yds. *Fury*'s 14in belt (amidships) was already inadequate and, furthermore, both Woolwich and Elswick claimed that 50-ton guns were within existing capabilities with even larger guns in the near future.

The early studies retained the main features of *Dreadnought* with the two twin 38-ton turrets augmented by a number of smaller guns *en barbette* amidships. In one such study a single 50-ton gun in a turret was squeezed in amidships. The 14in belt was retained amidships but the thinner belt at the ends was omitted and a thick transverse bulkhead fitted at each end of the belt. Thus the much admired end-to-end belt of *Devastation* was already abandoned for what must have been a very small saving in weight.

By this time Woolwich was speaking with confidence of a 60-ton gun and Barnaby was driven to a more radical solution. The main requirements seem to have been

set by Barnaby himself, though presumably after discussion with Board members and others. The armament was to consist of two twin turrets with 60-ton guns capable, if possible of being changed to 80-ton guns when available. White described the problem:[32] 'At first it was contemplated to have 60-ton guns and the ship was laid down on this basis. Finally, in 1874 it was decided to adopt 80-ton guns, which involved an increased weight aloft of 200 tons, and considerably modified the design, the draft and displacement having to be increased. There had been some previous instances of ships getting ahead of the settlement of their gun designs but never so serious one as this. Unfortunately, it was only the first of a long series of similar difficulties . . . .' The armour was to be concentrated over a short citadel with a maximum thickness of 24in. She was to be fast – 14kts – and capable of using the Suez Canal at light draught (24ft 4in). Barnaby's ideas were generally welcomed and the design was progressed incorporating some detail improvements mainly suggested by the DNO, Captain Hood, but with some later ideas from Barnaby. The following paragraphs describe the design as it finally evolved.

The design concept was of a very heavily armoured raft containing the machinery and magazines on which

Dreadnought, 1875, was started by Reed as a modified *Devastation* but was redesigned by Barnaby with the breastwork armour moved out to the side and slightly greater freeboard. She is shown here cleared for action at Malta. (Author's collection)

22. There was a useful tradition at the Admiralty Experiment Works, founded by the Froudes, that tests refer to models, trials to ships and this usage will be followed here.

23. Probably nine rolls with the 21in keels actually fitted to the ship.

24. It is hard to see where 400 men could get a clear run on this ship but the records are quite specific!

25. Henry Brunel correspondence, Bristol University Library. I am greatly indebted to the former archivist, Mr G Maby, for help with this material.

26. Later Director.

27. There is a nice story of this trial. When they rejoined the rest of the squadron, the band of *Sultan*, on which William Froude had previously carried out trials, struck up a popular song of the day 'Willy, we've missed you'. Froude had a great ability to get on with everyone.

28. A very long period (68-second) pendulum, now displayed in the Science Museum, London.

29. This shows that the crew ran on the deck itself and not on a temporary structure as has often been used in more recent trials.

30. Sir N Barnaby, 'On the Unmasted Seagoing Ships, *Devastation, Thunderer, Fury* and *Peter the Great'*, *Trans INA* (London 1873).

31. Sir William H White, 'The Principles and Methods of Armour Protection in Modern Warships', *Brassey's Naval Annual* (London 1904), p110. White would remember *Dreadnought* well as his frequent visits to Pembroke led, in 1873, to his engagement to Alice Martin, daughter of the Chief Constructor of that yard.

32. Sir William H White, 'Presidential Address'. *Proceedings ICE* (London 1904).

Inflexible, 1876, as completed with sails for training. Note the torpedo launching chute over the stem. (National Maritime Museum, London: HBU 1)

the two turrets were carried. The ends were protected by a strong armoured deck below the waterline, by close subdivision and by buoyant material whilst a light superstructure provided living space. Even if both ends were flooded, the armoured box was intended to have sufficient buoyancy and stability to float upright. This stability requirement led to a wide beam which, in turn, meant that the turrets could fire close to the axis past the narrow superstructure, limited by blast damage to the superstructure. She was fitted with anti-rolling water tanks to reduce the severity of rolling but these were ineffective.

The earliest studies of this configuration showed 60-ton guns though provision was made to mount 100-ton guns when they became available. Woolwich built an experimental 80-ton MLR which completed in September 1875 with a 14.5in bore. After tests, it was bored out to 15in and after further tests in March 1876 it was finally enlarged to 16in bore with an 18in chamber, accepting a 370lb charge. This gun fired a total of 140 rounds – 215,855lbs of iron from 42,203lbs of powder - mostly against what was known as 'Target 41' [33] which

had four 8in plates separated by 5in teak. The standard system of grooving used with studded shell proved troublesome and in final form it had thirty-nine shallow grooves ('polygroove') with a lead gas check at the base of the shell.

The production guns – 80-ton, Mark I – were mounted in twin turrets each weighing 750 tons and 33ft 10in external diameter. These turrets had an outer layer of compound armour (Chapter 5) with 18in teak backing and an inner layer of 7in wrought iron. The projectile weighed 1684lb and when fired with the full charge of 450lbs brown prism powder had a muzzle velocity of 1590ft/sec and in tests could penetrate 23in of wrought iron in either a single thickness or two plates spaced. The interval between rounds was said to be between 2½ and 4 minutes. To load, the guns were run out and depressed against ports in the deck through which hydraulic rams loaded the guns. Two of these monstrous guns survive on the train ferry pier at Dover, though the turret design is rather different [34] and an early studded shell is in the Naval Armament Museum, Gosport.

Inflexible's citadel was protected at the waterline by a strake of 12in plate, 4ft deep, backed by 11in teak containing vertical frames. Behind this was another 12in plate backed by 6in horizontal frames, filled with teak followed by the shell of two thicknesses of ⅝in plate. The total thickness of this waterline belt was 41in, weighing 1100lbs/sq ft and this thickness was preserved in the protection above and below, the thickness of teak increasing as that of the iron was reduced. Above the waterline strake there was a 12in outer plate and an 8in inner plate whilst below the thicknesses were 12in and 4in.

It is not clear why the armour was in two thicknesses

The design concept of *Inflexible* was of a raft, the citadel, which would float if the ends were destroyed or flooded. The ends were closely subdivided and protected by a thick deck. A light, unprotected structure above provided accommodation.

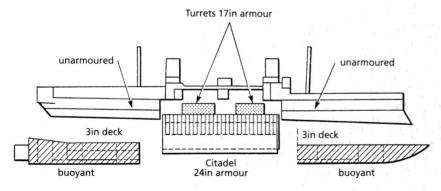

as a 22in plate was made by 1877 and it was already recognised that two plates are inferior to a single plate of the same total thickness. A test[35] in 1877 showed that a single plate 17-17½in thick was equivalent to three plates of 6½in. The waterline belt of 24in in total was the thickest belt ever carried on a battleship but it was only 4ft high and would have been of limited value. It does not seem that this protection was tried in final form. It was claimed that this protection was invulnerable to guns similar to those she carried and even to the 17.7in, 100-ton Elswick guns mounted in Italian ships but it was clearly the end of the road for wrought iron as the weight was already at the very limit of what could be carried.

The protection for the ends was a very sophisticated combination of measures. The first line of defence was a 3in wrought iron deck, normally 6-8ft below the waterline.[36] The space between this deck and the middle deck, just above water, was closely subdivided and used for coal and stores which would limit the amount of water which could enter from holes in the side. In addition, narrow tanks 4ft wide and filled with cork were arranged at the sides between these decks and extending 4ft above the middle deck. Inside these cork-filled spaces there was a 2ft coffer dam filled with canvas packed with oakum. All these fillings were treated with calcium chloride to reduce their flammability although tests showed this was not very effective. This scheme has much in common with that which Reed proposed to the 1871 Committee.

In 1877, Reed wrote to Barnaby and later to *The Times* claiming that calculations which he and Elgar had made showed that the stability provided by the citadel was inadequate if both ends were flooded. Despite a comprehensive rebuttal by Barnaby, an enquiry was set up chaired by Admiral Hope and consisting of three distinguished engineers, Wooley, Rendel and W Froude. Their investigation was extremely thorough, entering into aspects of naval architecture never previously studied.

Their report concluded that it was most unlikely that both ends would be completely flooded but that if this did happen, the *Inflexible* would a retain a small but just adequate margin of stability in terms of the GZ curve. Their comments on the difficulty of actually hitting the enemy ship are of interest – remember the *Glatton* turret and *Hotspur*'s initial miss! They listed the problems as the relative movements of the two ships, the smoke generated (470lbs of powder per round), the rolling and pitching of the firing ship, the lack of any way of determining range and the deflection due to wind. In particular, they noted that it was customary to fire the guns from a rolling ship when the deck appeared horizontal at which position the angular velocity was greatest. (Note also that Froude had showed that human balance organs are very bad at determining true vertical in a rolling ship.) All in all, hits anywhere on the ship would

be few and those in a position to flood the ends few indeed.

A shell exploding within the cork would destroy it locally but tests showed that a shell hitting light structure would explode about $\frac{1}{150}$ of a second later during which it would travel 6-10ft, clear of the cork. The canvas and oakum filling of the coffer dam was quite effective at reducing the size of the hole made by a projectile passing through. Both the cork and the coffer dam were tested full scale with the gunboat *Nettle* firing a 64pdr shell into replicas. The Committee also pointed out that shells were unlikely to enter the space between the waterline and armoured deck except at long range when hits were even less likely.

Though the Committee thought it was unlikely that the ends would be riddled (filled with water) and even less likely that they would be gutted (all stores, coal, cork etc, blown out with water filling the entire space), they examined these conditions with extreme care. Stability curves were prepared and Froude carried out rolling trials on a 1-ton model both in his experiment tank at Torquay and in waves at sea. The movement of floodwater within the ship acted to oppose rolling in waves, as in an anti-rolling tank. The effect of speed on the trim of the flooded model was also examined. Their conclusion was that the ship should survive this extreme condition but would be incapable of anything other than returning for repair.

This investigation was far more thorough than any

In 1885 *Inflexible*'s sailing rig was replaced by two military masts. (Imperial War Museum: Q39234)

33. Sir R S Robinson, 'On Armour Plating Ships of War', *Trans INA* (London 1879).

34. D Burridge, *The Dover Turret, Admiralty Pier Fort* (Rochester 1987).

35. C E Ellis, 'Armour for Ships', *Trans INA* (London 1911).

36. Note that in the very similar arrangement for protected cruisers, the deck was above the waterline at the centre. The weight and thickness of horizontal armour would steadily increase, an aspect rarely listed in comparative tables.

This diagram shows the GZ curves for *Inflexible* intact (1, loaded, 2, light) and with the ends riddled and flooded (3, loaded, 4, light). In the latter condition she might be able to get home if the weather was kind.

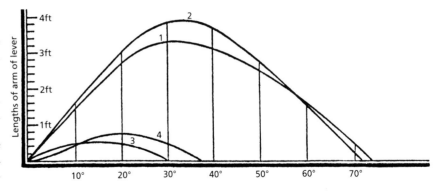

previous study of the effects of damage and owed much to White's calculations and Froude's experiments. It was the first time that GZ curves of stability had been drawn for a damaged ship and the importance of armoured freeboard was brought out and it must be a matter for regret that similar work was not carried out for later ships. With the invaluable gift of hindsight, one may suggest two aspects not fully brought out. The first was the vulnerability of the citadel armour itself, particularly bearing in mind the shallow 24in layer, in two thicknesses, and the increasing power of guns. The second point was the assumption that the watertight integrity of the citadel would endure even when multiple hits had riddled the ends. The *Victoria* collision was to show that doors, ventilation and valves do not remain tight after damage and *Inflexible* would probably have foundered from slow flooding into this citadel. Barnaby claimed[37] that she was designed to withstand a torpedo hit with the centreline bulkhead giving only a small heel – but he did not envisage flooding extending beyond one transverse compartment.

However, it is difficult to see a better solution to the design requirement and the concept received some vindication from the battle of the Yalu Sea on 17 September 1894 when two Chinese ironclads, *Ting Yuen* and *Chen Yuan*, to *Inflexible*'s configuration, but smaller, received a very large number of hits and survived. To some extent, the 1913 trial firings against the *Edinburgh* may be seen as justifying the concept. Opponents of the *Inflexible* mainly favoured protected cruisers whose *only* protection was similar to that at the ends of the *Inflexible* which they derided. White gives her cost as £812,000 though other, much lower, figures have been quoted. There were two diminutives which call for no mention.

'The Ship is a Steam Being'

Reed's letter, quoted at the beginning of the chapter, referred to the increasing use of auxiliary machinery. Some early examples include; a capstan in *Hercules* (1866), hydraulic steering gear, fitted to *Warrior* in 1870, and a steam steering engine for *Northumberland* as well as the turrets in *Thunderer* and later ships. The number increased rapidly and *Inflexible* was truly a 'steam being'. Her auxiliaries comprised:

1 steering engine
2 reversing engines
2 vertical direct fire engines
2 pairs steam/hydraulic engines to work the 750-ton turrets
1 capstan engine
4 ash hoists
1 vertical direct turning engine
2 40hp pumping engines, total capacity 4800 tons/hr
2 donkey engines for bilge pumping
2 steam shot hoists

4 auxiliary feed, similar to donkey engines.
2 Brotherhood 3 cylinder for boat hoisting
4 Brotherhood 3-cylinder fan engines
4 Friedman ejectors
2 horizontal direct acting centrifugal circulating pump

The list above does not mention ventilation fans but it is virtually certain that these were fitted. It was some time before satisfactory ventilation systems were developed. An electric searchlight was tried in *Comet* in 1874 and the first permanent fitting was in *Minotaur* in 1876. *Inflexible* had 800-volt d.c. generators by the US Brush company. These powered arc lights in the machinery space and Swan 'Glow' lamps elsewhere. The Swan lamps were connected in series and it was a year before the 800-volt system killed its first victim. She was even launched by electricity; when Princess Louise touched a button, a wire fused and the bottle of wine fell and weights crashed onto the dog shores.[38]

Steam boats

Steam boats had been tried from about 1850, the first satisfactory design being J S White's 27ft survey launch of 1861 for *Sylvia*. In 1864 J S White worked with Bellis on a lightweight engine weighing 4 tons which led to a successful 36ft boat burning 6lbs/ihp/hr. By the early 1870s the bigger launches were armed with either the spar torpedo or the Whitehead. *Inflexible* carried an advanced 42ft pinnace which White called the 'turnabout' boat. This was later developed into a 56ft pinnace with a speed of 15kts from 150ihp with a machinery weight of 6½ tons.

Compound engines

By 1860 the power available from the expansion of steam had been used for many years in single-stage engines[39] but there were limits to such use. As the pressure dropped in the cylinder, so did the temperature and this caused considerable heat losses from the alternate heating and cooling of the cylinder.[40] The changes in pressure during the stroke caused big fluctuations in the force on the crank which led to vibration and wear. The advantages of expanding the steam in two or more stages had been recognised at least since Woolf's patent of 1803 but the actual benefit was not great for steam pressures less than 60-70lbs/sq in. It was not feasible to use seawater in boilers at these pressures and it was necessary to use very pure fresh water which, in turn, needed reliable condensers. Many inventors demonstrated compound engines with impressive savings in fuel consumption but their reliability was poor, with leaking joints in the steam piping the most common problem.

Elder's patent of 1853 was the first reliable design and this was adopted in a small number of merchant ships from 1855 with claimed savings of up to 50 per cent in fuel consumption at the small expense of 5-10 per cent

37. Sir N Barnaby, 'Ships of War', *Trans INA* (London 1876).

38. B Patterson, Journal 4, Portsmouth Royal Dockyard Historical Trust. 1996.

39. This section is based on a series of articles by the author which appeared in the *Journal of Naval Engineering* 1993 entitled 'Marine Engineering in the RN, 1860-1905'.

40. R Sennett, 'On Compound Engines', *Trans INA* (London 1875).

41. E C Smith, *A Short History of Marine Engineering* (Cambridge 1937).

42. Said to be due to an overlong steam pipe and inexperience of the crew.

43. A later Chief Engineer, J Wright, pointed out that the normal 6-hour trial was for reliability rather than consumption since the weight of coal in each bag was not necessarily the same. Thirteen per cent of the weight of coal used was thrown away as clinker.

44. Wright said the higher-pressure boilers had a shorter life, say two commissions.

45. See also the author's *Before the Ironclad* for the earlier achievements of this great naval architect and marine engineer.

increase in engine weight. In 1860 the Admiralty installed a compound engine of Elder's design in the wooden screw frigate *Constance* which, in 1865, took part in a dramatic trial with two sister ships fitted with simple engines; *Arethusa* (Penn) and *Octavia* (Maudslay). All three ships used steam at 25-30lbs/sq in. The three ships sailed from Plymouth on 30 September 1865 heading for Madeira, the race ending on 6 October when all three ran out of fuel (see table below).

It was not a very convincing trial as there were doubts as to the differing use of sail assistance and the steam pressure was too low for compound engines to work at their best. Even so, *Constance* showed a considerable advantage though later her engines were said to be complicated, difficult to handle and unreliable.[41] In 1863 the *Pallas* was given a Humphrys compound and though this was economical and reliable, it was not repeated. In the late 1860s a number of ships, mainly corvettes, were fitted with different makes of compound working at 60 lbs/sq in and all proved economical and only *Spartan* is said to have been unreliable.[42] Briton with Rennie engines consumed 1.3lbs/ihp/hr at full power and 1.983lbs/ihp/hr at cruising speed. *Spartan*, *Monarch* and *Thetis* burnt about 2.5lbs/ihp/hr.

The Committee of 1871 had no doubts: '. . . the weight of evidence in favour of the large economy of fuel is overwhelming and conclusive . . . economy of fuel may mean thicker armour, greater speed, a smaller and cheaper ship or the power of moving under steam alone for an extended period'.[43] There are few contemporary accounts of early compound engines in service but it seems that the Royal Navy experienced more problems than did commercial operators and, in consequence, were a little slow in making the change.[44] The usage of warship machinery is very different from that of merchant ships. The latter operate continuously at maximum (sustained) power whereas it is rare for a warship to use full power and there will be frequent and rapid changes of load.

Surface condensers came into general use during the 1860s but erosion and corrosion problems were common at least up to the Second World War. A Committee on Boilers was set up in 1874 and its findings were incorporated into the first Steam Manual of 1879. Its many sensible recommendations included replacing tallow and vegetable oils by mineral oil, the treatment of feed water to reduce acidity and the use of zinc anodes in the boiler to reduce corrosion. New materials were introduced for joint sealing and piston packing to withstand higher pressures. Not for the first time – or the last – a major advance in engineering depended on apparently minor details.

The introduction of compound engines was the last achievement of the great Engineer-in-Chief, Thomas Lloyd,[45] who retired in 1869. As the Controller, Spencer Robinson, wrote: 'To Mr Lloyd, more than anyone else is due the successful application of the screw to the

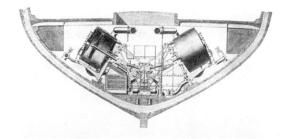

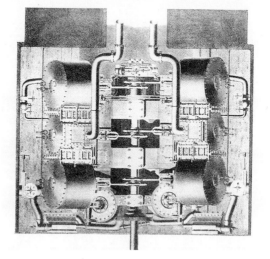

Above: Sir James Wright, Engineer-in-Chief 1869-87. (RNEC)

Left: The 6-cylinder compound engine of *Constance*. (Author's collection)

propulsion of steamships, and it was due to his enlightened knowledge and zealous exertions that the Royal Navy was able to take the lead in its application to ships of war.' He was followed by another civilian engineer, James Wright (later knighted).

Dreadnought and *Alexandra* were the first true battleships with compound engines and the latter's installation will be described in some detail. She had twin shafts, each driven by a Humphrys and Tennant three-cylinder compound engine with a 90in low pressure (LP) cylinder each side of the 70in high-pressure cylinder, all elaborately steam-jacked to avoid wasting heat. Earlier steam warships had horizontal engines which could be kept below the waterline for protection but *Alexandra*'s 12in belt was seen as sufficient protection and the simpler vertical arrangement was adopted. The engines were arranged on high seats to protect them from damage in the event of grounding, an all too com-

Fuel consumption of *Arethusa*, *Octavia* and *Constance*, 30 September-6 October 1865

	Distance from Madeira	Coal (lb/ihp/hr)	Hours steaming	Tons burnt	Tons/hr
Arethusa	200	3.64	134	224	1.7
Octavia	160	3.17	140	277	2.0
Constance	30	2.51	124	243	2.0

Alexandra shown late in life
after her little-used sailing rig
had been removed. Note the
two-tier recessed gunports
which generated clouds of
heavy spray and were not very
effective in permitting end-on
fire. (Imperial War Museum:
Q38109)

mon event in the nineteenth-century Navy.[46] They were
also braced to withstand the shock of ramming. There
were twelve cylindrical boilers arranged in four boiler
rooms separated by a transverse and a longitudinal
bulkhead; the working pressure was 60lbs/sq in and
there was 21,900sq ft of heating surface. The boilers
were arranged back-to-back against the centreline bulkhead so that the furnace doors would be handy for the
wing bunkers. Each boiler contained 200lbs of zinc
anodes which seem to have been effective since the boilers lasted 16 years before being replaced.

The surface condensers had 16,500sq ft of cooling
surface with ⅝in brass tubes, the centrifugal circulating
pumps being driven by their own steam engine.

Alexandra had an elaborate ventilation system with
steam-powered fans and, for the first time, valves were
fitted at each bulkhead to prevent the spread of fire and
smoke. The hollow lower masts, which were used as
ventilation exhausts, were seen as a particular fire hazard, as they could generate a very powerful updraught.
The engine-room complement consisted of a Chief
Engineer, ten Assistants and eighty stokers.

Alexandra (ld 1873)

Barnaby's *Alexandra* was an enlarged version of Reed's
centre battery ship and was obsolete in concept before
she was laid down. She was given a full sailing rig which,
it is said, was never used except for drill.[47] However, she
was an imposing ship and served at sea for 23 years as a
flagship. She mounted two 11in and ten 10in in a double-deck battery with recessed ports. These threw up
vast clouds of spray at speed and her effective end-on
fire was negligible. Her belt had a maximum thickness
of 12in iron and 12in of teak backing.

Temeraire (ld 1873)

The design of *Temeraire* commenced as a modified
Swiftsure and even the very different ship which completed can still best be seen in that light. In a paper dated
22 June 1872 Barnaby lists for the Controller a number
of options, most of which retained the centre battery
style of the *Swiftsure*.[48] In addition there was one turret
ship proposal which had a single turret mounting two
25-ton guns. The turret was 39ft in diameter with the

Temeraire, 1876. Her two 25-
ton guns on disappearing
mountings were effective but
very heavy. (Author's collection)

guns 19ft apart so that they could fire forward, either side of a narrow forecastle which carried the tripod (or quadruped) foremast. The Board had their usual and rational dislike for a single turret. She would have had a 6½-ton stern gun and four 64pdrs.

The beam was increased to 58ft so that ballast could be omitted and the weight saved used to increase the belt to 9in. The armament of the centre battery studies differed but usually had 18-ton guns in the main battery and a mix of 18- and 25-ton in the upper tier. An early variant (July 1872) had six 18-ton guns in the lower battery and four 12-ton in the upper with four 64pdrs. In December 1872 the preferred variant had two 25-ton, six 18-ton on the broadside and one as chase together with four 20pdrs.

Weights given were;
2 – 12in with carriage   78t-4cwt-2qtr-0
7 – 10in   196-14-0-0[49]

The first mention of barbette guns is on 3 February 1873 when they were said to be 'under consideration'. Instead of an upper battery with 8in armour and two 18-ton guns there were two barbettes with one 25-ton and one 18-ton gun in mounts 28ft in diameter. At a later date they were both 25-ton. These Rendel mounts were the only barbettes in British ships of the day. There was an armoured pit in the upper deck, fore and aft, each containing an 11in, 25-ton gun on a hydraulically worked, disappearing mounting. The gun was loaded hydraulically in the lower position and would then be raised to the firing position by further hydraulic rams, taking up a pre-set training angle as it rose, though elevation had to be applied manually. The normal crew was six but it could be worked by three if necessary (excluding ammunition suppliers) which compares well with a crew of nineteen for a similar gun on a broadside mount. One round could be fired every 105 seconds.

The after gun caused blast damage to bulkheads and fittings when fired on *any* bearing and hence three out of four of the annual practice firings were carried out with its crew manning the forward mount, damage being accepted once a year.[50] In many ways this mount was successful; it could be loaded, trained and fired quickly and accurately with a small crew but it was big and heavy and was not repeated. It is said that *Temeraire*'s single mount was the size and weight of a twin turret. Note that this account of the origin of *Temeraire*, well-documented, differs completely from both Parkes' and Ballard's (different) versions. In no way does it resemble the minority report of the 1871 Committee – nor, very much, that of the majority.

Shannon (ld 1873)

Shannon was officially described as a broadside, armour-belted, cruising ship complemented as a Second

The Royal Navy's first armoured cruiser *Shannon*, 1875. (National Maritime Museum, London: BKS/1)

Class battleship and may be regarded as the first armoured cruiser for the RN. She was not seen as a success, then or later, only spending three years of her 21-year life in an active role. She did have some novel features which should be mentioned here.

The 9in belt was carried to the stern, reduced to 6in but stopped on a 9in bulkhead 60ft abaft the bow. The fore end was protected as in *Inflexible* with a 3in deck, stepped down to support the ram,[51] and similar close subdivision. *Shannon* was the first ship to be protected in this fashion. Her two 10in, 18-ton guns were mounted on the upper deck and could fire forward through axial ports in the thick bulkhead which was wrapped round to give broadside protection to these two guns. The seven 9in, 12-ton were unprotected, mounted three on either side of the upper deck with one aft. It was intended that once these guns were loaded and trained, the crews would take shelter and the guns fired electrically.

Nelson and *Northampton* (ld 1874)

Even before *Shannon* was launched, it was appreciated that her fighting capability was very limited and two bigger cruisers were ordered. In these two ships, both ends relied on an armoured deck and subdivision for protection. Two more 10in were added aft, protected by a wrap around after bulkhead and there were four

46. A former Hydrographer, Admiral Roger Morris, suggests that the frequent groundings were often associated with compass problems. Though the master compass was fully compensated, the repeaters on the bridge were not.

47. Ballard, *The Black Battlefleet*.

48. Ship's Cover.

49. Ammunition carried for the 12in.
    Shell, filled   20 common, 4
                      shrapnel, 50 chilled
    Shell empty   30 common
    Shot   6 case, 60 chilled

50. Parkes, *British Battleships*. The willingness to accept actual damage at least once a year contrasts with the apocryphal stories of gunnery practice being omitted to avoid spoiling the paint.

51. The ram was detachable and stowed ashore in peacetime to reduce the hazard to other friendly ships!

Comparison of *Audacious*, *Shannon* and *Nelson*

	Audacious	*Shannon*	*Nelson*
Displacement (tons)	6010	5390	7473
Armament	10-9in	2-10in, 7-9in	4-10in, 8-9in
Belt	8in complete+battery	9in partial	9in partial
Total armour weight (tons)	924	1060	1720
Speed (kts)	12.5	12.25	14

The armoured cruiser *Nelson*, 1876. (National Maritime Museum, London: BAA/1)

William Froude, civil engineer, who developed a theory of rolling in 1860 and by 1870 had proved the value of model testing in improving hull form and reducing power requirements. (RINA)

unprotected 9in on either side. The side above the belt was constructed from 1in steel in *Nelson*, presumably to alleviate the problems of gunshot on unarmoured wrought iron. Since the steel was made by the Bessemer process, the end result may well have been worse.

It is interesting to compare these three cruisers with the slightly earlier Second Class battleships of the *Audacious* class (see previous page).

All these ships were intended to operate in distant waters against single enemy Second Class ships rather than in a battle line. Under these conditions, the armoured battery of the *Audacious* may well have proved invaluable. Barnaby's big cruisers were too expensive to be built in the numbers needed for trade protection and were incapable of fighting a true battleship.

William Froude and model testing

Until this date the power needed for a new ship was estimated by comparison with previous ships using the Admiralty Coefficient.[52] This was moderately accurate if both the hull form and machinery plant were closely similar to the previous ship and provided the speed was not too great. However, considerable errors were common and commercial owners faced losses with ships which were unable to make their intended speed or were burdened with engines which were unnecessarily big

and costly. The sloop *Amazon* of 1865 was one of many ships whose difficulties show the inaccuracy of power estimates.

She was intended for a speed of 13kts and a length of 212ft was suggested. To improve handiness, this was reduced to 187ft. On her first trial she failed to reach the design speed and a number of further trials were carried out with different propellers.

The two-bladed Griffiths propeller was better for sailing as well as more efficient and was chosen. It is interesting that the highest speed was achieved with almost the lowest indicated power. It was decided that the last two ships (*Blanche* and *Danae*) should be lengthened to the original 212ft and were reclassified as corvettes.

The British Association set up a number of committees from 1838 to 1870 with distinguished engineers and scientists to find a solution. It was generally agreed that model tests were misleading and that the use of the Admiralty Coefficient based on a number of full scale trials was the only possible approach. Froude[53] dissented from this view based on a series of model tests which he had carried out in the Dart from 1867 onwards.

He tried three pairs of models 3ft, 6ft and 12ft in length which he called the *Swan* and *Raven*. The latter was a conventional form with fine ends, loosely influenced by Scott Russell's Wave Line theory.[54] *Swan* was based on the bird and had fairly bluff ends. Froude first showed that there was no one optimum form as had been generally believed since Isaac Newton; *Raven* was best at low speeds and *Swan* at higher speeds. This is a most important development; if only a single optimum form had to be identified, it could, perhaps, be derived from a series of full-scale trials. With no one optimum, it was too costly to develop improved forms by building full-scale ships and model testing was essential. He then showed that the characteristics of the curve of resistance against speed were similar for each of the three pairs of models and developed Froude's law:[55]

The resistance per ton is the same for *similar* forms of different size at the same value of speed/√(Length)

This meant that new forms could be tried at model scale with full confidence that any benefits would be reproduced in the ship. In February 1868 Reed visited Froude to see his results and persuaded Froude to make a formal application for Admiralty assistance in developing his work. This application was received in December 1868, Froude proposing that a covered tank be built in which models could be towed to measure their resistance. He estimated the cost of building the tank and running it for two years would be £2000, offering his own services free for that period. It was too late to find the money in the 1869 Estimates but approval was given in February 1870 for expenditure under that year's Estimates, largely due to Reed's support.[56]

There were many practical problems[57] to be over-

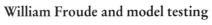

Amazon – various trials

No of blades	Pitch (ft)	rpm	ihp	Speed (kts)
4	15	75	1528	11.49
4	12-6	86	1941	12.08
2 (Griffiths)	15	88.7	1808	12.17
2	13-9	94	1663	12.4

come before the tank opened for full operation in May 1872. By this time Froude had refined his procedure and treated the frictional resistance of water over the hull separately which involved a number of tests of flat surfaces of different length and finish over a range of speeds. The procedure was validated by a careful trial in which the sloop *Greyhound* was towed over a range of speeds by the *Active*, the measured resistance agreeing well with that estimated from models. In 1873 Froude extended his model tests to include the performance of propellers, both in isolation and to measure the interference between propeller and hull flows when behind a hull. The dynamometer he built to measure propeller performance had a wooden frame and brass wheels, driven by leather bootlaces, and was last used for the *Abdiel* class fast minelayers in the mid-1930s.

From 1873 the emphasis was on matching hull form and power to the requirements of the whole ship. It is a mistake to think that the aim is some hydrodynamic optimum; *Inflexible* was amongst the first forms tested by Froude and it was well appreciated that her short, broad hull was not the best for speed but was necessary to provide the protection required. His novel use of wax meant that a model could be made in a single day and tested the next, after which it could easily be altered or melted down for re-use. Froude's work gave the Royal Navy an important lead over other navies[58] for many years. Never has £2000 been spent so well; Barnaby was to write[59] that he would be supported by shipbuilders all over the world in naming William Froude as the foremost worker in naval development during a wonderful century. William Froude died in 1879 and was succeeded by his son, Edmund, who ran the tank for the next 40 years, transferring to Haslar in 1887. Reed's contribution was important, showing his willingness to adopt and support new ideas whether they came from his own department or from outside.

Alexandria, 1882

The British intention in bombarding Alexandria was to silence the defences which were in the hands of nationalists trying to remove the Anglo-French 'protection' of Egypt. It is of interest that the Admiralty 'chartered a commercial cable vessel to pick up the cable 4 miles off Alexandria and act as a floating telegraph office, through which they controlled the operations of the fleet up to and after the bombardment of the city two weeks later.'[60] There were 8 main forts mounting in all 37 rifled guns, 182 smoothbores including 10 500pdrs, and 31 mortars. The defences may be considered in three main groups; to the north there were some old forts joined by a modern earthwork mounting twenty-six modern guns. Guarding the inner harbour was a more extensive but weaker line of old forts and modern earthworks, while at the western end was Fort Marabout which, with its seven rifled guns, was the

The original model towing tank opened at Torquay in 1872 by William Froude, sponsored by Edward Reed. (Author's collection)

The only known photograph of the sloop *Greyhound*. She was towed by *Active* (sister-ship of *Volage*) and her full-scale resistance measured, validating William Froude's use of model testing. She was also used for trials of bilge keels. (Imperial War Museum: A159)

52. The Admiralty Coefficient was used in two forms: (Appendix 3) Ad Cft = ihp/(mid sec. area x speed cubed) or ihp/{(dispt)$^{2/3}$ x speed cubed}.

53. Froude had first won a reputation as a railway engineer under I K Brunel and his work on rolling of the *Great Eastern* led him into hydrodynamics with his classic paper of 1860. See the author's 'William Froude and the Way of a Ship in the Sea' Devonshire Association, 1991 for further information on this fascinating man.

54. The Wave Line theory was quite wrong in principle but the emphasis on fine ends matched the needs of fast ships of the 1870s.

55. The French mathematician Reech had earlier developed a similar law but its importance and the way in which it could be used was not recognised.

56. The actual cost was much greater, Froude paying the excess out of his own pocket.

57. Including worm holes in the sides of the tank!

58. Tideman in Holland had developed a similar approach but his

progress was slower due to lack of funds. See J M Dirzwager, 'Contribution of Dr Tideman to the Development of Modern Shipbuilding', *Five Hundred Years of Nautical Science* (Conference, National Maritime Museum, Greenwich, 1981).

59. Sir N Barnaby, *Naval Development of the Century* (London 1904).

60. J D Brown, 'Overseas and oversea Communications 1814-1899', *Marine & Technique au XIX Siecle* (Paris 1987).

strongest individual fort. The fleet comprised eight ironclads[61] (total eighty guns, of which forty-three could bear on a broadside) and six gunboats.

Guns at Alexandria (omitting SB)

Guns	Fleet	Forts
16in RML	4	
12	4	
11	6	
10	38	5
9	16	18
8	8	12
7	4	2
Totals	80	37

In addition, the fleet mounted sixteen 64- and 40pdrs, forty-nine 20pdr BLR, thirteen 9.7in MLR, and seventy-one 1in Nordenfelt. The shore defences included 204 SB and 36 SB mortars (6-15in and 10–20in mortars), not all of which were manned.

Damage to *Alexandra* after the bombardment of Alexandria 1882. The first picture clearly shows the recessed gunports on two decks. (Naval Photograph Club)

The forts were badly constructed; the parapets were neither high enough nor strong enough, there were few traverses or expense magazines and much exposed masonry – misses were more dangerous than hits. There was no proper covered communication. The Egyptian defenders were deficient in everything except courage and were unused to rifled weapons.[62] From the Fleet's point of view:

Advantages. Very slight sea. Smooth water inshore. No mines or torpedo boats. Navigation was easy as the buoys were left in place.

Disadvantages. Smoke drifted out from the shore and there was a haze.

Rather surprisingly, the admiral divided his force with one group against each of the two main fortified areas; Fort Marabout was not engaged but its accurate fire soon became a problem and it was engaged by *Condor* and other gunboats firing from blind arcs. Firing began at 7:07am, 11 July and there was a heavy and accurate return fire.[63] Initially, the ships were under way but soon anchored to improve the accuracy of their fire which was made difficult by the vast clouds of black smoke from the powder charges.

The outer squadron, comprising *Alexandra, Superb, Sultan, Inflexible* and *Temeraire,* fired under way at 1600-3000yds but anchored at 9:30am at about 1100yds. The inshore group fired on Mex initially at 1100-1300yds, later closing to 400yds. Fort Mex was silenced by 10:30am and a landing party went in at 1pm-2pm. Adda exploded at 1:35pm. Pharos was silent by 3pm and by 5pm all guns were silent and the forts were in the hands of British landing parties.

Rounds fired

Heavy MLR	1746
64- and 40pdr	556
20pdr	627
9- and 7pdr	282
Nordenfelt	16,200
Gatling .65 and .45	71,000
Martini Henry	10,160

Examination of the forts after the battle showed that British gunnery had been very accurate but not very effective. Only seven out of twenty-six modern guns at Ras-el-Tin had been put out of action and only one out of seven in the southern batteries. Fuses had been very poor and many unexploded shells were found – one of *Penelope's* 8in shells was in the middle of 400 tons of powder! The scarp was penetrated to about 8-9ft but without practical damage. Eleven shell bursting on the 'superior' slope made a breach 18ft long for 4ft 6in depth. Out of thirty-seven heavy guns fired at, eight were hit directly and four by debris; a further five or six were damaged by their own recoil. Some 7000 rounds of Nordenfelt were fired at Fort Mex but only three hits were scored on the thirteen guns. All in all, a typical engagement in which a heavy but not very damaging bombardment led to evacuation of the forts.

The Navy lost six men killed and twenty-five wounded. There was no case in which armour was penetrated but several ships were hit many times – *Alexandra* sixty times. There were indications, as in other cases, that armour performed better on a ship than in a test butt. Ammunition handling, particularly in centre battery ships where the magazine was distant from the guns, was slow, difficult and could be hazardous – *Alexandra* was hit by a shell which could have caused an ammunition explosion had it not been dumped in a bucket of water.

Hits on ships

Ship	Total on hull	On armour
Alexandra	31	6
Inflexible	2	0
Superb	7	3
Sultan	12	5
Temeraire	0	0
Invincible	15	0
Monarch	0	0
Penelope	8	3
Totals	75	17

The greatest damage was to *Sultan*: a 3in indentation and two plates started. *Penelope* suffered from an 11in shot which entered a port, hit an 8in gun, stripped off the B tube for 6in and wounded ten men. White says of *Inflexible*: 'The blast from her huge guns was wrecking her boats and upperworks'.

Machine-guns

The first effective machine-gun was the French *mitrailleuse*, used in the Franco-Prussian War of 1870-71, which could fire some 250 rounds per minute. Various inventors came up with improved weapons and, following trials in 1870, the Royal Navy quickly adopted the Gatling gun. It was a revolver with 10 barrels of 0.56in bore and could fire 500 rounds per minute if all went well but it was prone to jam and was hard to keep steady.

The Gatling was soon superseded by the Gardner gun after trials in 1880 (in service 1884) with 1, 2 or 5 barrels side by side and which could fire 120 rounds per barrel per minute. This was soon followed, in turn, by the Nordenfelt, with 5 barrels, rifle calibre, firing a total of 600 rounds per minute. The RN used mainly a 5-barrelled, 0.45in version though there were some 4-barrel, 1in weapons (note the extensive use of machine-guns at

Alexandria in 1882). Finally, the Maxim single-barrel firing 600-650 rounds per minute was introduced in 1888 and which in developed form as the Vickers was to be used in considerable numbers in both World Wars. The original Maxim was chambered for the 0.45in Martini-Henry cartridge but later 0.303in and 0.5in were the standard calibres.

When the effective range for big guns was about 1000yds there was a very real role for the machine-gun in attacking exposed gun crews, particularly when mounted high up in fighting tops. The bigger guns, particularly the 1in Nordenfelt, were seen as capable of disabling or sinking a torpedo boat.

Coefficient of fighting efficiency

It seems appropriate to close this chapter by considering what features were seen by Reed and Barnaby as desirable in a fighting ship. The formula below was used by both of them in an attempt to compare the fighting effectiveness of various ships.[64]

$$\text{The Measure of efficiency} = \frac{A \times G \times H \times S^3}{100L} \text{ where:}$$

A is the weight of armour per ton displacement
G is the weight of protected guns and ammunition[65]
H is the height of port sill above water.
S is trial speed, kts
L is length, feet. (Used as a measure of 'handiness and quickness in manoeuvring')

This was used to compare tonnage, cost and efficiency for a number of ships.[66]

Tonnage, cost and efficiency

Ship	Tonnage (bm)	Cost (£x1000)	Efficiency
Monarch	5102	346	149.8
Hercules	5234	360	113.4
Captain	4272	330	83.3
Vanguard	3774	255	83.0
Minotaur	6621	430	61.1
Bellerophon	4270	343	58.6
Achilles	?	458	42.9
Also note			
Warrior			44.5
Defence			10.9

The parameters used indicate the importance placed on them in that day. It is perhaps surprising that if speed was used as the cube, that more efforts were not made to build faster ships. The attempt to balance cost against efficiency has a modern ring to it – and seems as unsuccessful as many modern cost-effectiveness arguments.

61. *Invincible, Inflexible, Monarch, Temeraire, Alexandra, Sultan, Superb* and *Penelope*.

62. *Gunnery Manual* 1892.

63. C S White, 'The Bombardment of Alexandria 1882', *The Mariner's Mirror* Vol 66 (London 1980).

64. There are indications that it was devised by Barnaby whilst working for Reed.

65. This is as written in the 1871 Committee report and elsewhere. One would expect G to be per ton of displacement as with A.

66. Constructors' Department report to 1871 on *Audacious*.

Steel for Ships, Armour, Engines and Guns

Five

Sir Nathaniel Barnaby, seen after retirement. (RCNC Archive)

FOR THE same strength, a steel structure is much lighter than one of iron. The use of steel in hull and in machinery saved a great deal of weight and, once open-hearth steel was available, steel was more reliable than iron. Steel alloys cover a wide range of properties and different steels were used in armour and in shells. In most applications, French industry was ahead of British companies.

Sir Nathaniel Barnaby, 1870-85

Barnaby came from a family of shipwrights and entered Sheerness as an apprentice in 1842. His ability won him a scholarship to the Central School of Naval Architecture and by 1855 he was working at Somerset House under Isaac Watts. Later, he was the senior assistant to Reed and, as has been discussed, contributed much to the designs for which Reed was responsible and to the development of the theory of stability. He took charge of the Department when Reed resigned but, in the confusion following the loss of *Captain*, Childers hoped to bring in Laird and Barnaby was only titled 'President of the Council of Construction', still with the rank of Assistant Constructor. In September 1872 his position was established as Chief Naval Architect, changed to Director of Naval Construction in April 1875.

He had a difficult task as he was not given the authority which Reed had under Spencer Robinson, funds were scarce and thinking on strategy and tactics even more scarce. Despite this, he produced some outstanding designs. He had a strong conviction of the moral worth of his work;[1] views which are difficult to summarise but the two short quotations which follow give an idea of his approach. 'Lasting good is only evolved in this world though strife and bloodshed' and 'Righteousness must come before peace'. He is said to have written a hymn. Barnaby resigned in July 1885 on health grounds but his grandson has written that the real reason was the continuous bitter arguments with Reed who had married Barnaby's sister and lived nearby.

Steel hulls

Barnaby[2] was well aware of the potential gains in using steel rather than wrought iron in ship construction but the change had to wait for a reliable source of the new material. In the middle of the century the meaning of 'iron' and 'steel' was ill-defined and all were very variable in their quality. The main difference lay in the amount of carbon in the alloy; wrought iron was the usual structural material with a very low carbon content of about 0.3 per cent, whilst cast iron had a carbon content of up to 6 per cent which made it run freely when melted. Steel was used to describe a wide range of alloys; when used structurally it had a carbon content of about 0.3 per cent up to an extreme 2 per cent. In general, an increase of carbon increased the tensile strength of steel but made it more brittle and liable to crack.

Steel had been used for centuries in tools and weapons but was too expensive for large-scale use until Bessemer developed his converter in 1856. By 1864 steel was being used in considerable quantities for the non-vital areas of warship hulls but the quality was very variable and cracking too frequent.[3] Because of this variability, it was always possible to find a good sample which would pass any test.

At low temperatures all metals become brittle and will crack easily. The normal methods of manufacture and working means that iron and steel in a ship will have many tiny cracks which will not spread when the plate or section is tough, above the transition temperature. Below this temperature, cracks may spread very quickly; such cracks can even spread across riveted seams though this is uncommon. The importance of the transition temperature was not appreciated until the end of the Second World War when cracks in all-welded ships could spread right round the ship. The few modern measurements on sample of earlier ferrous alloys are given below.

Ship	Transition Temperature, °C
Great Britain	50 (Iron)
Warrior	20 (Iron)
Titanic	20 (Steel)

In 1857, Siemens, a German working in London, developed a new type of reverberatory furnace for glass manufacture and in 1863 the Frenchmen Pierre and Emile Martin, father and son, realised this furnace could be used for steel manufacture. It took 6-15 hours to produce a load of steel compared with 30 minutes in a Bessemer converter but the longer time made the reaction much more controllable and led to a more consistent product. At this time the French iron industry in the Loire valley was in difficulty as the local ore had run out.[4] They decided to concentrate on steel using the Siemens-Martin, open-hearth process and, with a reliable material, the French Navy introduced the large scale use of steel.

The chief constructor at Lorient, de Bussy, decided to build the *Redoutable* almost entirely of steel and introduced new tools and working procedures. In October 1874 Barnaby and his assistant, William White,[5] visited the French steel works and Lorient. They were most impressed and, on return, Barnaby read a paper[6] to the INA in which he asked British industry to make steel of similar quality. In response, Riley, the manager of the Landore works in Wales (founded by Siemens) said that they were using the open-hearth method and could meet all requirements.

Iris *and* Mercury *(ld 1875)*

The 'despatch vessels' *Iris* and *Mercury* were ordered in 1875 to be built at Pembroke; their significance as 'cruisers' will be discussed in Chapter 7 while this section deals only with their many technical innovations. Pembroke was probably chosen because it was close to the Landore works but the fact that Pembroke had only limited experience with iron[7] may have contributed. Most yards (including Lorient) found that the techniques for using steel were learnt more quickly by men without previous experience in iron.

Early steel had a strength some 30 per cent greater than wrought iron and it was theoretically possible to reduce scantlings and hence weight *pro rata*. White wrote that for the *Iris* it was decided that no thickness would be reduced by more than 15 per cent and, of course, there were many areas whose thickness was determined more by durability than strength. Even so, there was an appreciable weight saving which could be put into fighting capability or, as in *Iris*, to aid in reaching high speed.

Initially, steel was much more expensive than iron – White says that in 1877 the cost was double. Much of the difference was because iron plates were usually not tested whilst this was always a requirement for steel. The Admiralty always asked for tests on iron plates and paid £20 per ton whilst untested plate could be bought at £9 a ton. In a test purchase of iron plates in 1874 two-thirds of the cheapest plates were found to be unfit for use when tested by the Admiralty. The price of steel dropped rapidly and a smaller weight of steel was needed so that commercial owners soon followed the Admiralty and by 1888 iron shipbuilding had died out.[8]

Steel in engines

Steel had been used in the boiler shells of warships since about 1870 but its use was much extended in the engines of *Iris* and her sister. Their two 3500ihp, 4-cylinder Maudslay compound engines had the 41in HP cylinders in line with the 75in LP cylinders with a stroke of 2ft 9in. The cylinders were horizontal and there was not room for two sets side by side so they were arranged in

Iris, 1877, the first steel ship for the Royal Navy following the successful introduction of the open-hearth process by the Landore works. (Author's collection)

separate rooms divided by a transverse bulkhead, the forward engine driving the starboard shaft. There were also two boiler rooms, the machinery occupying half the 300ft length. These two ships were unarmoured and the coal bunkers were outboard of the machinery to give some protection[9] and with four machinery spaces, cross-connected, these ships were quite resistant to damage.

The inboard section of the propeller shafts was of Whitworth 'compressed steel', 17in external diameter. As with all twin-screw ships of the day the external shafts (16½in wrought iron) ran inside a gun metal tube on *lignum vitae* bearings.

The twelve boilers, eight oval and four cylindrical, worked at 60lbs/sq in with a total grate area of 69sq ft and a heating surface of 15,900sq ft and were built entirely of steel, giving about a 10 per cent saving in weight. Sennett (Engineer-in-Chief) read a paper to the INA[10] in 1888 in which he demonstrated that merchant ship rules for boiler test pressures were illogical and could even be harmful. He proposed that the test pressure should not lead to stresses greater than $\frac{4}{9}$ths of the ultimate strength of the steel and the test should be 90lbs/sq in greater than the working pressure. These Admiralty rules would permit an 18 per cent saving in weight with equal or greater safety. Though there was considerable opposition to his views, experience showed he was right and that such boilers were safe. Steel construction facilitated the use of the corrugated furnace, developed by Fox in 1874, which came into general use from 1881. The corrugations provided radial stiffening, increased the heating surface and permitted expansion longitudinally. From 1882 brass boiler tubes were superseded, first by iron and later by lap-welded steel.

Richard Sennett was the first naval engineer officer to become Engineer-in-Chief. He trained in the Keyham Steam Factory before attending the Royal School at South Kensington where he graduated in 1870. He was very highly regarded and his widely-used text book *The*

1. See his *Naval Developments of the Century*, Ch 1 'Ethics of Naval Development'.

2. Several modern writers suggest Barnaby obstructed the introduction of steel, which is grossly unfair. The following paragraphs only touch on the problem of early steels.

3. D K Brown, 'The Introduction of Steel into the Royal Navy', *Journal of Naval Science* Vol 20 No 4 (1995). Note the failures of steel in *Audacious* and *Hercules* mentioned in Chapter 2.

4. T Ropp (ed S Roberts), *Development of a Modern Navy* (Annapolis 1987).

5. Probably as a result of this visit, White and de Bussy became good friends. See D K Brown, 'Interactive Design', Anglo-French Naval History Conference (Exeter 1996).

6. Sir N Barnaby, 'Iron and Steel for Shipbuilding', *Trans INA* (London 1875).

7. Mainly with *Inconstant*, which also used some steel.

8. J F Clarke and F Storr, *The Introduction of the Use of Mild Steel into the Shipbuilding and Marine Engineering Industries* (Newcastle 1983).

9. Trials showed that 2ft of coal was equivalent to 1in of steel as protection.

10. R Sennett, 'Working and Test Pressures for Marine Boilers', *Trans INA* (London 1879).

Above: Richard Sennett, Engineer-in-Chief 1887-89. (RNEC)

Right: The two engine rooms of *Iris.* She was too narrow for them to be arranged side-by-side. (Author's collection)

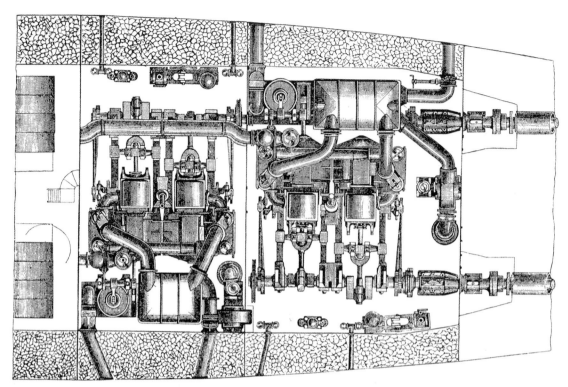

Marine Steam Engine was based on his lecture course at the RN College. He was only 40 when he became Engineer-in-Chief but resigned two years later to join Maudslay. His health soon failed and he died in 1891. White was to write of him '. . . a man who by what he had done and dared had helped the cause of marine engineering in many ways, and in a manner which had yet to be fully recognised'.

Speed trials

From the introduction of the steam ship, trials had been carried out to prove that the machinery worked reliably at its intended power and to determine the speed of the ship. Cheating was common in the early days[11] but largely eliminated by 1860. New ships on trial, run in optimum conditions, reached speeds considerably higher than those recorded in service, Reed putting the difference as about 1.5kts. Understandably, there were many who criticised the whole idea of measured mile trials and proposed that they be replaced by a lengthy run at sea in normal operating conditions. The counter argument, which the Admiralty accepted, was that the trial results, with everything (including wind and sea) at its best gave consistent figures which could be used to compare different classes; particularly important when the Admiralty Coefficient[12] was the only means for estimating performance of the next class. The load on the machinery in full-power runs served as a proof test, extended by a 6-hour full-power run. As the hull form was designed by the Admiralty, the contractor was

required to develop a specified power and not a particular speed.

The original trials of *Iris* in December 1877 were disappointing as she reached only 16.4kts instead of the 17.5kts confidently anticipated.[13] A set of progressive speed trials over a range of speeds was run in February 1878 using the procedures proposed by William Denny to the British Association in 1875. Two of the blades of the four-bladed propeller were then removed and up to half power these proved considerably more efficient – it was not thought safe to attempt full power with the mutilated propellers. A new set of four-bladed propellers was designed and manufactured in quick time with more pitch[14] and less diameter and blade area and when tried in August, *Iris* reached 18.6kts, making her the fastest ship in the world. A new two-bladed set was 0.014kts faster but not used as they caused heavy vibration.

During these extended trials it was found that by running the engines at full speed, with the shafts disconnected, internal friction in the engines absorbed 400ihp and friction on the shafts a further 170ihp. Froude carried out tests on large-scale replicas of shafts and shaft brackets and developed formulae for their drag which remained in use until well after the Second World War.

Pembroke Dockyard[15]

The little-known Pembroke Dockyard was formally established by Order in Council on 31 October 1815 though the first two ships were already well advanced at what had been called the Pater Yard. The new yard was strengthened by moving shipwrights from Plymouth Dock. It was developed as a specialist building yard, without refitting facilities, but even as a builder it had many deficiencies. Though there were thirteen building slips, most if not all with enormous timber frame roofs,[16] there was only one dry dock, no fitting-out basin and only one alongside fitting-out berth at Hobbs' Point.[17] Sometimes fitting-out had to be carried out in ships moored off shore at great cost in wasted time. The railway reached Pembroke in 1864 but it was still seen as an outpost. It was common for workmen to build their own houses and in the early twentieth century, Nicholls as an Assistant Constructor was able to rent a double fronted house with a garden and even a bathroom (cold water only) for £20 a year. Many men lived in neighbouring villages and would come to work in their boats.

In the early days, wooden ships sailed under jury rig to Plymouth or occasionally Portsmouth for their masts to be fitted and for rigging. Paddle ships usually had their machinery fitted at Woolwich but later First Class battleships and cruisers had machinery and turrets installed at Pembroke. At peak, the yard employed 3600 men.

Pembroke was the second yard (after Chatham) to be equipped for iron construction and *Penelope* was launched in 1867 followed by *Inconstant* a year later.[18] Few iron ships were built and in 1875 *Iris*, the first steel ship, was laid down on No 2 slip. She was followed by many major vessels with *Hannibal* of the *Majestic* class as the last battleship and *Defence* as the last big cruiser. Work in the yard was run down after the First World War and it closed in 1925.

Steel armour and the Spezia trial, 1876[19]

By the mid-1870s the Creusot works were capable of making steel armour by the open hearth process. They could cast ingots weighing up to 110 tons and had a 100-ton press for forging. The first serious test of steel armour in comparison with iron was at Spezia in October 1876 when a number of different plates were tried to make the selection for the *Duilo*. In those happy days there was no equivalent of the Official Secrets Act and these trials and many later ones were conducted before observers from other countries and reported in the press. The plates tried were:

22in Cammell iron
22in Marrel iron
12 + 10in iron sandwich from both manufacturers
22in Creusot steel

They were fired at first by a 10in shot, then a salvo of one 10in and one 11in and finally a shot from the 17.7in,

100-ton gun, all using Palliser chilled iron shot. As a result of these trials the Italian Navy selected steel armour for the *Duilo* as, although the 2000lb shot destroyed the steel plate, the shot also broke up, failing to penetrate the backing, whilst all the iron targets were pierced. Of the iron targets, the single plates proved superior to the sandwich. There were only slight differences between the iron from the two manufacturers, Marrels seems to have been a little harder which helped to break up the shot but left the plate more prone to cracking.

Compound armour c1880-90

At much the same date, compound armour was developed by men working for two Sheffield companies, J D Ellis of John Brown and A Wilson of Cammell's.[20] In this armour a hard steel face plate was welded to a tough iron back so that the face would break up a shot whilst the tough back would support the steel, hold it together if it cracked, as early steel was prone to do, and stop any fragments of the shot from penetrating.

The two inventors used different methods of manufacture. In both a wrought iron plate was made in the usual way and brought to red heat. Ellis then placed a steel plate in front of the iron, a small distance away, and molten steel was poured in between. This would melt the surfaces and, on cooling, form a weld with a fairly gradual transition from the hard steel to the softer iron. Wilson did not use the steel plate but poured molten steel on top of the iron. In both cases the plate so made was twice the final thickness and was rolled down to finished size. About one-third of the final plate was steel. There were some initial problems in ensuring a good weld, whose failure could lead to cracking, but these were soon overcome. Trials showed that compound armour was about 50 per cent better than wrought iron against chilled iron shot (figure of merit 1.5). The advantage against forged steel shot was less, about 1.25. It was used first on the turrets of the *Inflexible* and, soon after, for the belt of *Colossus* completed in October 1885. (The *Riachuelo* built for Brazil by Samuda, completed in February 1884, was the first to have a compound belt.)

During the 1880s both all-steel and compound armour were steadily improved, first one then the other gaining a slight advantage. Generalisations that one or other was 'better' should be avoided. In 1880 the French carried out tests at Gâvre against targets of compound armour and all steel from Schneider and Terre Noire. The results convinced the French Navy that compound armour was superior and it was adopted but Creusot refused to make compound plate and persevered with all-steel armour.

There was another trial at Spezia in 1882 aimed at the selection of the armour for the barbettes of the *Italia*. British compound plates from Cammell and Brown were compared with steel plates from Creusot. All

11. D K Brown, 'Speed on Trial', *Warship No 3* (London 1977).

12. Appendix 3.

13. It does not seem that model tests were carried out on the *Iris* before completion.

14. Barnaby's grandson showed that it was the changes in pitch and diameter which were important rather than the reduction in blade area as believed at the time. K C Barnaby, *The Institution of Naval Architects 1860-1960* (London 1960).

15. L Phillips, *Pembrokeshire County History* (The Pembrokeshire Historical Society 1993), Ch 6. Gives much more on the ships built at Pembroke.

16. A Nicholls, *They built ships of the line*, Unpublished typescript, MoD Library.

17. Carr Jetty was completed early in the twentieth century.

18. She was to remain afloat for 88 years, long after Pembroke had closed.

19. This trial is fully described in the *Engineer* of 29 December 1876 and this article is largely reproduced in J W King, *The Warships of Europe* (Portsmouth 1878). It is also discussed in Hovgaard, *Modern History of Warships*.

20. Note that both these firms were iron and steel manufacturers at this date though both would buy shipyards later.

plates were 19in thick with 20in backing. They were each fired on with two rounds of Gregorini chilled iron projectiles from the 100-ton gun. The compound plates were shattered whilst the steel plate was little damaged. Forged steel projectiles were then fired against the steel plate which proved much more effective.

The steel plate had many more bolts than the compound plates and it was argued that this caused the difference in performance. A second trial was ordered and held in 1884 to select the armour for the next ship, *Lepanto*. Similar 19in plates from the same manufacturers were used but all had twenty bolts to attach them. It was intended to fire one round from the 100-ton gun into the centre of each plate and one from a 10in into each corner but only the Creusot plate could resist this attack. The compound plates were demolished by two rounds from the 10in gun but similar projectiles were shattered by the steel plate. The shot from the 100-ton gun penetrated all three targets but were broken in so doing.

There were other tests in 1884 at Amager, near Copenhagen.[21] A Creusot steel plate was compared with compound plates from various manufacturers. The results were said to be inconclusive and the order went to Cammell, probably on cost grounds.

The situation changed again about 1886 with the more general introduction of forged chrome steel shot such as those made by the French firm of Holtzer, discussed later. Another set of comparative trials were carried out in 1888 at Portsmouth with two plates by Cammell. A compound plate was attacked in March and a steel plate in May. Both were 10½in thick and both were fired on by 6in, 100lb Holtzer forged steel shot as well as by Palliser shot with a muzzle velocity of 1976ft/sec. Wilson of Cammell claimed that the steel plate was superior to any Creusot plate since it did not crack under repeated impact[22] but there was no trial comparing British and French steel plate. This was said to be the first time that forged steel shot had been stopped and without cracking the plate. Barnaby showed photographs which indicated the compound plate was superior in resistance. He also referred to other tests at oblique impact in which the superiority of the compound plate was even greater.

Compound armour was further improved by Captain Tressider who hardened the face by chilling with cold water.[23] It is often claimed that the British use of compound was due either to conservatism or the inability of industry to make good steel armour. It would seem that there was very little difference until the late 1880s when steel began to show real superiority. There was a trial at Annapolis in 1890 in which 10in plates were compared; mild steel and nickel alloy steel from Creusot and compound from Cammell.[24] They were each fired on by four 6in Holtzer projectiles and one 8in Firth steel shot. The steel plates stopped all shot whilst the compound was penetrated by all. The shots went deeper into the

nickel steel than into mild steel but the former did not crack like the latter. Trials at Ochta in Russia, later the same year gave similar results.

Improved powder and the end of muzzle-loaders, 1870-82

The Royal Navy remained with muzzle-loaders until the end of the 1870s by which time most other navies had changed to breech-loaders. There were many good reasons for this apparent conservatism; the MLR was cheap and reliable, it could be worked in a turret of smaller diameter and, with Rendel's hydraulic loading, there were no great advantages for the breech-loader. It is also true that the Ordnance Board and Woolwich Arsenal were far from progressive and the Arsenal lacked facilities to build longer guns. As late as 1867, a comparative trial between a 9.4in Krupp BL and a 9in Woolwich MLR against an 8in plate intended for the *Konig Wilhelm* showed the muzzle-loader to be far superior.

During the late 1860s and early 1870s it was appreciated by several engineers that a slower-burning powder would be more effective. Larger grain powder was a small step in this direction and during the 1870s Major Rodman of the US Army developed a powder with large, dense grains with perforations which became known as 'prismatic' powder. The German Rottweil company made a further improvement in 1882 with prismatic brown powder, introduced in the RN in 1884. This was further improved in 1887 as 'slow burning cocoa' (SBC) from its colour. It was made from 79 per cent potassium nitrate, 18 per cent rye straw, partially converted to charcoal, giving the brown colour and 3 per cent sulphur. It is said that when the gun fired, only 43 per cent of the powder was burnt, the remainder forming enormous clouds of black smoke and also heavy deposits in the bore. (See photo of *Victoria*, Chapter 6.)

Breech-loaders from 1885

Longer barrels of 25-30 calibre were needed to take advantage of these slow-burning powders and the breech-loader became inevitable. Its arrival in the RN was hastened by an explosion in one of *Thunderer's* MLR in 1879 due to double-loading, an accident which could not happen in a breech-loader. After lengthy experiments, Woolwich finally produced a 12in BL for the *Colossus* in 1885. It was 25 calibres long and of mixed steel and iron construction. This design, the Mark II, was unsatisfactory and all were withdrawn from service after a similar gun failed on board *Collingwood* in May 1886 when firing a three-quarter charge.[25] The all-steel Mk IV was introduced in *Edinburgh* in July 1887, followed by three other marks before the 13.5in/30 cal was installed in *Rodney* in June 1888. Typically these guns could fire with a 2-minute interval between rounds.

21. Hovgaard, *Modern History of Warships*.

22. Sir N Barnaby, 'Armour for Ships', *Proc ICE* (London 1889).

23. It is not clear how much this process was used on compound armour.

24. Hovgaard, *Modern History of Warships*.

25. The history of the early 12in breech-loader is complicated and the following note has been supplied by John Campbell.

Mk I   Trunnioned gun for Horse Sand Fort.
Mk II   Naval version, no trunnions. Rejected by RN after *Collingwood* explosion and eventually modified as Mk I* for Horse Sand and No Man's Land Forts.
Mk III Elswick Ordnance Co design, originally trunnioned for forts but altered for *Colossus, Conqueror*.
Mk IV   ROF Design – *Edinburgh*
Mk V   ROF Design – *Hero*
Mk V*   Whitworth Design – *Collingwood*
Mk VI   Trunnioned version of Mk V and similar Mk VII for sea forts
Mks V & V* were interchangeable and some ships had a mix.

26. Contribution by Sir N Barnaby to W H White, 'On the Designs for the new Battleships', *Trans INA* (London 1889), p200.

27. Parkes makes much of what he refers to as the Froude ratio of length to beam. This is quite incorrect; the Froudes used the ratio of length/ ³√ (immersed volume) as the measure of high speed performance (or the inverse, volume/(length)³)

Edinburgh 1882, very different from the apparently similar *Ajax*. (Imperial War Museum: Q21209)

Almost every gun was different as problems were slowly identified and remedied and the completion of most battleships was delayed by late delivery of their guns. All these breech-loaders had interrupted screw breech-blocks with de Bange obturators. The block was not attached to the gun and was removed completely to load. Armstrong's were building similar but very large guns for the Italian Navy of up to 17in bore. These, too, had problems and delays and of the twelve similar guns made, few were identical. A pair of 16.25in variants of this gun was made for *Benbow* and others for *Victoria* and *Sans Pareil*. These were notable for using a charge of 960lbs, the largest used afloat, The interval between rounds was about 2½ minutes and the barrel life was 75-80 rounds. It is as well there was no war in this era as most navies were having problems with the new guns and their ammunition. France had long used breech-loaders and was a pioneer in all-steel construction but they do not seem to have been very powerful. Krupp produced a satisfactory breech-loading mechanism by 1869 but the Navy chose to stay with the small 9.4in gun until 1902.

Forged steel projectiles, mid-1880s

Chilled iron shot, such as the Palliser, would usually break up on the hard face of steel or compound armour. By the mid 1870s the French firm of Terre Noire were making satisfactory steel projectiles, first cast and later forged. these were further developed by other French firms – St Chamond, Firminy and Jakob Holtzer. Though Whitworth was making good forged steel shot by the time of the 1879 Spezia trials, the RN did not adopt forged steel shot until 1886 when 400 Holtzer

projectiles were purchased in France for the new breech-loaders.

It is perhaps appropriate at this point to quote Sir Nathaniel Barnaby on testing of armour and shells to show the efforts made by the Admiralty and by him personally.[26]

> There was never a target fired on for many years at Shoebury [*sic*] that I had not to go behind to see what had happened. For a great many years I was more familiar with the war that going on between armour and guns than any naval officer in any navy, and I can say that my experience of what happened behind these targets has been to me sometimes only too dreadful. I was always responsible for the way in which the target was made. I was responsible for the thickness of armour put against the gun belt, and when I saw these things flying to pieces, and huge masses driven far beyond the target, I used to be feeling always, there must be thicker and ever thicker armour.

Colossus and *Edinburgh*

These two ships, laid down in 1879, looked very similar to the *Ajax* but introduced most of the innovations discussed earlier in the chapter. Their hulls were of open hearth steel, their armour was steel-faced compound and they mounted 12in breech-loading guns, at first the Mk II, replaced by the Mk III and IV after the explosion in *Collingwood*. They were designed for 14kts[27] but both exceeded 16kts on trial. They were a little longer but with reduced beam compared with the earlier ships. Even so, they had a metacentric height of 9ft, so that

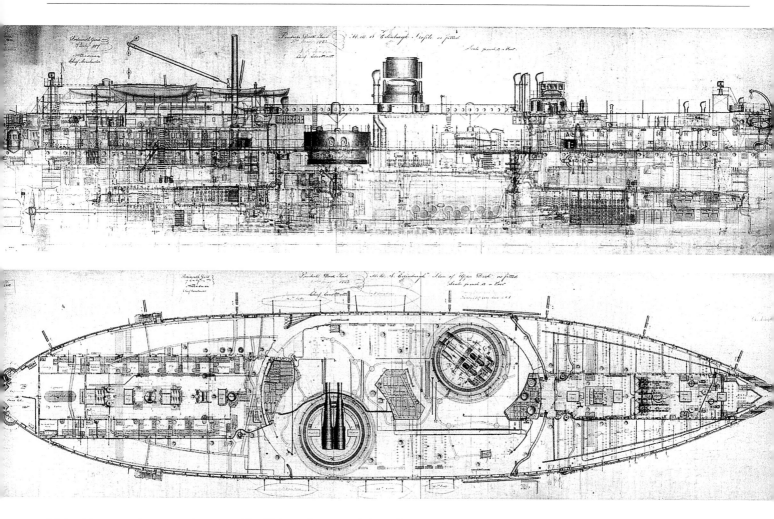

Edinburgh incorporated many new features – all-steel construction, breech-loading guns and a new hull form. The conspicuous searchlights, bow and stern, show that electricity had gone to sea. (National Maritime Museum, London: 9886, 9889)

there would still be sufficient stability after damage, which made them roll severely. Anti-rolling tanks were fitted but were too small to make much difference (see Appendix 5).

White[28] described the way in which their hull form was developed. It was intended to produce a form which with a length of only 325ft would need no more power up to 14.5kts than *Warrior* of 360ft. The form was developed using speed trial results of earlier ships and was then tested by Froude in the tank at Torquay. These tests showed that performance was a little better than had been anticipated and no changes were recommended. This form was also adopted for all ships of the *Admiral* class and speed trials of the *Edinburgh* in September 1883 confirmed its merit.

White is also probably referring to these two ships when he wrote[29] of a review which he carried out in 1878 into twin-screw propulsion. It had been thought that twin screws were less efficient than a single screw and were only adopted in shallow-draught ships or as a precaution against breakdown in those without sails.[30] White studied the trials of the *Audacious* and *Cyclops* classes and was able to show that the twin-screw ships

were, if anything, more efficient. Nearly a decade later, Thomas Ismay used this study in the design of the White Star liners *Teutonic* and *Majestic*, the first liners with a service speed of 20kts. Twin screws were also adopted by the Inman line at about the same time.

Conqueror and *Hero*, 1879 and 1884

Captain Gordon of *Rupert* suggested a number of improvements to that ship in February 1878. He wanted a high freeboard aft, one mast – also aft – and some 6in, saying 'The *Rupert* would commend herself to the judgement of naval officers as being a handy and convenient vessel.' In the Estimates for 1878 the new ship was described an improved *Rupert*. *Conqueror* (and her near sister *Hero*) had a 12in belt and citadel (8in ends). Her short 12in guns were close to the deck and could not be fired within 45° of the bow for fear of blast damage to the forecastle; they could not be fired abaft the beam because of blast on the bridge! It was a time of slow building and *Conqueror* took 7 years to complete; *Hero* a mere 4 years. The freeboard forward was 9½ft and she was always wet, rolling heavily as well. They went out

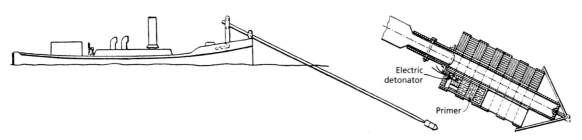

These two sketches show how the charge was lowered over the bow of a spar torpedo launch and also how the charge was made up of disks of gun cotton. Demolition charges were still made with a hole in the middle to take the spar until the Second World War.

on manoeuvres some half-a-dozen times but, other than that, did not go out of sight of land. Despite this, the concept was repeated in *Victoria* (Chapter 6). The report on the 1888 manoeuvres referred to her as a bad seaboat and also pointed out that the guns were too close to the deck, causing blast damage.

Torpedoes

The story of the torpedo is well known[31] and that of the mine only slightly less so, and hence these developments will only be outlined in this section, which will concentrate on defence against underwater weapons. Note that in the early years 'torpedo' was used to describe all underwater charges – Admiral Farragut's famous phrase 'Damn the Torpedoes' referred to what would now be called moored mines.

Spar torpedoes

The earliest 'practical' – if near suicidal – form of underwater attack involved the use of small steam launches with, by the later years of the century, a pole some 42ft long projecting 33ft over the bow and lowered 10ft below the surface and carrying two charges[32] each of 16¼lbs of wet guncotton. The pole charge would be lowered as the boat approached its target and would be exploded electrically when in contact at a depth of about

6ft. There were many attempts to use such weapons during the American Civil War and even a few successes. There were a few other successes; Russian launches sank the Turkish monitor *Seife* in the Danube on 26 May 1877 but a similar attempt shortly afterwards failed.[33] The French also scored a success in 1884, *Launch 46* sinking the composite cruiser *Yang Woo* in broad daylight and in 1885 sinking the tiny Chinese cruisers *Yu-Yen* and *Chen-Kiang*. The RN was slow to take an interest in such weapons and it is often suggested that this was because they were thought 'ungentlemanly'. It is more likely that it was a realistic appreciation of their lack of capability.

The Harvey torpedo[34]

This was an otter, similar to a paravane, towed behind and to the quarter of a ship. At speeds of over 6kts it would, if not tangled, stream out to 45° with a scope of 150yds. The charge was either 33lbs or 66lbs, initially fine gunpowder, later wet guncotton. It was introduced in 1870 and abandoned 10 years later to great relief.

Whitehead

In the early 1860s Captain Luppis of the Austrian Navy approached a British engineer, Robert Whitehead, for help in developing a remote-controlled spar torpedo boat. Though a model was made and tried, they decided

28. W H White, 'On the Speed Trials of Recent War Ships', *Trans INA* (London 1886).

29. W H White, 'Presidential Address', *Proc ICE* (London 1903), p45.

30. It is a pity that modern tanker owners do not recognise the need for twin-screw propulsion (and rudders).

31. G J Kirby, 'A history of the torpedo', *Journal of the RNSS*, Vol 27 No 1 & 2 (can be seen in the Imperial War Museum Library); J Campbell, 'Naval Armaments 1860-1905', *Steam, Steel and Shellfire*, Conway's History of the Ship (London 1992).

32. P Bethell, 'The Development of the Torpedo', *Engineering* (London May 1945-March 1946). He notes that until the Second World War guncotton charges still had a hole through the centre for the pole.

33. In this second attack the launches were commanded by Lieutenants Makarov and Rosjestvensky whose exaggerated claims won them promotion and later defeat in the Pacific.

34. Invented by Captain J Harvey and Commander F Harvey-Bethell.

Hero, 1885, a single-turret ram, derived from *Rupert* and equally unsuccessful. (Imperial War Museum: Q21343)

A spar torpedo being fired. The danger to the launch is obvious. (Author's collection)

that the scheme was not practical. Whitehead, who was manager of an engineering company in Fiume, continued to work on an automobile torpedo and, in 1866, built a prototype. It was propelled by compressed air, stored at 370lbs/sq in, working a rotary engine which drove a single propeller at about 100rpm. It had a speed of 6.5kts for 200yds and a further 100yds at reduced speed.

In this first prototype depth was regulated by elevators controlled by hydrostatic pressure, a system of control which led to violent fluctuations. Whitehead soon realised the problem and added a further control depending on pitch angle, which damped the variations in depth. Depth errors were reduced from ± 40ft to a claimed ± 6in. This control, based on a combination of pressure (depth) and angle (rate of change of depth), was known as 'The Secret' and remained substantially unchanged until after the Second World War.

In 1868 Whitehead demonstrated new designs, 14in and 16in diameter with a speed of 7kts for 700yds carrying a wet guncotton charge. The Austrian Navy was impressed but could not afford the sum demanded by Whitehead for exclusive rights. A committee of RN gunnery officers observed a demonstration in the autumn of 1869 and, as a result of their report, the Admiralty, in October 1869, invited Whitehead to bring two torpedoes to England; another demonstration of the nineteenth-century Admiralty's readiness to consider and adopt novel technology.

The Oberon *trials, 1870 and 1874*

Whitehead brought a 16in torpedo with a length of 14ft carrying 67lbs of wet guncotton and a 14in, also 14ft

long, weighing 300lbs with an 18lb dynamite charge. The speed of the torpedo was 6kts with an effective range of about 200yds. Preliminary demonstrations were convincing and in August 1870 the Admiralty purchased two 14in and two 16in for more extensive trials. These took place in the Medway and in September and October about 100 firings were carried out from the old iron paddle sloop *Oberon*, both from an above-water launcher and from a submerged torpedo tube. These torpedoes could attain 7kts for 600yds. The last of these tests involved sinking the old wooden corvette *Aigle* with a 16in torpedo fired at a range of 134yds. A hole 20ft x 10ft was blown in the side by a dynamite charge and the *Aigle* sank at once. The reliability of these torpedoes was impressive. The Admiralty then paid £15,000 for the non-exclusive rights to manufacture and for 'The Secret'. Production began in 1872 at Woolwich. The British example was soon followed by France, Germany and China.

In 1874 *Oberon* was prepared for a further series of trials, but this time she was to be the target. She was given a double bottom which represented, more or less, that of the *Hercules*. The existing single bottom of 7/16in plate was used to represent the inner bottom and a new outer bottom of 7/8 – 13/16in plates was built outside, supported by 7/16in bracket plates. The representation of *Hercules* was not exact, as *Oberon*'s original bottom was thicker and had much stronger and closer framing whilst she lacked the iron decks of *Hercules*.

The tests involved the explosions of a series of ground mines, each charged with 500lbs of wet guncotton, in 47ft of water ever closer to the ship. The first explosion

35. Lord Brassey, *Naval Annual* (Portsmouth 1885).

36. J Campbell, letter to author, based mainly on 1877 Torpedo Manual.

37. D Lyon, 'The RN and the torpedo', Paris 1987.

38. Ordered 12 February 1872, ld Pembroke 16 March 1873 and completed 11 September 1874.

39. Sir A W Johns, 'Progress in Naval Construction', *Trans NECI* (Newcastle 1934-5).

was 100ft from the outer plating of the ship and this was followed by further charges at 80ft, 60ft and 50ft. None of these ruptured the plating but *Oberon* was 'wrecked internally', typical of non-lethal, non-contact explosions.[35] The final – fatal – charge was exploded 38½ft from the keel. 'On the charge being fired, the ship appeared to rise bodily in the water; she had been struck amidships, and it was found that her back had been broken by the explosion.' She was kept afloat by her watertight bulkheads and, after emergency repairs, was towed into Portsmouth Dockyard.

The conclusions of the various trials as applied to *Hercules* were that a 500lb guncotton mine at 40ft depth would be fatal if under the ship and cause grave damage at 30-40ft from the side. Nets suspended 15ft from the side would protect against the 75lb charge of a Whitehead torpedo but a 33lb charge would cause serious and probably fatal damage if it exploded below the armour and within 4ft of the outer bottom.[36] It was as a result of these trials that Barnaby was to claim that *Inflexible* had been designed to resist a torpedo hit, though the consequences of a hit close to a transverse bulkhead, flooding two compartments, was still not recognised.

Delivery systems

In 1872 a 'Torpedo Committee' proposed four ways in which the torpedo could be launched at sea: from major warships, ships' boats, specially-built torpedo launches and purpose-built ships.[37] Within the next few years, all four would be tried and most major ships would have launchers – chutes – fitted. The first purpose-built ship was *Vesuvius*,[38] intended for stealthy attacks. Her boilers were designed to burn coke and what smoke these generated was intended to be discharged underwater. Her speed of 9.8kts was unspectacular and it would seem that she was never seriously tried in her intended role. She had a submerged bow tube 2ft in diameter and 19ft long with a sluice valve 4ft from the forward end. There were ten rollers top and bottom with side guide rails. She carried ten 16in torpedoes about 14ft long with a charge of 67lbs of guncotton.[39] Her only 'success'

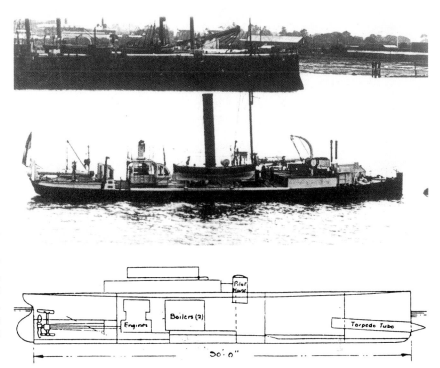

was as the firing ship in the *Resistance* trials, described later, though she remained in service until 1923. Experience then and up to the end of the Second World War showed that the great majority of successful torpedo attacks were made at night and at low speed. Almost certainly, *Vesuvius* was the right approach.

The *Polyphemus*

In the mid-1870s Barnaby and his constructor, Dunn, prepared a number of sketch designs for a fast, cigar-shaped ship whose armament was to consist of a number (usually five) of submerged torpedo tubes. The number of torpedoes carried would be between twenty-five and forty. The small, exposed upper portion was protected by 2in plate over a ⅜in skin. In the initial studies two parts of the flying deck were designed to

Top: Vesuvius, 1874. Designed as a 'stealthy' torpedo boat, she never seems to have been tried in her intended role. The tall funnel shown here was not part of the original design. (Author's collection)

Immediately above: The layout of the 'stealthy' torpedo vessel *Vesuvius* 1873.

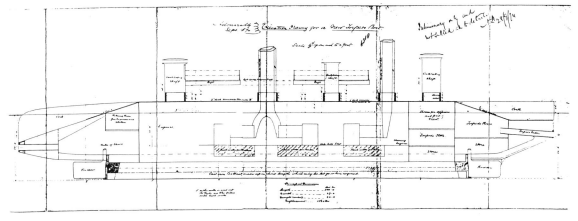

The Barnaby-Dunn torpedo vessel which preceded the *Polyphemus* 1881.

float off as life rafts but in *Polyphemus* these were replaced by boats on cradles, designed to tilt, allowing the boat to run into the sea.

There was a major change of concept when, on 13 December 1875, Barnaby wrote to Dunn:[40] 'It is desired to transform the smaller torpedo ship of high speed into a ram of the same general form and distribution of armour.' The design seems later to have been in the hands of Phillip Watts.

On 8 January 1876, Barnaby wrote to the Controller with a lengthy account of an unsatisfactory discussion with Admiral Sartorious, the leading advocate of rams. He wanted an unarmoured ram of 15-16kts with a light rig. This would cost £170,000 if similar to *Rover*. (In fact, Barnaby suggested the corvette *Rover*[41] was already what Sartorious was asking for.) He showed the model, 'made some time ago', of an armoured ship with torpedo tubes (forty torpedoes carried at this date, final number probably eighteen). At this time the design was for:

250ft (L) x 37ft (B) x 24ft (T) = 2340 tons
5000ihp = 17kts
Cost £142,000

Later the exposed steel hull was to have 3in or 2in protection (on top of the skin) of Whitworth compound armour. After lengthy trials the final protection consisted of an inner thickness of 'large' plates, 1in thick, with an ultimate strength of 45 tons/sq in and an outer layer of plates only 10in square with a strength of 60 tons/sq in,[42] hardened in oil. Hatch coamings were to be 4in thick with 8in on the CT. She had two boiler-rooms and two engine-rooms. There was a 250-ton cast iron drop keel, made in sections, which could be released in an emergency. There were two steel spindles through the length, one operated hydraulically and the other by hand, both had to be released for the keel to drop. Its working was tested fortnightly. She cost £226,000 but, at £30 per ton, the labour costs were low for such a novel ship.

Her torpedoes were 14in Mk II with a charge of 26lb of guncotton and a range of 600 yards at 18kts – the same speed as the ship! The cast steel bow cap of the for-

ward tube formed the ram and opened upwards through a hand wheel and spindle. A considerable number of model tests were carried out by William Froude[43] seeking the best shape for this 'ram'. It acted as a bulbous bow and its shape and position was found to have a considerable effect on the performance of the ship. A balanced 'two-bladed' bow rudder was fitted, arranged to retract into the hull when not in use. Trials showed that when going ahead the use of the bow rudder reduced the tactical diameter and the time to turn through a half circle by about 12 per cent. Going astern at 11kts with the stern rudder only at work the 'vessel was not well under control'[44] but with the bow rudder in use she was perfectly under control with a turning circle little greater than that going ahead at the same speed.

She is said to have behaved well in head seas but poorly in beam and quartering seas. Such behaviour would depend on the frequency with which waves were encountered and on both the transverse and longitudinal metacentric heights. The ventilation system worked well even when closed down for days on end. *Polyphemus* was the first ship to have electric lighting from a Siemens dynamo at 80 volts d.c. with earth return. She was the only ship of the day to be painted grey. As noted above, her torpedoes had about the same speed as the ship and were unlikely to be even as 'successful' as the ramming tactics discussed earlier. The failure of better torpedoes in the Russo-Japanese War confirms this criticism. It may be that she was intended to enter a fortified harbour, such as Cherbourg or Kronstadt, and torpedo ships at anchor.

Attack on a fortified anchorage – Berehaven, 1885[45]

The main object of the 1885 manoeuvres led by Sir Geoffrey Hornby with the 'Particular Service Squadron', assembled in the light of threatened conflict with Russia, was to try ships and their machinery, torpedo boats, offensive and defensive mines and other obstacles in the context of attacking a fleet in a defended anchorage such as Kronstadt. The real importance of this exercise has been obscured by the dramatic action of *Polyphemus* breaking the boom.

Booms were erected at either end of the passage behind an island; that at the east end being nearly 1 mile long. It was damaged by heavy seas on 18 June and also on 19 and 20 June but was repaired by the 22nd. The inner boom was made from light spars and lay 5yds inside the outer boom of heavier spars held by a 5in steel hawser. The booms were connected by light spars and there were ropes arranged as nets to catch propellers. Outside the boom there were four rows of observation mines, 10yds apart, 14ft below the surface. Near the shore there were electric contact mines also 14ft down and, even closer in, there were electro-mechanical mines against torpedo boats. The boom and minefield were covered by twenty-four field guns and twenty-four

40. Ship's Cover, Maritime Museum. I am indebted to David Lyon for bringing this passage to my attention. Note that this memo totally contradicts Barnaby's own account given many years later in *Naval Developments of the Century*.

41. 3460 tons, 14.5kts, generally similar to *Volage*.

42. C E Ellis. 'Armour for Ships', *Trans INA* (London 1911).

43. Reported April 1877 and August 1888. Reports would usually be written some time after the tests were carried out, preliminary results being passed by messenger or telegram.

44. Sir W H White, *A Manual of Naval Architecture* (London 1900), p700.

45. This note is based almost entirely on: Lord Brassey, *Naval Annual* (Portsmouth 1886).

Early torpedo vessels

	Vesuvius	Lightning	Polyphemus
Date, laid down	1873	1876	1881
Displacement (tons)	245	32.5	2640
Length pp (ft)	90	84.5	240
Ihp/speed (kts)	380/9.8	460/19	7000/18
Torpedo armament	1-16in bow, sub	2, dropping gear	5-14in tubes, sub (18 torp)
Other weapons			6 Nordenfelt MG

machine-guns. Some of the mines were also damaged in a storm. 'Of many hundred mines with 500lb and 72lb charges, the greater part were useless.'

On 23 June the *Mariner* was ordered to enter the minefield, small charges being used to show when the mines were actuated; only one mine failed because her draught was too small. That afternoon another TB broke down. At night, searchlights were used to watch the boom and minefields. *Shannon* had a 25,000 candle-power searchlight and, rather to everyone's surprise, it failed to signal 12 miles, perhaps due to moonlight. The *Oregon* (AMC) and Express joined on 26 June. The gunboats *Medina*, *Medway*, *Snap* and *Pike*, escorted by *Seahorse*, joined the next day having averaged 3kts on passage in heavy seas. In calm water, *Seahorse* could tow all four at 7kts.

The first attack was launched on the night of 29 June after the moon had set. There were three First and four Second Class TB, four armed launches, five steam pinnaces, two steam cutters and eight boats. The pinnaces laid five demolition charges on the boom (although rules said that the boom was broken if two (dummy) charges were placed on it the referees decided that 'heavy fire' would have prevented these charges being laid). The boom was attacked by TBs; their torpedoes could be tracked using Holmes lights and the steamboats had spar torpedoes. The rules said that a ship hit by a Whitehead was disabled and a dummy mine charge exploding beneath would render it 'hors de combat'.

On 30 June *Polyphemus* attacked using a 2-mile run-up at 17kts during which she evaded the attacks of six TB, dodging up to ten torpedoes, the mines having been removed. She went through the double boom and the 5in cable 'like pack thread'; no shock was felt on board, but the report is not clear if her passage made a gap big enough for TBs to pass. A mine was then exploded on the boom which was broken but with insufficient gap for TBs. The boom was dismantled and remaining spars replaced. The exercise continued – it was noted that there was a great reduction in sail exercises.

Author's comment

The date is significant; relations were strained with Russia and the exercise may be seen as preparation for an attack on Kronstadt. Most attention was focused on *Polyphemus*' spectacular attack on the boom but it was the combination of mines and shore batteries which was very effective and it must be doubted if the fleet's guns could have suppressed the field and machine-guns whilst mines were cleared. The boom was probably still needed to prevent the entry of shallow draught vessels such as torpedo boats though *Polyphemus* showed how easily it could be broken in the absence of mines. It was a serious and well planned exercise in war and there seems to be a noticeable loss of interest in attacking fortified harbours from this date.

Lightning *and early torpedo boats*

From 1874 onwards, John Thornycroft had been pressing the Admiralty to build a torpedo boat based on his fast launches. *Torpedo Boat No 1* (*Lightning*) was ordered in 1876 originally carrying two torpedoes in

Polyphemus, 1881, described as a 'torpedo ram', although she appears to have been seen more as a low-freeboard armoured torpedo boat. She was one of the first British warships to be given a grey paint scheme, presumably to reduce her visibility. (Author's collection)

TB 3 c1878, very similar to the original Lightning. (Author's collection)

TB 3 c1878, very similar to the original Lightning. (Author's collection)

frames which could be lowered into the water to release the torpedo. In 1879 these were replaced by a single torpedo tube on deck forward with a reload on a trolley either side amidships. She spent her service career as a tender to the torpedo school, *Vernon*, and was used for many experiments.[46] The fast launch, derived from *Lightning,* was seen as the right way ahead for torpedo vessels and large numbers were built in all navies.

From 1878 to the early years of the next decade a number of First Class torpedo boats similar to *Lightning* were built, together with a few experimental vessels. They were all fragile and were unable to make their design speed for long; most had been allocated to subsidiary duties by 1886. A number of smaller, Second Class boats were also built of 10-12 tons carrying two torpedoes in frames or, later, dropping gear. They were intended to be carried on larger ships but they proved even more fragile and were eventually replaced by the picket boat.[47]

The Hecla

Hecla was building as the merchant ship *British Crown* during the Russian scare of 1878 and was purchased, becoming a torpedo boat carrier and depot ship. She carried six Second Class boats and was used in a number of exercises in which her boats were launched against 'enemy' ports. She was apparently seen as successful since a purpose-built replacement, *Vulcan*, was built in 1888.

During most of her life she operated as a seagoing torpedo and mining school, spending the summer at Berehaven and the winter at Malta. The laying, and subsequent clearance of, a minefield off Grand Harbour was an important event each year.[48]

Early torpedoes

The early Woolwich torpedoes were 16in diameter, 14ft long with a charge of 106lb of wet guncotton. Air stored at 800lbs/sq in drove a 2-cylinder V engine giving a speed of 9.5kts for 250yds or 800yds at 7kts. The longer range was of little value as, at the slow speed involved,

the chance of a hit was remote. A 3-cylinder Brotherhood engine and contra-rotating propellers improved performance to 300yds at 12.25kts or 1200yds at 9kts. The introduction of contra-rotating propellers meant that the long fins over much of the length, needed to absorb torque reaction from a single screw, could be dropped. In 1883 R E Froude showed in his experiment tank that a blunt nose was more efficient, giving about 1kt increase in speed as well as making space for a bigger warhead.

Robert Whitehead purchased the Fiume works in 1872, trading as Silurifico Fiume. It was only six years since he had shown his first prototype end he was now the owner of a flourishing export business.[49] The RN had an insatiable demand for torpedoes and, as well as the Woolwich production, continued to buy direct from Fiume at about £320 for a 14in model (225 ordered in 1877). Even this was insufficient and in 1886 the RN bought 50 of the German Schwarzkopff torpedo as well as 200 from Woolwich and the same number from Fiume. By this time, Woolwich were producing the 14in Mk VIII with a charge of 78lbs of wet guncotton, working at 1350lbs/sq in which could reach 22kts for 1000yds. (This was estimated at 17-18,000 foot-tons, similar to the muzzle energy of a 12in, 45-ton gun.) Woolwich torpedoes had rudders and fins on the tail cone ahead of the propeller; Whitehead (Fiume) had control surfaces abaft the propeller.

Armed merchant ships

Early wooden commercial steamships differed little from warships as their strength had to be sufficient to withstand the concentrated weight of heavy engines and the vibration generated by the machinery and later the propeller. The use of armed merchant ships for trade protection was envisaged and outline plans prepared.[50] Gradually, merchant ships and warships diverged. In particular, merchant ships had iron hulls and their engines were arranged vertically so that the cylinders were largely above the waterline, exposed to gunfire.

46. See section on torpedo boats by David Lyon in *Conway's All the World's Fighting Ships 1860-1905.*

47. N B J Stapleton, *Steam Picket Boats* (Lavenham 1980).

48. 'Admiral Ballard's Memoirs, Part IV', *The Mariner's Mirror*, Vol 62 No 3 (London 1976). Ballard comments that when he became a Rear-Admiral, she was still performing the same seagoing duties as when he was a midshipman.

49. In 1912 Whitehead's granddaughter was invited to launch an Austrian submarine and soon after married her captain – Von Trapp. Their children became famous as the Von Trapp singers of the film 'The Sound of Music'.

50. Brown, *Before the Ironclad.*

51. Sir N Barnaby, *Naval Developments of the Century.*

52. Sir N Barnaby, 'On the Fighting Power of the Merchant Ship in Naval Warfare', *Trans INA* (London 1877).

From 1850, the Admiralty would not allow iron ships to hold contracts for carrying mail as such vessels were seen as the main source for wartime auxiliaries and iron hulls were thought too vulnerable to gunfire. In 1853 a Treasury Committee on Postal Contracts, decided, in agreement with the Admiralty, that the requirements for warships had diverged so far from those for warships that '...no expense should be incurred for the sake of giving a military character to the postal vessels'.

The American Civil War

The American Civil War, discussed in Chapter 1, demonstrated the importance of the war on trade, both as formal blockade by the Union and as commerce raiding by the Confederates. This led to the introduction into the RN of fast frigates and corvettes to hunt down raiders but the very high cost of such ships meant that they could be built only in very limited numbers and during the 1870s there was an increasing interest in the use of merchant ships as auxiliary cruisers. The Director of Naval Construction (DNC), Nathaniel Barnaby, was a great advocate of such conversions though well aware of the problems.[51]

Roles

In a paper to the Institution of Naval Architects (INA) in 1877[52] Barnaby listed the duties of a navy and showed that armed merchant ships could carry out some roles themselves and assist regular warships in others. The roles he considered for converted merchant ships were primarily patrolling and enforcing a blockade of the enemy coast and protecting British merchant ships from attack by enemy auxiliary cruisers. Like most writers of the day, Barnaby believed that: 'The speed with which fast steam ships can, in any weather, bear down at night upon slower steam ships and sailing ships, and the terrible nature of the attack which they can make on such ships with shells, the ram and the spar torpedo, will make it impossible to convoy successfully sailing ships and slow steam ships in the face of even unarmoured ships, provided they are fast and efficiently armed.' He did, however, continue 'And if . . . convoy is impossible, still less will it be possible to navigate such ships safely without convoy.'

The general belief was that trade routes and focal points should be patrolled and raiders destroyed. In particular, it was thought that such raiders would need to obtain coal at frequent intervals and if enemy coaling stations were captured or blockaded, it would be almost impossible for raiders to operate. The success of the Baltic fleet in the War with Russia in refuelling in quiet anchorages seems to have been forgotten.

The problem of protecting trade was a truly formidable one; Barnaby says that at the end of 1875 there were

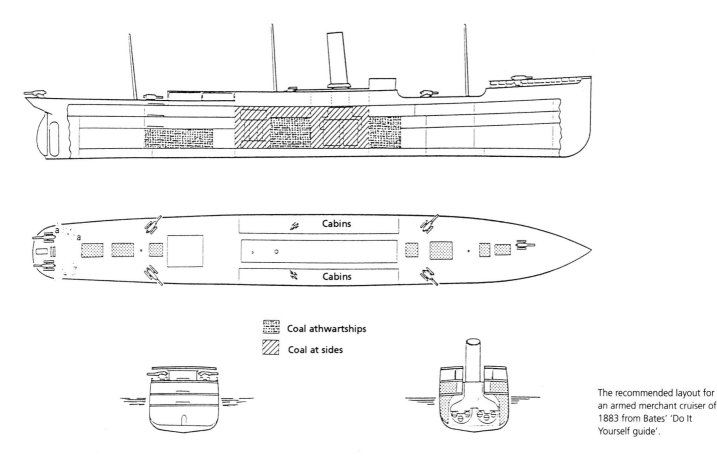

Coal athwartships

Coal at sides

The recommended layout for an armed merchant cruiser of 1883 from Bates' 'Do It Yourself guide'.

18,696 sailing ships and 3436 steam ships of over 50 tons. He thought about 300 steam ships had a speed of over 12kts.

Barnaby envisaged suitable merchant ships being armed with two 64pdrs in the bow, a ram and given a shot-proof screen ahead of the engines so that they could engage bow-on in safety. A similar arrangement could be applied at the stern. Though it might not be easy, some ships could be given a broadside battery of 64pdrs, protected by armour, 6in thick.

Technical problems

Iron hulls were still seen as the major problem, since a shot passing through the ship at a fairly low velocity would tear away a considerable area of plating on the far side. For this reason, most unarmoured warships were either of composite construction, with wood planking on iron frames or, if an iron shell was necessary for strength, it would be sheathed in wood. The *Simoom* tests in 1840 had shown that this fear was well-grounded, though giving little confidence in wood sheathing as a remedy. There are only two sets of modern tests of iron from ships and these show that the material from *Great Britain*[53] is greatly inferior in impact resistance to that from the *Warrior* of 1860.[54] Good-quality steel largely overcame this problem in the 1880s. Barnaby's idea of providing armour to the top of the engines was too difficult and protection was given by a layer of coal some 12ft thick, equivalent to 6in of iron.

Subdivision of merchant ships is discussed in Appendix 8 but the Admiralty's concern that armed merchant ships should float with a single compartment flooded had a major effect on merchant ship safety. In particular, Dunn's INA paper[55] showed both the need for subdivision and for bulkheads to be fully watertight to some distance above the flooded waterline, effectively to the upper deck. This caused problems as the Admiralty department responsible for troopships would only accept ships whose bulkheads stopped at the middle deck in order to improve ventilation and access! The DNC seems to have won this battle. Objections were also raised in the discussion of Barnaby's paper on grounds of strength and stability but he made it clear that any stiffening would be local – a 64pdr with its carriage only weighed 5 tons – and that the 10 tons of ammunition in the hold would preserve stability, at least until the day of battle.

Arming of merchant steamers on foreign naval stations

In 1883 the Admiralty (Constructors Dunn and Bate) prepared a 'do-it-yourself' guide[56] with this title on the arming of merchant ships. Commanders-in-Chief overseas were given a list of suitable merchant ships likely to be found in their area and, with this handbook, conversion should have been fairly straightforward. The armament had been approved by a committee of 1878 and

comprised four 64pdr, 71cwt MLR and one 40pdr, 35cwt BL. Sites were be selected to get as large an angle of training as possible, to allow for guns to be moved easily to the opposite side, to give end-on fire and, where possible, to use cargo ports. The engines and, where possible, the rudder head should be protected by 10-12ft of coal in bags. The ships on the list had been selected as having a real 'one compartment' standard of subdivision but outfitting authorities were required to check that the bulkheads had not been tampered with and that doors and valves worked easily and effectively. The guide lists, in minute detail, the stores required by such ships and arrangements were made to hold complete sets. Sketches of typical arrangements are given – it is interesting that these sketches show seven large guns and two smaller ones – note also *Oregon's* guns, below.

In 1885, when war with Russia appeared likely, sixteen liners were taken up and converted along the lines described above.[57] Bate, himself was responsible for the conversion of the *Oregon*[58] at Liverpool which was fitted with eight 9in MLR and eight 1in Nordenfelt machine-guns. It is likely that *Oregon* and *Hecla* (ex-*British Crown*) were the only conversions to complete.

Renewed subsidies

In 1878 Lord Ismay, of the White Star Line, proposed that, in return for an annual subsidy, his company would make available fast ships, with a large coal capacity, partially arranged for conversion and with a crew of which half would be naval reservists. The idea took some time to germinate but in 1887 agreement was reached along these lines for three Cunard ships and two from the White Star Line. They were to have fittings and platforms for guns installed. By 1901 contracts had been agreed for a total of twenty-eight (Cunard six, P & O fourteen, White Star five, Canadian Pacific three). The famous *Lusitania* and *Mauritania* were added later. The arrangements for conversion worked well in 1914 though it was found that fast, transatlantic liners were not satisfactory and smaller, long-endurance ships served better.

The Admiralty Experiment Works, Haslar

William Froude died in 1879 and was succeeded by his son, Edmund, who continued at Torquay until 1887 when a new tank was built at Haslar, opposite Portsmouth.[59] As more data on both hulls and propellers were accumulated, it was possible to arrange these results so that they could be used to give guidance for new designs. The first such compilation was the Iso – K book, revealed in 1888.[60] The results were presented in the form of graphs, one page for each speed/displacement ratio. Non-dimensional resistance would then be shown to a base of length/displacement ratio. A designer with a rough idea of displacement and speed could use the appropriate book – there were even-

53. J E Morgan, 'The Wrought Iron of SS Great Britain', RINA Historic Ships Conference (London 1996).

54. D K Brown and J Wells, 'HMS Warrior, the Design Aspects', *Trans RINA* (London 1986).

55. J Dunn, 'Bulkheads', *Trans INA* (London 1883).

56. A copy is held in the E R Bate manuscript collection in the National Maritime Museum.

57. R Osborne, *Conversion for War* (World Ship Society, Yatton 1983).

58. Brown, *A Century of Naval Construction.*

59. To ensure consistency, the model of the *Iris* which had been run at Torquay was re-run at Haslar. Later, a brass model was made and run each month as a check. This model was always known as *Iris* though it bore no relation to the original cruiser.

60. R E Froude, 'The "constant" system of notation of results on models used at AEW', *Trans INA* (London 1888). The method had been in use internally for some time before that.

tually ten volumes – to select an appropriate existing form which could be used for preliminary power estimates and as a basis for developing the lines of the new ship. The penalty for departing from the optimum could also be estimated.

Froude's Circular Notation

The basic unit was U, the cube root of the immersed volume

Length constant circ M L/U
Speed constant circ K V/(speed of a wave of length U/2)
Resistance circ C 1000 x Resistance/
constant (Disp x [CircK]²)

This notation sounds complicated and, indeed it was, but it was shorthand for some very difficult concepts. Edmund Froude tried to help users, inventing a special sliderule to evaluate the constants. Each page carried the resistance data, circ C for one value of circ K plotted to a base of circ M. The lowest curve would clearly be the 'best' but examination might show it to be unsuitable for the new design – too fine in way of the magazines or where the shaft left the ship. The 'Elements of Form', the basic shape corresponding to each resistance curve was also recorded in a standard form so that it could be adapted readily for the new ship.

In the discussion of Edmund Froude's paper, William

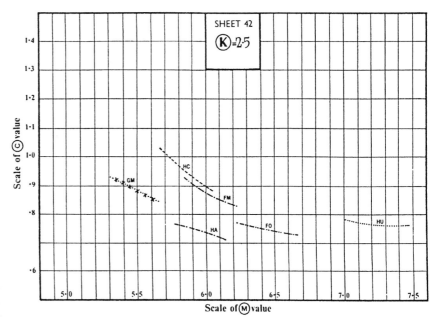

White said: 'It is not an uncommon thing for me to telegraph to Mr Froude that I am coming down to see him when some problem going beyond my experience has to be solved; and half an hour with Mr Froude, in company with these diagrams, places me in a position of secu-

One page (simplified) from Edmund Froude's Iso-K book. This page is for circ K = 2.5, a non-dimensional speed. The vertical axis gives a measure of the resistance whilst the horizontal axis shows length/displacement ratio. Curves for a number of forms are shown and while that labelled HA seems the 'best', it may well prove impractical for a new ship.

Edmund Froude's tank at Haslar, which opened in 1887, seen here in near original condition just after the Second World War. (RINA)

The Haslar documents associated with one design – the 'Improved *Medea*'. One may recognise the lines plan, experimental record and analysis leading to the power/speed curve and the final report to the DNC. (Author's collection)

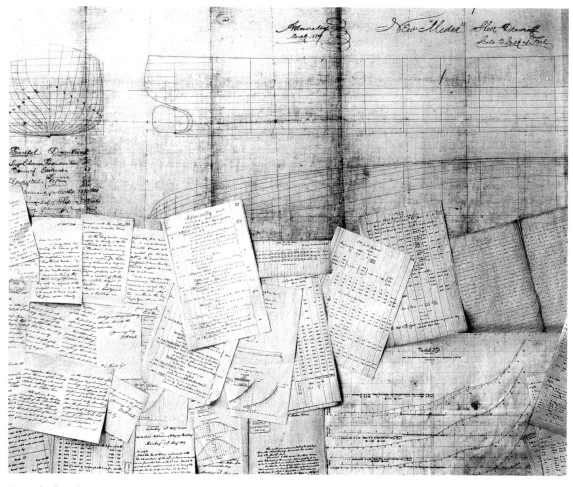

rity which otherwise could not be approached.' The value of these data books was enhanced by adding some methodical variations on a basic form – that of the *Vulcan* was chosen. These data books gave a good first shot at a suitable form but model tests of the forms of new ships were still needed as a form of quality control to ensure nothing had gone wrong and also to refine the form. Typically, some 3-5 per cent reduction in resistance was achieved – starting from a form which was already good – which, translated into fuel saving much more than paid for the tests. Model tests were then, and still are, a wise investment.

In a series of papers from 1883,[61] Edmund Froude published data on the way in which propeller thrust, torque and efficiency varied with diameter, pitch and speed, both forward and rotational. From these data it was possible to select the propeller geometry which would match machinery and hull characteristics most efficiently. The propeller data were so comprehensive that it was not usually necessary to test propellers for individual ships. At last the selection of a hull form, the design of the propeller and the estimate of power required was understood and expensive errors were rare. Froude and his tank, now known as the Admiralty

Experiment Works, gradually moved into other aspects of ship hydrodynamics. The controversy at the opening of the twentieth century over hollow versus full waterplanes led to a wave maker being installed in 1903. Tests were carried out on steering, vibration and, in 1904, on submarines. By the time Edmund Froude retired in 1919 some 500 forms had been tested for 154 classes of warship involving some 235,000 runs in the tank. The work of the Froude, father and son, gave the Royal Navy an important lead in warship design. The courses for constructors and marine engineers were moved from South Kensington to Greenwich when Wren's splendid naval hospital became the Naval College in 1873.[62] W H White was the instructor in naval architecture and Sennet for marine engineering, a brilliant pair. Initially, constructors and engineers did not wear uniform but this was soon remedied.

White published his Manual of Naval Architecture in 1877 as a simple summary for naval officers of all that was known in the subject. It is an easily-read blend of elementary theory, procedures and experience. It was translated into several languages and went into numerous editions, White acknowledging the help of W E Smith in the later ones.

61. R E Froude, 'A description of a method of investigations of screw propeller efficiency', *Trans INA* (London 1883).

62. Brown, *A Century of Naval Construction*. The author was at the College for its Centenary dinner in 1973.

The 'Admirals' | *Six*

THE YEARS 1878 to 1887 were a difficult time for the Navy; there was no strong threat from abroad and governments were dedicated to cutting expenditure. Technology was changing rapidly and, in doing so, affected both strategy and tactics, which were also affected by changes in all aspects of merchant shipping. All these uncertainties could be used as a reason for postponing new construction.

A paper by Barnaby of 9 September 1879 in which he compared the British and French fleets, drawing attention to the very powerful coastal defence vessels then building across the Channel, may be seen as the starting point for the 'Admirals'. He could offer a counter to these ships, based on *Agamemnon* with two 80-ton guns in barbettes, a speed of 14kts and armour as *Agamemnon*. If additional work was needed in the Dockyards,[1] such ships would be suitable but they should not be allowed to delay the completion of *Inflexible* and the four diminutives. (These five ships finally completed between October 1881 and July 1887!)

During 1879 Barnaby prepared four illustrative designs representing differing views of naval officers and others of the future battleship. The first was similar to the *Italia* with deck protection only, a type favoured by Armstrong and many others, but which had no support within the Admiralty. There were two variants on the *Inflexible*, one with sail and the other closer to Reed's ideas of 1871, neither of which was much liked. Finally, there was a variation on the *Dreadnought* design but with unarmoured ends.[2]

In October 1879, the Controller wrote of the need to get rid of the older ships and the need for modern vessels. A few days later the First Lord (W H Smith) doubted whether armour was necessary and asked if a small, fast, unarmoured ship with one gun would be better.[3] In December that year Admiral Hood drew a comparison between *Admiral Duperre* and *Colossus*; three single guns against two twin mounts. He claimed that all future wars would be decided at close range and therefore the turret, with better protection for the crew, was to be preferred. He preferred two 40-ton guns to a single 80-ton for the higher rate of fire. Admiral Keys concurred but wanted six 43-ton guns in twin barbettes with the guns 14¾ft apart. Four single 60-ton would be even better. The DNO thought that the French, German and Italian navies preferred the barbette, which was better for morale as the gun crews could see the enemy. Barnaby suggested a bulletproof boat deck over the barbette to protect the crews.

In 1880, Barnaby again drew attention to the French *Requin* class which, although described as coastal defence ships, were very suitable for use anywhere in the Channel, Mediterranean or Baltic. He offered a 7000-ton vessel with a speed of 14kts mounting two 80-ton guns, four 6in and with an 18in belt. Also in 1880, there was an influential paper from Rendel making an apparently impartial comparison of the advantages and disadvantages of the turret and barbette. The main problem with the barbette was the lack of protection for the crew and Barnaby suggested a shield, an idea which took a long while to mature.

There is a sketch in the Cover which probably dates from 1880 of a ship with the general configuration of the 'Admirals' but mounting two single 80-ton guns and four smaller weapons on the broadside, probably 6in, capable of penetrating 6in armour at 1000yds. The belt was 12in thick, 6ft deep and with a 2in deck described 'as *Polyphemus*', of Whitworth compound.[4] This ship would have been of 7-7500 tons and 325ft in length.

Consideration was then given to a lengthened DNC design of 7000 tons, 15kts costing £430-500,000. The forward guns were to be raised and each barbette would mount two 40-ton guns. Though Barnaby refers to having the *Requin/Caiman* in front of him, his design was very different, with a short, thick belt in place of the end-to-end of the French ship. With all this confusion of aim and restrictions on resources, it is amazing that the *Collingwood* was a success, reflecting great credit on Barnaby and his assistant, White. At about this time there seems to have been a relaxation permitting an increase in size to 'under 10,000 tons', still much smaller than the French *Formidable*. The armament was selected as two pairs of 12in, 43-ton guns.

The British ship was faster and the 12in, once its early

1. It is an interesting suggestion that the building programme depended more on providing work for the Dockyards than on the foreign threat.

2. It is usually suggested that Barnaby was disappointed by the rejection of these studies (Parkes, Burt) but it seems much more likely that they were 'stalking horses' intended to show admirals and others the consequences of their ideas which had not been fully developed. The fact that there were four very different styles strongly suggests that there was no favourite. There is no evidence either way but it may well be that Barnaby was as delighted by their rejection as I was by the rejection of a nonsensical 630ft LSL which I had produced to show the staff the consequences of their demands.

3. Smith's view is of interest as antedating the thinking of the *Jeune École*. See various papers in conference proceedings of *Marine et Technique au XIXᵉ Siècle*, Paris, 1987. His views may well have been influenced by Armstrong and Rendel.

4. Presumably the deck was in two thicknesses with small plates of very strong steel (60-ton) above larger plates of tougher material (45-ton).

Collingwood, Caiman and *Formidable*

	Collingwood	*Caiman*	*Formidable (Fr)*
Displacement (tons)	9500	7530	11,720
Armament, main	4-12in	2-16.5in	3-14.6in
secondary	6-6in BL	4-3.9in	4-6.4in
Belt (ins)	18 (compound)	20	22
Speed (kts)	16.8	14.5	15.0

5. W H White, 'The Principles and
Methods of Armour Protection in
Modern Warships', *Brassey's Naval
Annual* (London 1905), Chapter 5.
He says that it was the success of
the high mounts in *Imperieuse*
which led to this feature being
adopted but the dates clearly make
this impossible.

6. Two feet of coal was equivalent to
1in steel.

7. See Chapter 10.

8. W E Smith, *Distribution of
Armour in Ships of War* (London
1885). Based on lectures given at the
RN College.

9. W H White, 'On the Designs for
the New Battleships', *Trans INA*
(London 1889), p213 (one of the
longest discussions ever recorded).
This is a strange passage; no other
record of such a trial has been found
and most of those present seemed
surprised. Though White was a very
tough man in debate, there is no
instance in which he falsified the
evidence. (Note that by this time
White was very angry and his usual
clarity had left him. It is far from
certain what spaces were flooded
but it would seem that they were
extensive.) It is just possible, though
unlikely, that he confused the
calculations which follow with a
trial.

Collingwood, 1882, the first of Barnaby's very successful 'Admiral' class. (Author's collection)

problems were overcome, was probably a better gun than that in the French ships but to achieve this on a limited displacement the armour was thinner and less extensive. In both the British and French ships the main problem was the shallow belt and, in this respect, there was little to choose between them.

Collingwood

The long debate before design started seems to have cleared the air and there was a strong sense of purpose as the design was developed.

Configuration

Collingwood reverted to the *Devastation* arrangement of guns with a twin mount at each end, an arrangement to be followed in most other battleships up to *Dreadnought*, but she differed in concentrating the side armour between the turrets, the ends having cellular deck protection. The First Sea Lord, Cooper Keys, had recognised the superiority of broadside fire over end-on attack and it was probably his views which predominated, though there seems to have been little dissent from within the Admiralty.

Guns

The development of the early 12in breech-loader is discussed under *Colossus* and, once early problems had been overcome, including an explosion in *Collingwood*'s gun on trial, the later marks proved reliable and effective (penetration 20½in iron at 1000yds). A well-trained crew could fire with an interval of about 2 minutes between rounds. Almost every gun was different as one problem after another was slowly solved. Delays in

the delivery of guns was the main cause of the slow completion of battleships.

The barbettes for the main armament were a new design by Rendel and were considerably lighter than turret mountings, since only the guns themselves had to be turned. The saving in weight permitted the guns to be mounted at a greater height above water – and depression firing against an enemy's deck was still thought both important and possible.[5] The height certainly helped to keep the guns dry and this eased the gunlayers' task – though he was very much exposed to machine-gun fire – as did the abolition of narrow sighting slits, while the potential leak path round a Coles' type turret was abolished. Elevation and depression was not limited by the size of the port or the height of the roof, and ventilation was not a problem in an open barbette. Rendel overcame two of the problems of earlier barbettes as loading was below armour and the base was protected from explosions below by a 3in deck under the barbette structure.

The secondary battery was introduced to attack the unarmoured portions of enemy battleships with three 6in BL each side protected only by 1in splinter plating and a 6in bulkhead which extended from the barbettes as protection against raking fire. It is surprising that the secondary battery was given such thin protection in the light of the importance attached to it; even the displacement limit does not seem to excuse this weakness. Protection against torpedo boats was provided by lighter weapons; twelve 6pdr and ten 3pdr. She also had four above-water torpedo tubes.

Protection

The belt of compound armour stretched between the barbettes (140ft) and was 7½ft deep. The top 4ft was

18in thick, sufficient to keep out most projectiles at fighting ranges, from which it tapered to 8in (15in backing) at the lower edge. At the design draught there would have been 2½ft above water but she was overweight as completed, floating about a foot deeper so that the belt was nearly submerged at sea. The ends were closed by 16in bulkheads and there was a 3in deck over. Above this deck, deep coal bunkers were arranged along the side which provided considerable protection[6] but also helped to retain stability in the event of flooding above the belt and deck. The barbettes had 11in sides (10in rear) and the ammunition trunk was protected by 12-10in plate.

The ends were protected by a 2½in deck with closely subdivided coal bunkers over. This was a very well-conceived protection though not seriously proved in action.[7] Most criticism of the 'Admirals' was directed at their unarmoured ends and this aspect will be considered at length, both from contemporary views and with hindsight. The spaces below the deck were also closely subdivided but, as with all ships of the era, the effectiveness of the subdivision was compromised by drain valves in the bulkheads which always leaked and often jammed due to coal dust etc. It is probable that Froude's experiments on hull form were taken into account in the choice of hull form characteristics though detailed experiments on *Collingwood* did not take place until 1884. These would have shown the need for fine ends in a 325ft ship with a speed approaching 17kts and the flooding of such fine ends would not have a great effect on either trim or stability.

Sinkage with ends riddled

(from load draught, all stores and coal in place – worst case)[8]

Ship	Sinkage (ins)
Inflexible	23
Agamemnon	22
Colossus	18
Collingwood	17½
Camperdown	14

It would also appear that *Collingwood* was tried at sea with the ends flooded. In a discussion at the INA in 1889 on a paper by White on the *Royal Sovereigns*,[9] Reed was, as usual, attacking the lack of a belt to the ends and forecasting dire consequences if the ends were flooded. White replied: ' . . . we filled up the ship with water ballast; not merely over the ends, but in the large spaces in the hold. The ship went out ballasted with water with her ends chock full, and she manoeuvred and did everything quite satisfactorily, and quite justified the estimate which had been formed of her. The loss of speed due to filling the ends with water was only a quarter of a knot.' In responding to a question from Lord Charles Beresford, White confirmed that 80 tons of water had been put above the deck.

In the Ship's Cover there is a note of a calculation for *Rodney* by W R Perrett which showed that with both ends free flooding at a 'fighting draught' the new draught would be 27.18ft, the displacement 9939 tons (214 tons more than intended) and the metacentric height would fall from 5.5ft to 4.8ft. White then instructed Morgan on 5 April 1886 to consider flooding in the following four conditions:

1. All coals in place, 400 tons in hold, 408 tons in ends and 92 tons in main deck side

2. All coals consumed at ends.

3. All coals consumed in hold.

4. All coals consumed in hold and main deck leaving ends.

Condition	Mean Drt (ft)	Armoured freeboard (ft)	Metacentric Ht (ft)
1	28.92	0.33	0.63
2	28.67	0.58	-0.4
3	27.78	1.47	1.13
4	27.56	1.69	0.56

Similar figures for *Collingwood* were given as:

Collingwood, 1882. Her two pairs of 12in BL were mounted high up in Rendel's barbettes. They could have been worked although one may wonder if they could have hit anything in such conditions. The low ends made the class wet ships, a penalty accepted since it was thought that water on the low decks would reduce pitching. (National Maritime Museum, London: 8003)

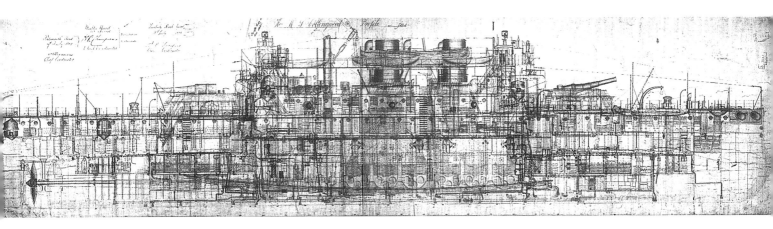

Condition	Mean Drt (ft)	Armoured Freeboard (ft)	Metacentric Ht (ft)
1	27.8	0.58	2.15
2	27.4	0.85	1.19

The conclusion was that coals should be consumed first from the hold and then from the centreline bunkers at the ends. Coal may not be consumed from the sides at the end. Clear instructions to this effect were inserted in the Ship's Book,[10] carried on board. These were very severe conditions and the damage more serious than ever likely and that the results were so favourable gives confidence in the design.

Barnaby was well satisfied with the protection within the overall limits under which he worked and White, after he left the Admiralty, made similar points in rebutting criticism. Barnaby claimed that a belt of limited length enabled better protection to the machinery and that the uptakes and downtakes were well protected. The guns, their machinery and crews were well protected and the magazines (and steering gear) were better protected than they would be by a thin belt. In particular, the combination of a protective deck sited below water with closely-divided coal bunkers above it was considerably superior to a higher deck and a thin belt. Since it was not possible to cover the full length with armour thick enough to prevent penetration by shells, subdivision was the better protection.

Speed and forced draught

To the engineers of the day forced draught must have seemed like something for nothing.[11] Pushing more air through the furnace enabled more coal to be burnt per square foot of grate area and hence more steam would be generated. The intention always was to use natural draught for cruising, with forced draught available to give extra speed for a few hours. One watch of stokers could just manage full power with natural draught but extra men were needed for forced draught. All torpedo boats from *Lightning* (1877) had forced draught; *Polyphemus* (1878) was the first larger ship.

Collingwood introduced forced draught to the battlefleet and she was considerably faster than the traditional 14kts of earlier battleships. She made 16.6kts with 8369ihp during her 6-hour, natural draught trial but only reached 16.8kts with 9573ihp under forced draught as her engines were unable to accept the extra steam. It was intended that forced draught should be used for short periods only and, even then, its use was 'generally attended with anxiety'. Contract trials consisted of a 4-hour trial with forced draught (1 hour in water gauge) followed by 8 hours maximum power at natural draught (½in wg). White, writing in 1890,[12] gives the following comparisons of speed in the table opposite.

Howe and *Medea*: comparative speed

Condition	*Howe*		*Medea (small cruiser)*	
	ihp	speed (kts)	ihp	speed (kts)
Forced Draught, trials	11,600	16.9	10,000	19.9
Natural Draught, Trials	8200	15.9	6300	18.0
Continuous Service Speed	4500	13.5	3500	15.75

Rodney 1884. The 6in secondary battery was much increased in this class. (Imperial War Museum: Q40000)

Even though *Collingwood* was 55ft shorter and 10ft wider than *Warrior* and 800 tons heavier, she required no more power than the older ship at speeds up to 14kts, a tribute to Froude's work on hull form.

However, the low freeboard, especially at the bow, meant that speed in anything except a dead calm was much reduced. There was considerable discussion of the behaviour of the 'Admirals' during the presentation of a paper by White in 1890.[13] He had been at sea in *Howe* for the 1889 manoeuvres and was very pleased with her behaviour in quite severe weather (swell 12-15ft high – sea state 5-6). The guns were 'worked', but not fired, without difficulty though the low ends were deep in water. She was put beam on to the sea and rolled 35-40° out to out in 5¼ seconds and again the guns could be worked. Under these conditions, the low turret of *Hero* was swept by seas and would have been unusable, a view confirmed by her captain. In discussion, Admiral Morant confirmed White's view of the 'Admirals'; he had been in *Anson*, in company with *Collingwood*, steaming at 8-9kts into a severe head sea and though the decks were awash, both ships could have used their guns. White took the opportunity to reject stories of poor ventilation in the class; the crew quarters were completely satisfactory and the officers' quarters needed only minor improvement.[14]

Follow-on ships (ld 1882-83)

The French ordered four more battleships in 1880 and the Board had to decide on an appropriate counter. Even though *Collingwood* had only just been started and was under bitter attack by critics such as Reed, the Board was aware that little had changed since her design was approved and there was much in favour of a homogeneous squadron of similar ships.

The first two, *Howe* and *Rodney*, had the same dimensions as *Collingwood* but the extra armament weight of 800 tons made them float some 18in deeper. The second pair had the barbette plating increased to 14-12in and the belt was lengthened to 150ft. To carry the extra weight they were lengthened 5ft and beam was increased by 6in. The extra immersion of these four ships meant that there was little of the belt above water and also considerably increased the frequency at which the decks were swept by waves. *Anson* cost £662,000, £150,000 less than *Inflexible*.

The new 13.5in, 67-ton gun developed at Woolwich was much more powerful and would penetrate the thickest armour afloat at battle range. Once again, there were considerable delays in completing satisfactory guns, cracking of the liners being the principal problem which, in turn, led to delay in the ships entering service.

10. The Ship's Book is not to be confused with the Ship's Cover. The former is kept on board and contains key documents on the operation of the ship, such as the stability statement and, as here, in any limitations on working fuel.

11. This passage is based on D K Brown, 'Marine Engineering in the RN', a series of articles in *Journal of Naval Engineering*, 1993-94.

12. W H White, 'Notes on Recent Naval Manoeuvres', *Trans INA* (London 1890).

13. Ibid.

14. He had been given the aftermost – worst – cabin over the propellers, always allocated to Constructors to rub their noses in vibration problems!

Early breech-loading guns

Bore (in)	Weight (tons)	Mk	Cal.	Charge (lb)	Proj (lb)	MV (ft/sec)	Penetration (in)*
12	45	III	25.25	259 Pris	714	1914	20.6
13.5	67	II	30	630 SBC	1250	2016	28
16.25	110	I	30	960 SBC	1800	1914	32

Notes: Pris = Prismatic, brown. SBC = Slow Burning Cocoa
*Iron at 1000 yds.

The building times of British ships were lengthy but the French were far slower.

Building times (years – months)

British Ships	Time
Inflexible	7-8
Agamemnon	6-10
Ajax	7-0
Colossus	7-4
Edinburgh	8-4
Conqueror	7-4
Hero	4-1
Collingwood	7-0
Anson	6-1
Camperdown	6-8
Howe	7-0
Rodney	6-4
Benbow	5-7
Victoria	4-11
Sans Pareil	6-3
Trafalgar	4-3
Nile	5-3

French Ships	Time
Caiman	10-0
Indomtable	8-8
Requin	10-0
Terrible	9-1
Amiral Baudin	9-2
Formidable	9-5

Benbow (ld 1887)

There were a number of reason why the sixth 'Admiral' was different; there were no suitable slips vacant in the Dockyards, so it was decided to use a private yard and, since it was desired to contract for a 3-year building time, it was essential that there was no delay in the supply of guns. Woolwich could offer no guarantee so it

was decided to mount a single Elswick 110-ton gun at each end. Similar guns had been supplied to Italy for the *Andrea Doria* class and those who worshipped size alone felt that 12in or 13.5in were inadequate even though the latter, at least, could penetrate any armour afloat. In service, the 16.25in was disappointing, with a life of seventy-five rounds, only able to fire one round every 4-5 minutes and also with a tendency for the muzzle to droop.

The 'Admirals'; criticism and justification

Criticism of the class centred on their lack of an end-to-end belt. Barnaby's defence has been given in an earlier section and seems valid with hindsight.[15] There was little official secrecy in those days which makes it even more strange that the trial flooding of the ends, mentioned much later by White, was not quoted in defence.

The real weakness was the shallow belt, so deeply submerged, particularly in the later ships. The deep coal bunkers above the deck gave some protection against small guns and splinters and would have helped considerably in preserving stability. Barnaby was aware of the problem and said that even if allowed a larger ship, with more weight for armour, he would not adopt an end-to-end belt but would increase the depth and thicken the existing belt and would also thicken the deck over the belt.

There was a reluctance in all departments to consider larger ships; politicians were not prepared to pay for them, and the Board realised that, in practice, bigger ships meant fewer ships. Even the constructors were reluctant to see the logic of size. Lecturing at the RN College, W E Smith[16] wrote; 'If we wanted a belt of armour 24in thick amidships and 18in thick at the ends, a belt by no means completely gun proof, four 150-ton guns, twelve 6in guns with a 3in side in front of them, a 4in inner bottom protection against torpedoes, 10ft in from the outer bottom, and 20kts speed, we should have

An unusual view of *Benbow* from above. Note the two enormous 16.25in guns on their barbettes, and also the large amount of flammable material stowed beside the funnels, though much would have been thrown overboard before going into action. (US Naval Historical Center)

a vessel of 20,000 to 25,000 tons displacement, and a cost for the completed ship not far short of £2,000,000. The ship, large and costly as she is, is still imperfect, her armour will roll out of the water and under the water. There is no protection against ground mines and the belt, especially at the ends, is still vulnerable. The length must be from 500 to 550 ft, the beam about 75 ft, the mean draught about 28ft and the indicated horse power about 30,000.' He saw such a ship as too big to be commanded by one man (!) and her length as too great for use as a ram.

Other navies perceived similar limits on size and adopted various compromises, all of which may be seen, with hindsight, as unsatisfactory. Benedetto Brin's *Italia* (13,850 tons) was the most extreme, with no side armour, a 3in deck 6ft below the waterline and with the space between this and the deck over subdivided and given cork and coffer dams, much as in the ends of the *Inflexible*. Her main armament consisted of two pairs of 17in BL (Armstrong) carried *en echelon* in a single redoubt protected by 17in compound plate. She also had a very powerful secondary battery of 6in BL which were entirely unprotected. *Italia* had a speed of 18kts, some 3kts more than most other battleships of the day, and could carry a large number of troops. The redoubt had a heavily armoured trunk to the magazines but the floor of the redoubt was unarmoured, making it very vulnerable to shells bursting in the unprotected spaces below, a common problem with barbettes of the day.

This style of protection was very common in the cruisers of the day and was strongly advocated by Lord Armstrong.[17] It seems unlikely that she would have survived a long action. The unarmoured secondary guns would soon have gone, followed by the main guns from hits below their barbettes. With the unprotected spaces riddled, there would be slow flooding below the armoured deck which would quickly disable her and eventually cause her to sink.

French ships of this era had a very thick but shallow belt from end to end (but thinner at the ends) with a high unprotected freeboard, and four single barbettes, one at each end and one either side close to amidships. There was also a powerful, but unprotected, secondary battery of 5.5in BL. For the narrow belt to be effective, the designer had to get the weight estimates correct so that she floated at the design draught whilst weight growth in service had to be controlled to prevent increase in draught (30 tons of added weight would sink them 1in deeper; not a lot with a belt 8ft deep at most and only 18in above water). There was an armour deck level with the top of the belt, typically 2¼in thick. Flooding above this deck, in unprotected spaces, would seriously reduce their stability and lead to capsize (as with *Herald of Free Enterprise*), particularly as tumble-home much reduced stability at large angles of heel in several classes.[18] White says that their subdivision was inadequate.

Budgets

The rising cost of ships combined with severe limits on spending meant that few ships could be built. Part of the increase in cost was due to the increased size of the new ships but the increased complexity had also caused a rise in the cost per-ton (Chapter 11). Though the total Navy Estimates were only slightly down from their peak, most costs could not be reduced and a disproportionate share of the reduction fell on new shipbuilding. Long building times almost always lead to greater overall costs as both men and facilities are under utilised. These delays also caused problems with Parliamentary accounting as money should be spent in the year for which it was voted.

Later coastal forts and minefields[19]

From the late 1870s there were a number of developments in coastal defence which made a successful attack much less likely. In particular, there was no successful clearance of a minefield protected by coastal guns even in exercises. The paragraphs which follow refer largely to British developments but they were paralleled in most cases by countries which the RN might have to attack. Dates should be read with care: it is not always possible to distinguish between the first installation and the date at which the equipment came into general use.

The guns used in coastal defence were usually the same as those mounted in ships, though the mountings and loading arrangements might differ. There was a limited use of iron armour on coastal forts and this, too, paralleled developments in ships. The earliest changes were to increase the elevation and hence the range of MLR guns on shore. There was a rather different approach from 1884 when some 9in and 10in MLR were given mounts suitable for high-angle fire.

To test the chance of hitting a mobile target with high-angle fire a trial was carried out at Warden Point in March 1888.[20] The target was a raft 100ft x 40ft fitted with small sails and drifting in the current. It was thought that the slow, erratic movement was similar to that of a bombarding ship. The gun was a 9in MLR on an extemporised high-angle mount giving 35° elevation firing 265lb shells with 25lb and 50lb SP charges and was controlled by a 'Watkins' position finder, 2000yds from the gun and 300ft above sea level. Despite a gale one day forty-one rounds were fired at 2500-9900yds (twenty-eight at over 6000yds) and seven hits scored. (It was estimated that there would have been eleven hits on *Inflexible*.) However, the time of flight was too long for there to be much chance of hitting a moving ship. (See Chapter 10 for the effectiveness of similar weapons against ships at anchor.)

The introduction of cordite c1893 made it less easy to see a battery as there was less smoke. Invisibility was enhanced when hydropneumatic disappearing mounts

15. Today's designers have to defend frigates of a third the displacement against far more powerful projectiles with no armour at all. Effective subdivision (and subdivision was NOT then very effective) is a very good defence. See *Victoria-Camperdown* collision. A thin (1-2in) belt to keep out machine-gun bullets and splinters might have been worthwhile.

16. W E Smith, *The Distribution of Armour in Ships of War* (London 1885).

17. One can only speculate as to whether Armstrong influenced Brin or *vice versa*.

18. As happened to the later, but similar, Russian ships at Tsushima. See Chapter 10.

19. Much of this section is derived from a paper by Anthony Cantwell, 'Later Developments in British Coastal Defence', read to the Ships v Forts Conference at Portsmouth in November 1995.

20. 1892 Gunnery Manual.

were introduced. These were mainly installed overseas though there were a few at home. The mounting limited elevation to about 20° and the rate of fire was slow. Since ships found it hard to see and hit a single gun anyway, the disappearing mount may be seen as unnecessary.

In 1885 a pit was dug on the tip of Portland Bill and a dummy 6in gun on a disappearing mounting installed in it. It was arranged so that every 2 minutes the gun would be raised for 20 seconds, discharge a puff of smoke and drop into the pit again. *Hercules* was brought up to do everything possible to destroy the gun. She opened with Gardner and Nordenfeldt machine-guns and fired 'hundreds' of rounds without hitting the gun or any bullets entering the pit. She then fired broadsides from her 10in and though some shots were close, none hit. Gunlayers then changed to independent firing and did even worse. During the time the heavy guns were firing, the 6pdrs were free to fire whenever the dummy gun was raised but not one hit was made on the gun or its emplacement. Hogg[21] makes the important point that the disappearing mount made little difference as the *Hercules* failed to hit the emplacement at all. It must be pointed out that hits in war would be less likely as the shore gun would be firing back.

By the end of the century the main coastal defence gun was the 9.2in BL, usually mounted in open barbettes, which it was thought quite big enough to disable any battleship. This view may well have been mistaken in the light of damage received in the Dardenelles and the twenty-two hits, mainly by 8.2in, which caused little damage to the weakly-protected *Invincible* at the Falklands. Captain H S Watkins introduced, in 1879, the depression rangefinder using a sight mounted high up whose angle of depression gave the range. A similar position finder followed. Though there were still a number of corrections needed to ensure that the shell hit a moving ship, these two instruments added greatly to the accuracy of coastal guns. The threat of torpedo boat attack meant that small quick-firers were added to the defences of ports and from about 1889 searchlights, too, were installed, usually in protected mountings.

In 1863 Sir John Burgoyne wrote a memorandum on the need to protect ports with mines and this was followed up by a joint Naval and Military committee.[22] Training began in 1867 and, by 1871, coastal mining was the responsibility of the Royal Engineers mining companies who laid a practice field annually. Controlled mines with a 500lb charge were laid on the bottom in about 60ft of water and, later, were under the control of Watkins position finders. There were also EC moored mines which, when hit by a ship, would send a signal to the control room who could decide whether to explode it. They could also be set for automatic explosion. There were a number of exercises which showed how difficult it was to clear a protected minefield. In one such, at the entrance to Portsmouth Dockyard in 1879, the umpires decided that the mines had been cleared but that all the

attacking ships had been sunk. The attacking force failed again at Milford Haven in 1886 and there was another exercise at Langstone Harbour in 1887.

In 1885 the Brennan torpedo was introduced. It was driven by propellers turned by long wires pulled out by winches on shore and by adjusting the tension, the torpedo could be steered. It had a speed of 22kts at 'short range', 19kts at 1000yds and 17kts for an extreme range of 1600yds.

There were a number of small trial firings which showed the navy had not entirely given up the coastal attack idea and brief notes follow. At Inchkeith[23] *Sultan* fired at a barbette 90ft above sea level. Bad fuses made it useless. Three series of ten shrapnel at 850-3500 yds had no effect. Also -

4-1in Nordenfelt fired 580 rounds in 5 min,		4 hits
2 Gardiner	650	12
13 MG	3874	27

all at 800-1100yds.

In 1898 *Arrogant*[24] fired against a dummy 9.2in mount on Steepholm to test a gun shield which was not penetrated with 6in shells. A trial of Lyddite shells was carried out in October 1895,[25] where 9.2in Lyddite shells were fired against an earthwork. Bursting in sand, the Lyddite was no more effective than blind shells. Common shell was no more effective.

In 1913 a target representing a battery of two 6in guns was erected on Oronsay in 1913 and fired on by *Formidable* using 12in common shell.[26] The battery was an a gentle slope, towards the sea, and below the skyline. It was a clear day with a gentle breeze (Force 2-3) across the range and with a bright sun behind the ship. The *London* was spotting for range from a position almost at right-angles to the line of fire.

Twenty rounds were fired in two series, the first of eleven rounds in 20 minutes. For the first two rounds, *Formidable* was stopped at about 9000yds after which she steamed in at 6kts, the guns being laid indirectly using the junction of black rocks and the beach as the aiming point. The target itself could not be seen outside 8000yds but inside this an indistinct blur assisted spotting for direction which was difficult as the target was indistinct and obscured by the dust and smoke thrown up. The second series of nine rounds in 6 minutes was fired with the ship stopped at 6000yds, the maximum at which the target could be seen. The conclusions reached were;

1. Given a clear point of aim, an isolated battery can be demolished quickly by firing from 12in guns.

2. The most practical way of carrying out such firing is for the ship to be under way but stopped (?) with another ship at right-angles spotting for range.

3. With a battery incapable of effective return fire,

21. I V Hogg, *Coastal Defences of England and Wales* (Newton Abbot 1974).

22. A Cantwell and D Moore, 'The Victorian Army and Submarine Minelaying' *Fortress* 18 (August 1993), pp32-47.

23. 1881 Gunnery Manual.

24. 1901 Gunnery Manual.

25. 1901 Gunnery Manual.

26. 1916 Gunnery Manual.

27. White, *A Manual of Naval Architecture.*

range should be selected for good visibility of the target.

4. Unless the battery is very clearly defined, indirect laying should be used.

It does not seem that those planning the Dardenelles attack were aware of this exercise or of the earlier trials showing the ineffectiveness of naval shells or those showing the difficulty in clearing protected minefields. The small number of exercises carried out does not support the thesis that the RN was planning to attack enemy forts at this date.

Sans Pareil and *Victoria* (ld 1885)

The origin of this pair of ships is obscure; they were seen as enlarged *Conquerors* with 13.5in, 63-ton guns in turrets. Cooper Key was still First Sea Lord when they were planned and it is not clear why his views on barbettes and broadside, as opposed to end-on fire, were overthrown. There were a number of design studies and, eventually, a design with one twin turret forward was chosen. The decision to mount 16.25in, 110-ton guns seems to have been for production reasons, as with *Benbow*. The principal defect of the 'Admirals', the shallow belt, was hardly improved since that in the new ships was just deeper. They did have some important innovations in machinery.

Triple-expansion engines (1881–85)

The introduction of steel for cylindrical–Scottish– boilers led to an increase in working pressure and this, in turn, led to suggestions of three-stage expansion. Dr

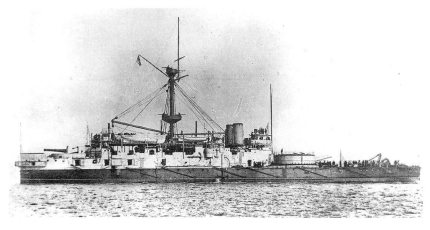

A C Kirk of Elders designed the first successful triple-expansion engines for SS *Propontis* in 1874 but their success was obscured by the failure of her unreliable water tube boilers. Kirk scored a clear success with the SS *Aberdeen* of 1881 which, on trial, burnt coal at 1.28lb/ihp/hr. The first RN ship with triple-expansion engines was the torpedo gunboat *Rattlesnake* of 1885 which was successful and led to these engines being chosen for the *Sans Pareil* and her sister, initially named *Renown*, later *Victoria*.

The best demonstration of the value of the triple-expansion engine came when the *Thunderer* was modernised in 1889-90 during which her old box boilers and trunk engines were replaced by cylindrical boilers and triple-expansion engines.

White[27] points out that on a run from Spithead to Madeira at 80 per cent power (4500ihp) the consumption was 1.67lbs/ihp/hr, about half that achieved by the old

Victoria firing one of her 16.25in guns. Note the vast cloud of smoke and the disturbance of the sea from the blast. The after 10in gun and the 6in battery can also be seen. (University of Newcastle)

Thunderer's machinery

	Original	*Triple-expansion*
Power developed (ihp)	6270	5500 (7000 forced)
Speed (kts)	13.4	13.25
Weight of machinery (tons)	1050	800
Coal (tons/mile/kts)	1350/4500/10	950/4500/10
Pressure (lbs/sq in)	30	145

machinery. He suggests that the older engines would not have been able to sustain power for 2600 miles but, if they had, they would have burnt 1350 tons of coal instead of the 650 tons actually used. Note that the reduction of 250 tons in machinery weight and of 400 tons of coal, both low down, could lead to stability problems.

The triple-expansion engine had a major influence on the economics of commercial shipping and the steam ship began to make rapid inroads into sailing ship cargo trade. It remained in commercial service until well after the Second World War. In the Navy, *Dreadnought* of 1905 (the end point of this volume) saw its replacement by the steam turbine. Strangely, the *Victoria*, the first battleship with triple-expansion engines, was also fitted with the first steam turbine in the RN,[28] driving a dynamo.[29]

The Victoria *and* Camperdown *collision*

The Mediterranean Fleet was preparing to anchor at Tripoli (Lebanon) on 22 June 1893 when Admiral Tryon ordered the two lines of battleships to turn towards each other. the lines were 1200yds apart and *Victoria*'s turning circle (35° rudder) was 600yds whilst that of *Camperdown*, who only used 28° helm, was 800yds.[30] Inevitably, the two ships collided at a speed estimated as about 6kts.[31] *Camperdown* struck the *Victoria* about 65ft abaft the stem at an angle of 85° (abaft the beam), slewing her bodily some 70ft to port which absorbed some of the impact. (This was estimated at 17-18,000 foot-tons, similar to the muzzle energy of a 12ins 45-ton gun.) Both ships were under full helm at impact and continued to turn through a further 20° while locked together. The stem of the *Camperdown* penetrated some 5-6ft into the *Victoria*'s upper deck with damage extending a further 4-5 feet. The ram projected 7ft and penetrated 9ft at 12ft below the waterline.

The gash in the side of *Victoria* extended 28ft down from the upper deck and was 12ft wide at that deck, about 11ft at the waterline and diminishing as it went down, giving an area of 100-110sq ft. Water would flow through an unobstructed hole of that size at the rate of 3000 tons per minute but, in the case of *Victoria*, there were only a limited number of spaces which could flood instantaneously. Every compartment used for storage was designed to be watertight and it is probable that those open to flooding would admit only some 500 tons in the first inrush.

The flooding then spread at a diminished rate – but still very quickly – into other spaces through doors and hatches which were open. White quotes the Chief Constructor of Malta, confirmed by survivors, as evidence that the doors and hatches were in 'good order and perfectly efficient'. Some more recent writers have

An official model of *Victoria* showing her on the point of sinking. The gash left by *Camperdown* can be seen under water, forward. The turret and battery are about to flood and the resulting loss of stability will lead to rapid capsize.

alleged that the rubber seals had been removed from the doors in the interest of 'spit and polish'. Even if the evidence to the contrary is thought to be biased, the story seems unlikely as extremes of smartness would not be applied to store rooms right forward, never seen by visitors. (White was not involved in the design of *Victoria* and his thorough investigation of the cause of sinking seems impartial.) With the crew at drill stations, doors could be shut in 3 minutes from the order. In the case of this collision, the order to close doors was given about 1 minute before impact and most of the crew were relaxing in their messes. Only in one case was it said that a sliding door could not be shut. Since this particular door was of exceptional strength and 35ft from the point of impact it is most likely that it was jammed by debris and not by distortion of the structure. Many doors closer were closed without difficulty.

Victoria's forecastle deck was only 10ft above the normal waterline and flooding brought it under in about 4 minutes; 2 minutes later men working on that deck had to leave. In about 9 minutes from impact the water was half-way up the turret and started to pour in through the gun ports and was also entering the 6in battery through an open door at the fore end. There was a sudden lurch and she capsized quite quickly to starboard. The table below shows how rapidly stability diminished as the waterplane was flooded.

Condition	Metacentric Height (ft)
Undamaged	5.05
Foc'sle under water	0.8
As above; turret and battery also flooded	-1.8

The sudden loss of 2.6ft of GM as the battery flooded caused the sudden lurch, vividly described by many survivors.

Camperdown's bow was torn by *Victoria*'s protective deck as she slewed and water spread through open doors, stopped only by a coffer dam built by her carpenter across the main deck.[32] At that time it is said that her metacentric height was close to zero. Both ships had drain holes in every bulkhead and every deck and, though these holes had valves, they were difficult to reach and some were jammed with dirt.[33]

White's conclusions were related specifically to the loss of *Victoria* and can be summarised as follows. There was insufficient time to close doors and hatches after the impact. The spread of flooding through these doors etc, despite efforts made to close them, led to the depression of the bow and loss of stability. Had all doors and hatches been closed prior to the collision, she would have been in no danger. Entering harbour is always hazardous and RN ships today always close watertight doors.[34] Even in the actual condition of the collision, had the doors and gunports in turret and battery been closed, *Victoria* would not have capsized though she

might have foundered slowly as flooding spread. White concluded with a strong passage on the need to be able to make superstructures watertight as, if not, freeboard is only to the lower edge of ports etc.

One cannot dissent from these conclusions on *Victoria*; the lessons for new design took a little longer to sink in and will be discussed in following chapters. White's report was dated September 1893 and the first of the *Majestic*s was laid down three months later.

The lessons learnt were that doors in bulkheads are best avoided[35] as they can be left open. Valves, too, should be reduced to a minimum and operated from high in the ship. The longitudinal bulkhead was blamed by many for the capsize and though White's careful inquiry showed it played little part,[36] it was removed in *Sans Pareil*. Implementation of these recommendations was slow as they made the ship more difficult to work and *Lord Nelson* was the first design in which unpierced transverse bulkheads were adopted.

The *Resistance* trials 1885-89

The old ironclad *Resistance* was used for a series of trials between 1885 and 1881. The first series were devoted to protection against gunfire, particularly of the secondary armament, the later sequence studying torpedo protection. These trials were carried out with a degree of secrecy unusual in the nineteenth century; White frequently mentioned these trials as justification for features of his ships but always concluded by saying that he could not go into detail. As a letter of 1888[37] says: '. . . every effort to be used to prevent unauthorised persons from witnessing the experiments, or gaining knowledge of the damage done when the ship is brought into harbour.'

The trials of 1885 were reported in *The Times* and summarised in Brassey's.[38] The first tests were to see if layers of rubber or spaces filled with asbestos could close up holes made in unarmoured structures by smaller guns. First, the gunboat *Pincher* fired a 6pdr shell into a compartment with sheets of rubber up to 1½in thick and then the *Blazer* fired a 5in shell. The rubber was a complete failure, totally destroyed by the explosion. A 6pdr shell was then fired into a tank filled with asbestos fibre[39] 'to which it would be imprudent to allude in detail'. This was partially successful as the asbestos formed a paste with incoming water and reduced the leak. These tests were quite elaborate but, since they were failures, they are only summarised here. The reference describes them in detail.

After *Resistance* had been recovered from the torpedo trials, she was prepared for further tests on the effectiveness of the novel HE shells in 1888. She was modified so that part of her hull represented the secondary battery of a modern battleship with a modern casemate (3in steel over 1in iron) and traverses of 1-1½in steel were built between the gun positions as well as rope mantlets.

28. The Engineer-in-Chief, Durston (and White) kept very closely in touch with Parson's work, making nonsense of the oft-repeated story that the Navy was surprised by *Turbinia*'s performance at the 1897 Review.

29. Eng Rear-Admiral Sir R W Skelton, 'Progress in Marine Engineering', *Trans Inst Mech Eng* (London 1930)

30. The author is pleased that he is not called on to explain why it happened.

31. *Report by the Assistant Controller and Director of Naval Construction (William White) based on the minute of proceedings of the court martial appointed to inquire into the cause of the loss of Her Majesty's ship Victoria* (London 1893).

32. Parkes, *British Battleships*.

33. So much for spit-and-polish!

34. The Ro-Ro ferry *European Gateway*, entering Harwich, sank following a collision, largely because the doors low down in the machinery spaces were open.

35. See Lord Charles Beresford, 'Watertight doors, and their danger to modern fighting ships', *Trans INA* (London 1896).

36. Reed's evidence to the 1871 Committee (Chapter 3), to the effect that longitudinal bulkheads are acceptable when the beam is small, is vindicated.

37. Admiralty to C-in-C Portsmouth 16 June 1888 (Ordnance Board Minutes).

38. *Brassey's Naval Annual* (London 1885) p 237.

39. The health risk to observers from asbestos fibres must have been very high.

A charge exploding against the old battleship *Resistance* during trials in 1887. ((©) MPL)

Dummy men were arranged and 'animals, if necessary, to be located in the battery'. Old guns, a torpedo and filled cartridge cases were to be positioned. The shells fired were mostly 6in or 4.7in steel common shell filled with powder, guncotton or Lyddite with a few powder-filled cast-iron common shells.

The results were summarised by the DNO on 3 April 1889 as follows.[40] Her 4½in armour would keep out all HE filled common shell whilst the casemate would keep out HE common shell up to 6in. 'Stronghead' 4.7in fired from a QF gun would penetrate the armour at up to 25° to the normal, empty or powder-filled. The armour would also prevent any fused HE shell from bursting inside. The 2in rear of the casemate was effective in keeping out splinters from 6in shell bursting nearby and the traverses were very effective. This trial was seen as particularly important in justifying the weight of case-mates to protect secondary guns. Coal bunkers were also very effective against HE shell.

The 1892 Gunnery Manual refers to trials using a 6in BL on a Vavasseur mount at a range of 120yds. Twelve out of fourteen shots hit despite considerable motion. Later, a 9.2in scored five hits from seven rounds. Palliser shot broke up on passing through armour but Holtzer projectiles penetrated without being distorted. It was noted that the 10in Palliser shot cost £3-10-0 whilst a steel armour-piercing projectile cost £30.[41] There was a lengthy debate as to the value of retaining Palliser as it was claimed that they were still effective against older ships with wrought-iron armour. Eventually, an outfit of 20 per cent steel AP was approved.

Lyddite was seen as having great promise but, at that time, its safety had not been fully investigated and there was concern of premature explosions in the barrel[42] and of detonation in long-term storage. HE shells formed a large number of small splinters and were not as damaging to structure as powder-filled shells with fewer, large splinters, though the HE, exploding on contact, made a

big hole in the shell plating. This accounts for the retention of thin armour at the ends and above the belt of RN battleships.

The Resistance *torpedo trials*

During 1885 the *Resistance* was prepared for a series of trials on the effect of guns and torpedoes and the protection against them. The spaces below the armour shelf over a length of 29ft on the port side were so arranged as to represent as nearly as possible the coal bunkers, etc used in contemporary ships for the protection of machinery spaces against torpedo attack. These spaces were subdivided by an iron longitudinal bulkhead (fitted at Devonport) and the space nearest the hull was filled with coal. The ship was towed out and moored fore and aft in Portchester Lake. On 21 September 1886, an 80lb charge was exploded 30ft from the side which shook her but caused no damage. This seems to have been in the nature of a calibration shot to see that all was well.

One of the main objects of the trial was to test the effectiveness of torpedo nets and to determine the minimum distance from the hull at which they would be effective. On 22 September, the torpedo vessel *Vesuvius* fired an old pattern 16in torpedo with a 91lb charge from her bow submerged tube against the nets which were rigged 30ft from the ship's side. The range was a mere 100yds, both to ensure the torpedo hit in the desired place and that it impacted the net at high speed. The explosion was impressive but the damage to the net was very localised, one supporting boom being un-shipped, and there was no damage to the ship.

Since the value of the nets had been demonstrated, it was possible to use static charges, hung from a boom, rather than 'expensive' torpedoes. A charge was exploded at 20ft from the side on 24 September which caused no damage. The next charge was detonated at 15ft from the side and caused some minor leaks in the plating. There was, however, a more serious leak which required 200 men at the hand pumps to control. This was due to a pipe which had fractured close to a hull valve. This was repaired and, after the ship had been inspected, trials were resumed on 18 October 1886. Nets had been rigged 25ft from the side and, at high tide, *Vesuvius* fired another 16in torpedo from her submerged tube at a range of about 200yds. There was no damage to the ship, confirmed by a diver's inspection.

On 2 November 1886 *Resistance* was moored in Fareham Creek in shallow water and a 16in torpedo (93lb charge) was lashed alongside her on the port side amidships, 8ft below the surface (just above the bilge keel). When the torpedo was exploded, she took up a small list but remained afloat. About 20ft of bilge keel had been blown off and the plating below much dented. Above the bilge keel three or four strakes of plating had been forced in and the seams opened up by 2-3in. Internally, skylights had been broken and the contents of the bunkers scattered. However, the bulkheads remained tight and confined flooding to a single compartment and hence *Resistance* could have remained in action.

There was then an interval until June 1887 while further alterations were made to the structure. It was intended to attack the port side again but abreast the engine-room. The wing passage with a width of three feet, tapering to nothing, was left empty. Eight feet inboard a new longitudinal bulkhead had been built of ³⁄₈in steel extending for 61ft. The space between this bulkhead and the inner bottom was packed with coal, 20ft high. The double bottom spaces had been altered to represent contemporary practice. Some 1½in plates had been worked on the outside at the upper part of the wing passage.

The first of the new series of trials was on 9 June 1887 and was intended to try a new design of Bullivant net. This used steel booms which were only half the weight of the old wooden design and with stronger hinge fittings. It was so designed that it could be got out or stowed very much more quickly than the older nets. Once again, *Vesuvius* was used to fire a 16in torpedo which tore the net but did not damage the ship. On 10 June, a 220lb charge was exploded 30ft from the side and 20ft down. Ill-informed observers feared catastrophe from this charge which was ' more destructive than any which is ever likely to be launched against an armour clad . . .' (!) The trials officer, Captain Long, had more confidence and had already promulgated the date of the next trial. The only damage was that some net booms were bent.

On 13 June a charge of 95lb of guncotton was exploded electrically from *TB 95* in contact with the double bottom and 20ft below the surface. The previous year's trials had suggested that, if the space adjacent to the shell was full of coal, it would transfer the shock of the explosion to the inner skin. For this new trial, the double bottom, 2½ft deep, was left empty though the bunker further inboard was left full. The charge was placed under the starboard side of the boiler room and, when it exploded, the whole ship seemed to lift, then heel 8 – 10° and finally settle on the mud. The battered hulk had sunk at last. The blast of the explosion had penetrated both the outer and inner bottoms and the inboard bunker bulkhead. The water spread through doors which had ceased to be watertight.

The lessons as given in the Naval Annual were:

Nets of the type in service will stop a Whitehead torpedo and if this explodes 25ft from the hull there will be no damage to the ship.

The new design of Bullivant net is equally effective and far easier and quicker in operation.

The structural design of contemporary ships is well adapted to resist torpedo explosions.

The compartment next to the skin is better filled with coal than empty.

To which one would add, with the benefit of hindsight, that the possibility of a hit on a bulkhead flooding two compartments had not been appreciated. This trial was seen as very important and as justifying the compartmentation of ships up to *Dreadnought*.

Nile and *Trafalgar* (ld 1886)

Though these ships have little of technical interest, the political manoeuvrings which led to them had an important bearing on future classes. Gladstone resigned as Prime Minister on 9 June 1885 and was replaced by Lord Salisbury heading a minority government, including Lord George Hamilton as First Lord. For the last time, an incoming government changed the naval Board members and Sir Arthur Hood became First Sea Lord. These changes coincided with Barnaby's resignation on health grounds.[43]

Hood was an ardent supporter of the low-freeboard, single-citadel turret ship[44] and wanted an improved *Dreadnought* for the two outstanding battleships of the Northbrook programme. In July 1885 the new Board seem to have approved a low-freeboard turret ship but with two citadels, apparently based on Barnaby's design C for the *Victoria*. After Barnaby had left and before White could join, Hood instructed Morgan and Crossland, the Chief Constructors, to develop a single-citadel design.

Barnaby heard of this and wrote to White and they wrote a joint memo expressing their unhappiness both with the way in which the requirements had been handled and with the new design. They jointly proposed a new Committee on Design[45] to examine the pros and cons of turret and barbette ships, the arrangement of vertical armour, the effect of quick-firers and the programme of work. They thought it was unwise to add a further £2 million to the £6.5 million already committed to the battleship building programme. They objected to the single citadel design and said that, should it be ordered, it should be signed by the Chief Constructors, marked 'By order of the Board'. The First Lord, Lord George Hamilton, was not pleased by this unasked-for advice and approved the single-citadel design.

Nile and her sister carried two twin turrets, each mounting two 13.5in guns and had a belt which was 20in thick at the waterline, amidships. It tapered at the ends, at the bottom and the upper belt had a maximum of 16in but they had the highest proportion of weight devoted to armour of any British battleship. The secondary battery was much increased; initially eight 5in BL with a total weight of 135 tons, it was changed in January 1890 to six 4.7in QF weighing 185 tons with the increased ammunition needed.

This and other changes led to them completing some 600 tons over weight which brought them a foot deeper in the water. In consequence, it was directed that all future designs should have a Board Margin of 4 per cent

40. Ordnance Board Minutes 611.

41. There is a table giving the costs of Palliser and armour-piercing for guns from 6in to 13.5in. 6in £1-15-0/8 to 13.5in £12-8-0/97.

42. See Chapter 10 for Japanese experience with prematures.

43. He was indeed sick at the time but the real reason was that he was tired of quarrelling with Reed, who was married to his sister and lived nearby. (Parkes, quoting K C Barnaby – grandson).

44. Lambert suggests that Hood and others supported the low-freeboard turret ship because of its value in attacking forts. It had better protection for gun crews, possibly a thicker belt and the poor seakeeping mattered less. A Lambert. 'The RN and the 'Cherbourg' Strategy', *Ships v Forts Conference,* Portsmouth, November 1995.

45. Manning, *The Life of Sir William White*, p185.

of the displacement to allow for changes during building.[46]

The success of the *Royal Sovereign* high-freeboard barbette ships has largely discredited these two ships but, at the time, they represented the views of many officers who believed that their low freeboard made them more difficult targets and who valued the thick upper belt and turrets to protect the gun crews. *Nile* and *Trafalgar* served mainly in the Mediterranean where their lack of freeboard was less serious. In moving the Naval Estimates for 1886, the Financial Secretary, Hibbert, said 'I may safely say that these two large ironclads will probably be the last ironclads of this type that will ever be built in this or any other country.'

Trafalgar 1887 (top) and *Nile* 1888, among the last of the low-freeboard turret ships. (Imperial War Museum: Q40357, Q39715)

46. In fact, the weight margin is of limited value as there is usually no corresponding space margin. Space margins are almost impossible to provide as space is not just an area but must be in the right place, both absolutely and relative to other spaces.

Cruisers and Smaller Craft | *Seven*

THE QUESTION of what was a cruiser in the 1870s was difficult to answer at the time and, even with hindsight, there are considerable difficulties. During the Napoleonic Wars, 'cruiser' described a role rather than a ship type; a Third Rate, 74-gun ship of the line operating alone would be described as a cruiser or serving on cruising duties. In the steamship era cruiser began to be used for a category of ships, though the range of duties was very large with a correspondingly wide range of size, cost and military capability.

Roles envisaged were scouting for the battlefleet, trade protection and 'showing the Flag'.[1] Rodger quotes Brassey listing cruiser tasks as 'the training of seamen ... exhibiting the British flag in foreign ports and especially in the harbours of semi-barbarous powers ... the repression of piracy and slavery, and the punishment of savage tribes'. A role which was not clearly set out was that of the 'ship of force', the capital ship, in more distant waters. This was explicit in some of the bigger cruisers such as *Shannon* and *Nelson*, but even the small cruiser would assume such a role when opposed by similar ships or sloops.

The problem of role definition was even greater for the smaller ships, the corvettes, sloops and gunboats. The nineteenth-century Admiralty did not set out roles for new ships in the way of today's Staff Papers. They saw the role as self-evident and, indeed, it is fairly clear from the way in which they were used. The main role of these small ships may be seen as acting as the policemen of the Empire, specifically showing the flag, aiding the civil power in peacetime and trade protection, coastal attack and defence and interdiction of coastal trade in wartime.

There were then many other duties for which they were used since they were available and cheap to run. These included training (particularly as gunnery firing ships), surveying and they were sometimes used to try new types of engines and equipment. Some consideration to the growth of trade is necessary before dealing with the ships needed for its protection.

The Carnavon Committee, 1879

A committee was set up in 1879 under Lord Carnavon, following the scare of war with Russia the previous year, to consider the defence of the Empire and its trade routes.[2] Their first report pointed out that the value of British ships and one year's freight was £900 million, of

Mercury 1878, with her sister *Iris*, was both one of the earliest steel ships and the prototype of the modern cruiser. (Author's collection)

which some £144 million was at sea at any one time. The true value of this trade was considerably greater as much freight in foreign ships was British property. Two thirds of seaborne trade of the world was British; half the food consumed in the UK was imported, as was the bulk of the raw materials used by industry. The Committee were particularly worried about the possible collapse of marine insurance in the event of war. They noted that the bulk of cable telegraph lines were British-owned.

In 1860 the British merchant fleet was equal to the rest of the world in tonnage and considerably more than half in value due to the predominance of steamships. There were very few ships with a speed of over 14kts and most of these were British; the majority had speeds of 8-12kts.[3]

Speed and tonnage of merchant ships

The figures in the table below show the number of British merchant ships within the given speed and tonnage bands.

Kts	Tonnage/1000				
	5	4	3	2	1
16	1				
15	3				
14	2	2	15		
13		4	9		1
12	2		2	25	6
11		19	56	86	8
10		9	33	138	75
9			4	126	256
8		1		4	172

1. This section leans heavily on a number of articles in *The Mariner's Mirror* by Dr N A M Rodger, though with minor disagreement in detail. N A M Rodger, 'The First Light Cruisers', *The Mariner's Mirror* Vol 65 (London 1979).

2. The Royal Commissioners appointed to inquire into the Defence of British Possessions and Commerce Abroad. Three reports, September 1881, March 1882 and July 1882 (plus summary February 1883). Held in PRO as PRO30/6/131.

3. These speeds were trial speeds and speeds in service were considerably less. Merchant ships were not sheathed and the anti-fouling paints available were not very effective until about 1890.

Note how few fast, large ships there were which were seen as suitable for use as armed merchant cruisers; the numbers for other countries, such as France, would have been even smaller. The overwhelming proportion were 2000 tons or less with speeds of about 9kts and these would be trial speeds with a service speed about 2kts less.

The Committee then went on to say: 'In the present circumstances of trade, merchant ships could not be protected by convoy even if ships of war could be spared for the purpose.' Unfortunately, the report does not attempt to justify this statement which was clearly seen as self-evident. They even contemplated merchant ships carrying guns on board in peacetime which could be mounted quickly in war. Both commerce and the Navy depended on coaling stations and, other than the overseas bases (Malta, Gibraltar, Bermuda and Halifax), they saw the following as vital in war.

Capetown and Simon's Town	Singapore
Port Louis (Mauritius)	Hong Kong
Aden	Port Royal
Colombo	Port Castries (St Lucia)

They recommended the expenditure of £2½ million on land defences, increasing the number of troops from about 10,000 to 18,600. There was an interesting comparison of the balance between sail and steam on various trade routes (1882):

Route	Type of Ship
North Pacific	Sail
W Coast, S America	Mostly sail, steam increasing
E Coast, S America	Steam
West Indies	Steam
Atlantic	Great majority steam
India	Equal
China	⅞ steam
Cape	Steam
Australia	Equal
Mediterranean	Steam
W Coast, Africa	Steam

The reports of the Carnavon Committee were kept secret and did not become generally known until the Colonial Conference of 1887. Though the Committee clearly demonstrated the weakness of the Navy, the Liberal government was dedicated to cutting government expenditure and no immediate action was taken. The reports, when published, provided ammunition for the agitation which led to the Naval Defence Act. During the 1880s there were some very important developments in the control of trade whilst some entirely new trades came into being.

The telegraph and the organisation of shipping

Between 1865 and 1880 the electric telegraph spread to most major shipping centres. This enabled owners to direct their ships to ports where there were known to be cargoes or at least a high probability of finding them. Ships could be re-routed from intermediate ports if their cargo had been sold. All this led to a considerable improvement in the effectiveness of cargo companies.

Rapid communications helped the organisation of Liner Conferences in which companies engaged in a particular route agreed on minimum rates to avoid cut-throat competition. The first of these was set up in 1875 for the Europe to Calcutta route. A British government investigation found, with reservations, that such restrictions on freight rates were not contrary to the public interest. The Baltic Exchange was opened in London as the centre for ship chartering, superseding the less formal arrangement centred in a coffee house. Lloyd's, too, established a worldwide network of agents and *Lloyd's List* enabled owners and shippers to find out where ships and cargo were to be found.

The military implications of this world communication network was soon recognised and plans were prepared to destroy enemy links at the outbreak of war. Many of the cruiser operations at the start of the First World War involved attacks on cable stations. Plans for trade protection relied heavily on the use of cable (and later wireless) to keep protection forces informed of the movements of both merchant ships and their potential attackers.

The new trades

Two-thirds of the first refrigerated meat cargo of 400 carcasses from Australia was inedible when it arrived in the liner *Orient* in 1881. However, the following year, all the first load from New Zealand arrived in prime condition. By 1900 7 million carcasses were arriving. The increase is show in the table below:

Year	Carcasses x 1000
1880	0.4
1882	66
1886	1187
1893	3889

Oil was originally shipped in barrels with a ton weight occupying 80cu ft or 2 'Tons' capacity. Later square 4-gallon tins, 2-3 to a case, were used. The first ship specially built as a bulk carrier, *Gluckauf*, entered service in 1886; with a gross tonnage of 2300 tons, she carried 2600 dwt tons of oil. (The *Marquis Scicluna* of 1655 tons was converted and operated the previous year by a South Shields Company.)

Initially, oil tankers were prohibited from using the

Suez Canal and although this ban was lifted in 1902, there were still severe restrictions and only in 1907 were the rules relaxed. By 1911 there were 48 sailing ships and 234 steamers carrying oil in bulk and this number was increasing very rapidly.

Atlantic liners

The development of the Atlantic passenger liner is of interest in at least two ways. They were the peak achievement of the commercial naval architect and marine engineer, usually being early users of new technology. They were also seen by the Admiralty and other navies as being the most useful ships for conversion to auxiliary cruisers in the light of their high speed. Many ships were given overt or covert subsidies and some even had stiffening for guns etc, fitted during building. Experience in the early stages of the First World War showed that this belief was mistaken; by then the Atlantic passage was short and the capacity of these ships in terms of fuel, fresh water and other stores was limited so that they could stay at sea for a few days only before replenishment. Their high sides made them very vulnerable to gunfire and it was found that the smaller, slower liner, intended for longer routes, made a more effective cruiser, both for the defence of and for attack on trade. The table below outlines the development of the fast Atlantic steamer from its origin.

They were splendid ships and the pride of their nations.

Freight rates and profits

Freight rates fluctuated wildly, as did profits. Wars such as the Crimean, Spanish-American and the Boer increased the demand for shipping and led to high rates. Major strikes could lock up large numbers of ships and have a similar effect on rates. It was possible to iron out these fluctuations to some extent by postponing building in difficult times and Kirkaldy[4] shows that many companies were operating at a loss in the early years of the twentieth century if due allowance is made for depreciation.

Fluctuations in freight rates
(homeward, 1900 = 100 per cent)

Year	per cent of 1900	Year	per cent of 1900
1884	95	1897	75
1887	95	1899	85
1889	125	1901	90
1891	95	1903	65
1893	85	1905	70
1895	80		

Atlantic steamers 1838-1907

Name	Date	Tonnage	Speed (kts)	Crossing (days-hrs)	Coal (tons/day)	Description
Great Western	1838	1340	9.0	14	28	Wood paddle
Britannia	1840	1156	8.5	14-8	31	Wood paddle
Great Britain	1843	3270			35-50	Iron screw
America	1848	1825	10.25		60	Wood paddle
Baltic	1850	3000		9-13		Wood paddle
Asia	1850	2226	12.5	10		Wood paddle
Persia	1855	3300	13.8	9-12	150	Iron paddle
Great Eastern	1858	18,914	13-14	10	280	Iron paddle and screw
Java	1865	2697	14	8-22		Iron screw
Russia	1867	2959	14.4	8-20	90	Iron screw
Oceanic	1871	3808	14.75	9-11		Iron screw
Britannic	1874	5004	16	8-20	75	Iron screw
City of Berlin	1875	5490	16	7-15	120	Iron screw
Servia	1881	7391	16.7		200	Steel screw
Umbria	1884	8127	19.5			Steel screw
City of Paris	1888	10,669	19	5-20	328	Steel screw
Teutonic	1888	9984	21	5-16		Steel screw
Campania	1893	12,500	22	5-9	485	Steel screw
Kaiser Wilhelm	1901	19,361	23.5	5-8	700	Steel screw
Celtic	1901	20,904				Steel screw
Mauritania	1907	31,938	25	4-11	1000	Steel screw

4. A W Kirkaldy, *British Shipping, its History, Organisation and Importance* (London 1919).

By 1904 the average dividend paid by cargo companies was 3.6 per cent of the capital employed increasing by 1912 to 6.8 per cent. Of twenty-four liner companies, the typical dividend in 1912 was 6 per cent but there were wide fluctuations, one company paying 60 per cent and five none.

Coaling stations

Coal varied considerably in heat content, weight and in price and was not always easy to obtain. Maintenance of coal stocks was a major task; in the 1870s the P&O line owned 170 sailing colliers to maintain its steamship service to India. The map shows some of the more important stations supporting trade in peacetime and Imperial communications in time of war.

Some typical coals

Source	Heat of combustion BTU	Cu Ft/Ton
Welsh best	15,788	-
Welsh average	14,858	42.7
Derbyshire	13,860	47.4
Scotch	14,164	42.0
USA (Bitum)	13,861	42.4

Prices varied from place to place: Welsh cost (1912) 23/- ton in Gibraltar, 26/- in Port Said, 36/- at Suez and 35/- at Singapore. Also at Singapore Natal coal cost 25/- and Australian 24/-. Prices at the pithead (1910) for comparison were Australia 7/6, India 5/1, Canada 10/5, South Africa 5/10.

Though Welsh was preferred, the price differential

was usually too great east of Suez and it was only used by warships.[5] Cheaper coal was bulky, quick-burning and with poor heat content and much ash. The lack of coaling stations in the Pacific (including the west coast of the USA) accounts for the survival of sail, both commercial and naval, in that ocean.

Trade protection

This was usually thought at the time to be the most important role for unarmoured (or lightly protected) ships and one in which there were several real difficulties and some other perceived problems which today we might consider imaginary. The Treaty of Paris (Appendix 2) attempted to regulate the conduct of trade war but the USA refused to sign, seeing the treaty as blunting its most effective weapon against England. The American Civil War had shown that a small number of raiders could inflict serious damage on merchant shipping and a very large number of ships would be needed to hunt them down. It was thought that there were an increasing number of merchant ships whose top speed was greater than most warships and, in many more cases, merchant ships had a greater sustained speed. The table given by the Carnavon Committee suggests that this view was mistaken or, at least, greatly exaggerated.

Part of the problem of cruiser speed was due to the need for British warships to carry a full sailing rig. This was not entirely due to conservatism but reflected the lack of coaling stations, particularly in the Pacific.[6] Prior to the introduction of the compound engine and, even more, the triple-expansion engine, it was not possible to carry sufficient coal to carry out a reasonable operation with enough left to reach the next bunkers. The triple-expansion engine had a double effect; not only did it

This map shows some of the main trade routes for both steam and sail in the late nineteenth century. Principal coaling stations are also shown.

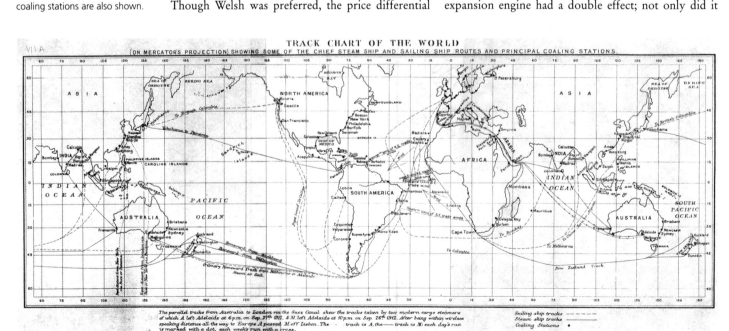

improve the endurance of warships but it made many more trade routes economical for commercial steam shipping which, in turn, led to more numerous coaling stations. However necessary, the added drag of a full rig cost about 1.5kts under steam and needed a larger complement, increasing the size of the ship.

Spencer Robinson, in evidence to the 1871 Committee (Chapter 3) had said that convoy was no longer possible and Barnaby put this view even more strongly *'I therefore repeat, as a challenge, in the presence of this distinguished Assembly,* the assertion that the successful convoy of sailing ships and slow steam ships in numbers, in the face of the attack of fast armed steam ships – especially attacks at night, and repeated night after night – is impossible.' (Barnaby's italics).[7] There were many other similar declarations by naval officers and others.

Nowhere are the reasons for this belief clearly spelt out. It would seem that the fear was that a fast raider – naval cruiser or armed merchant ship – could strike so fast that the escort could not get to the point of attack in time.[8] This view was almost certainly mistaken; it takes a considerable time to sink even a merchant ship by gunfire[9] – Barnaby envisaged raiders using the ram but experience showed that damage was, if anything, more serious to the aggressor.[10] The Admiralty of the day was ill-adapted to consider policy matters of this kind[11] as Childers' changes had virtually abolished the Board and there was to be no real Staff function for many years to come. The changes made after Reed's resignation and the loss of the *Captain* were intended to reduce the authority of the Chief Constructor (later DNC) and Barnaby can hardly be blamed for not setting a design policy on behalf of an ineffective Board.[12]

Barnaby realised that it would not be possible to build sufficient cruisers within then current naval budgets and proposed that trade protection should largely be provided by armed merchant cruisers. Since the vast majority of fast merchant ships were British this proposal had much to commend it. In brief, the main problem was the vulnerability of merchant ships, particularly their lack of subdivision and their tall, exposed machinery and problems of stability and strength in carrying an effective armament. All these problems were soluble and Barnaby and his staff (notably Dunn) made considerable progress, incidentally contributing much to the safety of merchant ships in normal trade.

The development of the cruiser

The technology of *Iris* and her sister has been discussed in Chapter 5; her lighter steel hull, improved hull lines and final success in propeller design made her the fastest ship in the world and led to a new style of cruiser. Her concept seems to derive from a visit by the Controller (H Stewart) and Barnaby to France in 1874[13] from which they concluded that the French were likely to pursue a *guerre de course*. Only a month later Barnaby

began the design of what was at first referred to as a fast corvette and later as a despatch vessel. It seems clear that she was designed to hunt French commerce raiders,[14] a view supported by her numerous medium-calibre guns (ten 64pdrs[15]) and by her generous coal supply. Her early compound engines would have burnt coal at the rate of about 2.2lbs/ihp/hr compared with a figure of over 3lbs/ihp/hr for the earlier, simple expansion engines; she cost £225,000. *Iris* and *Mercury* completed with a light sailing rig, which was soon removed.

She had no armour but was quite well protected. She had two boiler-rooms and two engine-rooms, below the water line and with deep coal bunkers outboard of them which would help to preserve both buoyancy and stability in the event of damage. The use of two engine-rooms was forced on the designer (White acting as head of section under Barnaby), because her narrow beam did not permit horizontal engines to be arranged side by side as was usual but the redundancy provided helped considerably in preserving her mobility.[16]

The *Comus* class (ld 1876–1881)
(nine ships and two more generally similar)

These ships appear as a step back from the *Iris* due to their heavy and not very effective rig. They were designed for distant waters and, despite the improved economy of their compound engines, sail was still deemed necessary in waters where coaling stations were few and far between. They were mainly of steel construction although because satisfactory steel was still scarce, some iron was used in the frames. They were sheathed and coppered with a gun-metal ram.[17] The design armament was two 7in, 4½-ton guns and twelve 64pdrs, all MLR, a numerous armament being needed to overcome a similar opponent quickly and they cost some £190,000. Speed was 13kts on trial and about 8kts sustained.

A number of schemes were tried for auxiliary rudders. The first seven had a second rudder built into the deadwood which could be brought into use if the main rudder was damaged. The next two had provision for this rudder but it does not seem to have been fitted. One of them, *Canada*, was given a retractable bow rudder but it was soon removed. Though all these devices were unsuccessful, it shows that the Admiralty was willing to try new ideas.

The most novel feature of their design was the introduction, for the first time in a small cruiser, of a protective deck. The fully-developed protective deck *system* is discussed in the next chapter but most of the essential features were evident in the *Comus*. It must be emphasised that it was a system and much more than a 1½in thick deck. Firstly there were deep coal bunkers (approximately 9ft, equivalent in resisting shot to 4½in iron) along the ship's side extending above the lower deck.[18] The protective deck was about 3ft below the lower deck which was at the level of the waterline. In a

5. This was not of mere academic interest; in 1904 the Japanese fleet used local coal as much as possible, reserving limited stocks of Welsh coal for the decisive battle.

6. See, for example, the dissenting report of the 1871 Design Committee.

7. Sir N Barnaby, 'On the Fighting Power of the Merchant Ship in Naval Warfare', *Trans INA* (London 1877).

8. This is very similar to the modern suggestion that convoys could not be protected against nuclear submarines and that 'Sea Lanes of Communication' should be defended instead. It was even claimed, mistakenly, that this would require fewer escort vessels.

9. See, for example, the efforts of the Vladivostok squadron in the Russo-Japanese war.

10. D K Brown and P Pugh, 'Ramming', *Warship 1990* (London 1990) (summarised in Chapter 1).

11. N A M Rodger, 'The Dark Ages of the Admiralty', *The Mariner's Mirror*, Vol 62 (London 1976).

12. It is even possible that the limits imposed on the DNC were in recognition of Barnaby's limitations in this aspect.

13. Visit to Brest, Lorient and Toulon by Sir H Stewart and Mr Barnaby. ADM 1/6329 – quoted by Rodger.

14. One might see the name 'despatch vessel' as disinformation to fool either the French or Parliament as to her true role. Her size and armament are too great for a simple messenger.

15. Rodger says this was based on 64pdr trials against a mock-up of *Shannon*.

16. It is far from clear that the value of this redundancy was recognised at the time.

17. The decision on whether a ship was to be sheathed had to made before building began. There could be no exposed steel and the ram, rudder pintles etc, had to be made of bronze.

18. The tops of these bunkers formed the seats for the outboard mess tables (G A Osbon, notes for the Naval Photograph Club).

normal action (as opposed to high-angle fire from forts),
it was unlikely that this deck would be hit and if it was,
it would only be a glancing blow which it was strong
enough to withstand. It would also stop most splinters
from shells bursting above.

The side bunkers were the first line of protection
against loss of buoyancy and stability; a full bunker
retaining, when flooded, some 63 per cent of its buoyancy and contribution to stability.[19] Then the space
between the protective deck and the lower deck was
closely subdivided and used for bunkers and stores, further limiting the extent of flooding and loss of stability.
This deck system extended for 100ft giving direct protection to engines, boilers and magazines. The protection to stability was far greater than is usually realised
since the inertia of the waterplane, on which the height
of the metacentre depends, is related to the cube of the

beam.[20] The midships body, where the beam is greatest,
contributes most and protection to the midships 100ft
preserves about three-quarters of the waterplane inertia.

Calliope *and the Samoa typhoon*

The survival of the *Calliope* in the Samoa typhoon of
1889 was rightly hailed as one of the great epics of the
Victorian navy. The political situation was 'confused'
and in dispute between the USA and Germany, each of
which had three warships at the island while there was
one RN ship, *Calliope*, to protect British interests.[21] On
15 March there were indications of an approaching
storm but the advice from local pilots was that it would
not be severe and the captains of the seven warships and
numerous merchant ships decided to remain at anchor
in Appia harbour, lowering topmasts and yards and
putting out more anchors, a seemingly sensible decision
since they had ridden out a previous storm in this fashion.[22] By nightfall the storm was increasing from the
exposed northerly direction and Captain Kane of
Calliope decided to make for the open sea, some
8000yds away. With power and revolutions for 15kts
Calliope was making only 2kts over the ground and
sometimes only 0.5kt. Eventually, she did get clear and,
returning four days later, she found all six of the other
warships were aground, seriously damaged, as were the
seven merchant ships.

The significance of this heroic episode lies in its
demonstration of the seamanship of the RN, the seaworthiness of the ship but, above all, in the reliability of
the machinery which had to work at full power for
many hours, combined with the dedication of the engineers. Captain Kane named seven men for commenda-
tion, including the two engineers. He particularly drew
attention to the fact that steam for full power was 'raised
with all despatch' and not gradually as was normal for a
full-power trial, imposing unusual thermal strains on
the machinery. He also pointed out that maximum
power was sustained for hours with the engines racing
as the ship pitched and the screw came out of the water.

Armour – belt or deck

Barnaby's views on armour are set out in a paper of
1889,[23] though these views changed from time to time.
He makes it clear that the increasing power of guns
necessitated changes in protection. Armour was first
introduced to protect gun crews and soon extended to
protection of the waterline (buoyancy and stability). By
the 1870s the biggest guns could penetrate any practical
thickness of armour and thick armour was concentrated
in a central citadel as in *Inflexible* (Chapter 4). A thin
belt is usually useless or worse and the protective deck
system, outlined above, would limit the effects of shellfire. In many cases the arguments between belt and deck
protection were fairly evenly balanced and it was logical
– not a sign of muddled thinking – to study alternative
designs.

Phaeton of the *Leander* class, 1883, developed from *Mercury*. (Author's collection)

One such comparison was for a *Boadicia* in early 1877 for which details of a belted and deck protected ship are given below.

	Belted		Protected	
	Tons	*per cent*	*Tons*	*per cent*
Displacement	6160		5660	
Armament	245	4.0	245	4.5
Machinery	1040	16.9	1000	17.7
Coal	520	8.4	500	8.8
Armour	795	12.9	350	6.2
Hull	3050	49.6	2910	51.4
Cost (£)	301,500		270,000	

Both were rejected by the Board who wanted a smaller and cheaper ship and though this was ordered as *Highflyer* in August, it was cancelled soon after.[24]

Leander *and* Mersey *(ld 1880-82)*

The *Leander*s were designed in 1880 after some dispute between Board members; Cooper Key wanted an enlarged, 15kt *Comus* whilst others wanted an improved *Mercury*; backed by the First Lord, Smith, the latter was chosen but, in order to fit a 1½in protective deck over 165ft amidships, she lost 0.5-1kt in speed and was a bit larger. The much better 6in BL was available and she carried ten of them, five on each beam with the forward and after guns each side on centre pivot mountings. She also mounted a heavy armament of machine-guns, sixteen in all (two Gatling, four Gardner, ten Nordenfelt). The protective deck differed from that in *Comus* by having the deck at centre just above the normal waterline and the sides sloped down to protect against shells entering at the waterline. Her compound engines were a little more efficient and with increased

coal supply she had an endurance of 8000 miles at 10kts. She had a light barque rig, similar to *Mercury*, and enough freeboard to make her a good seaboat.

Leander and her three sisters were very successful and may be seen as the ancestors of most cruisers for the rest of the century and beyond. Their general configuration was scaled up to the big First Class cruisers and down to the torpedo cruisers, whilst traces of the protected deck scheme can even be recognised in some sloops. The 1888 manoeuvres report criticised *Arethusa* for heavy rolling and recommended reducing top weight by doing away with her square rig.

The next step was the *Mersey* class of three ships whose main features were agreed only after prolonged debate. Cooper Key wanted a torpedo cruiser and in April/May 1882 the DNC prepared a design based on *Leander* of 2800 tons with a 2in deck, four 6in guns and ten submerged torpedo tubes. White, the head of section, was concerned that submerged tubes had not been tried[25] and would not be until *Polyphemus* ran trials later that year. Alternative designs carried two 9.2in and six 6in or fourteen 6in. The torpedo carrier was quietly dropped (see later) but when the first two ships were ordered in the spring of 1883 there were still great differences in armament under consideration. All variants had a pair of larger guns (9.2in, 8in or a new 7in) with a number of 6in; eventually, they completed with two 8in and ten 6in, costing £210,000.[26] The armour deck was increased to 2in on the flat and 3in on the slopes and ran from end to end, curving down at the bow to support the ram. The 1888 report saw them as very good ships but recommended replacing the 8in by 6in to reduce top weight.

Esmeralda

Lord Armstrong had long been an advocate of small, fast ships carrying very large guns, which culminated in

19. E L Attwood, *Warships, a Text Book* (London 1910). See also Appendix 4.

20. Inertia (second moment of area) = $\int y^3 .dx$. See Appendix 4.

21. D K Brown, 'Seamanship, Steam and Sail', *Warship* No 48 (London 1988).

22. N F Dixon, *On the Psychology of Military Incompetence* (London 1976). The author of this otherwise excellent book equates the decision to stay as the naval equivalent of the Charge of the Light Brigade and this has been copied by other authors. Since good advice had been sought and the season was late for serious storms, he is clearly wrong.

23. Sir N Barnaby, 'Armour for Ships', *Proc ICE* (London 1889).

24. Rodger, quoting Ship's Cover.

25. He must have meant submerged *beam* tubes since *Vesuvius*, completed 1874, had proved a bow submerged tube as indeed had *Oberon*.

26. Could the 8in have been to deal with small armoured ships like *Huascar*?

Severn, 1885, developed from the *Leander* class but with a full-length protective deck and two 8in guns. (Author's collection)

the *Esmeralda* laid down in 1881 to a design by Rendel. On completion in 1884 she caused a sensation and was often compared with the *Comus,* much smaller, four years earlier in concept and designed for a different role. Comparison with *Leander* in the table below shows the Admiralty in a better light.

Esmeralda's 10in guns particularly impressed journalists but they were too big for such a small ship, loading and training except in a calm were difficult and slow and her freeboard of 11ft forward meant they were frequently swept by the sea. Armstrong and others saw her as a battleship killer – perhaps she was if by 'battleship' one meant small ironclads such as *Huascar* – but most

people saw as an exceptionally powerful cruiser. Overall, one may see her big guns as a status symbol and, perhaps, the *Mersey*'s 8in as a copy. It is often said that big guns in cruisers enabled them to stand off and sink the enemy at long range. However, gunnery practice was still at about 800yds and the chance of any gun hitting at much over 1000yds was remote. The report on the 1888 manoeuvres thought that the armament of several cruisers was too heavy, recommending the removal of guns bigger than 6in.

The bigger cruisers – Warspite *and* Imperieuse (ld 1881)

As a result of the war scare with Russia in 1878, it was appreciated that there was a possibility of them using large armoured cruisers against British trade. The *Shah*'s action against *Huascar* may also have been seen as demonstrating the need for more powerful cruisers. In August 1880 Barnaby's office was working on two designs, an improved *Nelson* and a *Temeraire* derivative.[27] By November, the Board directed Barnaby to develop two designs for a big cruiser, one with a belt, the other with deck protection and both with the heavy guns in barbettes. His assistant, White, produced the designs by the 29th and Barnaby forwarded them to the Board, objecting to barbettes. On 1 December decided on a ship with a speed of 16kts and a 10in belt and on the 10th they ordered that the armament should be four 9.2in BL mounted, lozenge-fashion, in individual barbettes. They were slow to complete, with the first running trials in 1886.

Unfortunately, this lengthy gestation allowed time for numerous changes with a bigger crew, later and heavier marks of gun and extra coal, all of which

Comus, Esmeralda, Leander and Mersey

	Comus	Esmeralda	Leander	Mersey
Displacement (tons)	2383	3050	3800	4050
Armament weight (per cent)	6.4	7.6	4.4	
Armour (per cent)	5.8	3.5	5.3	
Machinery (per cent)	16.0	20.8	20.5	
Coal* Legend (per cent)	11.3	19.7	19.4	
Full (per cent)	14.9		24.5	
Hull (per cent)	55.8	42.6	41.6	
Trial speed (kts)	13.0	18.3	17.0	18
Endurance at 10kts	3600	6000	8000	
Armament	2-7in, 12-64pdr	2-10in, 6-6in	10-6in	2-8in, 10-6in
Armour	Partial 1½in deck	Complete, arched 1in	Partial 1½in	Complete, 2/3in

* Comparisons like this are difficult; coal and ammunition may be full or not and the distinction between hull and armour is uncertain.

brought the shallow belt deeper in the water. It seems that White, unusually, had produced incorrect weight estimates exacerbating the problem. They completed 25in deep with the belt almost submerged and initially only six of the intended ten 6in guns were mounted. The torpedo tubes were raised 2ft to keep them above water.

Some relief was obtained when the trials of *Imperieuse* in October 1886 showed that the brig rig with which they had been designed was useless; the use of sails while steaming reduced coal consumption by a mere 2.6cwt/hr. Typically, she took 16 minutes to tack. The masts were removed and replaced by a single military mast between the funnels saving 100 tons and *Warspite* was altered before completion. It was found that blast from the sided 9.2in prevented their use within 20° of the fore and aft line though otherwise they were reported to be very good gun platforms.[28] All these problems gave the ships a bad name but they were at least as good as contemporary foreign ships and had a reasonable service life, mainly as flagships of overseas squadrons – which is what they had been intended for. White wrote that their freeboard gave them an ability to use their guns in bad weather which would have enabled them to defeat larger ships.[29]

The Orlandos

On 15 September 1884 the journalist W T Stead published the first of a series of articles in the *Pall Mall Gazette* entitled 'The Truth about the Navy', which quickly led to a public demand for the Navy to be strengthened. Northbrook, the First Lord was abroad and in his absence it was decided to provide a further £3 million for the Navy which Northbrook announced in Parliament on 4 December[30] – just six months after he had said he would not know what to do with additional funds even if available!

Ironically, there was some truth in what he said as

there was some doubt about what cruisers should be built. The DNC Department had been working on two variants of an enlarged *Mersey,* offering the usual choice of belt or deck protection. Rather surprisingly, Rendel, who had been brought on to the Board as Civil Lord, came out in favour of the belted design. The role was never clearly defined but trade protection against small French armoured cruisers seems to have been the main task.

The seven ships of the *Orlando* class were very good value; on 5600 tons they carried two 9.2in and ten 6in with a 10in compound armour belt (16in end bulkheads) and a trial speed of about 19kts. As with *Imperieuse*, changes were made, including the welcome introduction of triple-expansion engines, and again the design calculations were incorrect so that they floated about 18in deep with the top of the belt on the waterline.

Despite this, they were good ships for their day with a citadel invulnerable to most cruiser guns, an armament which should have been able to destroy enemy cruisers quickly and good endurance. They were soon outdated by developments in weapons and armour but deserve a better reputation.

Torpedo cruisers – Scout

Cooper Key still wanted a torpedo cruiser,[31] an idea given further impetus when, in March 1883, Yarrow's proposed a large, armoured torpedo boat. Barnaby, who favoured a developed *Polyphemus*, reported on French small torpedo cruisers while Thornycroft proposed a lightly armoured, 600-ton torpedo boat.

Barnaby was directed to produce a small cruiser with two (later four) 5in guns and three torpedo tubes. His design for *Scout* and her sister came out at 1596 tons (legend)[32] with a speed of 16.7kts. They had one bow tube and two traversing launching carriages on deck,

27. She was originally a Second Class battleship derived from *Audacious.*

28. It is not clear whether this limited arc was that acceptable in peace and exceeded in war or whether it was an absolute limit. It was probably the effects of blast on the crew of the end mount which set the limit.

29. W H White, 'The Principles and Methods of Armour Protection in Modern Warships', *Brassey's Naval Annual* (London 1905). He actually wrote that their performance influenced the high mounting of guns in the 'Admirals' but the dates make this impossible.

30. N A M Rodger. 'The Dark Ages of the Admiralty', *The Mariner's Mirror* Vol 62 (London 1976).

31. Rodger ('The First Light Cruisers') suggests that Key was an early example of the naval officer who is fascinated by new technology and willing to support the introduction of novel craft provided that they are additional to and do not replace existing categories.

32. The word 'legend' causes confusion; it was intended to represent the ship in a typical seagoing condition as she might be when in action. To this end, about ½ to ⅔ of the total fuel was included. There was no attempt to deceive, at least prior to *Dreadnought*.

Imperieuse, 1883, one of a class of big armoured cruisers with the armament arranged lozenge-style. Their high freeboard greatly improved their fighting capability in bad weather. (Imperial War Museum: Q39201)

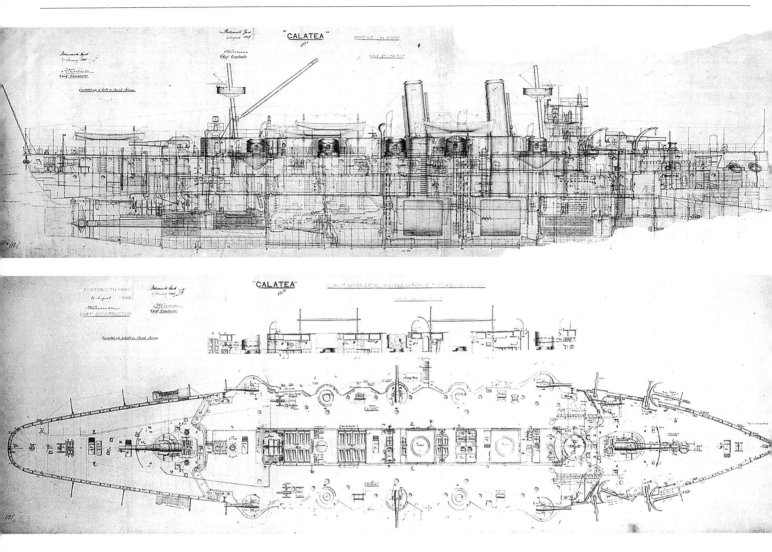

Above: Galatea of the *Orlando* class 1887. On a displacement of 5600 tons, these ships carried two 9.2in and ten 6in guns, with a 10in compound belt. They were good value and popular in their day, though perhaps a little too much had been attempted on a small ship. (National Maritime Museum, London: 17825, 17827)

Undaunted post-1897. Note the raised funnels. (Author's collection)

33. Measured from a photograph, the freeboard is about 14 ft, compared with 1.1 $\sqrt{L}$ of 16.5, better than many contemporaries.

34. There is a strongly-held view amongst naval constructors that scaling down from a larger design is likely to fail. Whilst this view cannot be proved, there are a number of examples which seem to support it.

35. Navy Estimates 1888.

fore and aft, which could fire through doors in the bulwarks either side. They were not successful, with poor stability, inadequate freeboard[33] and too slow to serve as fleet torpedo boats. Two fairly similar ships were built as despatch vessels – Admirals' yachts – and were intended to be unarmed but completed with four 5in.

Eight larger ships of the *Archer* class were built in 1885 with six 6in guns and these, too, were seen as unsuccessful, the 1888 report saying that they were unsteady gun platforms, probably because their armament was too heavy. They were the last ships with horizontal engines, which were arranged in two engine-rooms as in *Iris*. They had no direct successors, later small cruisers being reduced editions of *Medea*, described in Chapter 9. The much smaller torpedo gunboats seem to have been of similar style and may have been derived from *Scout*.[34]

Despite very muddled direction from the Board, Barnaby and White set cruiser design on a new path which was to lead to a very successful category over the next twenty years. *Iris* was the starting point with *Leander* as the first developed design.

Torpedo gunboats

Barnaby had long maintained that battleships should be defended against the threat of torpedoes by torpedo boat catchers – small gunboats – rather than armouring the bottom of the ship. Such vessels, which became known as torpedo gunboats (TGB), were designed just as he resigned; visually they seem very similar to the *Scout* though of only about one-third the displacement. Barnaby believed they were the smallest ships which could keep up with the battlefleet at sea. *Rattlesnake* even had a protective deck, although only ¾in thick, another clue to her cruiser origins. Diminutives, whose weight is scaled down from a bigger ship, tend to come out heavy which may have been part of the problem with the TGB. The form was much narrower and of less draught than *Scout* and was based on numerous tests by Edmund Froude at Haslar.

The first TGB was *Rattlesnake*, laid down in 1885 and, initially, she was reported on very favourably.[35] Doubts soon crept in and the report on the 1888 manoeuvres recommended a stronger hull, more freeboard and a turtle deck. There was doubt if the forward gun could be used in any sea and it was thought that it would be wrong to replace it with a 4.7in QF which added another 8½ tons.

The *Sharpshooters* were intended for 21kts but all except *Seagull* had the unreliable 'locomotive' boiler which meant that their trial speeds were about 19kts. Later, most were re-boilered and were then capable of about 21kts. They were immediately criticised as too slow, with trial speeds similar to those of torpedo boats or even less than the biggest boats entering service. It was an era in which trial speed differed greatly from

Scout 1885 and her sister were intended as ocean-going fleet torpedo boats, but their speed of 17kts (forced) was insufficient for the role. (Imperial War Museum: Q40129)

Torpedo gunboats

Class	Rattlesnake	Sharpshooter	Alarm	Halcyon
Date (ld)	1885	1888	1890	1892
No in class	4	13	11	5
Disp (tons)	550	735	810	1070
Length pp (ft)	200	230	230	250
Freeboard (F) (ft) approx	13	14.5	14.5	16.5
F/sq rt L	0.91	0.96	0.96	1.04
ihp/kts	2700/19.2	3500/19	3500/18.7	3500/18.2
Armament	1-5in, 4TT	2-4.7in, 5TT	2-4.7in, 5TT	2-4.7in, 5TT

Archer 1885, a Third Class torpedo cruiser, name ship of a class of eight. (Author's collection)

Top: *Rattlesnake* 1886, was the first TGB and was much praised when she completed. Later, she and her successors were thought to be too slow. (Author's collection)

Above: *Speedy,* 1893, was completed with Thornycroft water tube boilers and was both faster and more reliable than her sisters. She was the only three-funnel TGB. She appears to have minesweeping gear on the quarterdeck in this photograph. (Author's collection)

Below: *Halcyon* 1894 was one of the last class of TGBs with more freeboard and a poop to aid seakeeping. (Author's collection)

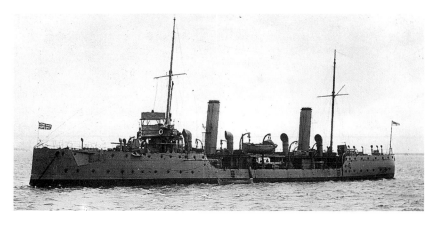

service speed, forced draught could only be used for a short time – in service, hardly ever – whilst the small torpedo boats lost speed very rapidly in a seaway.

The *Halcyon*s were bigger, with more freeboard forward and a poop, thought to be valuable when running before a following sea. Their machinery was heavier, though less powerful, in the interest of reliability. They could make 17-17½kts on natural draught and 19kts when forced. As well as protecting the fleet against torpedo attack they were seen as providing the inner line in a close blockade.

The TGBs were also seen as too big and expensive. However, the first successful destroyers (*River* class) were approaching the TGB in size and the TGB could outrun most early destroyers in a seaway, thanks to their adequate freeboard. They were much better ships than their reputation suggests and should probably have been re-thought as the basis for destroyers. The only successful torpedo attack of the nineteenth century was carried out by a TGB! During 1906 the survivors were converted for minesweeping.

First Class torpedo boats

Nineteen boats generally similar[36] to *Lightning* were built in 1876-80. Four larger torpedo boats of about 113ft (oa) were ordered in 1884 and then in 1885-87, during the war scare with Russia, some fifty boats of 125ft length were ordered. These were mainly from Thornycroft and Yarrow (five from J S White) and were intended as catchers against Russian torpedo boats. As such, they mounted two 3pdr guns and two twin Nordenfelt together with one fixed 14in bow torpedo tube. Alternatively, the 3pdrs could be replaced by twin 14in tubes. Many had a mixed armament of one 3pdr and a twin tube. The bow tube proved to throw up so much water that it was removed or, in later boats, not fitted. They had a trial speed of about 20kts and a crew of sixteen. Many survived until the First World War when they were used for local patrols. By this time most, if not all, had been refitted with water tube boilers.

Numbers of First Class torpedo boats

Type	Date	Number built	
Lightning and similar	1876-80	19	
'113ft'	1884-86	4	
'125ft'	1885-86	53	
Larger boats	1882-85	16	
'140ft'	1892-94	12	Contemporary with first TBD
Ex-Indian	1887-89	7	
'160ft'	1901-05	12	

Seven slightly bigger boats (c135ft) were built for India

in 1887-89 but were not delivered and taken over for the RN in 1892 (renumbered 1901).

In the mid-1880s a small number of larger boats were ordered and some others were purchased. In 1884 J S White began building a much larger boat of 137 tons, 153ft 8in long. She was purchased for the RN as *Swift* (later *TB 81*) and with four 3pdrs and three torpedo tubes together with a speed of nearly 24kts she anticipated the concept of the destroyer. The 140ft boats were enlarged versions of the 125ft boats with much the same armament and a trial speed of about 24kts. Later boats were bigger again with an armament of three 3pdr and three 18in torpedo tubes.

All these torpedo boats were short, and with a low freeboard they were severely limited even in moderate weather. Their light construction and reciprocating engines led to heavy vibration which partially accounted for the short life of machinery and hull.

Second Class torpedo boats

These small torpedo boats were intended to be carried on board larger ships, including the depot ships *Hecla* and *Vulcan*. Displacement increased from 11 tons in 1878 to about 16 tons in 1889 after which no more were built. They carried one or two 14in torpedoes in dropping gear and a machine-gun, having a speed of 15-16kts. The White 'Turnabout' boats of 1883-88 were seen as successful and were developed into the slower but more seaworthy 56ft picket boats for general use, including torpedo dropping. Between 1878 and 1889, sixty-four of these boats were built for the RN and about nine for colonial forces.

Novelty

Unlike the small sloops and gunboats described in the next section, there were a considerable number of experimental torpedo boats. Since their novel features were generally unsuccessful, they can be described only briefly here.

First Class

TB 13 was given a brass hull, presumably to reduce corrosion which was a serious problem in thin steel craft.

TB 34 introduced White's 'Turnabout' form with a long rounded cut-up and tandem rudders to give improved turning ability.

TB 79 had the first triple-expansion engine in torpedo boats.

TB 90 had water tube boilers and an experimental 4-cylinder engine, as did *TB 93*, the only twin-screw torpedo boat.

36. This section is based on *Conway's All the World's Fighting Ships 1860-1905* which should be consulted for details.

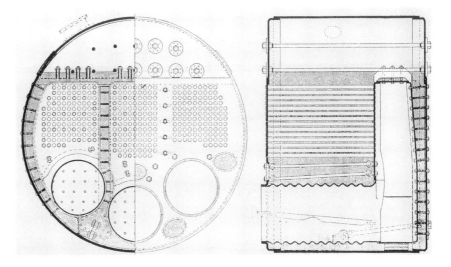

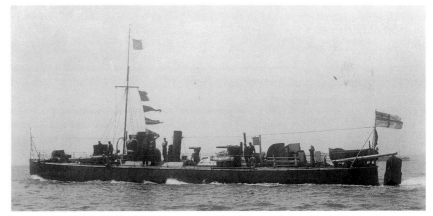

Top: A typical cylindrical boiler. Note the corrugated flue giving radial strength whilst permitting longitudinal expansion. (Author's collection)

Above: TB 25, built by Thornycroft in 1885 as the first of the 125ft boats. She carries a mixed armament with torpedo tubes forward and a gun aft. (Author's collection)

Below: TB 75, another 125ft TB built by Yarrow in 1887 and lost in a collision in 1892. Some of her sisters served as patrol boats in the First World War. (Imperial War Museum: Q41445)

Sirius, designed by Reed and laid down in 1868. Originally classed as a sloop, she was re-rated as a corvette. (Imperial War Museum: Q40635)

Second Class

TB 73 was the only warship ordered from a foreign builder – Herreschoff. She had a wooden lower hull with steel topsides. Her propeller was well forward and quite a distance below the hull. She had a coil boiler which was very efficient on the rare occasions when it worked. She was only used for experiments and did not enter service. The coil boiler was tried briefly in *TB 76* and *77* but was soon replaced by locomotive boilers.

TB 98 had Ruthven jet propulsion as described in Chapter 2.

Though none of these experiments were noticeably successful, they all seem to have been ideas worth trying and further damage the legend of a reactionary Admiralty.

Small, unarmoured warships 1860-1905

The smaller classes of warship had few technical novelties and it is convenient to treat the whole period of the book in a single section. All their perceived roles, both in peace and war, put an emphasis on numbers, which in the limited budgets of the day, meant they had to be cheap to buy and economical to run. It is easy to show that 'better' ships were possible but any comparison must be on the more difficult 'whole force' basis as better ships would be more expensive and hence fewer would be available. The conflict between quality and quantity is inevitable and there is usually no clear solution. However, the cheap ship, however numerous, must have adequate capability. It is not surprising nor is it necessarily a matter for criticism that these cheap and simple ships showed few technical innovations, other than a few selected for special trials of machinery etc.

It was seen as essential that these ships, usually operating far from coaling stations, should have full sail power. For a number of reasons, resistance to gunshot and ease of sheathing against fouling etc, it was seen as desirable that most of these ships should have a wooden skin. Both these points will be discussed later.

Numbers

The ships discussed in this brief section comprise fifty-five corvettes, seventy-two sloops, seventy-six gun vessels, sixty-eight conventional gunboats together with forty-two 'flatirons' and other unusual vessels. In addition, in 1860, there were a large number of older vessels available, many built during the Crimean War. These comprised:[37] twenty-eight screw frigates plus eighteen still building, twenty-two screw corvettes, twenty-six screw sloops, sixteen paddle frigates and thirty-six paddle sloops. There were also five sailing frigates and five sailing sloops and many[38] small gunboats of the Crimean War programme.

The majority of the new, small ships were built prior

Small warship building 1860-1904

Class	1860-4	65-69	70-74	75-79	80-84	85-89	90-94	95-99	00-04	Total
Corvette	5	14	12	12	12	-	-	-	-	55
Sloop	14	7	6	11	9	8	3	4	10	72
Gun Vessel	29	17	18	6	4	2	-	-	-	76
Gun Boat	-	20	9	2	14	10	9	4	-	68
'Flatiron'	-	4	21	15	2	-	-	-	-	42

to 1880 when their work was increasingly taken over by Second and Third Class cruisers derived from *Iris*.

Categories

The distinction between corvette – which soon became bigger than older frigates still in service – and sloop and also to a lesser extent between sloop and gun vessel was unclear; at least one class was reclassified. In appearance, layout and technical features, sloops were generally small corvettes. Corvettes were commanded by a captain, sloops and gun vessels by commanders and gun boats by lieutenants.

The hull

The material and style of construction breaks down as follows:

Category	Wooden	Iron	Composite	Steel
Frigates	18 (old)	3	-	-
Corvettes	23	6	13	11
Sloops	21	-	32	18
Gun vessels	45	-	27	2
Gunboats	20	-	44	4

The principal objection to an iron skin was that a shot passing through the ship would hit the far side at low velocity and, instead of puncturing a neat hole, would tear the seams for a considerable distance.[39] The three iron frigates had a wooden sheath to reduce the likelihood of such damage and make repair easier should it occur.[40]

Ships in distant waters would have little opportunity to dock and clean their bottoms, whilst fouling on an iron hull would be very rapid in tropical waters. It would have been essential to add wood sheathing with copper over as in *Inconstant*. Since the hull would have to be sheathed with wood anyway, it seemed sensible to use it as the skin, reinforced with iron stringers and frames. There was enough iron structure for strength in these short ships and also to resist the vibration from the propeller. Many of these composite ships had a very long life which suggests that their strength was fully adequate to prevent working and consequential rot in the planking.[41]

There was also a belief at the time that wooden skins withstood grounding better than iron hulls. White discusses this at some length[42] and, based on some admittedly limited tests by Fairbairn, concludes that an oak plank 3in thick is equivalent to ¼in iron whilst 6in of oak equates to 1in iron. (Planking resists as the square of thickness, iron linearly as thickness.) Metal ships with a double bottom were very satisfactory but smaller ships with a single bottom may well have been inferior in grounding to a wooden-skinned hull. There is little doubt that repairs to a planked hull would be easier when far from a dockyard though the wood or composite hull would be heavier than an iron hull.

Until 1873 the hull form was based entirely on experience but in that year William Froude began a series of model tests in his ship tank, completed the previous year. He compared the *Encounter* with the French *Infernet* showing that the greater length of the latter was beneficial at higher speeds giving her 1-1.5kts greater speed for much the same power. It was during this series of tests that Froude introduced his propeller dynamometer so that, for the first time, propellers could be designed to match the hull and engines.[43] This work shows that, though these ships were cheap and simple, proper attention was paid to every aspect of their design. Engines and boilers took up a great deal of space leaving little room for the crew forward and not much for the officers aft.

All these ships had good freeboard and hence were generally safe in all weathers. One of very few lost due to stress of weather was the *Condor* (1898) which foundered in 1901. Modern writers suggest that a principal cause of her loss was lack of experience in handling sailing ships.

The loss of HMS Condor[44]

The smaller ships of the era are usually described as very seaworthy but an article by Mrs J Faulkner suggests that some may have been lucky rather than safe. *Condor* was built of steel at Chatham in 1898 with a displacement of 980 tons, a length of 180ft and a beam of 33ft 3in. She had a triple-expansion engine of 1400ihp which gave her a speed of 13.5kts and was rigged as a barque. She was commissioned by Commander Sclater (Mrs Faulkner's great uncle) in November 1900 for the Pacific Squadron based in Victoria, British Columbia. As a result of experience on passage Commander Sclater complained to DNC of poor stability and heavy rolling, exacerbated by inadequate freeing ports in the high bulwarks. Mr Morrish, Assistant Constructor, did a simple calculation and decided that the captain was exaggerating.

Condor sailed from Esquimault on 2 December 1901

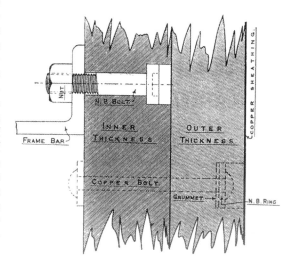

37. This table and much else is derived from H C Timewell's section on masted cruisers in *Conway's All the World's Fighting Ships 1860-1905*.

38. Some of the gunboats decayed early, having been built of green timber and it is uncertain how many were fit for service in 1860; a figure of 169 has been quoted but it is uncertain how many of these would have passed survey.

39. Barnaby makes it clear that this was his prime concern in several of his papers. Many writers say that it was fear of the plate shattering in brittle fashion but this was not the designer's worry; they were unaware of the effect of temperature and that wrought iron could have shattered in winter temperatures. This problem would also have affected the steel ships though possibly to a lesser extent.

40. Firing trials against replicas of the *Simoom* at Portsmouth in 1850-51 suggest this sheath would have been ineffective.

41. *Gannet* (1878) is slowly being restored at Chatham.

42. White, *A Manual of Naval Architecture*, p336.

43. This dynamometer remained in use until the fast minelayers of the late 1930s. It remained on display at Haslar, together with the original model of the *Encounter* propeller until 1995 when the museum was closed by the Defence Research Agency. The equipment is held in store at the Science Museum. It took some time to develop an accurate design process.

44. J Faulkner, 'HMS *Condor* is Missing', *The Mariner's Mirror* Vol 67 (London 1981).

This sketch shows the composite system of construction in which two thicknesses of timber were bolted to iron frames. Such ships were easy to repair, could be copper sheathed and were durable. *Gannet* of this style is currently (1996) being restored in Chatham Historic Dockyard.

Briton, a wooden corvette of 1868 designed by Reed. (Imperial War Museum: Q40814)

and was not seen again. There was a very heavy storm on 3 December; a lighthouse keeper on Vancouver Island reported wind Force 10-11, veering rapidly. Wreckage was eventually discovered spread over many miles of the coast.

In an annex to the article, Professor D Faulkner describes some modern experiments on a model of *Condor* at Glasgow University. The first step was calculation of stability particulars – allowing for 48 tons of coal which *Condor* carried on deck when she sailed.

Stability and capsize

Ship	Max GZ at angle°	Vanishing angle (°)	Fate
Condor	26	60	Disappeared 1901
Wasp	30	63 (gun vessel)	Disappeared 1887
Captain	23	54	Capsized 1870
Monarch	40	70	
Inconstant	50	Over 90	

It seems unlikely to be a coincidence that the three ships which sank had the poorest stability in terms of an early maximum GZ.[45]

It was found that *Condor*'s high bulwarks could trap at least 100 tons of water and possibly twice that amount. The freeing ports had an area of 18sq ft per side compared with 33.3sq ft for *Cutty Sark* of similar deck area. The 5ft model was tested in following and quartering seas of various lengths and heights corresponding to 15 to 25ft. A wind of 50-60kts in the direction of the sea was simulated. It was thought most likely that she had broached and early tests studied this possibility, but it

was found that the greatest danger came in fairly short following seas. A wave would pass the poop and break onto the main deck. The weight of water would cause her to loll, putting the freeing ports under. The next two waves would make things worse and she would capsize on the fourth encounter.

Professor Faulkner envisage two possible scenarios which could have led to the tragedy. In the first it is assumed that Commander Sclater, already worried about the stability of his ship, would keep head to sea. In the severe storm she would lose headway and fall beam to sea when she would be blown over. Alternatively, he may have run for shelter in Juan de Fuca Sound and capsized as described above. It seems that it was nearly 20 years since Commander Sclater had served in a sailing ship.

The rig of the surviving ships was much reduced and no more rigged vessels were built. In a lengthy passage, Admiral of the Fleet Lord Chatfield describes his concern on taking office in 1933 to find plans to re-introduce sail training. He felt the danger to be great because of the lack of experienced officers and petty officers, while there would be little benefit.[46]

Engines and boilers

Apart from a few deliberate experiments, the machinery of these ships followed the practice of the day. Timewell gives a breakdown:

Engine type	Frigates	Corvettes	Sloops
Simple expansion	20	16	22
Compound	1	37	24
Triple expansion	-	-	25

45. One may note the same result in the Great Pacific Typhoon of 1944 in which the three destroyers which sank had the poorest GZ.

46. Lord Chatfield, *It might Happen Again* (London 1947).

47. This was not seen as important; vibration was something you put up with until more delicate electronics had to be coddled after the Second World War.

Contemporary writers criticised these ships for their lack of speed and most recent writers have copied this view. In particular, it is pointed out that most of them were slower than the fast mail steamers of their day. The bigger vessels, corvettes, had trial speeds of about 13-14kts, sloops could make about 12kts until the late 1880s when speeds rose to about 14kts. Gun vessels were usually around 10kts as were most gunboats except the 'flatirons' which could only make 8.5kts.

However, they had a substantial speed advantage over most cargo ships, few of which made more than 9kts on trial and would lose speed to fouling far more rapidly than the copper-sheathed warships (see figures from Carnavon Committee). They were less fitted to chase raiders; it was generally thought that mail steamers with higher speeds would be used but the opening of the First World War showed that such fast ships were unsuitable either as raiders or escorts in consequence of their very high coal consumption. French cruisers of the period were a little faster (due mainly to greater length) but they, too, would have run out of coal quickly had they used full power for long. Since these British ships were so much better suited for escort rather than chasing, it is surprising that contemporary thought was so strongly opposed to convoy.

Speed is always useful but is also costly. *Encounter* made about 13kts from her 2000ihp and Froude's tests show that, had it been possible to double the power without increasing the size of the ship, her speed would only have increased to 14.5kts. In fact, such a ship would have been bigger, leading to a further increase in power and the cost would have increased dramatically. In most scenarios, two 13kt ships are more valuable than one 15kt vessel. This particularly applies to the earlier years; once a complete telegraph system was available it was possible to direct a smaller number of fast ships.

Full sailing rig cost about 1.5kts under steam due to air drag on the masts and rigging but was deemed necessary due to the lack of coal depots in distant waters. However, they were not good under sail either, as the aperture left by a hoisting propeller affected their handling whilst the drag of fixed, twin propellers was worse. Initially, twin propellers were used only on shallow draught ships such as the Crimean gunboats and the *Penelope* whose proportions were such that they were poor performers under steam or sail anyway. However, this performance was blamed on their twin screws which had a bad reputation in consequence. In fact, there was little to choose between single- and twin-screw propulsion as regards hydrodynamic efficiency but a twin-shaft machinery plant would be significantly bigger. Against that, the single screw would cause more severe vibration.[47]

Endurance

Endurance under steam was not seen as particularly important but a few typical figures are given in the following table.

Endurance of corvettes and sloops

Ship	Type	Launch	Engines	Endurance at 10kts (nm)
Amethyst	Corvette	1873	Cmpd	2-2500
Emerald	Corvette	1876	Cmpd	2-2250
Bacchante	Corvette	1876	Cmpd	3000
Satellite	Corvette	1881	Cmpd	6000
Calypso	Corvette	1881	Cmpd	4000
Nymphe	Sloop	1873	Cmpd	1000
Mariner	Sloop	1884	Cmpd	19-2300
Nymphe	Sloop	1887	T Exp	3000
Condor	Sloop	1898	T Exp	3000

Armament

From the early 1860s, corvettes and sloops received an armament of muzzle-loading rifles (MLR) with 64pdrs backed by a smaller number of 7in or even, in the biggest, 9in MLR. By about 1873, most ships in service re-armed with an all-64pdr armament. The breech-loader came in on new ships in the late 1880s and such weapons were retro-fitted to some of the more effective, older ships. Only the few sloops built in the 1890s received quick-firers.

The 64pdrs were almost always mounted on truck carriages at broadside ports. The larger MLR were normally mounted on swivel carriages with an elaborate systems of rails so that they could be traversed to either beam and often to bow and stern ports as well. It is doubtful if big guns could be moved in this way except in a calm. There was debate on whether small ships might have to fight on both sides and it was argued that the *Alabama-Kearsage* action showed that circling ships would usually present the same side to each other.

Fantome, a steel sloop of 1901. (Imperial War Museum: Q21244)

The *Alabama* was caught and sunk by the much more powerful USS *Kearsage*. Records of the battle are probably not too reliable but Wilson[48] suggests the following. Fire was opened at 900yds and *Kearsage* hit with the first round. The range closed to about 500yds and, in all, *Kearsage* fired 173 shells with 5-second fuse, claiming 40 hits. *Alabama* fired about 370 rounds of which 14 hit the hull of *Kearsage* and about twice as many hit the masts and rigging. Even on a calm, clear day it was not easy to hit at close range with a big gun from a small ship.

Cost

They were cheap ships; two late examples from 1888 were *Melita* (sloop) at £65,619 and *Pheasant* (gunboat) at £40,951. Some comparative costs for labour on the hull are:[49]

Category	£/ton
Corvettes	32
Sloops	32
Composite gunboats	31
Iron gunboats	46
Steel gunboats	47

Trials

Because these ships were cheap to build and run, they were often used to try new machinery, such as compound engines, and for firing trials of new guns. One interesting trial was of the Lumley rudder in which the rear section moved through double the angle of the forward part, very greatly increasing the force developed. This was tried in *Bullfinch* in 1862, the *Locust* in 1863 and in the sloop *Columbine* where the turning circle

was reduced from 818yds to 625yds. Similar ideas for flapped rudders have been tried more recently and have always been rejected on the grounds that such a vital item as the rudder should be very simple, although the flapped fin is often used in stabilisers.

'Flatiron' or Rendel gunboats

In 1865, Armstrong's were concerned by restrictions on their test site at Whitley Bay and mounted a heavy gun for test on a barge. This gave George Rendel the idea for a small gunboat mounting a heavy gun and he persuaded the Admiralty to purchase such a vessel. This ship, the *Staunch*, carried a 9in, 12½-ton MLR on a displacement of 200 tons and was the first RN ship without sails and was launched in 1867. The gun was mounted on a platform which could be lowered into the hold on hydraulic jacks for passage, the complete unit weighing 22 tons. It could be raised in 6-8 minutes even with the ship rolling up to 11° either way.[50] It was also loaded hydraulically and could be worked by six men instead of the usual crew of sixteen .

The gun fired over the bow and could be trained 5° either way by tackles; larger angles of train involved turning the vessel; with twin screws, working in opposition, she could turn in her own length (75ft) in 2 minutes 45 seconds and when moving ahead she could turn in three times her length in 2 minutes 15 seconds.

Rendel's original concept was for coastal defence where these ships, with a draught of about 6ft 6in, could use shallow water outside navigational channels and fire on an attacking force at close range. The weakness in this idea was the motion of small, shallow, flat-bottomed craft in the slightest sea. In these conditions it is very much easier to hit a small vessel from a large one than *vice versa*. Their rate of fire was so slow that they were vulnerable to attack by armed launches. Their attraction was the cost – *Staunch* cost £6719 – and twenty-seven somewhat similar vessels with a 10in, 18-ton MLR were built between 1870 and 1881 (two more later). They had a very long life, due in part to the heavy scantlings needed to accept the weight and recoil of such a big gun, and some worked off the Belgian coast in 1914-15 whilst others survived as lighters till about 1960.[51]

Spencer Robinson told the 1871 Committee that they also had a role in coastal attack and this is supported by work carried out by William Froude in his tank at Torquay. He was asked to develop a hull form which would give them 8.5kts under their own power and which could be towed in the open sea at up to 15kts. The form was derived from the Crimean gunboat *Snake* which had a resistance of 1.98 tons at 9kts, Froude's first design had a resistance of 1.5 tons cut to 1.28 tons by the thirteenth model. He thought the later forms would be safe to tow at 15kts.[52] The later, somewhat similar, *Medina* class carried a more practical armament of three 64pdrs. (See also the armoured gunboats in Chapter 2.)

48. See note 1.

49. Navy Estimates 1881.

50. R M Anderson, 'The Rendel Gunboats', *Warship International* 1/1976 (Toledo 1976).

51. The later *Drudge* is visible (1993) in a Portsmouth scrapyard whilst a similar Norwegian craft was in use as a car ferry well into the 1980s.

52. R W L Gawn, 'Historical note on the investigations at the Admiralty Experiment Works, Torquay', *Trans INA* (London 1941).

Staunch, 1867, the first of the Rendel 'Flatiron' gunboats and the first warship built without sails. (NPA)

White and the *Royal Sovereigns* | Eight

WILLIAM HENRY White was born at Devonport on 2 February 1845 and became an apprentice at the Dockyard there in March 1859. He passed into the Royal School of Naval Architecture at South Kensington in 1864 as top of the eight Dockyard students. He passed out three years later, still top, though pressed hard by W G John and F Elgar in particular. His early career has frequently been referred to in previous chapters and needs only to be highlighted here. Unusually, he excelled in every aspect of work; on the more theoretical side one should note his work on strength for Reed and his many contributions to stability, and he was just as successful in creative design work, in management and, less obvious, in teaching, from which sprang his most valuable – and readable – *Manual of Naval Architecture.*

In January 1883 he left to join Armstrong's as Warship Designer and Manager of Warship Building. His total Admiralty salary had been £651 while at Armstrong he was paid £2000 plus 2/- per ton for all warships and 1/- for merchant ships built by Armstrong's. During the next two years he designed several notable ships including the highly-regarded cruisers *Naniwa* for Japan and *Panther* for Austria.

Re-organisation, 1885

When Barnaby resigned in 1885 the First Lord, Lord George Hamilton, decided to re-organise the Controller's departments and persuaded White to return as DNC. This involved some complicated deals both with White and with Armstrong. White agreed to accept a considerable drop in income and the Admiralty agreed to release Philip Watts to take his place at Armstrong's. White was to be available for consultation for the remainder of his original 5-year contract, though only in respect of designs to which he had contributed.

White took up office on 1 August 1885 and commenced a review of the relationship between DNC and E-in-C, together with a re-organisation of the Royal Dockyards.[1] Both these areas had been subjected to frequent change in recent years and the Admiralty wished for a better and lasting organisation. White pointed out very clearly that a Dockyard was very different from a private shipyard, as it was a naval arsenal and even an operating base as well as a building and repair yard, whilst all these functions were subject to Parliamentary control. White proposed that the industrial role should

be separated as far as was possible and placed under a Chief Constructor, responsible through the newly-created Director of Dockyards to the DNC. White also proposed a new system of management accounting, independently audited.

Some idea of the relative size of the various Royal Dockyards is given in the table below giving the workforce of shipwrights, the key trade, and the total number at each yard. As well as shipwrights there were: caulkers, joiners, labourers, riggers, ropemakers, sail makers, sawyers, millwrights, blockmakers, boilermakers, brazers, bricklayers, toolmakers, coppersmiths, engine keepers, fitters, founders, gas makers, hosemakers, locksmiths, messengers, oarmakers, pattern makers, mast makers, painters, paviours, plumbers and stokers.

The Dockyard organisation was by far the largest industrial 'firm' in the country while the biggest individual yards were high up in size.

The Ritchie Committee, set up to supervise the re-organisation, approved White's proposals, as did the Treasury, and they were implemented in a Controller's Instruction of 1 February 1886. White was given the additional title of Assistant Controller and the E-in-C was to report to him. On the same day that these instructions were issued, the Government was defeated and Gladstone became Prime Minister with the Marquess of Ripon as First Lord. He appointed Dr Elgar as Director of Dockyards and made him independent of the DNC. Since it was soon clear that White was grossly overloaded, this change may well have been sensible but White saw it as a breach in the agreement by which he had returned. Matters were made worse since Elgar had been Reed's assistant and active in attacking both the Admiralty and White himself.

Since the Crimean War the Navy's guns had been ordered by the War Office, a seemingly sensible arrangement since both used the same suppliers. However, particularly when funds were scarce, friction was inevitable, even after the formation of a joint Ordnance Committee in 1879. In 1882 it was decided

Sir William White was the greatest warship designer of all time and also a superb manager. (Author's collection)

1. Brown, *A Century of Naval Construction.*

Numbers in the Dockyards

	Chatham	Sheerness	Portsmouth	Devonport	Pembroke	Total
Shipwrights	618	367	831	749	373	4839
Total workforce	1428	858	1973	1810	735	6370

A view of one of the Dockyards with an early TBD. (RCNC Archives)

that the cost of naval guns should be paid from naval votes and there was a transfer of design responsibility to the Admiralty. The 1886 re-organisation also created a Naval Ordnance Department under Captain John Fisher, at last largely giving the Navy control over its own guns, though there were initial difficulties in transferring funding, finally cleared as part of the Naval Defence Act financing.

Most of White's changes survived, making the vast new building programme possible by making the Dockyards into by far the fastest builders in the country and the world, so demonstrating White's managerial skill.

The Naval Defence Act of 1889[2]

The fears for the capability of the Navy initiated by the 'Truth about the Navy' articles in 1884,[3] discussed earlier, had not been quelled by the small Northbrook building programme. By the end of that year there was a real danger of conflict with Russia and in 1885 a 'Particular Service Squadron' was commissioned under Admiral Hornby as a Baltic expeditionary force. The exercise carried out by this force at Berehaven, simulating a naval attack on a heavily-defended anchorage, was of great value (see Chapter 5) but further exposed the weakness of the Navy.

In July 1886 the short-lived government headed by Gladstone was replaced by Lord Salisbury as Prime Minister and Lord George Hamilton as First Lord. The Naval Lords were headed by Sir Arthur Hood with W Graham as Controller and including Captain Lord Beresford. Initially, the Board's concern was for reform of the Admiralty itself; Beresford was pursing the very real need for a Naval Staff in the guise of the Intelligence

Department but, after achieving limited success, he resigned and used his seat as an MP to agitate for a stronger navy. White's reforms of the dockyard organisation and his changes to the accounting system gave confidence that any additional funding would be used quickly, efficiently and economically.

In June 1887 White, who had been in office for a year and was only 42 years old, sent a memo to the Board drawing attention to the number of ships which were obsolescent, or would become so within the next 5 years. His paper included very detailed proposals for the number and type of replacement ships together with planned building schedules and a detailed estimate of the rate of spending. Altogether, he proposed the scrapping of seventy-two obsolete ships and their replacement by modern vessels at a cost of £9 million.[4] Reaction within the Board was mixed; the First Lord told the Parliamentary Select Committee that '. . . I was not certain that either the Controller or the First Naval Lord would acquiesce in the recommendations of the Director of Naval Construction.' The First Naval Lord and the Controller did, indeed, propose an alternative programme and the full Board then considered both proposals.

There was a strange report in June 1888 that the Naval Lords were satisfied with the strength of the Navy and did not recommend a large building programme. This may merely have been the tradition support given by public servants to their minister but the First Lord's statement accompanying the 1888 Estimates suggests a more fundamental cause. He said that there had never been a full study of the naval requirements of the Empire; that the procedure had been for the First Lord to get as much money as he could from the cabinet and for the Board to do the best they could with those funds. White's memo and the questions raised about it by Lord Hamilton had forced a more fundamental examination. Hood's objections were probably related to his wish for turret ships rather than White's proposal for guns mounted in barbettes with high freeboard.

The final proposal was for a somewhat bigger programme than that put forward by White but differing little in principle. The Board proposed that over the following five years the building programme should include ten battleships, thirty-seven cruisers and eighteen torpedo gunboats. This was put to the Cabinet in a memo dated 1 December 1888.[5] The Chancellor, George Goschen, had only the previous month opposed increasing expenditure on the Navy on the grounds that more warships were not needed. One may suspect that this was a ritual protest as Chancellor; he had been First Lord and was aware of the weakness of the Navy and the success of the eventual Act owed much to his clever handling of the funding.

There was further pressure for a stronger navy from a forceful speech by Beresford in the House in mid-December. In February 1889 a report[6] on the naval manoeuvres of 1888 was presented to both Houses of Parliament. This report showed that the Navy was 'altogether inadequate to take the offensive in a war with only one great power . . . and . . . supposing a combination of two great powers to be allied as her enemies, the balance of maritime power would be against England.' This restatement of the Two Power Standard carried great weight even though the Admiralty tried to show that all was well.

Finally, on 7 March 1889, Lord George Hamilton introduced the Naval Defence Act authorising the building of seventy ships between 1889 and 1894 at a cost of £21.5 million. He re-iterated the traditional but often neglected 'Two Power Standard' going even further in proposing that the RN ships should be larger than foreign equivalents to allow for the greater endurance needed. Hamilton also said that '. . .if there are any nations abroad who do wish to compete with us in naval armaments, the mere enunciation of this scheme will show to them the utter futility of their desire', a hope which was not to be fulfiled. The ships were:

7 *Royal Sovereign* plus one *Hood*
2 *Centurion*
9 *Edgar*
8 *Astraea*
21 *Apollo*
4 *Pallas*
18 *Sharpshooter* TGB

It is hard to make a valid comparison of the strength of leading navies at that date. The following table compares the number of 'effective' ships in various categories for Britain, France and Russia but there is considerable doubt over the effectiveness of some ships

included, *eg Warrior* and *Black Prince* as 'cruisers', and the many wooden-hulled ships in the French list. Building was even slower in France than in England and it is uncertain which ships were actually available. The comparison is even more difficult of the technical factors affecting operational effectiveness such as compound versus steel armour, the value of armour piercing projectiles, reliability of boilers and engines in sustained high speed etc. Only thirty ships, mostly small, were removed from the effective list so that the new construction appeared as an addition. The Navy had to wait for Fisher's much needed pruning of 1904 to get rid of obsolete hulks.

Comparison of fleet strengths 1889[7]

	Britain	*France*	*Russia*
First Class battleships	22	14	7
Second Class battleships	15	6	1
Armoured cruisers	13	7	8
Coast defence ships	11	6	7

White's very detailed planning took into account the availability of slips and other facilities. Since the new ships were to be much longer than earlier vessels, there was a shortage of long slips and some of the Dockyard ships would have to be built in dry-dock. Pembroke had to be provided with better lifting gear to install machinery and so on. White is understandably famous for his design work but it is arguable that he was even greater as a planner and manager. At this date, battleship building was primarily done in the Royal Dockyards. From *Warrior* to *Trafalgar* twenty-seven battleships were built in the Yards and eighteen in private shipyards, mostly in the early years (purchased ships excluded). From *Royal Sovereign* to *Dreadnought* thirty-two were built in the Dockyards and eighteen in private yards. Once the Dockyards learnt the technique of working in metal, they were usually much faster than private shipyards. It is likely that better management following White's reforms and greater investment in equipment led to their success.[8]

The financial provisions of the Act were cleverly conceived and departed considerably from normal practice; indeed, the whole Act, committing expenditure for five years ahead, was a breach of Parliamentary custom. Six battleships, twenty cruisers and twelve TGBs were to be built in the Royal Dockyards at a cost of £11.5 million provided under normal Estimates. In addition, a further £4.75 million was provided to complete ships already building in the Dockyards. The total sum of £16.75 million was to be available in five equal installments but money not spent in any year was not, as usual, to be returned to the Treasury but placed in a special account for use in later years. Should it be necessary to spend

2. Based on Sumida, Parkes and Manning together with re-examination of PRO papers referenced therein.

3. See Chapter 7 – *Orlandos*.

4. If the five surviving *Audacious* class were retained as effective, this figure could be reduced to £7.5 million.

5. Naval Estimates 1888-89. Lord George Hamilton, PRO CAB 37/22.

6. By Admirals Dowell, Vesey Hamilton and Richards.

7. Parkes, *British Battleships*, p353.

8. B Newman, Research Papers 1 and 3, History of British Shipbuilding project, University of Glasgow.

more than the allocation in any one year, the extra was to be made available by the Treasury from the Consolidated Fund or by borrowing.

The funding of the contract-built ships – four battleships, twenty-two cruisers and six TGBs – was an even bigger departure from traditional financial rectitude. The total cost of £10 million was to be paid into the special fund mentioned above in seven equal, annual installments. Since it was planned to complete the ships in five years, this implied a deficit in funding until the sixth and seventh installments were paid which would be met from the Consolidated Fund or borrowing. Other financial changes introduced at the same time reduced the impact of this considerable increase in spending on the budget as a whole.[9]

Expenditure on shipbuilding increased by about £2.5 million a year whilst the continuity of work proposed meant that both management and labour would be encouraged to improve productivity. Like most great changes, the Naval Defence Act of 1889 involved bringing together a number of topics – the demand for a bigger navy largely triggered by Beresford, a government which supported a strong defence, Goschen's clever financing together with White's vision of the future navy supported by his Dockyard and accounting

reforms to be followed by his brilliant designs for the ships approved. There were some problems in the execution of the programme, discussed in later sections, which added £1.35 million to the cost and delayed completion by a year but, by and large, the programme was very successful.

The *Royal Sovereign*s

In August 1888 White was recalled from sick leave to attend a special meeting of the Board, held at Devonport, to consider the designs for the new battleships. The First Sea Lord, Hood, was a strong supporter of turret ships and White was directed to prepare a design for an improved *Trafalgar*. Hood was probably surprised by the effect of his improvements on size and cost.

Improving the *Trafalgar*
Increase natural draught speed to 17kts – 70 per cent more power, machinery weight by 50 per cent, 560 tons

Increase endurance – 300 tons coal

Increased length of armour to cover bigger machinery – 240 tons

Royal Sovereign 1891, White's first battleship as Director. Bigger than earlier ships and with a high freeboard, they were then regarded as excellent seaboats. The 6in QF guns were an important part of the armament, intended to demolish the unprotected areas of a battleship. The weight of ten such guns, with their casemates and enhanced ammunition supply, was very considerable. (National Maritime Museum, London: 20010, 20012)

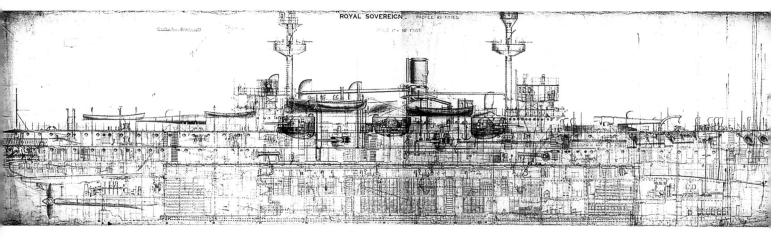

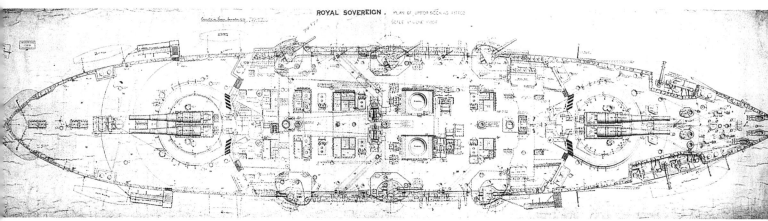

A 13.5in barbette aboard a *Royal Sovereign*. The guns had to be trained fore-and-aft to load. (Author's collection)

Raising guns 2ft – 120 tons of turret armour
Secondary armament – 270 tons
Bigger hull to carry above – 1000 tons
Larger complement – 540 to 700 with more space and
  stores.

The new ship would displace 16,000 tons and cost about £1 million, 25 per cent more than *Trafalgar*. The way in which different factors interact is well described by Admiral Sir R Bacon writing of a later *Dreadnought*:[10] 'I did not, at the time, appreciate that the 350 tons increase in armament weight would mean, approximately, over 1000 tons in weight to the ship; for, in order to float the extra 350 tons, the hull would have to be increased in length; and the increase in length of hull again meant more horsepower to obtain the same speed; moreover, the armoured deck and side armour would also have to be lengthened, so that a considerably larger displacement than that merely due to the weight of armament would become necessary.'[11]

White also submitted other designs for turret ships down to 11,700 tons for comparison with the French *Brennus* and also a range of barbette ships. Another meeting was held on 16 November 1888 to consider these proposals and agree on the principal features of the new ships. The main topics for discussion were:

Turret ship versus barbette.
The guns of both main and secondary armament and
  their arrangement.
Height of freeboard, noting that top weight virtually
  precluded a high-freeboard turret ship.

Whether the armour should be used over a single citadel
  or whether there should be separate redoubts for each
  main gun mounting.
Speed

It should be noted that both professional and naval opinion was divided on all these questions and that there were a number of lesser but still important aspects to be decided. It would seem that the meeting was aware that considerable extra funds would become available since all their decisions favoured bigger, more expensive designs.

The meeting decided that seven ships should be high-freeboard barbette ships with a twin mount in a separate redoubt at each end. There seems to have been a preference for a new 12in gun but it was clear that it would not be available in time and it was agreed to stay with the 13.5in, 67-ton gun. The secondary armament was to consist of ten 6in QF, widely distributed both longitudinally and vertically.

The main belt was to be 18in of compound armour with an upper belt of 4in of steel armour, backed by coal bunkers. This would stop any high-capacity HE shell from penetrating and would make it unlikely that the 3in deck would be hit by an intact projectile.

Narbeth has described the atrocious conditions under which the design team worked:[12] 'Ship designs were prepared in attics in the roof of the old Admiralty building, and in various rooms in the old shops extending from the Admiralty towards Charing Cross. Men were crowded into these miserable, unhealthy places, and the whole staff was inadequate for the burden of that day –

9. J Sumida, *In Defence of Naval Supremacy* (Winchester (Mass) and London 1989).

10. Admiral Sir R Bacon, *From 1900 Onwards* (London 1940).

11. Student naval architects used to be taught the 'weight equation', a mathematical process which modelled the effect of adding a weight while preserving other characteristics such as speed, endurance etc. Depending on speed, the increase in displacement was 3-5 times the added weight. Though crude, it was the forerunner of modern computer design algorithms.

12. J H Narbeth, 'Fifty Years of Naval Progress' *The Shipbuilder* (London November 1927).

preparing for the Naval Defence Act. For instance, in attic rooms No. 86 and 87 Mr W H Whiting and Mr Richards prepared the design of the *Royal Sovereign* class and of HMS *Barham* etc. . . . Mr E Beaton occupied the ground floor of an old saddler's shop next to the passage way to Spring Gardens, which is now closed – and there prepared the designs of HMS *Hood* etc.' At this time, the Controller's department comprised:

1 Director	1 Engineer-in-Chief
1 Surveyor	2 Inspectors
2 Chief Constructors	4 Asst Engineers
3 Constructors	1 Chief Inspector of
9 Asst Constructors	Timber
(1st class)[13]	1 Curator
6 Asst Constructors	
(2nd class)	
8 Draughtsmen	

The design department moved into the new building in St James' Park about 1894.

The *Royal Sovereign*s were generally seen as a success at the time, though there was considerable opposition from supporters of turrets and from advocates of thicker and more extensive armour. On 10 April 1889, White read a paper to the Institution of Naval Architects[14] describing the design in considerable detail, explaining the reasons for the various decisions. Reed and other opponents were present and their objections were destroyed by White's factual evidence. In service, they were found very successful, with a few minor problems. Most were disposed of before war broke out and hence they could not be proved in action.[15] Factual descriptions of these ships are readily available and will not be repeated here. Instead the following section will review the design, in the light of modern knowledge and of the changes which White himself made in later classes, to identify the causes of their success and point out a few weaknesses.

A Critique of the Royal Sovereign

The first reason for their success was that they were considerably larger and more expensive than previous classes. All design is a compromise but there are fewer and less critical compromises in a big ship. Tabular comparisons with foreign ships on guns, speed and armour will always favour the big ship. A big ship may still be a failure if there are faults in important aspects but the Naval Construction Department was by now a very professional organisation with a great fund of experience and expertise. It was this fund which enabled White to demolish his opponents in debate; he could produce sound theory, model tests or full-scale trials in support of each decision.

There were many opposed to large battleships, including Sir Nathaniel Barnaby. He supported a strange proposal for ships of 3200 tons armed with two

9.2in and light protection, arguing that five of these toys could be bought for the price of one 'Admiral'.[16] White demolished such arguments in a Cabinet paper of 1895, the main points of which are included in the following paragraphs.[17]

Reed argued that though the new ships were intended to be considerably faster than the *Trafalgar* and were bigger, power had not been increased in proportion. White pointed out that the power required was based on Edmund Froude's model tests,[18] now a well-proven procedure. It should also be appreciated that the initial form sent for testing was developed using an increasing basis of knowledge from earlier tests. In this case, the *Royal Sovereign* form was relatively longer than that of the *Trafalgar*. Performance depends on many aspects of form but the most important for faster ships is the ratio of length to the cube root of the underwater volume.[19] Reed's failure to understand is surprising as he was instrumental in sponsoring William Froude's work.

The main armour protection consisted of an 18in belt of compound armour, 8½ft deep, extending from the fore to aft barbettes (reduced to 14in at the ends), capped by a 3in steel deck and with thick bulkheads at either end. Though guns afloat – including her own – could penetrate such a belt on the range at normal impact, it was effectively invulnerable under action conditions. The days of compound armour were numbered and it is, perhaps, a little surprising that all-steel armour was not used though any difference in performance at that date would have been small.

The barbettes rested on a solid redoubt of 16-17in plate, extending down two decks to the protective deck, enclosing the ammunition supply and operating machinery and protecting the barbette itself from explosions underneath. This was a great advance on previous ships, much reducing the vulnerability of barbette-mounted guns. There was still opposition to the barbette since it was claimed that the crew was unprotected. There seems to be very little to support this statement; the guns were loaded under armour and most of the crew of eleven men per twin mount would be protected. The gunlayer, alone, was exposed though he had a shield against machine-gun fire. Realistically, it was noted that the magazine crew (twenty men) and shell room crew (twelve men) were trained to replace casualties. Even so, White provided an armoured shield in later classes. The gun had to be trained fore-and-aft to load and it was argued that in this position the barrel itself was a big target. Since gunners of the day had difficulty in hitting a ship, the chance of a gun barrel being hit cannot have been great.

There was a belt of 4in steel over the deck height above the protective deck between the barbettes.[20] This was the main point of attack by critics who wanted thick armour but to increase to 18in would add 500 tons directly and much more in consequential increase. White knew from the *Resistance* trials (Chapter 6) that it

13. Plus one at Torquay as assistant to Mr Froude.

14. W H White, 'On the Designs for the New Battleships', *Trans INA* (London 1889). It closely followed the First Lord's statement on the Navy Estimates, 1889-90.

15. The *Fuji* and *Yashima* of the Russo-Japanese War were very similar in design.

16. Sir N Barnaby, 'The Protection of Buoyancy and Stability in Ships', *Trans INA* (London 1889).

17. Sir W H White, *The Characteristics and Dimensions of Battleships*, PRO CAB 1/2.

18. Tests were reported by Froude between November 1888 and February 1889. At the time of writing, the whereabouts of these reports is unclear; it is believed that the PRO copies are being transferred to the NMM whilst the Froudes' Museum, Haslar, copies are at the Science Museum store.

19. Froude called this Circ M = L,ft/3√(35.Dispt-tons). Length/beam ratio is unimportant for most forms.

20. At the time White read his paper to the INA it was uncertain whether this upper belt should be 4in or 5in and both figures are given on different pages. This seems to have been the first extensive use of steel armour in the RN.

21. There is a well-known saying in design offices that 'the best is the enemy of the good-enough'.

22. There were sixteen 6pdr and twelve 3pdr against torpedo boats.

23. White points out that this weight was very nearly equal to the total armament weight of *Fury*.

24. *Blucher* at Dogger Bank and *Defence* at Jutland are obvious examples of the hazards associated with ammunition passages.

25. For example the similar *Yashima* when mined.

Resolution 1892. The primitive wing bridges fore and aft show clearly. The upper deck 6in gun shields were later replaced by casemates. (Imperial War Museum: Q39971)

was likely that a 4in plate would explode any shell filled with high explosive and it was backed by closely divided bunkers 10½ft deep to protect buoyancy and stability. White said that if more weight became available, he would thicken this belt but it was 'good enough'.[21] The ends of the ship were protected by a 2½in deck, below water, which forward curved down to support the ram, with close subdivision above it. There were the usual objections to 'unprotected' ends but, as White said during the debate, the ends of the *Collingwood* had been flooded with little loss of capability (Chapter 6).

The secondary armament was an important and costly feature of the design. The 6in QF was still under development but its significance was appreciated. It was not an anti-destroyer weapon as in later Dreadnoughts[22] but was intended to destroy the unarmoured structure of battleships – the justification for the upper, 4in belt. The weight of these mounts and associated equipment was 500 tons compared with 140 tons in *Trafalgar* as designed (185 tons as completed).[23] The secondary battery needed eight men per gun together with eight more in each of the two magazines and seven in each shell room (total 110). There was also an ammunition party of about thirty men who would carry ammunition for the 6in, 6pdrs and 3pdrs.

To prevent more than one of these guns from being put out of action by a single hit, they were to be widely separated along the length and arranged on two decks. Consideration was given to the use of turrets for the secondary armament, but it was thought that the fixed armour of the casemate would provide better protection and the gun in a casemate could be hand-worked, making it less likely to be put out of action due to loss of power. The two guns each side on the main deck were protected by casemates, another lesson of the *Resistance* trials. The casemate had 6in protection on the face and 2in rear; each weighed about 20 tons. The problems of main deck casemates are discussed under cruisers. There were also six lighter guns each side on the main deck. As completed, the upper deck 6in were mounted in the open with light shields but in 1902-05 casemates were added.

An ammunition passage ran from the forward to the after barbette, on the centre line, just below the protective deck. This was the biggest weakness of the ship and perpetuated in later designs. The passage could transmit flash from an explosion[24] and could also spread flooding. As arranged in *Royal Sovereign*, it meant that the engine-room and both boiler-rooms were divided, port and starboard, which could – and did – lead to large angles of heel, even to capsize, in the event of damage.[25] The design office were only partially aware of the problem; the heel was calculated for flooding one such space but damage on a bulkhead, flooding two spaces was not considered. The reason for this was that the effects of extensive, asymmetric flooding were just too difficult to calculate before computers. It was assumed that the effect of flooding two spaces could be estimated by adding the effect of flooding each one singly but, very often, it is much more serious. Damage to ships of the era is considered in Chapter 10; all too many ships of all nations capsized, often very rapidly.

Hood 1891. Admiral Hood was a devotee of the turret and one of the *Royal Sovereign*s was so completed. Her stability was poor, as was her seakeeping. She was scuttled in 1914 to block the southern entrance to Portland Harbour and her remains can still be seen on a calm day. (Imperial War Museum: Q21356)

26. W H White, 'The Qualities and Performances of Recent First-Class Battleships', *Trans INA* (London 1894).

27. This trial was still quoted in my university course in 1949.

28. R A Buchanan (ed), *Engineers and Engineering* (Essay by D K Brown) (Bath 1996).

29. W H White, 'The Qualities and Performances of Recent First-Class Battleships', *Trans INA* (London 1894). His definition of 'load' is not entirely clear but includes armament, armour, coal, ammunition, stores and equipment. Also PRO CAB/1.

30. Whiting graduated from RN College in 1876, Beaton in 1878, both with second class certificates. White was Instructor in Naval Architecture until 1877.

The barbette design enabled the designer (Whiting) to give them an adequate freeboard (19ft 6in forward, about 10 per cent less than a modern guideline). The eighth ship of the programme, *Hood*, was a turret ship with a design freeboard of only 11ft 3in which meant she had difficulty in steaming fast even in calm water and lost speed rapidly as wave height increased. The low freeboard had other implications; since stability at large angles depends on freeboard, it was necessary to give *Hood* a much greater initial metacentric height, partially to offset her lack of freeboard.

As these figures show, *Hood* was still inferior to the barbette ships at large angles and when casemates were fitted for the upper deck 6in of the barbette ships in 1902-05, it was decided that *Hood*'s stability was insufficient for this work to be done. Roll period is roughly proportional to beam/√GM and this would imply that *Hood*'s roll period was some 7 per cent shorter than that of her half-sisters. In turn, this would lead to a more rapid roll, making accurate gunnery more difficult.

Hood finally showed that the turret ship as then understood was a failure. She was used in 1913-14 for successful tests of anti-torpedo bulges and, on the outbreak of war, she was scuttled to block the southern entrance to Portland harbour where, on a calm day, her remains are still visible.

Completion and service

It was intended that these ships should be completed three years after they were laid down and this was nearly achieved, a tribute to White's re-organisation of the Dockyards. *Royal Sovereign* was pushed on even more rapidly, completing in 2 years and 8 months at Portsmouth, already the fastest building yard in the United Kingdom and in the world.

In a later paper[26] White showed that the designers' intentions had been realised in almost every aspect. The calculated displacement was almost exactly correct allowing for 250 tons of approved additions which had been deducted from the Board Margin. This meant that the remainder of the margin could be used for extra coal if desired. The centre of gravity was 1.75in below the calculated position in *Royal Sovereign* (4in in *Ramillies* due to heavier machinery) and the bunkers had been arranged to give the least possible variation of GM with load (3.6ft load, 3.55ft light).

White intended these ships to have a metacentric height of about 3½ft as experience showed this was adequate for safety whilst giving a long roll period which would favour accurate gunnery. The roll period was not measured but White says the full period was about 14-16 seconds. Heavy rolling occurs when the period of the waves impacting on the beam of the ship is the same as the period of the ship – resonance (Appendix 5). Waves of the period of the *Royal Sovereign* would have a length of well over 1000ft and, while such waves are not common, they do occur for about 1 per cent of the year in the North Atlantic. He decided that since waves which would cause rolling were uncommon and the square bilge would provide good damping, bilge keels would not be fitted on completion.

Stability of *Royal Sovereign* and *Hood*

	Displacement (tons)	GM	Max GZ	at °.	Vanishing angle,°
Royal Sovereign	14,262	3.6	2.3ft	37	63
Hood	14,532	4.1	?	34	57

Even uncommon wave lengths do occur and there were complaints about heavy rolling as soon as the ships entered service. In particular, *Resolution* met very severe conditions in December 1893. There were grossly exaggerated accounts of her behaviour and of the damage she sustained and it was even alleged that she was in actual danger. It was said that she rolled to 30-40° from the vertical and that the waves were up to 42ft from trough to crest. The problems of estimating roll are explained in Appendix 5 but in brief, as White said in his 1894 paper, a pendulum mounted on the bridge as in *Resolution* can indicate a roll angle of about double the true angle. For much the same reason, human balance organs are disturbed and the most conscientious observer will greatly overestimate roll angles. This distortion of the true vertical also makes it difficult to estimate wave height.

There is no doubt that *Resolution* did experience extremely unpleasant rolling and is virtually certain that a long underlying swell was the cause and not the 300ft waves which were estimated visually by the ship's officers. The actual damage was slight – the total cost of repairs was £440 – and water only entered the ship because severe conditions were not expected and some openings were not fully secured.

Bilge keels were then fitted to *Repulse*, 200ft long by 3ft deep, and in a comparative trial she rolled 11° whilst *Resolution* without keels rolled through 23°. In a more scientific trial with *Revenge* it was found that, before keels were fitted, it would take forty-five to fifty swings to reduce a roll of 6° to 2° whilst when keels were fitted the same reduction took place in only eight swings. It was found that the keels had no measurable effect on speed but, somewhat surprisingly, the turning circle was considerably reduced.[27]

It is surprising that White designed the ship without bilge keels, as in a series of papers from 1860 William Froude explained the behaviour of a ship in waves and went on to demonstrate how model tests followed by a clever but rather difficult graphical analysis could predict the behaviour of ships and the effect of keels. White's error becomes the more surprising when it is realised that the clearest description of Froude's procedure is given in White's own *Manual of Naval Architecture*! No wonder that Froude told the Committee on Scientific Education in 1872 that the principles of rolling had not been 'scientifically applied' even in the most recent ships.[28]

White maintained that their size was justified by their load-carrying capacity. He compared their load[29] with foreign battleships of the same length and 12,000 tons, saying that his ships carried 1600 tons more. He also claimed that they were not unduly expensive, thanks to the more efficient British shipbuilding. Dockyard-built ships cost £770,000, exclusive of armament and 'establishment charges' (overheads – cost approximately £900,000 if these are included) compared with £950,000-£1,000,000 for the foreign ships on the same basis, or a little less than *Inflexible*.

Royal Sovereign at sea: even these relatively high-freeboard ships were wet. (National Maritime Museum, London)

The class were well liked in service but became obsolete fairly quickly as they were overtaken by the developments described in the following chapter. They were generally seen by contemporaries as handsome ships and most modern writers agree with this view. It is often said that 'If it looks right, it is right'; I would put it the other way round, saying 'If it is right, it will soon come to be seen as looking right'. White and his assistant and former student, Whiting deserve every credit for a fine class and poor Beaton[30] did the best he could with *Hood*.

Second Class battleships – *Centurion* and *Barfleur* (ld 1890)

The provisions of the Naval Defence Act included two 'Second Class' battleships and though White, at least, was well aware of the fallacy of the cheap and nasty, there was some justification in this case as their intended role was as a ship of force in China and the Pacific. Their likely opponents were big Russian cruisers, whilst shallow draught (26ft) was essential to operate on the

Redoutable (ex-*Revenge*) off the Belgian coast during the First World War. The list is probably to increase the range of her guns. The original 13.5in had been replaced by 12in. (Imperial War Museum: SP1912)

Centurion 1892, a Second Class battleship, similar in style to the *Royal Sovereign*s. (Author's collection)

Chinese rivers. The hulls were sheathed against fouling. It should be noted that the decision on whether a ship was to be sheathed had to be taken at the design stage. In a sheathed ship all exposed metallic parts had to be bronze, including major components such as the ram and rudder pintles.

The first two ships were very much miniature *Royal Sovereign*s with four 10in as their main armament and a belt with a maximum thickness of 12in. They were to be about 0.5kt faster which presented some difficulty in selecting proportions and form.[31] The 10in guns had the remarkable elevation of 30° (though only half charges could be used over 15°), presumably for shore attack. They were hand-loaded and trained by a steam engine with emergency hand operation. Since this exposed a considerable number of the crew, a 6in shield, open at the back, presumably to allow smoke to disperse, was provided and this was to develop into the modern turret.

There was an interesting discussion of the pros and cons of hand-worked guns in the Navy Estimates for 1890. The hand-worked gun needed larger ports because the trunnions were differently placed and more of the gun was exposed. In order that the heavy weights of gun and shell could be worked manually, delicate mechanisms were necessary and breakdowns were more frequent than in power worked mounts. To prove that hand-working was possible, one gun of *Trafalgar* fired four rounds in 9½ minutes.

White proposed three different styles of armour:

(a) As *Royal Sovereign*, 12in belt, flat 2½in deck, 4in upper belt.
(b) Uniform 5in armour from 5ft below the waterline to 10ft above with a 2½in sloping deck behind.
(c) A thick belt, light upper belt and sloping deck behind. This would be 300 tons heavier than (a) or (b).

White had suggested a uniform thin belt for the *Royal Sovereign*s with a protective deck as *Blake* (see following section) but the Board chose (a). Despite an expensive modernisation in 1901-04, these two ships had a short active life. Roles for second-rate ships are best filled by ageing first-class vessels.

White's earlier cruisers

These interesting ships cannot be described in any detail and the following sections will concentrate on innovations in technology.

Belts and decks

Since the Design Committee of 1871 there had been numerous advocates of deck protection only, at least for cruisers. The minority report had suggested deck only for all ships and this was adopted by Brin for his *Italia* class battleships. White was later to suggest a similar arrangement for battleships.[32] It is not sufficiently appreciated that the 'protective deck' described an elaborate system of protection in which the deck itself was

31. R A Burt, *British Battleships 1889-1904* (London 1988), p91.

32. There are many claims for the 'invention' of deck protection including Reed, Lord Armstrong, Brin and Bertin (1872–SPHAX 1884). The first two seem to have a good claim, Brin may well have been a separate creation. Brin probably read the Design Committee report.

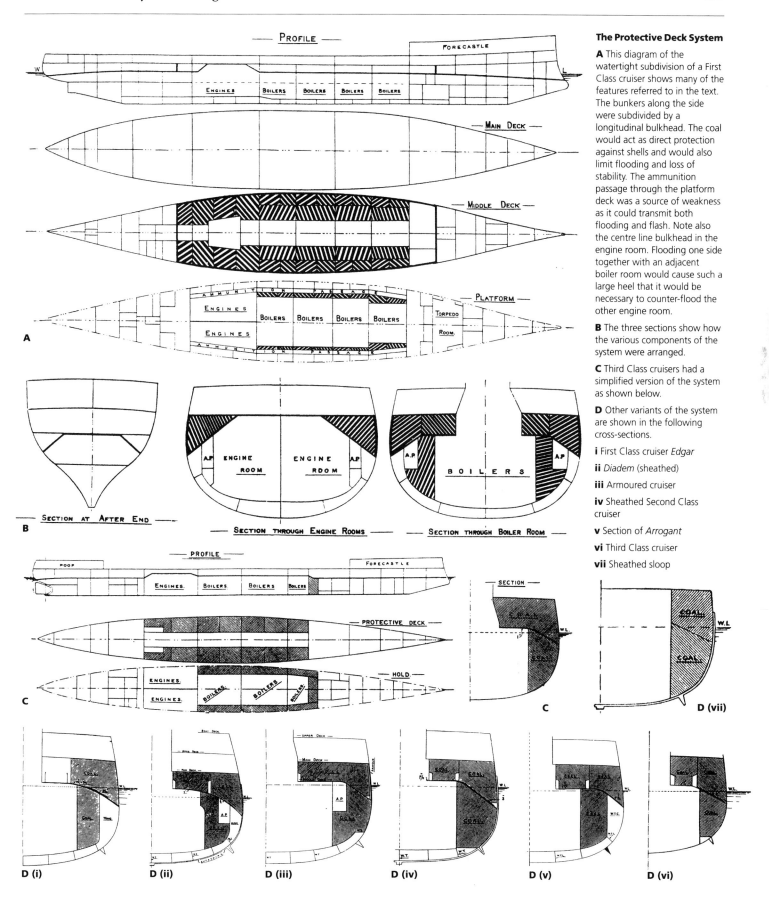

PROFILE

FORECASTLE

ENGINES — BOILERS — BOILERS — BOILERS — BOILERS

MAIN DECK

MIDDLE DECK

PLATFORM

AMMUNITION PASSAGE

ENGINES

BOILERS — BOILERS — BOILERS — BOILERS

TORPEDO ROOM.

ENGINES

AMMUNITION PASSAGE

A

SECTION AT AFTER END

B

A.P — ENGINE ROOM — ENGINE ROOM — A.P

SECTION THROUGH ENGINE ROOMS

A.P — BOILERS — A.P

SECTION THROUGH BOILER ROOM

PROFILE

POOP

ENGINES. — BOILERS. — BOILERS. — BOILERS.

FORECASTLE

PROTECTIVE DECK

ENGINES. — BOILERS — BOILERS — BOILERS

HOLD.

C

SECTION

COAL

COAL

C

COAL

COAL

D (vii)

COAL — A.P — COAL

D (i)

BOAT DECK — UPPER DECK — MAIN DECK — A.P — COAL

D (ii)

UPPER DECK — MAIN DECK — A.P — COAL

D (iii)

MAIN DECK — COAL — A.P — COAL — W.T.

D (iv)

COAL — COAL — W.T.

D (v)

COAL — COAL — W.L.

D (vi)

The Protective Deck System

A This diagram of the watertight subdivision of a First Class cruiser shows many of the features referred to in the text. The bunkers along the side were subdivided by a longitudinal bulkhead. The coal would act as direct protection against shells and would also limit flooding and loss of stability. The ammunition passage through the platform deck was a source of weakness as it could transmit both flooding and flash. Note also the centre line bulkhead in the engine room. Flooding one side together with an adjacent boiler room would cause such a large heel that it would be necessary to counter-flood the other engine room.

B The three sections show how the various components of the system were arranged.

C Third Class cruisers had a simplified version of the system as shown below.

D Other variants of the system are shown in the following cross-sections.

i First Class cruiser *Edgar*

ii *Diadem* (sheathed)

iii Armoured cruiser

iv Sheathed Second Class cruiser

v Section of *Arrogant*

vi Third Class cruiser

vii Sheathed sloop

Blenheim 1890, was the earliest
First Class cruiser without side
armour, relying on the
elaborate protective deck
system. (Author's collection)

only one aspect, albeit the most important. In its later form the deck was just above the load waterline on the centreline curving down in *Edgar*. In *Diadem*, later still, it angled down to some 4ft below LWL. In many cases the maximum thickness extended only over a small section of the slope and much thinner on the flat.[33] Over the machinery, the centre third had no deck and protection depended on gratings. Rope mantlets were often suspended below the gratings to catch splinters. There was usually a thick glacis round the tops of the cylinders in the engine-room which projected above the deck.

The 'tween deck above the deck was closely subdivided and used for the stowage of coal. This coal was a vital part of the protection and stability was calculated with the lower bunkers empty and the upper ('tween deck) ones full. The coal served as additional protection – 2ft coal = 1in steel. It was also known from trials that coal absorbed some of the effects of a shell bursting within a bunker. Perhaps more important was the value of coal in reducing the effect of flooding; the coal occupied $\frac{5}{8}$ of the volume so flood water could only fill $\frac{3}{8}$ of the bunker.[34] This also applied to loss of waterplane inertia which governs the height of the metacentre *so that coal reduced loss of stability on flooding*, an important point often neglected. Note that Second and Third Class cruisers were similar and the arrangement of bunkers in sloops was selected to provide some protection and aid stability when damaged. In some classes the protective deck system did not extend to the ends but these were too fine to make much contribution to either buoyancy or stability. A good deal of thought was given to getting coal from the upper bunkers to those adjacent to the stokehold. Some of the later opposition to oil fuel

derived from a proper recognition of the value of coal in protection.

The bunkers were subdivided, typically two layers each side and one transverse bulkhead between each major watertight bulkheads. In general, the lower 3-4ft of these internal bulkheads were fitted with coffer dams, 12in wide, stuffed with oakum and canvas to seal leaks from splinters. Sometimes 18in spaces were fitted and used as hammock stowages. Hatches were given deep coamings. This deep, cellular layer provided also very good protection against sinking from underwater attack.

Below the protective deck, there were further deep coal bunkers outboard of the machinery which would provide some protection against plunging shells, limit loss of buoyancy and give some protection against underwater attack while torpedo warheads were still very small. These were the working bunkers and had inevitable weaknesses; the inner doors had to be open in use and would be hard to close in an emergency due to bits of coal jammed in the slides. This was realised and they could be shut from the deck above, sometimes power-operated, but they would be certain to leak after damage if the structure was distorted. An ammunition passage would run fore and aft through these bunkers, conveying ammunition from magazines to guns. Inevitably it also carried fire and flood and was a major weakness in all ships of the day.

When this system of protection was introduced the shells it had to face were either powder-filled, common or Palliser (these latter were usually unfilled shot), though high explosive fillings were coming into use. At the relatively close range envisaged (less than 6000 yds)

33. Also thin over top of the double bottom to allow frames through- fig 22.

34. E L Atwood, *War-Ships, A Text Book* (London 1904).

35. *Blake* and *Blenheim*.

36. There was still some uncertainty over this feature as the side plating, 1in thick, was worked flush so that a belt could be added later, if desired. (Lecture by D Topliss at NMM).

37. White, p224.

38. Casemates first appeared in *Edgar* design, retrofitted to *Blake* whilst fitting out.

39. C C Wright, 'Impressive ships', *Warship International* 1/70 (Toledo 1970).

40. *Crescent* and *Royal Arthur*.

projectiles would travel horizontally and there was virtually no chance of a shell hitting the deck directly. The greatest hazard would be from the very large fragments from common shell which would probably be stopped by about 3in steel (or coal equivalent). However, HE shells fired from quick-firing guns could cause massive damage to the unprotected sides above the protective deck. Following the *Resistance* trials, the casemate was seen as an essential feature of the protected cruiser to protect the guns' crews. (See Chapter 10 for the few examples of damage to protected cruisers.)

Blake *and* Blenheim *(ld 1888)*

These two ships[35] were among the first cruisers designed by White as Director following his return from Armstrong's who had such a high reputation for cruisers. They were also the earliest First Class cruisers without side armour, relying entirely on deck protection[36] though, as described in the previous chapter, such protection had been adopted by Barnaby in *Comus* and *Mersey*.

They were planned as trade protection ships and were originally intended to carry eight 6in BL (QF were fitted in place of BL), with a speed of 20 to 22kts. Coal was to be provided for 6½ days at 20kts or 80 days at 10kts[37] (much greater than the *Orlandos*). The *Resistance* trials (*qv*) led to major changes with heavy casemates,[38] 6in thick for the four main deck guns (weight of conning tower + casemates 276 tons). Presumably the weight involved, high up, was too much for protection for the upper guns. In their day they were highly regarded

except for their high cost – *Blake* £440,701.39 They had a fairly short active life: *Blake* paid off in 1898 and *Blenheim* in 1901. White refined his ideas on bigger cruisers in the design of *Vulcan* – which, in turn, fed back into the somewhat smaller *Edgars*.

The Edgars *(ld 1889)*

These ships were generally similar to *Blake* but cost less with a slight reduction in speed and in deck thickness. Even the earlier ships, with low freeboard, are described in the Ship's Cover as 'excellent seaboats' but two ships[40] completed with a high forecastle, partly to provide more accommodation but partly to improve seakeeping. This raised forecastle was seen as very successful and White's proposals for later classes usually

Vulcan 1889, a torpedo boat carrier and depot ship. Note the large hydraulic cranes to lift the torpedo boats in and out. (Author's collection)

Gibraltar of the *Edgar* class 1892, slightly reduced versions of *Blake*. (Author's collection)

These photographs of the builder's model of *Latona*, 1890, show deck detail typical of cruisers of the period. Note the lack of weather protection to the bridge and the numerous boats. (Author's collection)

de Lôme noting that they cost £367,000 against £416,000 for the French ship. Their guns could easily penetrate the soft armour of the *Dupuy de Lôme*, while they were faster and generally superior.

Powerful *and* Terrible *(ld 1894)*

These two ships were designed to counter the *Rurik*[42] but, as so often, the threat was greatly exaggerated and, in this case, White seems to have exacerbated the problem. The original proposal was for an all-6in armament of twenty guns but the DNO proposed four 8in, fourteen 6in[43] and after considering various schemes, the Board decided on two 9.2in Mk VIII[44] and twelve 6in.[45] The fore and aft 6in either side were carried in double casemates, extending over two decks, a feature which may be seen as a White trademark. The protection given by these casemates may have been less than was believed; see Chapter 10 for an explosion in *Iwate* involving three casemates.

Powerful and her sister, *Terrible*, were criticised as underarmed but White pointed out that the weight of armament and protection was some 10 per cent greater than in previous First Class cruisers; the great size of these two ships was a consequence of their speed and coal capacity. There was no space for more magazines and more guns would further increase their size. White said that stability was not adequate for additional casemates – but in 1902, four more 6in, with casemates, were added. The deck was 4in on slopes amidships but the bottom 1ft where the frames passed through was only 2½in (any lucky shell passing through this thin strip would have the whole depth of the coal bunker in front of it). They were the first ships with the ammunition passage just below the protective deck so that ready use stowage in the casemate (the cause of *Iwate*'s explosion) could be done away with. The original intention was to fit cylindrical boilers but the Engineer-in-Chief, Durston, encouraged by White, decided to use the water tube, Belleville boiler, discussed in the next section.

The Diadem*s (ld 1896)*

The eight ships of the *Diadem* class were slightly reduced versions of the *Powerful*. They were slower, the deck a little thinner and each of the 9.2in was replaced by a pair of 6in with shields. They were designed in the first quarter of 1894 for the 1895-96 programme. Their duties were said to be trade protection on distant stations and they were to be capable of dealing with any existing cruiser or building. Vibration was always a problem with high power, reciprocating engines and those of the second group of ships were altered to improve matters. The first group had cylinders arranged – High pressure, H, Intermediate, I, Two Low, L, L but the cylinders of the second group were arranged as L, H, I, L and this redesign also gave another 1000ihp and 0.25kt in speed.

referred to the need for freeboard as in these two ships. Several of these ships were used early in the First World War to maintain the blockade north of Scotland where it was demonstrated that their freeboard was totally inadequate; even *Crescent* with the raised forecastle suffered serious damage to her bridge.[41] The main deck guns were only 10ft above the waterline.

Freeboard

Ship	Freeboard (F) (ft)	F/sq rt L
Edgar	17.4	0.9
Crescent	26.1	1.3

In 1897 White compared them with the French *Dupuy*

Water tube boilers – Bellevilles[46]

There had been a number of earlier attempts to produce a water tube boiler; *Janus* had been built in 1844 with a boiler of Lord Cochrane's design and in 1865-70 four more ships were fitted with similar boilers designed by his son.[47] In 1875 a very high-pressure boiler was ordered from Perkins for *Pelican* but it was not completed due to contractual problems.[48] None of these was reliable and the first water tube boiler to achieve success was the Thornycroft boiler fitted in *TB 100*, completed in 1886.

The great advantage of the water tube boiler for warships was its flexibility, the ability to change steam flow rapidly, up or down. The boilers were smaller and, because they could be dismantled, large openings in the deck above were not needed. The torpedo gunboat *Speedy* was re-boilered with the Thornycroft water tube design in 1891 and a long series of trials were carried out which demonstrated the expected flexibility and proved the reliability of this boiler. Thornycroft gave the following figures on weight saving.[49]

Water tube boiler, with auxiliaries	68
Locomotive boiler, torpedo boat	48
Locomotive boiler, latest torpedo gunboat	43
Anson (cylindrical)	21.3
P & O liners	16.6

After a visit to France by White in 1892, it was decided to fit Belleville boilers, working at 245lbs/sq in, in the torpedo gunboat *Sharpshooter* in place of her unreliable locomotive boilers. She then ran a series of prolonged trials, similar to those of *Speedy*, and the Bellevilles proved flexible, reliable and able to sustain full power for long periods. Belleville had built his first water tube boiler about 1850 and by about 1880 all *Messageries Maritime* mail ships used them and it was adopted by the French navy from 1889. A Royal Navy engineer officer from Jersey, Eduard Gaudin, 'who could be mistaken for a Frenchman', was sent to Australia and back[50] in a French liner and his favourable report had much to do with the Admiralty's selection of the Belleville.

The Belleville was chosen for the *Powerful* in 1892 without waiting for the *Sharpshooter* trial and the forty-eight boilers were required to develop 25,000ihp for short periods and 18,000ihp for 'as long as the coal lasted'. Each boiler had eight groups of tubes passing backwards and forwards ten times like a flattened spiral over the furnace. The tubes were 4½in in diameter with a thickness of 0.38in in the lower ones and 0.19in for the upper tubes. Seamless tubes had been used in small tube boilers and their use became universal as seamless tubes became more readily available following the bicycle boom from 1894. *Powerful* and *Terrible* were re-tubed in 1900. Marine engines were increasingly dependent in

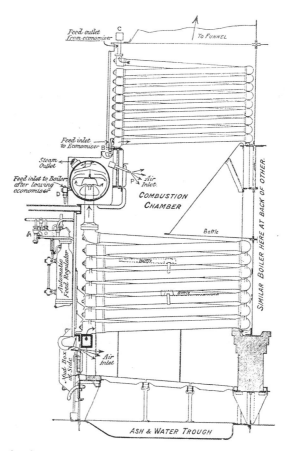

A Bellville boiler. (Author's collection)

developments in other industries; see footnote on *Renown* (Chapter 9).

Trials in *Powerful* were very successful with consumption per ihp/hour of 2.06 tons at 20 per cent full power and 1.83 tons at 72 per cent while the Belleville outfit weighed 20 per cent less than a cylindrical plant of the same power. There were also savings of engine weight associated with the higher pressures used. Bellevilles were adopted for all new battleships and cruisers but other large tube designs were tried in torpedo gunboats, *eg* Niclausse in *Seagull* and Babcock and Wilcock in *Sheldrake*. Problems for which the Belleville was rather unfairly blamed are discussed in a later section.

The torpedo boat destroyer

By 1892 it seemed that the torpedo gunboat was too big, expensive and slow to form an adequate defence against torpedo boats. The big torpedo boat, such as *Swift* (*TB 81*), showed promise but were still too small. The Controller, Fisher, saw the solution and, following discussions with Yarrow and Thornycroft,[51] ordered the first 'torpedo boat destroyers'. These were enlarged torpedo boats of 275-280 tons, a speed of 26kts on trial, and an armament of one 12pdr, three 6pdr and three 18in torpedo tubes, After the first six boats, the speed was increased to 27kts, the bow torpedo tube was omitted

41. D K Brown, 'Sustained Speed at Sea in the RN', *NEC 100* (Newcastle 1984).

42. Manning, *The Life of Sir William White*, p306.

43. R Burt, '*Powerful*', *Warship 48* (London October 1988).

44. Descriptions of these guns are to be found in – 9.2in *Warship 23*; 6in *Warship 28*.

45. The 9.2in had shallow barbettes plus 6in on turret. Rates of fire were 9.2in 2rpm; 6in 4rpm; battle practice.

46. D K Brown, 'Marine Engineering in the RN: Part III', *JNE*.

47. *Oberon, Chanticleer, Audacious* and *Penelope*.

48. E C Smith, *A Short History of Marine Engineering* (Cambridge 1937).

49. J I Thornycroft, 'Water Tube Boilers for Warships', *Trans INA* (London 1889).

50. This mission is mentioned in: Scott Hill, 'The Battle of the Boilers', *JNE* (London 1985) and in W H White, 'Presidential Address', *Inst CE*, (London, 1903). Both accounts imply his trip was secret and it is likely that he pretended to be French and possibly served as an engineer on the ship.

51. D Lyon, entry in *Conway's All the World's Fighting Ships 1860-1905*, also *The First Destroyers* (London 1996).

and the guns increased by two 6pdr. They were about 200ft in length with a turtledeck forecastle.

In all, there were 111 generally similar boats, the 6 original 26-knotters, 36 '27-knotters', 66 '30-knotters' and 3 special '33-knotters' (which failed to achieve their speed). Large numbers of generally similar boats were built by other navies. Three turbine boats are dealt with later. The 30-knotters carried the same armament with a trial speed of 30kts on a displacement of 350-380 tons and a length of 215-220ft. They can be broken down by date of order and by builder as follows:

Destroyers – date of order

26-knotter	1892	4
	1893	2
27-knotter	1893 initial	6
	1893 follow on	30
30-knotter	1894-5	8
	1895-6	21
	1896-7	16 + 3 specials
	1897-8	6
	1899	9 + 6 purchased in 1900

Success 1901. This view shows all the obstructions on the forecastle which would generate spray as the bow pitched under. (Author's collection)

Destroyers by builder

Builder	26kt	27kt	30kt
Yarrow	2	3	0
Thornycroft	2	3	10
Lairds	2	3	13
Doxford		2	4
Palmer		3	13
Earls		2	2
White		3	-
Hanna Donald		2	-
Fairfield		3	6
Hawthorn Leslie		3	5
J G Thompson – J Brown		3	8
Naval Construction & Armament Works – Vickers		3	5
Armstrong		2	-
Thomson		1	-

NB. 33kt 'Specials': one each by Thornycroft, Laird and J Brown

It is strange that the popular view of the destroyer as an exclusive preserve of Yarrow and Thornycroft is so wrong. Yarrow's had a contractual dispute with the Admiralty[52] after the early boats and built very few for some years while Laird and Palmer built most, the latter seemingly the favourite of commanding officers.

The glamour associated with these small, fast ships has concealed the facts that they had appalling seakeeping, unreliable machinery and hulls which were barely strong enough. Their trial speeds were far in excess of those which could be reached at sea whilst, in the wars in which such craft were involved, very few successes were obtained. These harsh criticisms will be justified in the following paragraphs.

Seakeeping

Though the principles of the behaviour of ships in waves were set out by William Froude in a series of papers from 1860[53] it was not until big computers became available that theory could be used directly in design.[54] Following the loss of the *Cobra* in 1901, the Admiralty set up a Committee[55] to study the safety of destroyers in general. These studies will be further considered later but the Committee circulated a detailed questionnaire to commanding officers on seakeeping whose results will be interpreted in the light of modern theory in the following paragraphs.

The effect of severe weather can degrade the operational performance of a warship by damage to the ship itself or by reducing the ability of captain, officers and crew to perform their duties. Damage to the ship is most likely to occur when she is slamming into a heavy head sea. Plating and frames near the bow can be ruptured by the heavy impact forces. Less obvious, the whole ship

flexes and the deck or bottom plating amidships may split or buckle. Repeated loading of this kind may lead to fatigue failure in the form of cracks. Damage may also occur to superstructures from the impact of green seas sweeping the deck.

Seasickness is the most obvious effect of rough seas on people.[56] People vary, one from another, and from time to time so guidelines are imprecise but sickness is most likely to be caused by vertical accelerations, the combined effect of pitch and heave, greater than about 0.8 m/sec^2 at a frequency of 0.18-0.3 Hz (cycles per second). Tired men are more susceptible than are those who are alert and roll is tiring, but the direct effect of rolling on sickness is slight. Most people get used to motion after a few days but almost all are sick occasionally.[57] Pitch and heave are mainly a function of length and early destroyers were short. It is known that decision making is also affected by motions and particularly by vertical acceleration but such effects have not yet been quantified. Vibration, noise and exhaustion due to cold and wind will also reduce the ability to reach a correct decision – and all were present in these early destroyers and in the light coastal craft of the Second World War.[58] Manual tasks – loading and training a gun etc – are governed mainly by the lateral acceleration due to roll.

The key question asked by the 1901 Committee was: 'Describe the differences in the behaviour of the destroyer in a *fairly heavy head sea* at speeds of 17kts, 15kts, 10kts and 8kts respectively'. Few respondents had dared to try 17kts under these conditions. The first difficulty is in interpreting the meaning attached by commanding officers to the words italicised but from answers to other questions it would seem that they generally took it as the sea corresponding to Beaufort Force 8 winds (then defined as 23-28kts). There is no exact relation between local wind speed and wave height but for seas such as the Mediterranean and English Channel,[59] from which most accounts came, a typical wave height would be 6½ – 7½ft, which occurs for well over half the year.[60]

A typical, overall comment reads: 'Against a heavy sea a TBD steaming at 17 or 15kts would tear all her packing out, sweep everything off the upper deck, carry away the platform and bridge rails, and probably sweep someone off the bridge. She would race, jump, kick, labour, eventually lose her steam, and after a short time be a mass of defects. At 10kts she would be wet and at 8kts fairly comfortable.' The results of a modern computer study of *Star* confirm this graphic description.[61] The effects on ship and men outlined above will be considered in turn using appropriate quotations.

Damage

There are frequent reports of the bridge being swept in head seas. The young Commander Roger Keyes said that at higher speeds he steered from the aft position as

52. Yarrow's had developed light machinery which caused less vibration than most and the Admiralty passed the Yarrow drawings to other builders. Since Yarrow could get all the orders they wanted abroad, they did not tender for RN work.

53. The Papers of William Froude 1810–1879, INA (London 1955).

54. D K Brown, 'Weather and Warships, Past, Present and Future'. RINA Conference, '*Seakeeping and Weather*', London 1995.

55. The Torpedo Boat Destroyer Committee, 1901-03.

56. It is no coincidence that the word 'nausea' derives from the Greek word for ship.

57. The author would claim to be a bit better than average as regards motion sickness based both on experience at sea and in navigating a rally car.

58. D K Brown, 'Fast Warships and their Crews', *Small Craft*, RINA, No 6, 1984.

59. Several COs note that they could steam faster in longer Atlantic waves.

60. I have used the 'Coastal Code' relationship for wind of limited fetch.

61. D K Brown, 'Sustained Speed at Sea in the RN', NEC 100, Newcastle 1984.

Banshee in what appears to be Sea State 5–6, wave height c4m. The wind speed would be about 35kts, Beaufort 8. Note the inadequate canvas screen to the bridge. (WSS)

the bridge was feet deep in green seas. The bridge was a canvas screen around the 12pdr, about 40ft abaft the bow and 15ft above the static waterline (see photo of *Banshee* above). Minor damage was frequent. The rivets connecting the frames to the plating below the waterline failed frequently, CO *Handy* reporting 'I visited the fore mess deck on several occasions and observed the bow plates panting and frames giving inwards and back, about 2in play.'

These light ships flexed visibly. 'The upper deck is practically always on the wave when the vessel is at sea'. This would weaken and loosen rivets, starting leaks, and keeping the Dockyards busy with repairs. *Seal* reported a more serious incident in which the upper deck plates were split for 5ft 6in in from the port side and for 11in down the side – and the splits growing at 3in an hour. Buckles ran down both sides 'as far as you could see', and the keel was buckled. Slamming under the stern was confined to Thornycroft ships which had a semi-tunnel stern.

Motions

None of these early destroyers had bilge keels as completed[62] and there were many complaints of heavy rolling. Bilge keels were fitted to *Star* in 1901 – at a cost of £250 – which reported that in comparison with *Sylvia* in company, she was rolling 25° compared with her sister's 30°. There was some dispute over this trial[63] but eventually bilge keels were fitted to all. It was also noted that the higher bow and greater flare of *Star* made her much dryer than *Sylvia*. There are many such reports praising Palmer's ships but they are difficult to understand as the difference was slight whilst all had a freeboard only about half that which would have been given to a ship of that length in the Second World War.

It is surprising that there are few reports of broaching, a serious hazard to small, fast ships. One report says: 'I consider they were in real danger when running before a heavy sea with half their length out of water for considerable periods . . . With a heavy swell on the quarter, the ship yawed rather badly, at times the rudder having practically no effect.' The replies to this question-

naire are fascinating and numerous but space demands that the section is closed by the following quotation which says it all.

> A destroyer could not steam 50 miles at more than 10 or 12kts with a fairly heavy sea right ahead and expect to be fit for service at the end of it . . . On 10th and 11th October, 1901, *Crane* was the sole survivor of eight TBDs after steaming 10kts for 200 miles against a moderately heavy sea, and she had to seek shelter for repairs to damage caused by trying to increase to 15kts with the sea right ahead.

At high speeds, even in calm water, the pattern of waves generated by the ship led to a serious loss of stability. This is a complicated phenomenon, still to be guarded against in modern fast patrol boats, in which the area of the waterplane is reduced.

Living conditions were appalling and the 'hard lying' money paid to the crew was well earned. There was no insulation on the sides and the mess decks were like ovens in summer and a freezer in winter. Tuberculosis was rife. This extreme discomfort which would cause exhaustion must have contributed to their poor performance in action.

Machinery problems

The early destroyers – 26- and 27-knotters – had a variety of boilers. In order to get her to sea quickly the first, *Havock*, was given the unsatisfactory locomotive boiler, reaching 26.1kts on trial, soon passed by Thornycroft's *Daring* at 28kts with water tube (WT) boilers. The first forty-two boats had a variety of boiler designs

Boilers	Number of ships
Locomotive	6
Yarrow WT	10
Thornycroft WT	8
Blechynden	3
White	4
Normand	8
Reed	3
Du Temple	1

Technology was pressed to the limit or beyond. Thornycroft's *Boxer* was briefly the record holder at 29.7kts but was handsomely beaten by the Russian *Sokol*, built by Yarrow's, the first past 30kts. The leading French designer, Normand, claimed 31kts for *Forban* – though none of her sisters got near that speed. It was Normand who said that a TBD was 'a machine designed to run a trial trip'. Every trick, legitimate and other, was employed to squeeze out the ultimate as there was usually a penalty of £1000 per knot (2½ per cent of the cost) for every knot down – and sometimes a bonus for going faster. Trial speed had little meaning as a report of 1900[64]

62. Bilge keels increase resistance though only slightly. Faced with a heavy penalty if the contract speed was not achieved, it was simpler to leave out bilge keels. Even recently, bilge keels tend to be small if there is a penalty on speed.

63. D K Brown, 'Sustained Speed at Sea in the RN', NEC 100, Newcastle 1984.

64. Ship's Cover.

65. Froude's earlier work had showed that for slower speed propellers, which did not cavitate, small blade area increased efficiency. For cavitating propellers, a much larger area was needed but no one could say how large.

66. Now held in the Science Museum store.

67. Lyon, *The First Destroyers*.

gives the service speed of the 27-knotters as 19-22kts and that of the 30-knotters as 26-27kts, both in calm water. In rough seas there were cases of TBDs being beaten by the despised torpedo gunboats.

A destroyer's machinery at full power was an awesome sight with pistons moving at 1100ft/min, cranks rotating 400 times a minute and steam leaking at 250lbs/sq in. An anonymous engineer wrote: 'There was heat, noise and vibration everywhere, while in the engine-room men worked in a smother of oil and water thrown off by the rapidly revolving cranks. It was often a case of "pour on oil and trust in Providence".'

Providence did not always prove worthy of such trust. *Foam* had a cylinder break in 1898, the connecting rod going through the bottom. *Bat* broke the bottom end bolt on a connecting rod, the piston coming out through the upper deck before falling into the sea. *Bullfinch* on trials in 1899 broke a connecting rod at nearly 30kts which fractured a cylinder, eleven men being killed by escaping steam.

Vibration was inevitably a severe problem with fast-moving machinery and cavitating propellers. The engines were the major problem as Yarrow showed about 1884, running a torpedo boat at full rpm with the propellers removed. Later, in 1892, Yarrow showed that machinery vibration could be greatly reduced by balance weights worked by eccentrics off the crankshaft. The maximum amplitude of vibration of a First Class torpedo boat at 248rpm had been reduced from $^{27}/_{64}$in to $^{7}/_{64}$in.

Many destroyers had difficulty in meeting the trial speed due to cavitation losses on the high-speed propellers. If pressure is reduced, the boiling point of water is reduced – the best-known example is that of a kettle at the top of a mountain which boils at such a low temperature that it does not make decent tea. The pressure on the back of the propellers of these early destroyers was so low that the water 'boiled' at sea temperatures causing a serious loss of thrust. Charles Parsons investigated the problem during trials of *Turbinia* and it was clear that an increase of blade area was desirable but there was very little hard evidence, experimental or theoretical, to guide the designer. Some writers have suggested a feud between Edmund Froude and Parsons on the subject which is quite untrue.[65] Their extensive correspondence[66] shows that there was no disagreement, but neither would claim fully to understand the problem, let alone propose a solution. Many destroyers ran trial after trial before they reached contract speed – worn out. Worse could happen; in 1904 *Chamois* lost a blade off her propeller at high speed. The out-of-balance forces broke the shaft bracket and the whirling shaft ripped open the bottom, sinking the ship. This disaster led to an involved, semi-empirical method for calculating the strength of shaft brackets which remained in use – particularly in College exams – till well after the Second World War.

Chamois sinking in the Gulf of Patras on 29 September 1904 after a propeller blade broke off and the whirling shaft penetrated the hull. (Author's collection)

The '33kt Specials'

These three boats were ordered in 1896 with a contract speed of 33kts, which none of them even approached. They represented the ultimate reciprocating engined destroyer and are worthy of note on that account (see table below).

It is not generally realised how much Henry Deadman RCNC contributed to the design of the early destroyers.[67] Deadman was born in 1843 and, after an apprenticeship at Deptford and Chatham, he was one of the first entry to the Royal School of Naval Architecture in 1864. His early years were spent mainly overseeing contract-built ships but much of his career was spent in various dockyards. By 1886 he was Chief Constructor of Portsmouth and that yard's reputation for rapid building owes much to his direction.

He returned to Whitehall in 1892, retiring as Assistant Director in 1906. Though he had charge of various designs, it is his work on destroyers which was important. His detailed specification of the structure ensured that the problems mentioned earlier in these lightly-built ships were not fatal. He was a key member of the TBD Committee following the loss of *Cobra* (Chapter 11).

Experimental destroyers 1896

	Arab	*Express*	*Albatross*
Builder	Thompson	Laird	Thornycroft
Displacement (tons)	470	465	430
Boilers	4 Normand	4 Normand	4 Thornycroft
Pressure (lbs/in²)	250	240	250
Stroke (ins)	18	21	20
Revs/min	390	400	380
Indicated HP	8600	9250	7500
Machinery wt (tons)	208	208	190
Speed, trials (kts)	30.9	30.9	31.5

Nine

A *Majestic* Fleet, 1893-1904

Renown, 1895, a Second Class battleship, introduced a new style of armour deck which was used in all White's later battleships. Note that the sheer is greater than in other contemporary ships contributing to seakeeping as well as to a handsome appearance. She is shown here during a Royal Cruise, for which she was painted white. (Author's collection)

THE BATTLESHIPS described in this section are generally lumped together under the rather derogatory heading of 'pre-Dreadnoughts' which conceals the fact that, until Dreadnoughts were at sea in numbers, these ships commanded the sea – there was even a German squadron of similar ships at Jutland.[1] Though they were of similar style, lumping them together also conceals the major developments in armour, guns and in many other items, including the hull itself, which took place in this decade.

Renown may be seen as setting the definitive style for a generation of battleships, but the application of that style varied from class to class as there were important differences in the roles envisaged. To explain these developments, each class will be described briefly followed by more detailed consideration of the main aspects such as armour, guns and gunnery, hull design and building times and machinery.

Renown (ld 1893)

This ship formed part of the 1892 programme, which included the first three of the *Majestic* class, was designed round the new 12in, 50-ton gun. When it was realised that this gun would not be ready for some time, it was decided to build a third *Centurion* to keep Pembroke Dockyard busy. The new Controller was J A Fisher, then a strong advocate of the 'lightest practicable big gun and the heaviest secondary gun', and he let White develop a much superior design. *Renown* had the same four 10in guns but with hydraulic training and electric elevation, though they were still loaded manually. The shield now had a back to it and was virtually the modern turret. She was given a heavy secondary armament of ten 6in QF in casemates.

Her novelty lay in her armour; the main belt was 8in of the new Harvey material, discussed in a later section, and far superior to earlier armour. This belt was 210ft

Pre-Dreadnoughts: main features

Class (ld)	No. of Ships	Armour Belt Type	Thick (ins)	Equivt Cmpd	Speed (kts)	Disp (tons)	Notes
Royal Sovereign (89)	7	Compound	18	18	16.5	14,150	
Hood (89)	1	Compound	18	18	16.5	14,150	Turret ship
Centurion(90)	2	Compound	12	12	18.5	10,500	Second Class
Renown (93)	1	Harvey	8	12.8	18	12,350	Second Class
Majestic (93)	9	Harvey	9	14.4	17	14,560	
Canopus (96)	6	Krupp	6	12.5	18	13,150	
Formidable (98)	3	Krupp	9	18.8	18	14,500	
London (99)	3	Krupp	9	18.8	18	14,500	
Duncan (99)	6	Krupp	7	14.6	19	13,270	
King Edward VII (02)	8	Krupp	9	18.8	18.5	15,585	
Lord Nelson (05)	2	Krupp	12	25	18	16,090	

long and 7½ft deep with a 6in Harvey upper belt. The middle deck at the top of the main belt was 2in thick at the centre but sloped down at 45°, 3in thick, at the sides to meet the lower edge of the belt. The sloping edge of the deck provided a very strong support to the belt but, more important, any intact shell which penetrated the main belt would be slowed in doing so and then hit the 3in slopes at 45°, which it would be unlikely to penetrate. This style of protection was used in every British ship up to *Hood* and in the German Navy up to *Bismarck* where it did fairly well in her final, close-range action.[2] White wrote to her designers, Dunn and Beaton,[3] that a 6in QF could only just penetrate 10in of ordinary steel (say 8in Harvey) at 1000yds and hence *Renown* was invulnerable to all 6in shells beyond that range and also to larger HE-filled shells.[4]

Unusually for the day, *Renown* had considerable sheer forward which made her a very handsome ship and may have helped to keep her dry. There were fewer interruptions to the side plating forward which may also have helped to keep her free of spray.[5] She was Fisher's favourite and carried his flag on several occasions. Much of her short life was spent as a yacht for Royal cruises, a role for which her appearance fitted her.

Her machinery was contracted to Maudslay who sub-contracted a great deal of work to thirty other firms. Items sub-contracted included; steering gear, air compressors, dynamos, evaporators, capstans, hydraulic equipment, pumps, boat hoists, crank shafts, pistons and piston rods, connecting rods, cross heads, cylinder covers, springs, condenser tubes, boiler plates, furnaces and boiler tubes. Shipbuilding was already becoming an assembly industry, depending on a wide and capable base. Rather surprisingly, *Renown* was sheathed even though fairly effective anti-fouling paints were available.

The *Majestics* (ld 1893-95)

These eight ships may be seen as First Class developments of *Renown*. Their main belt was increased to 9in Harvey in both the upper and lower belt, giving a thick wall of steel some 16ft deep and 220ft long, closed by thick bulkheads. The ends were unprotected, a feature discussed later. They marked a further increase in size compared with the *Royal Sovereign*s which White justified as due to British ships' need to keep the sea for longer periods. He claimed[6] that in the earlier ships, load–equipment, armament and coal–totalled 3500 tons with a displacement of 14,200 tons whilst a French 12,000-ton ship would carry only 2300 tons; about 80 per cent of the British equipment, 62 per cent of the armament weight and 64 per cent of the coal.

A new design of 12in gun was introduced in the

Majestic, 1895, the name ship of a large class of First Class battleships based on *Renown*. (Author's collection)

1. When *Hood* was sunk by *Bismarck* in 1941, d'Eyncourt remarked that she was as outdated as would have been White's *Majestics* at Jutland, an exact parallel in dates.

2. W H Garzke, R O Dulin and D K Brown, 'Sinking of the *Bismarck*' *Warship 1994* (London 1994).

3. Ship's Cover.

4. White was not entirely consistent in his claims for penetration, even allowing for the improvements in armour.

5. Her freeboard/sq rt length ratio was a respectable 1.1.

6. PRO ADM 116/878. Contains White's design submissions.

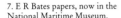

7. E R Bates papers, now in the
National Maritime Museum.

8. For *Powerful* (500 x 71.5 x 45ft),
Harland proposed 530 x 68 x 43ft.

9. The maximum draught for the
canal was 25ft 4in until 1902 when it
was increased by a foot. *Canopus'*
load draught was 26ft 2in (about
18in less than in *Majestic*) and she
would have had to transit light.

10. The French tried a 5.9in
howitzer in the gunboat *Dragonne*
but the results did not justify
further work. High-angle firing,
with a long time of flight from a
ship pitching and rolling is unlikely
to be accurate. See also Chapter 10
for the effectiveness of howitzers.
The boat deck of *Canopus* was to be
strengthened to mount six to eight
howitzers (Ship's Cover).

11. However, an instruction dated 5
November 1895 laid down that the
height of the mast above water was
to be 160ft in battleships and First
and Second Class cruisers, 140ft for
Third Class and 120ft for TGB.

12. Similar plates in First World War
light cruisers proved able to keep
out all 4in shells and HE shells of
6in calibre.

*Majestic*s, and improved loading arrangements tried,
discussed later under armament. A full shield, later
known as a turret, was fitted to the 12in guns. They had
twelve 6in QF as a secondary armament, all mounted in
casemates, four on the main deck and two on the upper,
each side.

There was a rather strange proposal from Sir Edward
Harland that warships should adopt longer, narrower
forms, similar to liners. Bates[7] investigated this proposal for *Majestic*.[8]

	Majestic	*Harland proposal*
Dimensions (ft)	390 x 75 x 45	450 x 70 x 42
Load displacement (tons)	14,900	15,330
Metacentric height (ft)	2.75	2.1

The metacentric height of the Harland proposal would
have been unacceptable and a further increase of displacement would have been needed.

Canopus class (ld 1896-98)

At this date, Japan was seen as an increasing threat in the
Far East, especially in the light of her reinforcement by
capture of Chinese ships in the Sino-Japanese War. The
Canopus class were required to have a draught shallow
enough to transit the Suez Canal[9] and to operate in
Chinese rivers. Confusingly, it was later decided that
sheathing was not necessary as they were not intended
for distant waters. Weight was saved by reducing the
thickness of the belt to 6in though, with the new Krupp
armour, this was equivalent to about 8in of Harvey.
There was a light extension of the belt forward to the
stem of 2in plating. This is often dismissed as of value
'only' against splinters and light shells but the loss of
speed due to splinter damage was a serious threat to a
pursuing ship. The main deck was increased to 1in as
protection against howitzers, which it was believed the
French were fitting.[10] This deck would explode all shells
containing high explosive. Thought was given to
mounting the 6in in turrets but casemates were again
preferred since turrets would have involved power
operation, itself vulnerable to damage. Ramming was
still seen as important and *Canopus* had a long beak supported by the 2in bow belt.

This class was the first design of battleship with water
tube boilers – Belleville – giving a further weight saving.
This saving, low in the ship, meant that the beam had to
be increased to obtain satisfactory stability. Possibly to
save weight high up, only one top was fitted to each
mast, reducing the number of 6pdrs to six. White
instructed Dunn and his staff that the foremast was to

Formidable, 1898, name ship of
her class. She was torpedoed
and sunk in 1915 by *U24* off
Portland. (WSS)

be 'as light as possible'.[11] Protection against torpedo boats was increased as twelve 12pdrs were fitted instead of eight. Wood was to be avoided except for the deck, admiral's quarters and the wardroom to reduce the fire hazard.

There is an interesting note in the ship's cover showing how the first estimate of the hull weight was deduced from the *Renown*.

Hull weight of *Renown*	4640 tons
Thicker bottom	75
Bilge keels	35
Ten feet extra length	105
Two feet extra beam	105
Barbettes 38ft/29ft	180
Citadel change	20
Total *Canopus*	5160 tons

Formidable and *London* classes (ld 1898-1901)

The first three ships of the 1897-98 programme were originally described by White as 'Modified *Majestics*' though in most aspects they were better described as more heavily-armoured *Canopus*. White suggested that, since improvements in armour manufacture had made an 8in plate as effective as the earlier 9in, the belt could be reduced to the lower thickness, saving 160 tons and reducing cost by £47,000. The Board decided on the 9in belt, though they rejected a suggestion to increase the secondary armament to fourteen 6in. The main belt was 218ft long, 15ft deep and its effectiveness was considerably enhanced by increasing the slopes of the protective (middle) deck to 3in. The bow splinter protection was increased to 3in,[12] 12ft deep whilst similar protection was added aft, 1½in thick and 8ft deep. The five follow-on ships were ordered after the *Duncan*s and incorpo-

Prince of Wales of the *London* class 1902. This view shows the arrangement of the numerous boats carried at that time. (Author's collection)

rated many of the improvements of that class, notably the rearranged deck protection.

Both the 12in and 6in guns were of new models adding 150 tons high in the ship, exacerbating the stability problems associated with lighter machinery. White was reluctant to push gun-mounting designers into smaller barbettes, as in some foreign ships, since he accepted that improved reliability and rate of fire justified the larger mounting but the new loading arrangements required an even larger-diameter barbette.

They had inward-turning propellers, which it was thought would enable the machinery controls to be better grouped, giving a more compact engine-room. Edmund Froude showed that this would give a very slight improvement in propulsive efficiency at the cost of making turning at rest more difficult when the propellers were run in opposition to turn the ship.[13] It is not usually realised that the turning moment on a twin-screw ship at rest and using the shafts in opposition is due much more to the pressure forces acting on the hull than to the thrust in the propeller shafts.

The *Duncans* (ld 1899-1900)

The first four ships were built under the 1898 supplementary estimates in response to big building programmes in France and Russia. It was believed that the latter navy was building faster battleships and, in consequence, the *Duncans* were a knot faster at 19kts than earlier ships. This meant more powerful engines and, for the first time in a battleship, 4-cylinder, triple-expansion engines were adopted while it was also necessary to test a new hull form. These changes delayed the start of their building and the first two *London*s were laid down before any of the *Duncan*s.

Mainly for economy, the *Duncan*s were to be 1000 tons smaller than the *London*s and this combination of high speed and small size presented White with a difficult problem. The Board agreed to a reduction in the

thickness of the belt to 7in KC. The forward armoured bulkhead was eliminated in favour of extensions to the belt, reducing through 5in, 4in to 3in at the stem. This was not an economy measure but something White had advocated for some time. Fear of high-capacity shells bursting high in the ship led to the thick protective deck being moved up to main-deck level, discussed later. The middle deck was reduced to 1 inch, even on the slopes, further weakening protection at the waterline. The DNC's efforts at weight saving in the hull had a major effect in this class. To reduce the target formed by upper works the big cowl ventilators were replaced by wind sails.

The cost breakdown of several classes is compared in the Ship's Cover for *Duncan*.

Cost £ x 1000	*Canopus*	*Formidable*	*Duncan*
Hull	318	337	330
Armour	240	330	275
Machinery	123	135	155
Gun mountings	76	80	80
TOTAL	757	882	840

The figures for *Canopus* are actual costs, those for the other ships are estimates. Note the big jump in cost for Krupp armour compared with Harvey in the *Canopus* and also the high cost of *Duncan*'s more powerful machinery.

The *King Edward VII* class (ld 1902-04)

The heavy intermediate battery fitted in USS *New Jersey* and the Italian *Bennedetto Brin* caused concern and it was decided that the three ships of the 1901-02 programme should carry four 9.2in in single turrets, the number of 6in being reduced to ten. This increase in armament, together with a slight increase in speed to 18.5kts added 1000 tons to the design displacement. Increased concern for gunnery also showed in the abolition of the old 'fighting tops' in favour of fire control positions.[14]

The weights of complete mountings, including ammunition, were given as:

Weight of mounting

Turret	rpg	Tons	Casemate	Tons
Twin 12in	105	1015	7.45	100
Twin 10in	105	620	6	61
Single 9.2in	105	230	4.7	45
Single 7.45in	100	132		
Twin 6in	100	147		

In the early stages of the design, White was sick and his place was taken by the senior deputy, H E Deadman.[15]

Albemarle of the *Duncan* class, 1901, which were slightly smaller and faster than the *Formidable*s but with only a 7in belt. (WSS)

Commonwealth of the *King Edward VII* class 1903. The 9.2in guns at the corners of the superstructure could not fire fore and aft because of blast effects on the 12in turrets. (WSS)

He asked the head of the battleship section, J H Narbeth (Assistant Constructor), to prepare a number of alternative studies based on the *Duncan* from which the Board selected one with four twin 7.5in turrets. On return to office, White suggested these should be replaced by single 9.2in. According to Narbeth, the blast effects of the 9.2in on the 12in turrets were forgotten and the usable arcs of the 9.2in were limited in consequence.[16]

The armour disposition followed that of the *London*s in most respects but because the upper deck was congested by the 9.2in turrets, the 6in had to be arranged in a battery rather than the traditional casemates. The battery was subdivided as far as possible by traverses but White felt it was a compromise forced on him.[16] The barrels of these main-deck 6in would dip into the sea at 14° roll. The battery armour was 7in thick on the side which increased the area protected against HE shells and enabled some reduction in deck armour. The weight estimates for the design were reduced in the light of the savings achieved in the *Duncan*s but even so, further savings were made, discussed later. Though White played only a small direct part in the design of this class, they are properly seen as the culmination of his '*Majestic* fleet'.

Lord Nelson **and** Agamemnon **(ld 1905)**

These two ships were overshadowed by the *Dreadnought* and it is not sufficiently appreciated how many new features they themselves introduced. The 6in battery was eliminated[17] and they had ten 9.2in in lieu. The combination of 12in and 9.2in proved impossible to control as ranges increased since the splashes of the two calibres could not be distinguished.[18] The main belt was greatly increased in thickness to 12in with an upper belt 8in thick. The extensions fore and aft were also considerably increased in thickness. Since there was no need to protect a 6in armament these big increases in the belt could be made with very little overall increase in armour weight. Both the increase in armour and the abolition of the 6in battery were the results of studies initiated by the Controller, Admiral Sir W H May, which showed the value of big guns and thick armour (discussed in Chapter 11). Both ships were frequently hit at the Dardanelles with little serious damage (Chapter 10). The requirement for the 9.2in to fire at 5° across bow and stern proved impossible to meet because of the risk of hitting the 12in turret but it was claimed that 2° was possible.

A requirement was that these ships should be capable of using certain docks[19] which limited the beam and constrained the shape of the midship section. In turn, this meant that the centre 9.2in turret on each side had to be a single mounting. The main transverse bulkheads in the machinery space had no doors[20] or open pipes penetrating them and ventilation was separate for each space, greatly increasing their resistance to underwater explosions.

These ships were intended for the 1903-04 programme but their many novel features took longer to develop than expected and when the time came to place the orders, there was still uncertainty over the beam and, even more, over which docks they could actually enter. The Controller, May, decided to defer the new design and order three more *King Edward*s instead.[21]

Reduction in hull weight

Reduction in the weight of the hull has always been seen as important by the naval architect; Reed's efforts in this direction have been discussed in Chapter 2 and it is unlikely that he was the first to try. Since the hull is the major component of the all-up weight – displacement – of the ship, a small percentage saving can be most valuable. The table below shows how the weight of the hull of both battleships and big cruisers diminished with respect to dimensions during the White era.

13. R E Froude, 'Experiments on the Direction of Rotation in Twin Screw Ships', *Trans INA* (London 1898). Note that this explanation, supported by evidence, differs from that usually given which attributes the change to an attempt to achieve a marginal gain in efficiency.

14. In practice, control of three different calibres was almost impossible.

15. J H Narbeth, 'Three Steps in Naval Construction', *Trans INA* (London 1922). The contribution to the discussion by Deadman is important, contradicting some of Narbeth's paper. The position of Narbeth is discussed in Chapter 11.

16. Sir W H White, 'The Principles and Methods of Armour Protection in Modern Warships', *The Naval Annual* (London 1905), Chapter 5.

17. The earliest study in the Cover shows four 12in, eight 9.2in, twelve 6in and a 7in belt on 14,000 tons.

18. It should have been possible for the different calibre guns to fire alternately, making spotting easier.

19. No 9 at Chatham and No 5 at Devonport.

20. Lifts were provided for officers only.

21. W H May papers, National Maritime Museum. May sounds very angry over errors by Watts.

Agamemnon 1906. Her mixed armament of 12in and 9.2in guns was not a success. She had thick and extensive armour which stood her in good stead at the Dardanelles where she received numerous hits with little damage. (Author's collection)

armour or vastly more expensive guns without increasing the total cost. There remain good arguments for lighter hulls; a heavy hull will need more powerful engines to drag it through the water and will burn more coal in consequence. Instead of thinking just of savings in hull weight, the designer should seek the cheapest overall package of capability in guns, armour and speed etc, though unnecessary weight should always be eliminated.

It is often not realised that the definition of 'hull weight' includes many items other than structure. For example, the hull weight of *King Edward VII* is given as 5,900 tons (36.1 per cent of displacement) of which only 3,340 tons (20.4 per cent) was structure. The remainder (15.7 per cent) included 510 tons of supports for equipment, 550 tons of magazine fittings, ammunition service and gun supports, 600 tons of engine and boiler seats and uptakes etc, 480 tons for pumping, ventilation and other services together with 420 tons for paint, cement and miscellaneous fittings.

There is often some doubt as to whether a thick deck is all in the hull weight group or partly or wholly in protection. There is also some doubt as to which fittings appear in hull as opposed to equipment or machinery. Finally, in making a comparison on dimensions there can be difficulty in deciding which deck to take in selecting the value of depth – *eg* breastwork ships – or how to deal with a step in deck level such as *Dreadnought*'s long forecastle. For these reasons, comparisons between ships of roughly the same date and design style are fairly accurate whilst long-term studies from *Warrior* to *Dreadnought*, such as those in the final chapter, can only be seen as broad generalisations.

The designers of *Topaze* used this comparison of weight over product of dimensions for smaller ships.

Reduction in hull weight is always presented as an absolute virtue, a view which needs careful examination. Hull weight is a large part of the load displacement, some 40 per cent, and a small reduction in this group will make weight available for guns and armour. A saving of 100 tons may only be about 2 per cent of the hull weight but it is 5 per cent of the armament weight. Stated in this form, the argument is fallacious implying that cost per ton is constant, that fairly cheap structure can be replaced by the same weight of more expensive

Hull weight and dimensions

Battleships	L	B	D (ft)	$LxBxDx10^{-3}$	W_H	$W_H/L.B.Dx10^{-3}$
Renown	380	72.0	43.3	1185	5040	4.25
Majestic	390	75.0	41.1	1200	5650	4.70
Canopus	390.3	74.5	43.4	1262	5310	4.20
Formidable	400	75.0	44.75	1342	5650	4.21
Bulwark	400	75.0	43.60	1308	5625	4.30
Duncan	405	75.0	43.00	1306	5400	4.13
KE VII	425	78.0	43.25	1434	5900	4.11
L Nelson	410	79.5	40.6	1423	5720	4.01
Dreadnought	527	82.0	61.3	2649	6100	3.28

Armoured Cruisers	L	B	D (ft)	$LxBxDx10^{-3}$	W_H	$W_H/L.B.Dx10^{-3}$
Blake	375	65.0	41.75	1018	3502	3.44
Diadem	500	71.6	40.00	1432	4450	3.10
Cressy	440	69.5	39.75	1216	4780	3.93
Monmouth	440	68.5	38.75	1168	4030	3.45
Devonshire	450	68.5	38.75	1194	4350	3.64
D of Edinburgh	430	73.5	40.25	1420	5150	3.62
Warrior	480	73.5	40.50	1428	5190	3.63
Swiftsure	436	71.0	41.7	1291	4630	3.58

	$W_H/L.B.Dx10^{-3}$
Daring	2.2
Rattlesnake	3.98
Halcyon	4.18
Pelorous	3.67
Apollo	3.91
Talbot	3.34
Express	1.69
Sharpshooter	3.21
Barham	3.80
Medea	3.80
Bonaventure	3.95

Notes: *Daring* was built of mild steel; *Express* of HT steel. *Bonaventure* and *Talbot* were sheathed.

The depth of ships with poop and forecastle was taken as –

Depth to upper deck + 7 x (Length of poop + forecastle)/L ship

White's battleships

The reduction from a ratio (W_H/L.B.D) of 4.7 in *Majestic* to 4.0 in *Lord Nelson* reflects the attention paid to weight saving within the battleship section. The low figure for *Dreadnought* is not strictly comparable because of her long forecastle configuration but suggests that further weight saving had indeed been achieved. There was some concern over the loading on dock blocks under these short, heavy ships. In *Majestic* the load was over 40 tons per foot run of blocks.

Cruisers

The cruiser table shows a hull weight ratio of about 3.6, considerably less than for contemporary battleships, reflecting the general use of lighter fittings and scantlings. It is interesting that Reed's *Swiftsure*, which White maintained was derived from his cruisers, fits the cruiser weight family, as indeed does *Dreadnought*.

Narbeth[22] explains in some detail how this reduction was achieved and his writing will now be summarised. The estimated hull weight for the *Majestic* was 5650 tons and the *Majestic*, herself, was weighed at 5717 tons, the same within the limits of accuracy of the weighing process.[23] A sister-ship in a commercial yard weighed 6030 tons. A big effort was made during the building of the *Formidables* with every fitting challenged and alternatives sought if too heavy. This shows the fallacy of equating weight and cost even within the hull group; a special lightweight fitting is almost certainly more expensive than a readily-available but heavy item. White argued[24] that cost does not depend directly on displacement; in particular, complement will vary with armament and horsepower. The first three ships showed an average saving of 40 tons, the next three of 125 tons whilst a redesign of the boat deck in the last two helped to a saving of 630 tons.

The requirement for speed in the *Duncans* made weight saving even more important. The methods used to achieve these savings were incorporated into the specifications for later classes and the weight estimates adjusted downwards in consequence. Even so, the *King Edwards* saved 250 tons from the reduced estimate. With the exception of *Russell*, the dockyard ships were usually the lightest. Machinery development, which led to further important weight savings, is discussed later. It was noted that weight growth in service sank the ship deeper by about ¾in per year. A rule of thumb was that one ton of weight was added for every £150 spent on the ship.

A broad comparison such as this conceals much important detail. Narbeth explains how builders were encouraged to reduce weight in the hull, shown in the table for *Duncan* as 5400 tons. The first two ships saved 90 tons whilst *Russell* (Palmers) was no less than 530 tons lighter. The specification for future ships was rewritten to ensure that such savings as detailed above were repeated. In consequence, the design figure for the

King Edward VII was reduced by 250 tons to the 5900 tons shown above. Some further important savings were made in this class by:

Abolition of fighting tops
Surrender of the 40ft steam pinnace
Surrender of the stream and stern anchor
Reduce storing from four months to three.

In all, a saving of 75 tons.[25]

One of White's Assistant Directors, W H Whiting, was a leading advocate of weight saving believing that the battleship was there to carry guns and resenting any alternative weights (carried to excess when he objected to rangefinders). In a paper to the INA[26] Whiting made the obvious, if rather simplistic, point that a saving of 5 per cent on the 2000-ton hull of a 9000-ton cruiser corresponded to 100 tons, which is 14 per cent of the 700-ton armament weight.

The actual weight increase from a simple change will usually be much greater than expected; a few years before, battleships carried two 9-ton steamboats. These were replaced by two 18-ton pinnaces, a much more capable boat but the weight increase was not 18 tons. The bigger boats needed heavier derricks, rigging and winches and the load increased by about 70 tons. If the power had been increased to restore the loss of speed and the bigger engines protected in the same way the displacement would have gone up by about 250-300 tons.

Whiting listed seventeen items which he thought could be reduced in weight–anchor and cable gear, duplicate systems (electric light had replaced oil but the oil lamps were retained in case of electrical failure), excess paint–up to 2lbs/sq ft[27]–the tendency of store keepers to keep everything they can lay their hands on, etc.

Building times

The building times for the *Majestics* to *Lord Nelson* are of interest, The sixteen built in commercial yards averaged 41 months (42.9 months if the cruiser-like *Swiftsures* are omitted) whilst the twenty-five ships built in the Royal Dockyards averaged 36.6 months. Portsmouth was notably the best averaging 32.6 months compared with 38.5 months for the other yards. The main reason for the difference is the lack of strikes in the Dockyards but this, in turn, must be attributed to better management at both professional and foreman level. This, too, explained the innovative methods used in the Dockyards such as the early introduction of electric lighting at Portsmouth.[28] It is possible that the Dockyards were also helped by greater investment in machinery.

In a little-known paper of 1892, Deadman, latterly Chief Constructor of Portsmouth Dockyard, describes

22. J H Narbeth, 'Three Steps in Naval Construction', *Trans INA* (London 1922).

23. Weighing a ship under construction is not a very accurate procedure. Every item going to the building slip is weighed as it arrives (if there is a queue at the weighbridge some will slip by). The recorder notes the weight, the group he thinks it belongs to and the position in the ship but these are not always easy to recognise. Items removed from the ship such as scrap metal and paint tins are weighed (if they are not just chucked overboard) and deducted from what was thought to be the figure for their arrival. The weighed figure is always heavy.

24. PRO ADM116/878.

25. This complies with the well-known design rule 'If in doubt, leave it out'. Attempts to find a lighter or cheaper unit rarely succeed – cut it out.

26. W H Whiting, 'The effect of modern accessories on the size and cost of warships', *Trans INA* (London 1903).

27. In recent years *Leander* class frigates have been found with eighty coats of paint. Stripping these off saved some 45 tons.

28. H E Deadman, 'On the Application of Electricity in the Royal Dockyards and Navy', *Trans I Mech E* (London 1892).

the impact of electric light on shipbuilding at Portsmouth. If the ship was fitting out near the electric shop, leads would be carried to her on temporary poles but for the building slips and more distant berths, a shed would be erected with a boiler, engine and dynamo. The cost, including depreciation of the plant, for the cruiser *Royal Arthur* was estimated at £1200 which was little, if at all, greater than that of candles. The vastly superior light enabled work to be done better, more quickly and under better supervision as well as the improvement to the '. . . health and comfort to the workmen' which would have justified a higher cost. As Deadman concluded the '. . . celerity and cheapness of construction, which have lately been attained in Portsmouth Dockyard, could scarcely have been realised without the aid of the admirable illumination afforded by the system of incandescent lighting.' In discussion, White said that he had used electric light at Elswick in the building of the *Victoria*, though not to the same extent as at Portsmouth.

During the same period, the average building time for twelve French battleships was 60 months. A French government report suggested that their build costs were about 20-25 per cent greater than British.

French building effort

	C Martel	Charlemagne	Gaulois
Weight at launch (tons)	3512	3511	3500
Man days work/1000	548	396	336
Days/ton	158	113	95

Armour

Harvey armour (1891-93)

There were at least two rapid developments in the armour itself at this time; reference has already been made to the first, Harvey armour. The principle of compound armour was sound; a hard steel face which would break up attacking shot, backed by a tough material but it was unsatisfactory in use. The transition from face to back was too sudden and the weld would fail whilst the backing iron did not provide sufficient resistance to stop shot or splinters which had passed through the face. Various schemes were tried to overcome these difficulties and the US engineer, H A Harvey, was the first to achieve success. In tests in 1891, at Indian Head, his plates proved considerably superior to all other armour.

In his process the face was 'cemented' – heated in contact with carbon – and was then cooled with water giving a very hard face. The whole plate was annealed which gave a tough back. Harvey himself used the process on a nickel steel alloy but British tests showed that resistance to penetration was as great without nickel[29] though the toughness was less, particularly when the face was chilled using the Tressider process. Initial tests gave a figure of merit of 1.3 but this was soon improved upon; tests in 1893 showed a figure of merit of 2.0.[30]

Resistance to penetration by uncapped projectiles[31]

15in of wrought iron is the same as:
12in of compound
12in of all steel
7½in of Harvey
5¾in of Krupp

There were a number of tests of various types of shell and armour in 1892-93.[32] An AP common steel shell with the point of an AP, a larger capacity HE (Lyddite) filling and a base fuse would pass through one calibre steel or compound. Holtzer 6in shot were broken up by Harvey or Tressider 6in plate in a trial on *Nettle*. On 4 August 1892 five 6in Holtzer all broke up on Ellis Tressider plate and on 1 November Harvey steel by Vickers broke up more Holtzer shot. On 18 January 1893 6in Vickers Harvey broke up four heavy-charge

29. Statement on Navy Estimates 1894.

30. In comparing the figure of merit of one type of armour with another, it is important to state the type of projectile used. For example, Palliser chilled shot had virtually no chance of penetrating any cemented armour. It is not certain what type of projectile is referred to in the table but it is likely that it corresponds to forged steel shells such as the Holtzer.

31. 1915 *Gunnery Manual*, p 96.

32. *Brassey's Naval Annual 1893* (London 1893).

These sections show the changes in the main armour protection of White's ships. Note the introduction of the sloped deck in *Majestic* and how the thickest deck was raised to the top of the belt in bulwark.

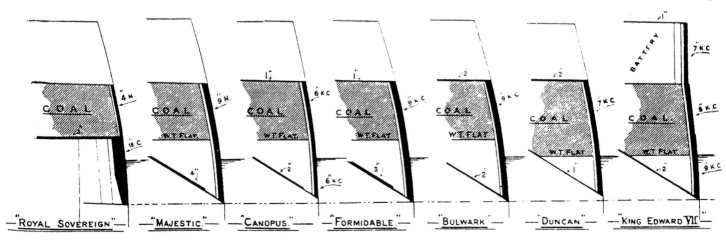

"ROYAL SOVEREIGN" — "MAJESTIC" — "CANOPUS" — "FORMIDABLE" — "BULWARK" — "DUNCAN" — "KING EDWARD VII"

Holtzer shot which would have penetrated 10½in steel.

Harvey armour, almost certainly without nickel alloy, was used for the 9in belt of the *Majestics* (laid down 1894) which enabled a larger area to be protected. They were the only major ships with a Harvey main belt before the process was superseded by the superior Krupp method. Early studies for the *Canopus* showed Harvey armour and it was noted that improvements made a 6in plate equivalent to earlier 6¾in plates.

Krupp armour (c1896)

Though the Harvey process was a great improvement, it was soon found that the back was not tough enough when attacked by forged steel projectiles. Krupp developed an improved process in which the low carbon steel was alloyed with 3½-4 per cent nickel, 1½-2 per cent chromium and a small percentage of manganese (some molybdenum may also have been used). The steel was then melted in an open-hearth furnace and then cast into an ingot of up to 60 tons weight and allowed to cool until it was solid enough to be lifted. After re-heating to a uniform temperature the ingot was pressed to a slab in a hydraulic press and the unsound portion, perhaps as much as one-third, cut off.

The pressed slab was then passed back and forth through the rolling mills until it was a little thicker than the finished size. At each pass the rollers, driven by engines of up to 15,000 horsepower, moved some ¼–½in closer. After rolling, the plate was placed in a low temperature furnace, softened by sprinkling with water, and set flat when the face was planed flat. The plate was then arranged face up on a truck and covered with a mixture of animal and vegetable charcoal to a depth of 6in and another plate laid on top. The whole was then covered with sand and run into a furnace where it was kept at a high temperature for up to three weeks. Immediately after being withdrawn, the plate was bent to the final shape and toughened by re-heating and cooling in an oil bath. The edges were cut to final shape and all holes were drilled and plugged with clay.

The face was then heated to a higher temperature than the back by protecting the latter in the furnace and the plate was suddenly chilled on both sides by water jets. The face was now very hard whilst the back, which was not carburised, and was heated to a lower temperature, remained tough. The shape was checked and any adjustment made in the press with the plate nearly cold. Any final adjustments were made by grinding as the face was now too hard to cut but holes in the back could still be drilled and tapped. The process was complicated, temperature control being vital, and took a considerable time, manufacturers quoting 9 months for delivery from receipt of orders. The hard face was deeper in Krupp plate than in Harvey and could not be varied independently of the hardness required. Note the greater cost shown in the table under *Duncan*.

The changes in the nature of armour to Harvey and

Albion of the *Canopus* class, the first ships with Krupp armour. (Imperial War Museum: Q38101)

then to Krupp, combined with a big building programme, meant that armour production limited the number of big ships which could be ordered. 1898 was seen as the worst year after which new plant came on line giving about 28,000 tons in 1899-1900. At £95 per ton, it was big business.

The figure of merit was at least 2 but varied with thickness as the optimum depth of hard face was not attained in either thin or thick plates. Hovgaard quotes;

Plate thickness	Figure of merit
4in	2.25
6in	2.67
12in	2.33

The first RN ship with a belt of Krupp armour was the *Canopus* (laid down 1896) where it was 6in thick. Many writers have denigrated the *Canopus* class for their thin belt, failing to note its superior performance and the much greater height covered. This class also introduced thin armour extending to the bow; though flooding for-

A typical armour bolt. Note how the bolt is necked so that the screw tread is not the narrowest part of the bolt.

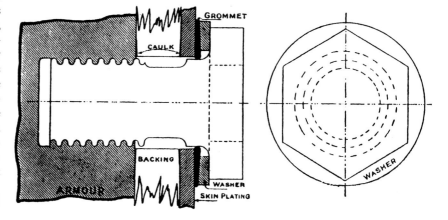

ward posed no danger to the ship, it would reduce speed and cause inconvenience. The 2in plate would be effective against small QF and splinters from larger HE shells bursting in the sea.

For a short time, Krupp armour put defence ahead of attack but gunfounders were soon busy. It was noted that *Formidable*'s belt could resist all older 12in shells at over 3000yds but capped shells would penetrate at 5000yds and the 9.2in at 3-4000yds. The basic Krupp armour process remained in use until the end of the battleship era, a remarkable achievement, though Britain and Germany (but not the USA) improved performance by about 30 per cent *c*1930 by improved heat treatment and minor changes in composition which enabled a still more gentle transition from hard face to the back.

Armour distribution up to Dreadnought[33]

The distribution of armour did not change in principle between *Canopus* and *Dreadnought* but there were subtle changes between each class showing that careful consideration was given each time. The *Formidable*s had a 9in belt of Krupp cemented and had a thin belt to the stern as well as the forward belt of *Canopus*. The upper edge of the belt was at main deck level, 9ft 6in above the waterline. The *Bulwark*s were similar to the *Formidable*s but the area covered by the main belt was a little greater and the deck thickness was increased between the barbettes.

The *Duncan*s sacrificed armour for speed, having a 7in main belt. The forward belt was increased both in area and thickness with the aim of maintaining speed after damage. There was a much more radical change in horizontal armour arrangement with the main deck, at the top of belt, becoming the thickest deck. The middle deck was reduced to 1in, even on the slopes. White[34] had been advocating this arrangement for some time out of concern for the effects of high-capacity shells bursting above the belt. He pointed out that with only a 10° roll or list, the projected vertical height of the deck would be about 13ft compared with a height of 9½ft for the belt. The chance of a shell hitting the deck, even when the trajectory of the shell was near horizontal, was considerable and the effects could be serious. The uppermost deck (main deck, level with the top of the belt) should be strong enough to prevent the shell from penetrating and, since the impact would be oblique, 2in would be sufficient. However, this deck would be seriously damaged by the explosion of a large shell and a second deck (middle), 1in thick, would be needed to stop splinters and debris from reaching the machinery and other vital spaces.

Deck protection is expensive in terms of weight; 1in of deck protection weighed as much as 5in on the belt. White was probably right in principle but the reduction in thickness of the middle deck slopes considerably reduced the effectiveness of the side protection. One may also wonder if the gunnery of the day was capable

of hitting an enemy ship at all with a roll of 10° either way.

The *London*s were similar to the *Duncan*s in arrangement of decks but with a 9in belt. The *King Edward*s were similar in principle to *Bulwark* with variations to suit the main deck battery which had 7in armour between main and upper deck.

The *Lord Nelson*s were changed considerably. The main belt was increased to 12in amidships at the waterline with 8in to the main deck and reduced to 4in aft. Barbette armour was simplified and slightly thinner. Deck armour was also slightly thinner. A number of tests had been held with a thin de-capping plate in front of the main plate but these were not successful.

Tests of armour

Sample plates were submitted for test by the manufacturer and, sometimes, a plate would be selected from a production batch for test. Plates of 160lbs upwards were tested unbacked, supported on two edges only, and fired on by salt-filled capped common shell (160lb and 200lb plates) or APC for thicker plates. Thinner plates were supported on substantial wood backing and fired on with common shell. The striking velocity was specified. Test pieces were taken frequently for mechanical and chemical testing. Note that armour weighs 40.8lbs/sq ft per inch thickness. The specification was usually in terms of weight, *eg* 240lbs, which is 5.88in and referred to as '6in'. Manufacturers were also allowed a small tolerance on finished plates which usually resulted in the finished plate being slightly thinner.

Armour details

The introduction of face-hardened armour with a tough back meant that there was no need for substantial timber backing. Some packing, about 2½in of teak to give a fair surface, was all that was required. Bolts changed little. They retained a neck which would stretch under load rather than tearing at the threads.

Inevitably, there were many openings in armoured decks. Hatches closed in action were made of material as thick as the deck, usually with a counterbalance weight. Coal-bunker hatches often had a horizontal sliding cover. Funnel and ventilator openings had to leave a clear air passage and were protected by armour gratings. The opening in the deck is subdivided by girders and a grating is fitted in each space. For a 2in deck the grating of cast steel would be 7in deep, made up of ½in members, 2½in apart. Some of these gratings could be opened in the same way as ordinary armoured hatches. Splinter nets were fitted 12in below the gratings in the engine-rooms to stop debris reaching machinery.

The *Belleisle* trial (Chapter 10) showed that gratings were most effective if the bars were perpendicular to the line of flight of the shell, *ie* fore and aft.[35] Gratings and nets were of little value in keeping out the very small splinters from lyddite shell. A later trial, in 1913,

33. Burt, *British Battleships, 1889-1904*.

34. W H White, 'The Principles and Methods of Armour Protection in Modern Warships', *Brassey's Naval Annual 1905* (London 1905).

35. This does not seem to have been adopted.

36. The BVII mount in the *Irresistible, Venerable, Prince of Wales, Albemarle* and *Exmouth* could load at any angle but in service usually loaded at 5° suggesting that the design was not satisfactory. The *King Edward*s had the BVIIs for loading at any angle.

Victorious of the *Majestic* class 1895. Note the many openings and projections in the sides which would generate spray and also admit water if she was damaged. (Imperial War Museum: Q40506)

involved exploding 9.2in powder-filled common shell over gratings, both cold and heated to 1200°F. The hot gratings worked better but a considerable number of fragments, up to 8lbs weight, passed through.

The use of rope mantlets to prevent splinters flying round a battery was tried in 1893 and they were found to be almost useless. The value of splinter nets under the boat stowage was tested on shore in 1892 and during the *Belleisle* trial and were found to give very little protection. An 1899 trial of 9.2in AP shells at 30° impact showed that both capped and uncapped shell could penetrate 7in KC at 1950ft/sec (2000yds for a Mk VIII gun, 3200yds for the Mk X).

Armament

Twelve-inch guns

All British battleships from *Majestic* to the early *Dreadnought*s mounted 12in guns in twin turrets but there were significant improvements in speed of loading, in muzzle velocity and a considerable reduction in the size and weight of the mounting.

Up till the *Majestic*s all big guns had to train fore-and-aft for loading and were carried in a large pear-shaped barbette. The last two ships of the class, *Caesar* and *Illustrious* (ld 1895) were given circular barbettes in which the guns could be loaded at any angle of training. It is surprising that this feature was so long delayed as Armstrong had used it in his mounts for the *Re Umberto* (ld 1884). The mountings for these two British ships introduced, for the first time, a break in the ammunition supply as a precaution against flash, with a loading chamber below the gun containing twenty-four ready-use shells.

Three different designs of mounting were fitted to the *Canopus* class. The first ships had mounts similar to *Caesar*, then to speed up loading another mount was introduced which abandoned the break in the ammunition chain. Finally, *Vengeance* (ld 1898) introduced a mounting in which the guns could be loaded at any elevation. It is claimed that this reduced the interval between rounds from 48 to 32 seconds but there seem to have been problems and loading at any elevation was not standardised[36] until the *King Edward VII* class. The *Formidable*s introduced an improved loading chamber.

British turrets were larger than those of other navies which made them easy to work but also made them very heavy. The *Duncan*s had barbettes reduced in diameter by 1ft to 36½ft. In the *King Edward*s this was further reduced to 34ft and in *Lord Nelson* (and *Dreadnought*), with the new 45-calibre gun, to 27ft. The table below shows the improvement in performance of the gun itself.

Twelve-inch gun particulars

Mark	Length (cal)	Wt gun (tons)	Wt shell (lbs)	MV (ft/sec)	Penetration* (in)	First fitted
III-V	25	45	714	1914		1887 *Edinburgh*
VIII	35	46.1	850	2417	11.5	1895 *Majestic*
IX**	40	50.8	850	2567	13	1901 *Implacable*
X	45	57.7	850	2725	14	1905 *Lord Nelson*

* Of KC plate by APC at 5000yds, normal impact. (Capped shells entered service *c*1908.)
** *King Edward*s had a heavier charge giving MV of 2612ft/sec

Triumph with anti-torpedo nets spread. Note the length of the 7.5in guns. The muzzles would go into the sea if the ship was rolling. (Imperial War Museum: SP2458)

Secondary armament

The secondary battery, usually twelve 6in, was intended to attack the unarmoured portion of enemy ships; 12pdrs and smaller were mounted to protect against torpedo boats. Many officers believed that the enemy would be disabled by such a 'hail of fire' and only then would the 12in guns fire, sinking the opponent with AP shot at close range. This belief was probably the origin of the procedure in which AP shell were tested only at normal impact.

In British ships the secondary battery was normally protected by casemates. Whatever the scheme of protection, a considerable amount of ammunition was exposed to hits from the enemy big guns behind fairly thin armour in ready-use stowage and while in transport from the magazine. At Jutland, *Malaya* was to show the danger of a lightly-protected battery.

Projectiles

The introduction of the forged steel projectile of the Holtzer type proceeded only slowly in the RN, it would seem mainly on cost grounds. During the 1890s AP projectiles had no bursting charge but as compounds such as Lyddite (picric acid), which could (sometimes) resist impact without detonating, came into use, a burster charge of about 2 per cent total weight was added. Fusing to burst after penetrating armour remained a problem till 1918. In 1902 there were still large numbers of Palliser shot in the magazines which were almost useless against hard-faced armour. There were a number of Holtzer projectiles, imported from France, which were unlikely to defeat KC armour.

In 1902, Vickers and Armstrong's agreed with Krupp on price-fixing and also on sharing a number of patents. Vickers already had a licence for the manufacture of Krupp armour and this agreement was extended to share a number of other patents. The most important of these concerned the use of Krupp fuses[37] which were widely adopted by both the Army and the Navy between 1905 and 1912. The Krupp-Vickers agreements stipulated that both sides should transfer all later developments, but this condition was increasingly evaded.

There was an interesting trial in 1878 in England.[38] A compound plate was accidentally installed the wrong way round and a chilled iron shot easily penetrated the plate when hitting the soft side first. It was then found that if the plate was the right way round but with a thin wrought iron plate in front of the hard steel, the shot would still penetrate. Finally, an engineer officer, Captain English, suggested putting a cap of soft iron on the head of the shot which was then capable of penetrating the hard face. The results of this test were ignored and capped projectiles were not used until tried by Russia in 1894.[39] When an uncapped projectile (or a soft-capped shell with striking velocity below 1750ft/sec) strikes hard-faced armour the plate will be dished, spreading the force of impact. The point of the shell will be forced back into the body, breaking it up. The hard face of the plate may be broken up but the back will usually remain intact. Should the armour be grossly over-matched by the shell, a cone-shaped piece of plate will be forced out and flung into the ship. The diameter of this cone will be about that of the shell at the face and up to three times that at the back.

Capped shell had about 15 per cent greater penetration provided that the velocity on impact was sufficient (*c*1750ft/sec) and the angle to the normal was not more than about 15° (some benefit up to 30°). Capped shell were first introduced from about 1904 but were neither numerous nor satisfactory for some years.

About 1903, Firths produced an AP shell which they called the 'Rendable' and proved very effective. Vickers, Armstrong and Hadfield[40] were given the chance to produce competing products but it was July 1905 before the first successful 9.2in shell was produced and the 12in was still awaited. The performance of shells during the Russo-Japanese War is discussed in the next chapter but it would appear that in neither battle did shells of either navy penetrate thick armour and burst inside. Improved alloys enabled complicated hardening techniques to be used on the head whilst the body of the shell was annealed to make it tough.

The 1915 gunnery manual says that APC, filled either with powder or Lyddite, will seldom penetrate even medium armour if hitting obliquely. They will usually burst, 'explode, not detonate', in passing through the plate. If such shell hit normally, HE-filled shell would burst about three-quarters of the way through a thick plate, projecting fragments into the ship. Powder-filled HE at 1960ft/sec would penetrate 12in KC and burst a few feet behind. Thin-walled HE shell would be stopped by armour ⅓ calibre in thickness.

Testing shell

From each 'Lot' of 400 shells, two were tested. One was fired against armour (sand-and salt-filled) and the other fired for recovery to ensure that the shell was not deformed during firing. The shell fired against armour was required to perforate, *ie* if it broke up and fragments passed through the plate, the batch was passed.

Uncapped AP shell were tested against KNC armour at 20° inclination (6in) and 30° (9.2in, 12in).

Gun	Striking Vel (ft/sec)	Thickness (in)
6in	2020	4.5
9.2in	1900	7
12in	1850	10

If the shell failed this test, another one was tried and, if that passed, the batch was accepted. The procedure for a second failure was complicated but was almost equivalent to allowing the manufacturer to go on till he got a pass. A very high proportion of failures could be accepted in this way.[41] Since the shells were unfused and without burster, these vital functions were not tested.

Safety of ammunition

A considerable number of tests were carried out on the effect of shells hitting 6in and 4.7in shell stowed in racks. If a powder-filled shell was struck, it would explode but neighbouring shells would not be affected. A Lyddite shell would not explode if hit by a powder-filled shell but would explode if hit by a Lyddite-filled shell and would also set off shells within a few feet.

There were a number of trials of cartridges, usually singly. In all cases the cartridge would burn fiercely but not explode. There were several cordite fires in the Russo-Japanese War, notably when a 12in shell burst in the after turret of *Fuji* which ignited eight quarter charges. These burnt fiercely for some time but the flash did not spread and six HE shells exposed to the fire did not explode. (A cut hydraulic pipe contributed to the fire.) A study by the DNO of the Russo-Japanese War specifically concluded that cordite charges would not explode. Accident was seen as a greater hazard to ammunition than was enemy action.

With hindsight, one can see that these tests were inadequate in that they did not simulate a fire in a large quantity of cordite in a confined space. However, it is clear that safety of ammunition was studied and there was considerable evidence that it was not a major hazard.

Target practice

Gunnery practice from 1860 to the end of the century was carried out quarterly against a stationary target, with the firing ship steaming slowly on a steady course at about 1500yds range. Stories of practice ammunition being thrown overboard to avoid damage to the paint should be treated with caution; even if true, such actions were the exception. Note, for example, *Temeraire*, mentioned earlier, where actual structural damage was accepted once a year from the after barbette and its crew trained on the forward mount in the other three quarterly firings (Chapter 4). Though these conditions for practice were unsatisfactory, they were not entirely unrealistic since lacking fire control, and even range-finders, the chance of hitting at over 1500yds was thought to be remote. However, on 10 August 1904, both the Japanese and Russian battleships were capable of fairly accurate fire at 12,000yds.

By the end of the century it was clear that guns, if pointed correctly, could score hits at much longer ranges. However, the first step was to improve hitting under the artificial conditions of the gunlayers' test. This had now been formalised; the firing ship steamed at 8kts past the target, opening fire at 1600yds with a closest approach of 1400yds. Each gun fired in turn for about 6 minutes. Under these conditions, 20-40 per cent hits was usual though many ships were worse. Note that *Majestic* only scored about 40 per cent hits on the bigger target of *Belleisle*. Practice in other navies was generally similar; at the end of the century, the USN carried out a practice to RN rules scoring about one-fifth of the hits which would be expected from a British ship – which matches their performance against Spain.[42]

Any complacency was shattered in May 1899 when Captain Percy Scott's cruiser, *Scylla*, fired seventy rounds, scoring fifty-six hits – 80 per cent. The following year, now commanding *Terrible*, on the China Station, he scored 77 per cent hits with the 6in (average ship 28 per cent) with 5.3 rounds fired and 4.2 hits per minute from each gun while the 9.2ins achieved 64 per cent hits. The following year she did even better but others had learnt the lesson and in 1902 *Terrible* was only fourth-best in the China squadron. Scott's methods were strongly supported, both by junior officers, who copied them, and by senior officers; the Commanders-in-Chief of both the Mediterranean and China Fleets presented shields for competition and the Admiralty awarded a sleeve badge for marksmanship. The results of the annual tests were reported in the press and a good result was seen as essential for promotion both for the gunnery officer and the captain. In 1903 Scott was appointed as captain of the gunnery school.

There was a well-publicised scandal in 1904 when *Centurion*'s gun sights, passed by the Admiralty, were found to be defective. In 1905 Scott was given the new post of Inspector of Target Practice and, thanks largely to his efforts, it was the first year in which hits exceeded misses. Jellicoe was appointed Director of Naval Ordnance in 1905. Between 1897 and 1907 the percentage of hits rose from 32 to 79 per cent, despite an increase in range in 1904.

37. K I McCallum, 'A Little Neglect? The problem of defective shell in the RN 1914-18', *Journal of Naval Engineering* (London June 1993).

38. Hovgaard, *Modern History of Warships*.

39. It does not seem that Russia used capped shells in the war with Japan.

40. D Carnegie, 'The Manufacture and Efficiency of Armour-piercing Projectiles', *Proc ICE* Vol 153 (London 1903).

41. Marder claims that 30-70 per cent *were* dud shells – I suspect a misquote and should be 30-70 per cent *may* have been dud. The tests were not good enough to say 'were'.

42. It is said that the French were somewhat better but no evidence has been found. In 1898 *Redoutable* and *Amiral Duperre* fired 625 rounds at 3000yds while at anchor in a calm sea scoring 23.2 per cent hits. Campbell refers to firing against *Zenta* in 1914 with poor results.

Battle practice, in which all guns were fired simultaneously, was introduced in 1905 with firing at 5-7000yds for 5 minutes. Initially, the target was stationary but, from 1908, it was towed slowly whilst the ship manoeuvred. The results were about 0.8 hits per gun per minute. Scott invented and used several training aids to improve performance including a loading trainer, the 'dotter' to teach the layer to keep his sights on the target from a rolling ship and, a little later, a similar deflection trainer. In no way does it detract from his leadership to draw attention to the support which was quickly given at all levels. Genius functions best when it is the trigger to a critical mass.

Rate of fire

At 1000-1500yds the time of flight was negligible, the projectile travelled almost horizontally and there was no need for elaborate fire control. Rate of hitting should have been almost the same as rate of firing and no explanation has been given for the 80 per cent of shots which missed though it seems likely that rolling accounted for a large proportion.

The table below lists the interval between successive rounds for various guns. The conditions under which these results were achieved are not known but it is likely that they were the best which a well trained crew could achieve, under ideal conditions and without undue attention to aiming.

Rates of fire[43]

Ship	Interval between shots (min-sec)	
Sans Pareil	3-24	
Benbow	3-0	
Trafalgar, Hood	2-9	
'Admiral' 13.5in	3-9	
R Sovereign	2-11	
Colossus	3-21	
Conqueror	3-21	
Collingwood	3-0	
Thunderer 10in	1-13	
Devastation 10in	1-14	
Barfleur	1-25	
Prince George and class		*Majestic* and
any position	1-8	*Magnificent* differ
fixed position	1-30	
Caesar	1-12	BIII mount, all round loading

43. 1901 *Gunnery Manual* per J Campbell.

44. 'H M Ships *Dreadnought* and *Invincible*', Tweedmouth Papers, MoD Library.

45. PRO ADM116/878.

46. Commander S King-Hall, 'The Evolution of the Cruiser', Naval Staff Monograph,1928.

47. In 1889-93 a plate of 10½in needed to resist 6in Holtzer at 2000ft/sec. Now 6in plate will do so with a 100:57 advantage in weight.

In 1906 Jellicoe, as DNO, compared rates of fire in the simple gunlayers test with those achieved in battle practice and noted that the latter was very similar to the rate of fire by Japanese ships at Tsushima.[44]

Rate of fire (rounds/min)

Gun	Gunlayers	Battle practice
6in	12	4
9.2in	5	2
12in	2	1

As range increased, it became necessary to spot the fall of shot before firing the next round to correct range and defection. It was this, more than anything, which led to the immense superiority of the big gun. The smaller gun, whose apparent advantage was in rate of fire, could not achieve this rate at longer range.

The changes in gunnery procedure, outlined above, greatly increased the fighting capability of warships but involved few changes in ship design. The chance of being hit was greatly increased and the danger of the unarmoured parts of the ship being destroyed was enhanced.

Armoured cruisers, 1898-1904

During 1893-94 considerable thought was given to the future building programme, particularly for cruisers. The starting point was to match the thirty French and Russian First and Second Class cruisers.[45] The overall building programme for the five years up to April 1899 was large – and expensive. The proposal was:

Number and Category	£ ship + engine	£ Armament (both x 1000)
7 First Class battleships	5600	1500
1 First Class cruiser	800	200
6 as *Blenheim*	2900	600
1 *Vulcan*	380	60
12 *Talbot*	3000	800
6 Fleet Rams (*Arrogant*)	1800	300
4 Imp. *Barham*	500	170
7 Torpedo gunboats	525	150
74 TBD	2700	570
30 TB	550	170
TOTAL £x 1000	18,755	4470

Further consideration of cruiser requirements came a little later. Each battleship 'needed' two cruisers so, with eighteen battleships in the Mediterranean and eight to ten in home waters, fifty-six cruisers were needed for fleet work. Trade protection demanded another 18 cruisers, together with eighteen armed merchant ships. This totalled seventy-four against sixty-three modern ships in service and twenty older cruisers. It was proposed to build three *Blakes*, four *Talbots*, one *Vulcan*, two new design and five *Barhams*. In March 1894 approval was given to a programme very similar to the table above.

This then led to a projection of cruiser numbers as follows:-

Cruiser numbers

Category	Date	England	France	Russia	Combined
1st Class	1895	19	10	5	15
	1896	21	13	6	19
	1897	24	15	9	24
	1898	29	17	9	26
2nd Class	1895	12	13	5	18
	1896	12	13	5	18
	1897	12	13	6	19
	1898	12	15	7	20

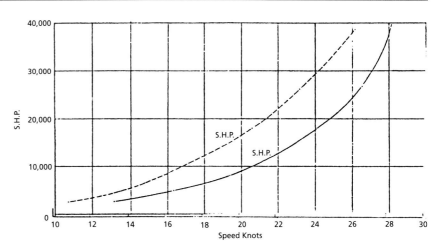

White's personal contribution to the philosophy of cruisers as well as to their design was important. Writing much later, a staff officer[46] wrote; 'Suddenly, the naval officers would receive a short statement from the DNC (White) in which he would point out that time was getting on . . . and that action was necessary in the shape of a decision. "In order to assist their Lordships to reach this decision" he submitted a design.' Faced with a *fait accompli* the Board would usually agree with White. While exaggerated, the files in the Public Record Office and the ships' covers show that White did push the Board in somewhat this way.

Cressy *class (ld 1898-99)*

The introduction of Krupp armour meant that big cruisers could be given a worthwhile belt without an undue increase in size. Whilst on leave, White saw the Italian *Garibaldi* and the *Cressys* were his response to them and to the French *Montcalm*. A 6in belt would keep out AP shells from 6in (the largest true QF gun) at most fighting ranges and would explode most HE shells outside the ship.[47] To a considerable extent *Cressy* was a belted *Diadem*, her protection weighing 2500 tons (21

The upper curve shows the power required to drive a cruiser with fouling accumulated over 176 days out of dock. Compared with the lower curve for a clean bottom, power is almost doubled for a given speed.

In the design of *Drake*, 1901, White and his team tried to reduce the superstructure, partly to give a smaller target and partly to reduce the risk of fire. This made the funnels even more conspicuous, making them (in the author's view) the most impressive of White's cruisers. They were powerful ships in their day and it was thought that their belt of 6in cemented armour would permit them to join the battle line if required. The double tier casemates were a feature of White's ships and provided far better protection than in most foreign ships. (National Maritime Museum, London: 35011, 35011B)

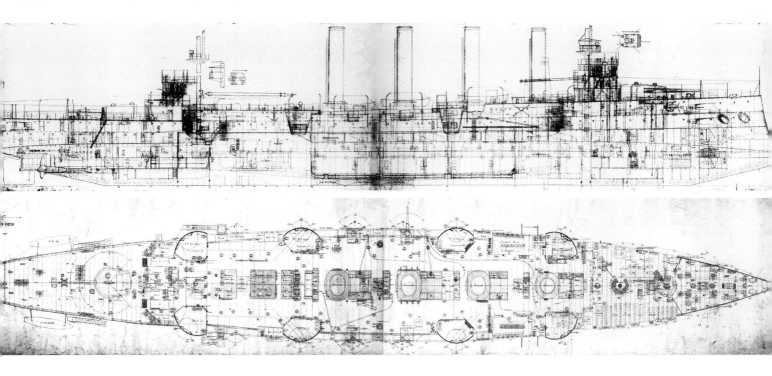

per cent) compared with 1809 tons (17.1 per cent) for the ship without a belt. (Overall, this led to a 1000-ton increase in displacement.) She had a 6in belt 230ft 6in long extending from 5ft below to 6ft 6in above. The main deck was 1in and the second deck 1½in, curved down to meet the bottom of the belt. The space between was used for bunkers, subdivided as in protected cruisers. It should be noted that the thickness and disposition of the armour was virtually identical to that of *Canopus*, making it realistic, as White suggested, to use the *Cressy*s in the line of battle.

They introduced a more powerful mark of 9.2in gun as well as twelve 6in QF.[48] They were the first ships to use fireproofed wood.[49] None of this class was sheathed as successful anti-fouling paints were available,[50] saving some £40,000. It had been estimated that sheathing would increase draught by 9in, displacement by 550 tons, cost by £40,000 and reduce trial speed by ½kt. Anti-fouling paints of the day had a life of about a year, after which the ship would be docked for recoating. Even so, White says that 6 months' fouling in home waters would increase the power required for a given speed by about 20-25 per cent and at the end of the year, power would be increased by 50 per cent. In tropical waters these increases would be doubled.

They had a metacentric height of 3.25ft light, 3.5ft deep and the maximum righting lever was at 35°. They completed with a draught 6in less than designed, a saving of 300 tons due to weight-control measures as described earlier under battleships.

The captain of *Cressy* (Tudor) was pleased with his ship which he saw as a good seaboat but she was very wet – 'the waves in a very slight seaway, dash against the projections – casemates, shoots etc – and squirt up the side coming down in sheets of spray over the boat deck'. She also took in a fair amount of water through the ports of the lower casemates.

Drake *class (ld 1899)*

Though the *Drake*s were not dissimilar in appearance to the *Cressy*s, they had a number of important changes. They were White's counter to the *Jean d'Arc*. Evidence to the Fane Committee[51] by two of White's senior Assistants show how he operated. Smith said:

The DNC would then confer with one of the Chief Constructors – in the case of *Drake* it was myself – to whom he would show the Controller's minute, and from our general knowledge of what is practicable, we would see at once in our minds some sort of a cruiser near the mark.

Another senior Assistant, Whiting, describes the next step:

'I wish a design to be prepared for a ship of the following dimensions and I wish Mr ——, Assistant Constructor, to take charge.' The Chief Constructor

would then go into the Assistant Constructor's room and request him to make a rough drawing, indicating the disposition of armour and the arrangement of guns and other things, and to make what we call preliminary calculations as to the weights of all the principal features and to consider the disposition of weights longitudinally to see that the vessel would float properly. The Assistant Constructor would also make an outline calculation of stability to see that the vessel would have sufficient stability to float properly.

White seems always to have followed up these preliminary discussions with a short, formal memo confirming what was to be done. One interesting such note is for the Second Class cruiser *Talbot* where having decided the displacement, White asks what thickness of deck can be afforded.

Considerable effort was expended in reducing the area of the target in *Drake*. The depth of the hull was determined by the draught limitation of the Suez Canal,[52] together with the height of the boiler-room, bunkers above and the 6in casemates on the main deck. The freeboard at the bow was taken as 30ft though this apparently high freeboard was compromised as regards stability at large angles, particularly after damage, by gunports and other openings (these obstructions would also generate a lot of spray). A version with only 24ft freeboard and reduced sheer, giving a height to the gun axis of 28ft, was considered. Though it would have saved 50 tons, the cost saving was not thought worthwhile in view of the loss of speed in bad weather.[53]

The boat deck was abolished to save weight and also reduce both the target and the fire risk, which was probably a natural extension of the work started on earlier classes to reduce the fire hazard but also included the lessons of the Spanish-American War (Chapter 10). The 6in belt extended from 6ft 9in above the waterline to 9ft 5in below. Instead of the 5in armoured forward bulkhead of the *Cressy*s' the *Drake*s had a 2in extension of the belt to the bow. This would have been very valuable in protecting the fore end against splinter damage from HE shells bursting in the sea. Even though such damage would not be fatal, it would reduce the speed of the ship. The 5in bulkhead aft was retained. There was considerable thought given to reducing the longitudinal subdivision in the bunkers since the transverse bulkheads were more effective in torpedo protection.

The number of 6in was increased to sixteen for attacking unprotected areas but the 9.2in were seen as essential to penetrate armour and thick decks. Small, ready-use magazines for the amidships guns were considered, and rejected, as an alternative to the ammunition passage. As far as possible, magazines were kept away from machinery to avoid the heat. The big guns normally stowed 100 rounds per gun though there was space for 150. It was noted that fire would be opened at about 6000yds.

48. They could carry twelve 6in with 100 rounds per gun or 10 guns with 200 rounds. Twelve guns with 200 rounds would increase displacement by 3-400 tons.

49. This use must ante-date the lessons of the Spanish American War. Hindsight suggests it may not have been very effective; modern warships use untreated wood as the 'fireproofed' material gives off toxic fumes when in a fire. There were contemporary complaints that the fireproofing tarnished gold braid on uniforms.

50. Holtzapfel – 'International' from 1879 and 'Moravia' from about the same date. Early anti-fouling paints were a wonderful brew of copper, arsenic and mercury salts and probably killed many painters as well as barnacles. But sheathing was still discussed later.

51. Brown, *A Century of Naval Construction*.

52. Then 25ft 4in.

53. The loss of speed would have been very small since 24 ft freeboard is equal to !.1√Λ.

54. W H White, 'Presidential Address', ICE 1903.

55. Manning, *Life of Sir William White*, p398

56. G Bennett, *Coronel and the Falklands* (London 1962).

57. Hovgaard quotes the mining of *San Diego* in the First World War. Calculated heel due to longitudinal bulkheads was 17½° but gun ports on 2nd deck went under at 9½° and she capsized – as did many others.

58. K McBride, 'The *Devonshires*', *Warship 47* (London July 1988).

The metacentric height was 2.6ft deep and 1.7ft light with a maximum righting lever of 1.5ft at 35°. Much consideration was given to the type of boiler to be installed; the weight for 28,000 ihp being:

Type of Boiler	Draught	Weight (tons)	Trial (hrs)
Cylindrical	Natural	2000	8
„	Mod. force	1680	4
„	High force	1400	3
Belleville	Natural	1250	8
„	Mod force	1030	4
Small tube		1000	3-4
			(estimate only)

They completed with forty-three Bellevilles.

Though the *Drake* made her design speed of 23kts on trial there were indications that propellers with greater area and less pitch would be better.[54]

	Dia (ft)	Pitch (ft-in)	Area (sq ft)	rpm	ihp	Speed (kts)
Original	19	24-6	76	116	30,860	23.05
Revised	19	23-0	105	122.4	31,450	24.11
	-	-	-	116	26,000	23

At full power, the new propellers gave an extra knot of speed, whilst at the same speed as reached in the original trial, 4860 less horsepower were needed.

Monmouth class (ld 1899-1901) [55]

These were relatively cheap ships for trade protection, to counter the French *Kleber* class (eight 6.84in) and ten could be built for the cost of seven *Drakes*. White produced a comparison showing that the ten *Kents* would have about the same gunpower as the seven bigger ships, less endurance, very much inferior protection and would need 550 more men; quality versus quantity is never easy.

The side armour was 4in of non-cemented Krupp, 11ft high. This would keep out 6in HE and all types of 4in at fighting range, although in the *Belleisle* trials three out of four 6in shells penetrated such plate at 2450yds. At the Falklands *Kent* was hit thirty-eight times by *Nurnberg*'s 4.1in shells of which four hit the belt and did not penetrate, twelve hit rigging, funnels etc and twenty-one hit the upper hull. During this battle she was hit by a 4.1in shell on the gunport of A3 casemate which ignited one or more charges in the casemate and flash went down the trunk to the ammunition passage. Sergeant Mayes threw away the charge at the bottom and flooded the compartment.[56] It does not seem that the significance of this near-disaster was fully appreciated; it seems a general rule that we don't learn from victories!

Berwick, 1902, a *Monmouth* class small armoured cruiser designed for trade protection. (WSS)

There was usually a longitudinal bulkhead in the engine-rooms of White's cruisers but, in the later ships, it was not fitted in boiler rooms as asymmetric flooding was recognised as a hazard.[57] The head of section, Whiting, wrote a strong memo to his staff on the need to keep weights low in the ship and they all signed it.

They had very hollow waterlines forward which was much criticised at the time but was probably the right shape for their speed-length ratio though it would very slightly have increased pitching. They had a new design of electrically-operated twin 6in turret fore and aft but the operation was unreliable, the turrets were cramped and the guns were difficult to align as they were in a single cradle. However, these turrets worked well at Falklands. White answered criticism by saying he gave the Board what they asked for and, indeed, they were better fighting ships than usually given credit for.

This class had much the same propeller problems as the *Drakes* and new propellers had been ordered even before they went on trial.

Propeller problems

	Dia (ft-in)	Pitch (ft-in)	Area (sq ft)	rpm	ihp	Speed (kts)
Original	16-3	20-0	54	147	22,500	22.7
Revised	16-3	19-6	81	140	22,700	23.6

On the 30-hour trial, with 16,500ihp, the earlier propeller gave 20.5kts, 21.64kts with the revised set. It is a little surprising that the original propellers for these two classes were so far out as they were designed using model tests and experience with earlier cruisers.

Devonshire class: 1901-02 programme (ld 1902) [58]

The design was intended to be a more powerful version of the *Monmouth* with only a slight increase in size; in particular, they were to use the same machinery with a 0.75kt drop in speed.

Argyll of the *Devonshire* class,
1904, with a mixed armament
of 7.5in and 6in guns. (Author's
collection)

At a meeting on 17-18 March 1902, four possibilities were considered:

1. Increase *Monmouth* armour to 6in – which would reduce freeboard by 6in giving a displacement of 10,600 tons and an increased cost of £50,000.
2. Lengthen by 30ft to float at the same draught and make same speed at 22,000ihp. This would give a displacement of 10,900 tons, and an additional £80,000 cost.
3. Increase length by 25-30 feet and beam to give 6in armour and
   (a) Eight 7.5in twins fore and aft and eight 6in on main – 11,700 tons, cost 0.25kt or 600ihp more, or

(b) six 9.2in, singles at ends, twins amidships and eight 6in which was thought too expensive.

The final compromise involved 10ft on the length and 2ft 6in on the beam with the twin 6in of the earlier class replaced by single 7.5in turrets. While building – after the first three had been launched – the double casemates forward were replaced by single 7.5in turrets. After considerable debate they were given an anti-TB armament of eighteen 3pdrs and pom-poms in place of 12pdrs.

Carnavon at the battle of the Falklands fired eighty-five 7.5in and sixty 6in shells, mainly Lyddite, at ranges of 11-12,000yds.

Duke of Edinburgh *class 1902-03, two ships
(ld 1903)*[59] *(also* Warrior *class 1903-04,
four ships, ld 1905)*

These ships derived from the larger studies for
improved *Monmouth*s outlined above. It is often said
that their increased armament reflected the views of
Phillip Watts rather than White but this is incorrect, the
armament was a Board requirement and W H Whiting
was in charge of both designs with C J Croxford as head
of section.

There were a considerable number of design studies,
sketches of which appear in MacBride's article. Design
A had a forecastle, much as finally built, whilst B lacked
the forecastle but had a twin 9.2in forward. Design C
had four twin 6in turrets and was rejected as it was
thought a battery was easier to control. Arguments over
boilers were continuing and D was as C except for
cylindrical boilers; the comparison is interesting-

Design	Boiler	Length (ft)	Displacement (tons)
C	Water tube	480	13,275
D	Cylindrical	526	14,500

Variants on Design A with a mix of water tube and
cylindrical boilers were also considered. There was a
belt of 6in KC for 260ft, tapering to 4inch forward, 3in
aft. The main deck was intended to be 1½ inch, later
much reduced. The ammunition passages ran fore-and-
aft outside the boiler rooms. Mention is made of flash
precautions but these passages were to prove disastrous
in the coming war. When it was realised that the 6in
were even closer to the waterline than the main deck
guns of *Drake*, which had proved unsatisfactory, consideration was given to twin turrets on the upper deck
but it proved difficult to give them end-on fire. To meet
the order date, the original battery was accepted. The
6in were the Mk 9 with a longer barrel which somewhat
limited the bow arcs of the forward guns. It was not
possible to fit the longer 9.2in.

It was thought necessary to carry eleven boats weighing in total 50 tons, to which must be added the weight
of ancillary equipment.[60] They were the first class with
standardised machinery in which all components were
interchangeable, reducing spares holdings and making
maintenance much easier. Surprisingly, serious consideration was given to sheathing them. It would have cost
£40-45,000 and added 600 tons.

The low and unsatisfactory 6in battery was replaced

59. K McBride, 'The *Dukes* and the
Warriors', *Warship International*
4/90 (Toledo 1990).

60. Whiting loathed weight not
devoted to armament – he must have
been angry.

Minotaur 1910, more
powerfully armed than the
Warrior class but more
congested. (Author's collection)

after the battle of Coronel with between six and eight guns in shields on the upper deck. The 1903 programme ships were given four single 7.5in turrets instead, a decision based on experience with *Cressy's* lower guns.

At Jutland, *Defence* was hit by seven heavy and three medium shells and fire spread along the ammunition passage. *Warrior* was hit by fifteen heavy and six medium shells, mostly at main deck level. One heavy shell penetrated the 6in armour at the waterline entering the port engine-room and leaving through the bottom to starboard.

Minotaur *class (ld 1905)*[61]

The Controller, W H May, wrote to Watts on 5 August 1903 concerning the ships of the 1904 programme. The design was still run by Whiting who was asked to consider various combinations of 9.2in. 7.5in and 6in guns. McLeod, the DNO, objected to close spacing of guns, did not want any 6in and nor would he accept versions with the 7.5in as the largest gun. He favoured two 9.2in and 7.5in but would like to see two twin 10in. It was generally agreed that the Board wanted the best, almost regardless of cost. There was even some consideration given to a design with 12in guns.

Guns	MV(ft/sec)	Penetration
US 10in	2800	
Swiftsure 10in	2920	11.3in @ 3000yds
9.2in 50cal	3030	10.1in @ 3000yds

It was decided that the advantage of the 10in did not justify introducing a new calibre in place of the well-liked 9.2in. A secondary armament of ten single 7.5in in turrets was selected. Twelve-pounders were fitted against

torpedo boats. The armour was very similar to earlier ships though with the secondary armament on the upper deck, no need was seen for an upper belt; the turret tubes were 7in.

The boilers were all water tube. At Controller's suggestion, *Shannon* was given a different hull form with 1ft more beam and 1ft less draught – she was nearly 0.5kt slower.[62] During the development of the *Duke of Edinburgh* design, the Controller (May) asked for model tests to compare hollow and straight waterlines and it may be that *Shannon* incorporated such changes. Froude complained, rightly, of the difficulty of making such a comparison as it is almost impossible to change one parameter of the form without affecting several others. The straight line form was more resistful but possibly pitched a little less.

Smaller cruisers

Second Class cruisers were required in considerable numbers, mainly for trade protection, and hence they had to be cheap, whilst having the speed and armament quickly to overwhelm armed merchant raiders and small enemy cruisers. There can never be a complete answer to a dilemma of this sort and White's designs of smaller cruisers were frequently criticised. The *Medea* class for the 1887 programme may be seen as the starting point. On a displacement of 2800 tons they mounted six 6in BLR (later changed to QF) and had a design speed of 18kts (natural draught) which they achieved. It was expected that they would reach 20kts with forced draught which was all but reached. The continuous speed was 15.75kts. Fouling was still a problem and three of the class were sheathed for tropical service[63] which cost 0.25kt and added 150 tons to their displacement. White seemed pleased with them claiming that in

Marathon, 1888, a Second Class cruiser of the *Medea* class. (Author's collection)

the manoeuvres of 1889, held in bad weather, the *Melpomene* could fight her 6in guns with ease and in these conditions she could defeat a low-freeboard turret battleship.

The *Medea*s were generally recognised as too small and the 'Improved *Medea*', which became the *Apollo* class of the Naval Defence Act, was much bigger at 3400 tons (unsheathed). Ships which were sheathed were 3600 tons, ¼kt slower and £10,000 more expensive. The sheathing needed cleaning in dock after 1½-2 years. This class of twenty-one ships were about 0.5kt faster thanks to their increased length and their triple-expansion engines were more economical. A typical instruction from White, showing his direct involvement, to a section head (Dunn) is in the Ship's Cover.

> I think the better course will be to take the form of the Australian cruisers, increase the length by pulling out the sections to 265-285 feet making the displacement about 3000 tons or else arrive at this displacement by pulling out Medea which may be more economical at 20 knots. We must also investigate if 41 feet beam is sufficient. Cost should be about £145-150,000.

A note in the *Talbot* Ship's Cover shows that the preliminary power estimate was made using resistance data from Froude's model tests. The propulsive coefficient (the ratio of ihp/shp) was assumed to be similar to previous cruisers – 47 per cent taken – giving the ihp needed. There is an intriguing note that the *Edgar* trials were considered unreliable (see Chapter 7).

Their armament of two 6in and six 4.7in, all QF, was thought to be too light. The last eight ships of the Naval Defence Act, the *Astraea* class, were 1000 tons bigger, 20 feet longer and increased freeboard to improve seakeeping. Armament was slightly increased by a pair of 4.7in.

The nine *Eclipse* class were a further 1000 tons heavier with an initial armament of five 6in and six 4.7in, later changed to eleven 6in. All these ships had a protective deck, usually 1in on the flat and 2-3in on the slopes. The four *Arrogant*s of the 1895-96 programme were originally described as 'Fleet Rams', apparently intended to finish off disabled enemy ships. The ram was very strong and supported by the protective deck and was beamy for strength though this caused some loss of speed. The conning tower armour was increased to 9in in view of their intention to fight at close range. Though of similar displacement to *Eclipse*, they were 30ft shorter with 4ft more beam making them a little slower. They had a big, balanced main rudder and a smaller one ahead of it which together with a considerable cut up at the stern gave them a small turning circle of 380yds[64] compared with 650yds for *Astraea* of the same length. They cost £300,000. The five *Highflyer*s were virtually repeat *Eclipse*s with an all-6in armament as built. Some thirty Third Class cruisers of about 2000 tons had little of technical interest and must be omitted.

Furious, 1896, one of four ships rated as Second Class cruisers but designed as 'fleet rams'. (Imperial War Museum: Q42735)

It is interesting that Second Class battleships were unsuccessful, expensive in terms of capability and with a short service life. One might think of the *Audacious* classes as an exception but, as hinted earlier, these ships are probably better considered as large cruisers. On the other hand, Second Class cruisers were built in large numbers and seen as valuable. The balance between quality and quantity is always difficult to draw and it would seem that the nature of cruising duties tipped the balance to numbers for these ships. On the other hand, a battleship had to be able to fight any ship of the enemy.

Scouts

These ships seem to have derived from ideas of Vice-Admiral Fitzgerald[65] about 1901. He thought a small, fast cruiser with good endurance and seakeeping was needed to watch enemy ports. His paper was criticised in discussion as, on the one hand, too small and, conversely, too expensive, particularly in terms of manpower. In 1903, the Admiralty issued a specification for a scout which owed much to the Admiral's views but with a primary role of supporting destroyer attacks. To this end, coal stowage had been much reduced so that their value as 'Scouts' was lessened.

Pairs of ships were ordered from each of four builders to their own design and important features are identified below.

Armstrong; L = 395ft, circ M[66] 8.77, no side armour, protective deck, focsle.
Fairfield; L = 379ft, circ M 8.17, 2in belt over M/C, deck at ends, focsle and poop.
Laird ; L = 379ft, circ M 8.13, 2in belt over engine-room, deck, focsle.
Vickers; L = 381ft, circ M 8.19, protective deck, turtle back focsle, no poop

61. R A Burt, '*Minotaur*', *Warship 42* (London April 1987).

62. The index to the Haslar reports describe model PR as 'normal' and mention PQ2 as an alternative. The full reports are inaccessible at the time of writing.

63. For some reason, the sheathed ships had horizontal engines as opposed to the vertical compound of the others.

64. Attwood, *Warships – a Text Book.*

65. C C P FitzGerald, 'A Design for a Fast Scout', *Trans INA* (London 1901).

66. Circ M is Length/(displaced volume)$^{1/3}$.

Four 'Scouts' designed by their builders to a loose specification. *Top right: Attentive* 1904 (Armstrong). *Immediately below: Skirmisher* 1905 (Vickers). *Below right: Pathfinder* 1904 (Cammell Laird). *Bottom left: Foreward* 1904 (Fairfield). (Author's collection)

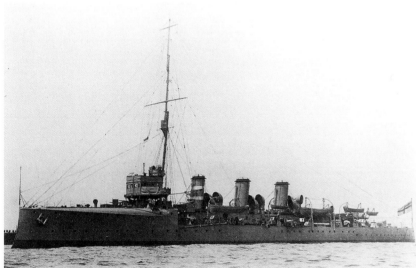

Circ M is the most important factor affecting the resistance of fast ships and, not surprisingly, the Armstrong ships were significantly faster than their rivals though all met the required 25kts.

Their original armament was ten 12pdrs, soon increased to twelve. This was seen as inadequate and in 1911-12 they were re-armed with nine 4in. Discussion of a second paper by Fitzgerald[67] shows that most naval opinion saw the original armament as satisfactory at the time they were ordered. Though they were too small and too weakly armed to be seen as entirely successful, the Armstrong style (due to Phillip Watts) was liked and formed the basis for many Admiralty designs. As so often with 'improved' ships, displacement increased more rapidly than length and circ M fell.

Machinery developments

The Battle of the Boilers[68]

The excellent results obtained with the Belleville boiler in early trials did not seem to be repeated in service though most of the problems were actually due to the increased pressure rather than the boiler itself. In 1900 *Hermes* had to return home after only a year in commission; in 1903 *Spartiate* broke down on trials due to faulty condensers and bearing problems. *Europa*'s passage to Sydney took 88 days, 58 steaming and 30 coaling due to leaky condensers with an overall consumption of 5lbs/ihp/hr.

From 1900 there were attacks on the Belleville in Parliament, led by Sir William Allen, and in the press led by the magazine *Engineer*. As a result the Admiralty appointed a committee of enquiry into water tube boilers under Admiral Sir Compton Domville. The only other Admiralty representative was the Chief Inspector of Machinery, J A Smith, the other members having a Merchant Navy or Lloyd's background. Their interim report of 1901[69] saw several important advantages for water tube boilers such as the ability to raise steam quickly, reduced risk of action damage because they were smaller and the ease of replacing a damaged or worn boiler because they could be dismantled.

On the other hand they saw some apparent disadvantages in the Belleville design. Mainly they did not like the automatic feed control and the high feed pressure or the long travel (50ft) of the steam and water through the boiler but they also criticised a number of other details. They recommended that Bellevilles should not be fitted in new ships unless already committed and that Babcock or Yarrow large tube boilers should be used in battleships.[70] They also recommended a mix of water tube and cylindrical boilers, which was adopted to a limited extent and proved to be a mistake. Smith concurred with most of the recommendations but said that the Belleville '. . . is a good steam generator, which will give satisfactory results when it is kept in good order and worked with the required care and skill.'

In their final report of 1904[71] the Committee confirmed their earlier views and described a series of trials on alternative designs. By this time Admiral Domville was flying his flag in the *Bulwark* which had Bellevilles. He wrote 'My experience with Belleville boilers on the Mediterranean station has been very favourable to them as steam generators, and it is clear to me that the earlier boilers of this description were badly made and badly used.' The committee recommended small tube Yarrow boilers for smaller ships but insisted that the tubes be straight, an error which was to cause many problems during the war.

There were a few real problems with the Belleville but they were minor. The problems in the RN were due partly to a decision to replace Belleville's patent packing in the feed system with a cheaper substitute but more to the fact that crews were not trained to use this fairly complicated equipment and there was not even a handbook. With experience, the Belleville became both reliable and economical: during *Terrible*'s first voyage to China in 1902 she averaged 11.2kts, burning 200 tons of coal a day but in 1904 she made the same voyage at 12.6kts burning only 100 tons a day. Bellevilles lived on until 1939 in the Royal Yacht *Victoria and Albert* with few, if any, problems.

Trials with alternative boilers

Ship	Type	Wt of Boiler Room Equipt (tons)	Lbs Steam/ Hr per ton Boiler wt
Minerva	Cylindrical	558	280
Hyacinth	Belleville	454	394
Medea	Yarrow	330	478
Medusa	Durr	314	503
Hermes	Babcock	481	380
Sheldrake	Babcock	125	351
Espiegle	Babcock	95	261
Seagull	Niclause	135	359
Fantome	Niclause	77	297

The Babcocks of *Hermes* were marginally more efficient than the Yarrow or Bellevilles but all were well ahead of the Durr, Niclause and cylindrical designs. The Yarrow was much easier to clean, an important point. All of the water tube boilers needed more careful stoking than the cylindrical but Yarrow was seen as the best. Boiler pressure was reduced from 300 to 210lbs/sq in but was soon raised to 250lbs/sq in where it was to remain for many – perhaps too many – years.

Engines and condensers

> A life in the engine-room,
> An odour of oil and grease
> A rattle of valves and rods,
> Never a moment's peace.   Eng Rear Ad G C Boddie

In the twenty years between the introduction of the triple-expansion engine and its replacement by the turbine, there were considerable reductions in the weight and space required by the machinery. Steam pressure rose from 135 to 250lbs/sq in , piston speed from 700 to 1000ft/min (destroyers 1300ft/min) and shaft rpm from 100 to 140 (400). The most powerful reciprocating machinery for the RN was the 4-cylinder, twin shaft installation for *Drake* (1898) which developed 30,000ihp.

There were steady improvements in balancing which reduced vibration and in forced lubrication which was tried in the destroyer *Syren* in 1899 and introduced in battleships from about 1903. Conditions in the engine-room of a high powered, reciprocating engined ship were frightening; noise, vibration (despite the improve-

67. C C P FitzGerald, 'The New Scouts', *Trans INA* (London 1906).

68. D K Brown, 'Marine Engineering in the RN', *Journal of Naval Engineering* (1993-94).

69. 'Water tube Boilers in the Royal Navy', *Engineering* (London 15 March 1901).

70. The extra weight and space for large tube boilers was considerable.

71. 'Report on the Committee on Naval Boilers'. *Engineering* (London, 5 August 1904).

A torpedo boat, possibly *Countess of Hopetown*, undergoing vibration trials. (Author's collection)

ment), steam leaks, hoses playing on hot bearings etc – no wonder that Fisher compared conditions with a snipe marsh!

Used hard, the triple-expansion engine was never very reliable.[72] In November 1906 the 2nd Cruiser squadron[73] raced from New York to Gibraltar. *Drake* was the fastest despite using American coal – the others had Welsh – and though using only ⅘ths power[74] for 30hrs, averaged 22.5kts for a total time of 7 days, 7 hours and 10 minutes. *Berwick* was only a mile behind and *Cumberland* a further half mile; the others were crippled and far behind. All required extensive repairs to the hull as well as the engines since many rivets had been shaken loose by the vibration. In another trial in 1907 *King Alfred* averaged 25.1kts for 1 hour, 24.8kts for 8 hours. They were reputed to use 11 tons/hr at 19kts.

Attempts were made to improve economy by cutting out cylinders at low power or, as in *Blenheim*, by using two engines per shaft with one disconnected for cruising, but none of these schemes helped much. A trial of water consumption in *Argonaut* ended a long debate by showing that steam jackets on the cylinders increased consumption rather than reducing it as was intended. Some benefit was found in using the exhaust from auxiliaries in the main engines or for feed water heating.

The early condensers leaked very badly but improvements were pushed through by the Admiralty over an often reluctant industry. From about 1870 the condenser shell was made of brass or gunmetal instead of cast iron. Leakage again became a problem about 1890 due to increased pressure and could occur either at the gland or in the tubes. Gland leakage was largely cured by better design and improved fit. Tube leakage was never entirely cured but was reduced by tighter control of the composition of the brass (from 1890) and by tests involving 'jarring' whilst under load. From 1901 all tubes had to be drawn over a mandrill and in 1904 the test pressure was raised from 300 to 700 lbs/sq in (later 1000lbs/sq in), all surface defects had to be removed and rules on purity were tightened. The table below shows how the improvements discussed above led to reductions in weight, space and cost.

Ship	ihp/ton	Coal (lbs/ihp/hr)	Floor (sq ft/ihp)	Cost £/ihp
Royal Sovereign		8.34	2.0	0.54
Prince George		7.9	1.82	0.56
Terrible	10.76	2.0	0.42	7.6
Diadem	10.93	1.76	0.39	9.5
Canopus	11.17	1.72	0.42	
Drake	12.24	1.81	0.35	10.1
Albemarle	11.37	1.96		
Amethyst	18.51	1.45	0.31	10.4
				Turbine
Black Prince	10.87	2.11	0.39	12.8
Shannon	12.37	1.82	0.39	11.9

Sir William White

During his long career as Director, White served six Boards with five First Lords and six Controllers, working with three Engineers-in-Chief, six DNOs and three Directors of Dockyards. Unhappily, his last years were marred by the errors in the design of the Royal yacht, *Victoria and Albert* which resulted in a breakdown in his health.

White was responsible for the design of the Royal Navy for 16 years during which he designed forty-three battleships, twenty-six armoured cruisers, twenty-one First Class protected cruisers, forty-eight Second Class, thirty-three Third Class and seventy-four smaller ships worth £80 million 1909 pounds. The Royal Corps of Naval Constructors was a creation of his, he was responsible for a major and successful re-organisation of the Royal Dockyard which led to great reductions in building times. He led in a number of theoretical investigations and was a superb teacher. As a warship designer and manager he remains unsurpassed.

72. See, for example, Second World War frigates and corvettes.

73. Boilers were – Belleville; *Drake, Essex, Bedford, Cumberland*. Babcock; *Cornwall*. Niclause; *Berwick*.

74. Perhaps it was the reduced power which gave her better reliability.

Proved in Battle | *Ten*

DURING THE period covered by this book there were few naval wars and none of these involved the Royal Navy. The Admiralty of the day studied foreign wars very carefully and both tested the lessons and supplemented them by a considerable number of full-scale trials of weapon effectiveness. To these one may add the results of some later trials which throw light on the 'battleworthiness' of these ships together with relevant lessons from the actions of the First World War .

The Sino-Japanese War, July 1894-February 1895

Hostilities[1] broke out in July 1894 without a formal declaration of war, perhaps itself a lesson for the future. There was one important battle, off the Yalu, on 17 September 1894 between a Chinese squadron whose most important ships were of the centre citadel style (as *Inflexible*) and a Japanese force including several protected cruisers mounting heavy guns. The main action was fought at ranges of 2000–2500yds and the Japanese scored about 10 per cent hits, the Chinese 5 per cent. The two Chinese battleships were hit frequently; *Chen Yuan* c150 hits, *Ting Yuen* 200,[2] the latter suffering serious fires. Reed's attack on the *Inflexible* had been based on the impression that numerous hits on the unarmoured ends of a centre citadel ship would lead to capsize, an impression that this battle did something to dispel.

The war was carefully studied; for example, in submitting[3] the design for *Canopus*, White refers to a hit by a Japanese 12.6in (32cm) shell which only dented the Chinese 8-14in compound armour to a depth of 3-4in. At the battle range of 2500yds such a shell would have been expected to penetrate 23in of iron or 18-19in of compound. White suggests that this showed that armour did better in battle than on the test range.[4] He does not seem to have considered the alternative hypothesis that the Japanese shell or fuse failed to function properly.[5] There were few other lessons from this war though the Japanese interpretation of the legality of attacks on neutral merchant shipping caused some concern.

The Spanish-American War, 1898[6]

War was declared on 21 April 1898. There were two battles, both very one-sided. In the first, at Manila on 1 May 1898, an American squadron of four protected cruisers and two gunboats destroyed a Spanish squadron, at anchor, of one small and unseaworthy cruiser,

five gunboats and some small, old vessels. The range varied between 5000 and 2000 yards. The Spanish cruiser burnt furiously before sinking as did at least one of the gunboats. After the Spanish surrender the wrecks were examined and an estimate made of the number of hits scored.[7]

US gunnery at Manila, 1 May 1898

Calibre (ins)	Rounds fired	Hits	Per cent
8	157	14	9
6	635	7	1
5	622	22	3.5
6pdr	2124	31	1.5

The US squadron received a few hits which caused no serious damage and there were no casualties; the Spanish squadron lost 167 killed and 214 wounded.

On 3 July a Spanish armoured cruiser and three protected cruisers attempted to escape from Santiago, Cuba, and were destroyed as they left by a USN force of four battleships and an armoured cruiser. The 11in guns of the Spanish protected cruisers were defective and they were short of ammunition for their 5.5 inch. The 10in guns of the new armoured cruiser were not mounted. The first to leave, the protected cruiser *Teresa*, burning furiously, was beached to save her crew and, shortly, her sister, *Vizcaya*, suffered an identical fate. The armoured cruiser *Colon* followed and was close to escape, with little damage, when poor coal caused her to slow drastically and she, too, was beached to save her crew. *Oquendo*, like her sisters, burnt furiously and was beached. Again, the USN examined the wrecks and compared rounds fired with hits.

US gunnery at Santiago, 3 July 1898

Calibre (ins)	Rounds fired	Hits	Per cent
13	47	0	0
12	39	2	5
8	219	10	5.5
6	271 }	17*	2
5	473 }		
4	251	13	5
6pdr	6553	76	1

* It was difficult to distinguish between 5in and 6in hits.

1. H W Wilson, *Battleships in Action* (London 1926, reprint 1995). A most important source for battles of the period. See Review of Sources.

2. The number of hits seems almost unbelievable but photographs show that hits were indeed very numerous. See, for example, those reproduced in H W Wilson, *Ironclads in Action* (London 1896).

3. PRO ADM 116/878.

4. This was a widely-held view, then and later, which was still thought a valid argument in developing the protection of the *King George V* class in the 1930s.

5. The Japanese adopted Shimose (picric acid) fillings for their shells in the mid-1890s. It is at least possible that this was in recognition of the poor performance of earlier shells.

6. The sources for this section are Wilson, *Ironclads in Action*, and J R Spears, *The American Navy in the War with Spain* (London 1899).

7. It is difficult to be sure that every hole has been found but the figures should be fairly accurate for the bigger shells.

The appalling rate of hitting, particularly against stationary targets at Manila and when return fire was negligible, was the most conspicuous lesson. Percy Scott had already formulated his ideas on improving British gunnery, demonstrated the following year in *Scylla*, but the failures in USN gunnery probably helped to win ready acceptance for his ideas at all levels in the RN.

The main cause of Spanish losses was fire; the upper two decks of the protected cruisers were of wood on steel beams, *ie* no steel deck plating, which dried in tropical heat, burnt readily.[8] The British Admiralty seem to have carried out a review of the fire hazard before the war started as the cruisers of the 1897-98 programme, the *Cressys* already had a much reduced amount of wood and much of what was fitted was treated to make it fire-resistant. Further improvements in the *Drake* class concentrated on reduction in the extent of superstructures. Two of the Spanish protected cruisers were damaged by the explosion of their own torpedoes and the USN decided that above-water torpedoes should not fitted in battleships and cruisers. The light shields to Spanish guns were inadequate and casualties were heavy – at Santiago the Spanish lost 323 killed and about 200 wounded, the USN losing 1 killed and 10 wounded. White's preference for casemates, based on the *Resistance* trials, was given further justification.

The USN force off Cuba was burdened with four old monitors which proved useless.

The *Belleisle* trials, 1900

The firing trials carried out off Selsey Bill against the old ironclad *Belleisle*[9] in the summer of 1900 form an interesting contrast to the battles mentioned above. The *Majestic* fired for about 7 minutes, starting at 1700yds abaft the port beam of the target, steaming past at 10kts with a closest range of 1000yds and continuing until the range was about 1700yds again.[10] It was possible to count the hits which amounted to some 40 per cent of

the rounds fired; much better than Manila in fairly similar circumstances but not all that good against a large, stationary target.

The objects of the trial were:[11]

(a) To ascertain the risks of fire in action on account of wood fittings, where such precautions have been taken as may reasonably be expected in a well-disciplined ship.
(b) To give officers a more accurate idea of the extent of damage likely to have been caused by various descriptions of projectiles when fired under conditions as nearly resembling an actual engagement as possible.
(c) To give means of determining the best means of making good such damage as might occur.

The *Belleisle* had steam up and was cleared for action and officers' and crew's effects were in their normal position for action. Boats and spare spars were left in place but 'normal' precautions were taken against fire; the decks were flooded by hoses. There were six minor fires, all of which were easily put out. The large clouds of smoke which were observed were due to the bursting charges of some 1000lbs powder and 500lbs Lyddite. It was, however, reported that all fire mains and hand pumps were destroyed in the unarmoured portion of the ship and no water could be obtained on the forecastle or quarterdeck. The boats were all completely destroyed but none caught fire – there was no difference between those covered with wet canvas and those without. All signal halliards were cut. *Belleisle* was an old ship and was not modified for this trials suggesting that fire precautions in more recent ships were indeed adequate.

Belleisle trial: rounds fired (all fired with full charge)

No.	Type	Hits*	Notes
7	12in AP	0	No hits found. Probably shot.
8	12in common	5	
100	6in Lyddite	} 75	Aimed at bow and battery
100	6in common		Aimed at stern
400	12pdr common	80	
750	3pdr AP	35	

* Brassey. *cf* report of 40 per cent overall ratio of hits. If these figures are accurate, they add further justification to the big gun's accuracy.

No hits from the 12in AP could be identified, but it is possible that they passed through light structure and the holes were obscured by other damage. *Belleisle*'s weak armour, 8in and 12in wrought iron, was pierced by two 12in common shell and one 6in common as a result of

The remains of *Belleisle* after gunnery trials off Selsey Bill in 1900. (Author's collection)

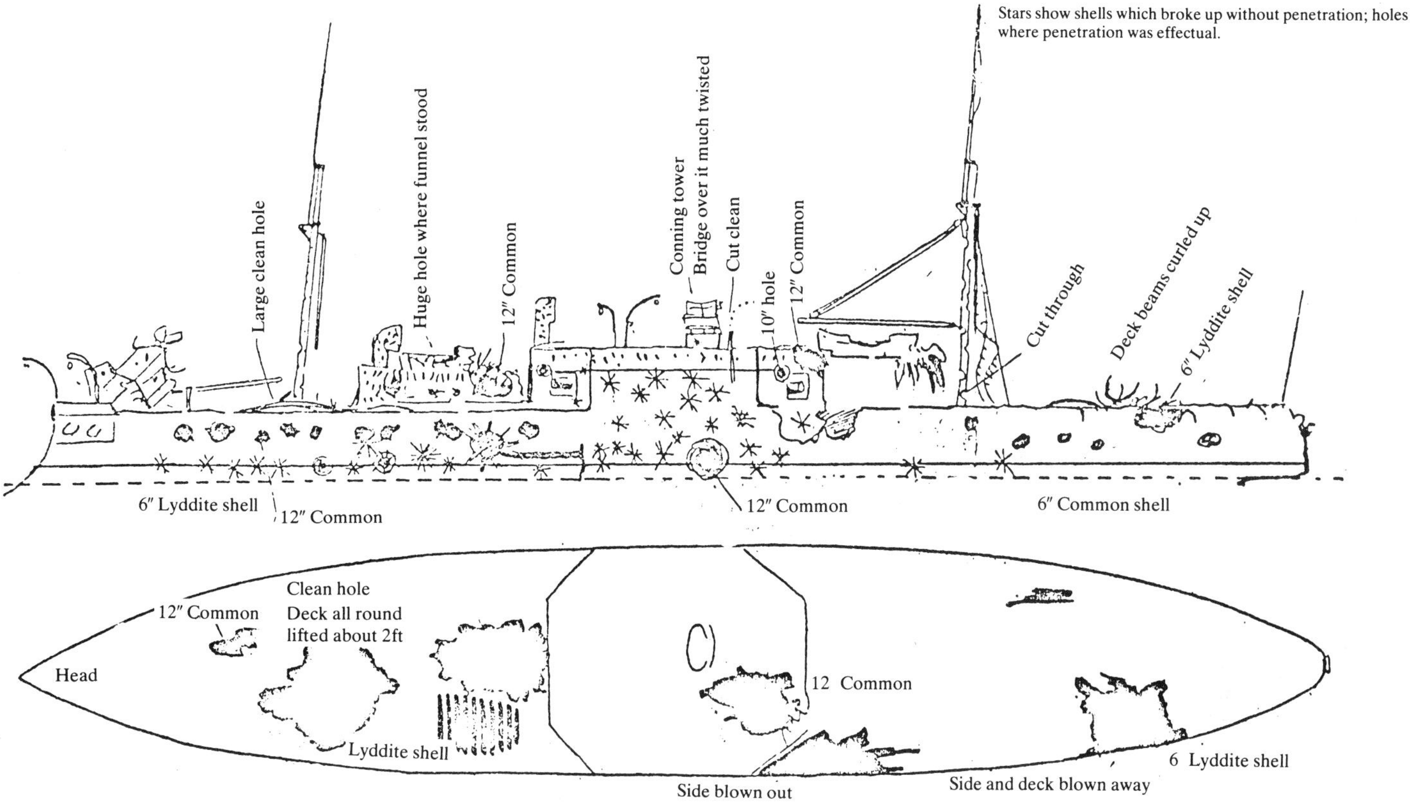

Stars show shells which broke up without penetration; holes where penetration was effectual.
Large clean hole
Huge hole where funnel stood
12″ Common
Conning tower
Bridge over it much twisted
Cut clean
10″ hole
12″ Common
Cut through
Deck beams curled up
6″ Lyddite shell
6″ Lyddite shell
12″ Common
12″ Common
6″ Common shell
12″ Common
Clean hole
Deck all round lifted about 2ft
Head
12 Common
Lyddite shell
6 Lyddite shell
Side blown out
Side and deck blown away

Damage to the *Belleisle* in the trials off Selsey Bill in 1900.

which she sank – but she was moored with only a few feet of water under the keel and was easily salvaged for examination. There was a marked difference between the effects of 6in common (powder-filled), fired at the after end and Lyddite shell, aimed at the fore end. The former broke everything 'as with an axe' but the latter reduced everything to powder 'as in dry rot'. The effect of Lyddite shell was to make large irregular holes in the unarmoured parts, which would have been impossible to repair at sea. Lyddite shell bursting between decks bulged and tore the deck above, unlike powder-filled shell. 'High-capacity shell will do great damage and demoralise the crew.' The retention of areas of thin armour in British ships up to the Washington Treaty was justified as even thin armour would keep out most Lyddite shell. Though difficult, repair of holes from common shell could usually be made with wooden plugs.

One hundred and thirty dummies had been placed round the ship and traverses were found to be effective in reducing 'casualties'. Coffer dams filled with old canvas were struck in many places (as used in protective deck systems) but none caught fire.

In 1902 a mock-up of 6in KC plates, representing the *Drake*'s casemates, was fired on. It successfully resisted two cast steel, 6in AP shot at a striking velocity corresponding to 2300yds but was penetrated by two 9.2in shells at a speed corresponding to 5800yds. The plate backed by a coal bunker was more severely damaged than the unbacked plate but the coal absorbed blast and splinters and reduced the overall damage.

An arrangement of 4in KC was erected to represent the *Monmouth* casemate and this was penetrated by three out of four 6in at an equivalent of 4100yds and by two 9.2in. The 9.2in was seen as particularly effective and, as before, the danger was noted of mounting fittings on the armour, which could be thrown off on impact.

Technical lessons of the Russo-Japanese War

This was the only major war at sea between 1860 and 1905 and was carefully studied at the time even though, in most aspects, the British Admiralty saw it as an old-fashioned war and thought many of its 'lessons' had already been overtaken by the changes forming part of the *Dreadnought* revolution. The picture was further confused by Admiral Fisher as he quoted the war as justifying all his rapidly changing ideas. However, a number of problems were identified and rapid and effective actions were taken. This short account[12] will consider lessons as perceived at the time and the actions taken and will also reconsider those lessons with hindsight.

Purely operational problems and tactics[13] are not discussed but they merge into a group of topics such as speed, the 'all-big gun' armament and range, the value of torpedoes and mines etc, which dominate the requirements for new ships. Then there are purely ship design

8. It is likely that most US shells were powder-filled with a powerful incendiary effect.

9. D K Brown, 'Attack and Defence, Part 5', *Warship 34* (London April 1985).

10. Based on account in the *Brassey's Naval Annual* (London 1901) which, in turn, was based on articles in *The Times* and *Engineer*.

11. 1915 *Gunnery Manual*.

12. D K Brown, 'Technical Lessons of the Russo-Japanese War', *Warship 1996* (London 1996). The same theme is explored in greater depth.

13. For a general account of the war see H W Wilson, *Battleships in Action* and J S Corbett, *Maritime Operations in the Russo-Japanese War* (originally completed as a Confidential Staff History in 1915, reprint Annapolis 1994).

aspects such as arrangement of armour, underwater protection, fire resistance etc. The requirement and the technical solution cannot be entirely separated since, for example, the size of gun and the range adopted for battle will have a major effect on the thickness of armour, its extent and its arrangement.

There were two main battles; the first in the Yellow Sea on 10 August 1904 (usually referred to as 10 August) and the second at Tsushima on 27 May 1905. There were also cruiser encounters whilst heavy losses, particularly from mines, were experienced away from formal battle. The RN was very well-informed of the events of the war since Japan was an ally and allowed a number of British observers[14] to sail with their fleet and they also made available a number of their own confidential reports.

Speed

On 10 August, the two fleets were fairly evenly matched in speed and the Japanese had difficulty in closing. At Tsushima, the Japanese fleet speed was about 15kts while the Russians could only make 9kts, limited by older ships and by about 3kts loss due to fouling. The War College had been set up under Captain May in 1902

as a think-tank and his early studies seemed to show that speed was of little value as the slower fleet could manoeuvre to keep the faster fleet abeam. After the war, his successor, Captain Slade,[15] showed that when the slower fleet was constrained by a coastline or by the need to reach a specified destination such as Vladivostok, the value of speed increased. In a later paper, the DNO, Jellicoe, prompted by Watts, took the pragmatic line that speed was useful if the cost was not too great.

Guns, gunnery and shells

There was a considerable difference in the way in which the two big battles were fought. On 10 August, the Russians opened fire at about 15,000yds and, by the time the range had fallen to 12,000yds, they were remarkably accurate; remarkable since their ships had not been fitted with telescopic sights. Most of the firing at this battle was at ranges of between 9500 and 6500yds at which hits were fairly frequent. Pakenham was led to believe that the ranges were some 3000yds greater than these figures as he had relied on short (4ft 6in) Japanese rangefinders. He then argued that, since British gunnery was superior, they should be thinking of opening fire at

Rossiya damaged off Ulsan in 1904. There were heavy casualties among her gun crews. (S A Lilliman)

20,000yds and that 10,000yds would be seen as close range.

The Japanese fleet had no great superiority in speed in 1904 and Togo may have been unwilling to seek close action, wishing to preserve his fleet for a second battle against the Baltic Fleet. Tsushima was fought at much closer range. There was no fire control instrumentation in either fleet throughout the war. Sims[16] noted there were few hits when the range was changing rapidly.

Most eyewitness accounts mention the great difference between the performance of Japanese shells in the two battles. At the outbreak of war there were two types of shell available for the bigger Japanese guns. Armour-piercing had a 5 per cent bursting charge[17] and high explosive a 10 per cent charge, the filling in both cases being Shimose – picric acid, very similar to British Lyddite. During 10 August three out of sixteen Japanese 12in guns burst from premature explosions of the shell in the barrel and the fuse was redesigned before Tsushima. Pakenham's report on these less sensitive fuses has been read as implying that the later shells had improved armour-piercing capability but this is an incorrect view.

Before Tsushima, the Japanese introduced a powder-filled, high capacity shell[18] which was usually, if incorrectly, referred to as 'HE'. Japanese accounts differ as to the number of each type of shell fired at Tsushima but there seem to have been no penetrations of armour thicker than 6in and descriptions of Russian survivors suggest that a large proportion of the hits were from powder-filled shells. On 10 August the Japanese fired 279 AP shells of which at least 10 hit Russian armour, mainly turrets, and not one penetrated. At Tsushima, the *Orel* was hit frequently and inspection after her surrender revealed one hit by a 12in shell (type unknown) on her 5¾in belt which had failed to penetrate.

Russian shells were filled with wet guncotton which, being less sensitive than Shimose, gave them a slightly superior armour-piercing capability. On the other hand, a considerable number failed to detonate; one unconfirmed report[19] says that the shells of the Baltic squadron were given a higher than usual water content to allow for tropical conditions and that such shells rarely exploded. Two of sixteen Russian shells which hit on 10 August failed to explode as did four out of fifteen at the cruiser battle of Ulsan while at Tsushima eight out of twenty-four failed. One 12in did penetrate the 6in belt of the *Shikishima* and burst behind, perhaps the only successful AP round of the war.

Armoured cruisers

Once Togo had lost two of his six battleships to mines, he was forced to use his powerful armoured cruisers in the battle line and, since the Russian fleet had many second-rate (or worse) ships at Tsushima, their value was over-rated. It does seem as though *Osliabia* was mainly sunk as a result of fire from cruisers but she was a strange ship. Her main armament was four 10in, barely more than the latest cruisers, and she was fast for the day. She had a fairly thick belt (9in Harvey) but it was very shallow and her towering sides made her a fine target for cruiser guns.

Several protected cruisers suffered heavy casualties amongst their gun crews due to inadequate shields. White was right in insisting on casemates though even these could fail. During the battle of Ulsan on 14 August 1904 the *Iwate* was hit by an 8in shell at 7am in the forward upper 6in casemate and the ready-use ammunition detonated. The explosion spread to the lower casemate and to the neighbouring upper deck casemate as well as disabling a 12pdr. One officer and thirty-one men were killed and forty-three wounded of whom nine died later. This should have alerted the RN to the dangers of ammunition explosions.

The Japanese seem to have relied on destroyers for scouting, based on the Elliot Islands though they were always supported by cruisers. This was used by Fisher in arguing that nothing was needed between a big destroyer and a battlecruiser.

Mines

There were heavy casualties on both sides from mines; the Japanese lost a third of their six battleships in one day, whilst the sinking of *Petropavlovsk* off Port Arthur on 13 April 1904 killing Admiral Makarov deprived the Russians of their only competent leader. *Pobeida* was damaged on the same occasion.

In all, the Japanese lost to mines the *Hatsuse* and *Yashima* (battleships), *Hei-Yen*, *Takasago*, *Miyako* and *Sai-Yen* (cruisers) and five smaller ships. The Russians lost *Petropavlovsk* while the *Sevastopol* was mined twice without being sunk. British reports suggested that a single mine explosion would only be lethal if a magazine was detonated.

There is very little published information on RN work on minesweeping as a result of the war but many hints show that such work was extensive, effective and implemented. By January 1908, Fisher told a subcommittee of the Committee for Imperial Defence that mines could easily be cleared but he would not explain the technique as this would 'throw away one of the deepest secrets' possessed by the Navy.[20] That year the conversion began of thirteen torpedo gunboats to carry the new sweeping gear. The nature of the sweep is not known but it is likely that it was a wire sweep between two ships using kites to depress the wire. By 1913 it was reported that sufficient gear had been stockpiled to equip eighty-two trawlers and a special reserve force trained to sweep mines was ready.

Torpedoes

During the war the Japanese fired some 350 torpedoes scoring very few hits, whilst the Russians scored no hits. The war opened with a surprise attack on the Russian

14. The senior British observer was Captain Pakenham, whose reports are held in the Ministry of Defence Library and have been used extensively in this account.

15. Captain J W Slade, *Speed in Battleships*, War College, 31 May 1906.

16. Commander W S Sims, USN, *Big Battleships of High Speed*. Originally written for President Theodore Roosevelt, this paper was passed to Admiral Fisher (with permission) and later, with only slight changes, published.

17. This was a large charge for an AP shell and may have contributed to their poor performance in penetration.

18. *A Study of the events of the Russo-Japanese War from the Point of View of Naval Gunnery*. Originally CB 47, probably written by Captain Harding RMA, 200 copies circulated. An excellent technical history.

19. A Novikoff-Priboy, *Tsushima, Grave of a Floating City* (London 1937). The author was a steward in *Orel* and, though sensational in style, his account seems accurate.

20. R F Mackay, *Lord Fisher of Kilverstone* (Oxford 1973).

Pallada (left) and *Pobieda* under attack from Japanese howitzers at Port Arthur, December 1904. (S A Lilliman)

fleet at anchor off Port Arthur. Nineteen torpedoes were launched against the almost unprepared Russian ships (although the watertight doors were shut and the nets out), scoring three hits on the stationary targets.[21] The 18in torpedoes had a warhead of 198lbs of gun cotton which caused severe damage.[22] There were no docks capable of accepting the damaged ships and the Russian constructors devised ingenious cofferdams which permitted repairs to be made afloat. This took time and *Retvizan* completed on 28 May, *Tsessarevitch* on 8 June and *Pallada* on 16 June. The RN was impressed by the damage resistance of *Tsessarevitch* which they attributed to her thick inner bulkhead, though it is almost certain that the hit was abaft the protection. As a result, tests of a similar scheme were carried out and incorporated into *Dreadnought* at a late stage of the design (Chapter 11). The RN may have misread this lesson but action was quick and effective.

There were a number of other torpedo attacks off Port Arthur, notably when the Russian fleet was returning on 23-24 June, where sixty-seven torpedoes were launched; the *Sevastopol* was hit forward, needing six

weeks for repair, and *Pobeida* and a cruiser were also damaged. A very similar action occurred when seventeen destroyers and twenty-nine torpedo boats launched seventy-four torpedoes against the Russians returning from the 10 August battle without scoring any hits. In all these actions the lack of success is blamed on the Japanese policy of attacking individually rather than co-ordinating attacks, and also in firing at too great a range in the confusion of a night action.

In December 1904 the *Sevastopol* moored out of sight of the Japanese howitzers and was the object of numerous torpedo attacks. She was protected by nets and had the support of a gunboat. In all 104 torpedoes were launched for one hit and two which exploded in the nets sufficiently close to cause damage.[23]

Tsushima was the only occasion when big ships used their submerged tubes – *Mikasa* fired four, *Shikishima* two and *Iwate* four (believed to be the only gyro-fitted torpedoes used in the war), scoring no hits. Destroyers and torpedo boats fired a considerable number during the day for one hit on the disabled and helpless *Suvorov* which finally sank her.

The weather was bad at Tsushima and many of the smaller torpedo boats had sheltered during the day. They came out at night and joined with the destroyers in a series of brave but uncoordinated attacks on the demoralised Russian survivors. The total number of torpedoes fired is uncertain; the Staff History[24] says eighty-seven were fired during the night but it is likely that this included those fired during daylight. There was a hit on the cruiser *Monomakh* which was scuttled the next day to avoid surrender. This was probably the only hit of the war on an undamaged, moving ship. *Nakhimoff*, already damaged, was hit forward and scuttled the next day and *Sissoi* was hit in the stern disabling the rudder and one propeller and she sank the next day. *Navarin* was sunk by mines dropped ahead of her by destroyers.[25]

The 350 Japanese torpedoes had scored few hits and had little effect on the war. To a considerable extent, one may see the same pattern at Jutland.[26] The speed of a torpedo was only about 1½ to 2 times the speed of the target ship and hence the lengthy running time made it likely that the target's movements would not be predicted correctly. It seems likely that night torpedo attacks by surface ships could only be effective when good voice radio was available and, possibly, radar. By the time of the war, RN torpedoes had mostly been fitted with gyros and the first trials of heater torpedoes had taken place. Fear of the torpedo was a major factor in the drive for increased gun range; this fear was almost certainly exaggerated but it had a real influence on tactical thinking.

High-angle fire at Port Arthur

The surviving ships of the original Russian Pacific fleet sank in Port Arthur prior to the surrender of the port on 2 January 1905. They came under fire from Japanese Army 11in howitzers in December 1904 and some were scuttled in the hope of preventing serious damage. There seem to have been about thirty hits by 480lb shells of which seventeen reached the protective decks. *Peresviet* was hit by twelve shells of which six reached the protective deck. Of these four penetrated, causing little damage. Demolition charges (torpedo warheads) were exploded against the sides of several ships before the surrender, probably explaining one account claiming that severe damage had been caused by near-miss shells.

Fire

At Tsushima, most Russian battleships were disabled as a result of serious fires long before they were in danger of sinking. Observers comment on the incendiary effect of Japanese shells, Semenov,[27] saying that there was a marked difference from 10 August. It is almost certain that this was due to the powder-filling of shells which were better firelighters than Shimose-filled shells. There are specific references to paint catching fire, with flames either spreading along the surface or fire spreading from dislodged flakes of burning paint. It is said that the red lead primer did not burn.[28] *Orel* is said to have been stripped of woodwork during the passage and her remaining boats were soaked in water before the battle but this did not prevent major fires.

A single fire is easy to put out if the firefighters are unhindered but it is more difficult when they are being fired on. If there are several fires and firefighting is hindered by casualties and cut hoses, both from numerous splinters, they will spread and join to a single massive conflagration. Ammunition fires seem fairly common and it is surprising that only the *Borodino* blew up, though *Iwate* was very close to it. The vulnerability of the lightly-armoured ammunition supply routes (and ready-use storage) for the secondary armament may be recognised. Harding[29] suggests that the serious fires at Tsushima and the long time for which they burnt was due to the coal carried high in the ship. As discussed earlier, the RN had done much to reduce the risk of fire and the measures taken seemed adequate in the light of the *Belleisle* trial. There were few serious fires in the First World War; exceptions being *Good Hope* and *Monmouth* at Coronel and in *Black Prince* at Jutland. It is probable that these fires were the result of frequent hits overwhelming the fire parties as described above, though they may have involved cordite charges.

Flooding

From Russian accounts one can see a number of common factors; a gradual breakdown of command due to injuries to senior officers – inadequately protected by the conning towers – and the difficulty in passing orders as voice pipes were cut, and access obstructed by debris, structural damage and fires, together with a hail of splinters on the upper deck.

Splinters also affected the stopping of holes above the waterline; not difficult if unhindered but virtually impossible under fire. This led to a build-up of water above the protective deck as the ship rolled in heavy seas, reducing stability and possibly giving a heeling moment. Firefighting water added considerably to the problem. *Suvorov* had quite severe flooding through a lower-deck gun port.

Sinking

The centre of gravity was high in the Russian ships of French style, with towering sides, and a satisfactory intact metacentric height was obtained by increasing the beam.[30] Much of the benefit of beam is lost when extensive flooding occurs and it is virtually certain that the stability of these ships after damage was very poor. The centreline bulkhead in the machinery spaces would lead to large heeling moments if one side was flooded, whilst the righting moment would be seriously reduced if hits had made the upperworks non-watertight and the tumblehome[31] would further reduce the righting moment. It

21. Corbett as 13 above.

22. *Annual Report of the Torpedo School, 1903*. PRO ADM 189/23.

23. CB 47 says only eighty-five were fired.

24. Corbett, *Maritime Operations in the Russo-Japanese War.*

25. This incident seems to have made a deep impression on Jellicoe who saw the dropping of mines ahead of a fleet as a major threat.

26. D K Brown, 'Torpedoes at Jutland', *Warship World* Vol 5/2 (Liskeard 1995).

27. V Semenov, *The Battle of Tsushima* (London 1908)

28. It is interesting that these accounts refer to *Suvarov*s which were new ships and, as such, would not have had too many coats of paint.

29. CB 47.

30. It is suggested by Klado and others that weight growth during building left the *Suvarov*s with an inadequate metacentric height when completed.

31. The French battleship *Gaulois* was rebuilt with vertical sides after the Dardenelles, much improving her stability.

Damage to *Orel* after Tsushima, 28 May 1905. After her surrender to the Japanese, her damage was closely investigated. (S A Lilliman)

was a combination of a high centre of gravity, asymmetric flooding and reduced righting moment which led to capsize, although in the case of *Alexander III* and *Osliabia* flooding of the lightly-protected ends was a contributory factor.

Pakenham drew attention to the dangers of centreline bulkheads in several of his reports. No attention seems to have been paid to this point which was probably the prime cause of capsize. At the time, capsize was blamed on the extreme tumblehome, a feature which was incorporated only to a small extent in British ships prior to the First World War. He also pointed out the need for unpierced bulkheads and, quite reasonably, it was felt that efforts already in hand following the loss of *Victoria*, eg *Lord Nelson* and *Dreadnought*, were adequate. There was always a problem with doors to coal bunkers which could be jammed by bits of coal. The Japanese tried to reduce the risk by stacking two hours' supply in the stokehold and keeping the doors firmly shut.

Most of the postwar debate centred on whether the Russian ships were destroyed or disabled by the effects of 12in shells or by the 'hail of fire' from smaller guns, particularly 6in, but due to the failure of shells, there was no certain guidance. Jellicoe in two papers written in justification of the 'all-big gun ships'[32] largely ignores the war and bases his arguments for the 12in on the rate of hitting during RN battle practice.

The senior Royal Navy observer, Captain Pakenham, gave his views in the following well-known quotation:

The 10in guns of the *Peresviet* and *Pobeida* were of 45 calibres, and may also be of greater range, but the effect of every gun is so much less than that of the next larger size, that when 12in guns are firing, shots from 10in pass unnoticed, while, for all the respect they instil, 8in or 6in guns might just as well be pea shooters, and the 12pdr simply does not count. This must be understood to refer entirely to the moral [*sic*] effect.

The basis of this statement is unclear though it seems consistent with accounts by Russian survivors, particularly from the *Orel*. It should be noted that Pakenham refers specifically to morale effect, a sentence too often omitted.

Damage to Orel

The damage to this ship is well documented both from official inspections after the battle and from a fascinating, highly coloured but generally accurate account of the battle by a survivor.

The *Orel* was hit many times, and large numbers of shells struck the near-by water, drenching us with spray. The sea appeared to form a wall, barring our progress. Vomits of black and brown smoke, jets of flame, fountains of spray thrown up by the bursting shell, created an elemental tempest. [33]

Hits on *Orel*

Calibre (in)	No (lbs)	Wt shells (lbs)	Wt burster (lbs)
12	5	4200	405
10	2	980	96
8	9	2250	207
6	39	3400	351

The table above shows that the few 12in hits account for most of the weight of shell and burster hitting the ship whilst her survivors speak of the morale effect of the explosion of large shells.

The lessons

The RN was generally correct in seeing the war as an old-fashioned one from which few lessons could be drawn. However, it is clear that the war was studied very carefully, that some lessons were drawn and, in most cases, swift and effective action was taken to implement necessary changes. The war was seen as confirming many existing ideas and was used to support much of the Fisher revolution. Poor Nebogatov's third squadron showed that obsolete ships were a hindrance of no value and the value of speed was reconsidered.

The main debate after the war was between supporters of the all big-gun ship and the hail of fire enthusiasts (including White) both of whom claimed that the war supported their views. With hindsight, it seems clear that 10 August demonstrated the possibility of long-range fire – over 12,000yds – which made a considerable number of 12in essential for salvo firing. Tsushima was fought at closer range and the evidence seems less clear. However, closer examination of the damage, such as the table of damage to *Orel*, demonstrates the destructive power of the larger shell. The value of the hail of fire in disrupting firefighting and leak-stopping is often neglected, even by supporters of the 6in.

The RN was already concerned over the destructive power of the big, high-capacity shell, probably as a result of the *Belleisle* trial. It was this which led them to retain a lighter upper belt and light protection to the waterline at the ends rather than an all or nothing scheme as in the later USS *Nevada*. It was probably the same reasoning which led British designers to pay a lot of attention to protection and duplication of *Dreadnought*'s fire control communications.

The Admiralty were satisfied with their fire precautions and the First World War largely justified their confidence. They also were satisfied with subdivision, but this was not entirely justified. Pakenham had warned of the dangers of longitudinal bulkheads but these were to topple many ships in the coming war. Spread of flooding through vent trunks etc, remained a problem even though unpierced bulkheads had already been introduced in *Lord Nelson*.[34] Mines took a terrible toll of

32. Two papers by Jellicoe and Watts – Building Programme of the Royal Navy. *The Lessons of the Russo-Japanese War in their application to the Building Programmes of Britain, Germany and France* and *H M Ships Dreadnought and Invincible*. Held in the Tweedmouth papers, MoD Library. These are summarised in D K Brown, 'Battleship Design', *Warship World* Vol 4/1 (Liskeard 1991).

33. Novikoff-Priboy, *Tsushima, Grave of a Floating City*.

34. See Beresford's views, Chapter 8.

Hero after trials in 1912.
(Author's collection)

Two views of *Empress of India*
under fire November 1913.
(Author's collection)

would eventually be overcome. Since most tests of penetration were at normal angle to the plate and mostly carried out with unfused shell (often inert-filled), these failings were not apparent.

Though the lack of success with torpedoes was recognised, it was thought that the introduction of the gyro and of heater torpedoes, faster and of longer range, would overcome these problems. Fear of the torpedo was to influence both tactics and ships design.

The Admiralty were well aware that simple comparative tables of guns, maximum belt thickness and speed meant little but it was a lesson which naval correspondents should have learnt. Such a comparison of the *Suvorov*'s with the Japanese ships might well have suggested a Russian victory.

	Mikasa	*Suvorov*
Displacement (tons)	15,140	13,516
Armament	4-12in, 14-6in	4-12in, 12-6in
Speed (kts)	18	17.8
Belt armour (in)	9	7½

There is little difference in the figures above though the greater displacement of the *Mikasa* hints at more extensive armour. Warship design had already become so complex that the figures given in reference books gave only the slightest indication of fighting capability. The next generation of battleships depended to an increasing extent on the effectiveness of fire control and on the performance of their projectiles, neither given in tables.

More trials 1906-13

There were some other British full scale firing trials in the years up to the outbreak of war. There were trials against *Landrail* in 1906 and *Hero* in 1907, both aimed at the development of fire control. The percentage of hits by the big gun in the latter trial is of interest.

12in	43 per cent
9.2in	32 per cent
6in	19 per cent

A more detailed trial, to examine the effectiveness of different types of shell and protection took place in 1909-10, using the old battleship *Edinburgh*.[35] Many of the individual tests relate to a later era but some can be related to ships discussed in this volume. The charge for the shells was adjusted to give a striking velocity corresponding to a range of 6000yds and for the tests of deck protection the ship was heeled to 10° to allow for the angle of descent plus some rolling. The shells used were the newly introduced 13.5in as well as 9.2in and 6in, both Lyddite and powder-filled.

The lessons learnt as affecting ships described in this book are as follows.

ships in 1904-05 and the British actions were prompt and sensible though not entirely adequate.

The one serious failure was in not recognising that Japanese problems with over-sensitive shell fillings of picric acid (Shimose or Lyddite), and AP fuses which detonated before penetration applied to the RN as well. New shells were being introduced at this time and it is probable that it was thought that any such problems

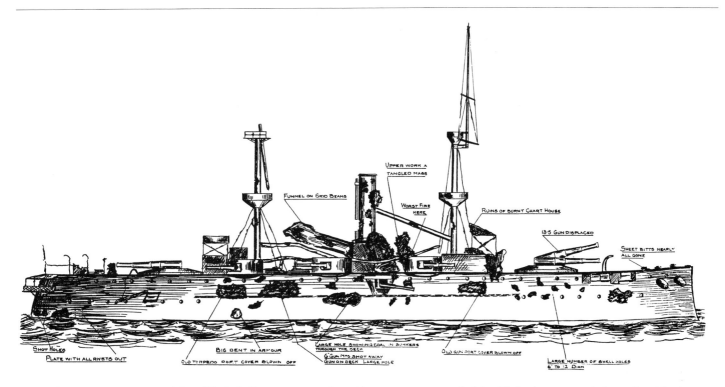

Labels on illustration: SHOT HOLES · PLATE WITH ALL RIVETS OUT · BIG DENT IN ARMOUR · OLD TORPEDO PORT COVER BLOWN OFF · FUNNEL ON SKID BEAMS · UPPER WORK A TANGLED MASS · WORST FIRE HERE · LARGE HOLE SHOWING COAL IN BUNKERS THROUGH THE DECK · 6 GUN MTG SHOT AWAY GUN ON DECK LARGE HOLE · RUINS OF BURNT CHART HOUSE · 13·5 GUN DISPLACED · SHEET BITTS NEARLY ALL GONE · OLD GUN PORT COVER BLOWN OFF · LARGE NUMBER OF SHELL HOLES 6 TO 12 DIAM

An impression of the damage to *Empress of India* in the 1913 firing trials.

(a) High capacity HE, *ie* Lyddite, filled shells were extremely formidable weapons. They caused tremendous local 'smashing effect', opening up the ship and breaking decks and bulkheads. The splinters were small and did not always penetrate even one bulkhead but were so numerous that they would have caused numerous casualties and cut all electric cables. Against heavy structure the blast effect was very localised. Important equipment should not be sited on the deck below an armoured deck. There is an interesting sequel as after Jutland nose-fused Lyddite shells were withdrawn as they were judged to be ineffective against armoured ships.

(b) The big splinters from powder-filled common shell (CPC) were far more damaging to structure than HE Lyddite-filled shells, tending to follow the line of flight of the shell. It was recommended that a mix of the two types of shell should be used. (One may see (a) and (b) as reinforcing the lessons from the *Belleisle* trial.)

(c) Sections of structure intending to represent cruiser protection showed that even quite thick decks were vulnerable to the effects of large HE shells while thin side armour was effective in keeping most of the blast and splinters outside the ship.[36]

(d) The effect of a large HE shell bursting on the funnel casing could be devastating. The gratings were quite effective in keeping splinters out of the boilers but the blast would have blown the contents of the furnace into the stokehold. Overall, the value of exten-

sive side armour, even of thin (4in) plate was emphasised.

There was a trial at Shoeburyness in 1906-07 of a casemate representing that of the *Devonshire*s. This had 6in KC with a ¼in mild steel screen behind to carry the instruments. It kept out 7.5in common shell at an equivalent 6-8000yds but was easily penetrated by capped shell.

In 1913, firing trials were carried out against the *Empress of India*, mainly to give officers and men some idea of the effect of live shell against a real target. It was also intended to study the problems of firing from several ships at the same time. The intention was to repeat this at longer range but the target had sunk and was too damaged for further trials. In the first sequence the cruiser *Liverpool* fired 6in and 4in HE shell at 4750yds, hitting the large, stationary target with seven out of sixteen 6in and twenty-two of sixty-six 4in. The battleships *Thunderer*, *Orion* and *King Edward VII* then fired common shell at 9800yds scoring seventeen hits from forty 13.5in, five from sixteen 12in, seven from eighteen 9.2in and five from twenty-seven 6in.

Finally, *Neptune*, *King George V*, *Thunderer* and *Vanguard* fired ninety-five common shell from their main armament at 8-10,000yds scoring twenty-two hits in 2 minutes. By 4:45pm the *Empress of India* was blazing furiously and down by the stern, sinking at 6:30pm. In all, she had received over forty hits from large calibre shells and it is not surprising that an elderly ship sank. It was noted that her upper decks were planked-over beams without steel deck plating accounting for the fires as in the Spanish cruisers at Santiago.

35. D K Brown, 'Attack and Defence, Part 5', *Warship 34* (London 1985) (based on the 1915 Gunnery Manual). This trial will be discussed in more detail in a later volume.

36. Probably the origin of the *Arethusa*'s light belt.

Firing against torpedo boats and destroyers

A considerable number of trials were carried out with a wide variety of guns and projectiles to find the best way of sinking or disabling an attacking torpedo craft in the short time it was in range and before launching its torpedo. In 1889 a large replica torpedo boat was built at Shoeburyness. One-pounder shells were found to be ineffective, whereas 3pdr common shells were satisfactory when fired against the broadside but ineffective in the more realistic end-on shots, bursting long before they reached the vitals. Further trials were held in 1894-95 with 6pdr and 12pdr shells. The conclusion was that only the 12pdr could be relied on to stop a torpedo boat with a single shot. Presumably, this led to the adoption of 12pdrs as the *Dreadnought*'s anti-torpedo boat armament. Tests were also carried out in 1895 to see if the boilers of torpedo boats could be protected by hanging the spare fire bars on the bulkhead – '. . . the results were not encouraging'.

The old destroyer *Skate* was used for further trials in 1906 against 3pdr, 12pdr and 4in (25lb shell). The ship was moored so that she was either end-on to the line of fire or 13° off the line. The 3pdr was ineffective in end-on fire, many rounds glancing off the sides, and even at 13° it was thought that damage would not cripple the torpedo boat.

The 12pdr caused much more severe damage but this time the conclusion was that it could not be certain of disabling a destroyer with one hit. The 25lb shell of the 4in gun caused severe damage. There was a marked difference between the effects of Lyddite and powder-filled shell, the former making a much bigger hole when bursting on the side whilst the bigger splinters from the powder-filled shell caused damage over a greater extent. It was concluded that either powder-filled or Lyddite 4in or 12pdr would disable the destroyer if the engine-room were hit but, outside the machinery, Lyddite shell had a far better chance of disabling or sinking.

A large number of trials[37] were carried out using shrapnel shell from guns of 6in to 12in. The object was to determine the optimum size of ball to disable the craft or its crew. Though severe damage was caused in some cases, the danger area was quite limited and it was thought that it was unlikely that the fuse would function with sufficient accuracy at the short ranges involved. Even case shot, fired from a 12.5in RML, was tried and rejected because of the likely damage to the rifling of the gun.

Loss and damage in the First World War

The years from the launch of *Dreadnought* to the outbreak of the war were ones of very rapid development and the ships described in this book were obsolete, used in secondary roles and often exposed to weapons far more powerful than those they had been designed to withstand. However, it is still possible to draw some valid conclusion from their behaviour.

Perhaps the most interesting example is the well-documented case of damage to *Agamemnon* from Turkish guns at the Dardanelles[38] in early 1915. On 25 February, whilst engaging the outer forts, she was hit seven times out of an estimated fifty-six shells landing close. These were probably from Fort No 1 with two elderly 9.4in firing Gruson cast iron shells (similar to Palliser). The hits were:

1. Hit derrick, passed through funnel, nine casualties.

2. Hit forecastle while weighing anchor, some casualties.

3. Hit S2 9.2in turret on armour. Glanced off and burst, penetrating upper deck. Damage to electric leads.

4. Hit forward funnel, bust on winch. Scattered cordite charges for 12pdrs.

5. Grazed topgallant mast.

6. Passed through 25lb side plating about 4ft above armour, then through two 5lb minor bulkheads. It then broke up in penetrating the 2in armour deck, starting a small fire in a hydraulic machinery room. This was soon extinguished. Denham notes that the machinery room was between two magazines and had the hit been a little to either side, the consequences could have been very serious.

7. Hit 8in belt without damage.

Agamemnon had fired 123 9.2in shells of which 12 were Lyddite, several of which burst prematurely, soon after leaving the muzzle. On 7 March, engaging the forts at the Narrows, she was hit several times on the armour without damage and three hits outside which caused large holes, suggesting they were medium calibre HE (probably 5.9in). *Agamemnon* fired 8 12in and 145 9.2in shells. In the same action, *Lord Nelson* was hit on the flying deck, splinters entering the conning tower, slightly wounding the captain and others.

On 18 March *Agamemnon* was hit five times on the armour and six times outside, by medium calibre, HE howitzer shell. One shell which burst on the armour of S3 9.2 turret caused flash in the after 12in and a splinter damaged the inner tube of the left 12in. Other hits wrecked the capstan, badly damaged the fore shelter deck, wrecked the after funnel and destroyed two 12pdrs. In these three actions, *Agamemnon* received some twenty-six hits but they were mostly medium calibre (probably 5.9in, possibly 8in), some 9.4in, and were probably chilled iron shot, and only the damaged 12in gun affected her fighting capability. On the other hand, she was close to a magazine explosion from hit 6 in the table above, despite having the best armour protection of any of the ships in this account.

37. Gunnery Manual 1915

38. H M Denham, *Dardenelles, a Midshipman's Diary* (London 1981), augmented by material from J Campbell.

Underwater damage

The table below lists underwater damage to British battleships earlier than *Dreadnought*.

Ship	Weapon	Cause of Sinking
Majestic	Torpedo	Capsize
Ocean	Mine	15° list
Goliath	Torpedo	Capsize
Formidable	Torpedo	Capsize
Irresistible	Mine	Sank upright
Cornwallis	Torpedo	Capsize
Russell	Mine	Severe heel
King Edward VII	Mine	Capsize
Britannia	Torpedo	Capsize
Triumph	Torpedo	Capsize

Other fatal damage

Bulwark	Magazine explosion	
Montague	Grounded	

In many cases there was a rapid initial heel, 8° seems typical, which sometimes increased steadily to capsize but, more often, they would hang for a considerable time at this angle. There would then be a lurch and further rapid heel to capsize. This could be spread of flooding to a new compartment (possibly associated with bulkhead failure) or free surface high up destroying stability. Heel was often reduced by dramatic counterflooding. In some cases the ammunition passage was identified as spreading flooding.

Of the ten ships sunk by underwater explosion, seven capsized, two were abandoned with severe heel and one sank with 6-7° list. Almost certainly, these losses can be attributed to the off-centre flooding due to a centreline bulkhead in the machinery spaces; something which Reed had warned against in 1871. The *Irresistible*, which sank with a small list only, is in fact the clinching evidence as reports say that the centreline bulkhead between the engine-rooms was damaged in the explosion.

A very crude calculation, based on *Canopus*, suggests the following figures for heel:

Space flooded	Angle of heel (°)
Engine-room	9.6
Boiler room	6.8
Both	16.6

It is assumed that the coal bunkers are flooded but the coal remains in place preserving ⅝ buoyancy. There are frequent references to shoring up bulkheads in damaged ships which suggests the 'lurch' often referred to, could be the failure of a bulkhead.

One may sum up White's ships as having adequate armour for their era, well arranged. Their fire precautions were satisfactory in all but his earliest ships but the centreline bulkheads were a fatal flaw. Even though the risk of flooding through ventilation ducts, pipes etc was recognised and action taken, it was not fully adequate. Main deck casemates were a weak point, not exposed during the Russo-Japanese War.

Ocean, which was mined and sunk in the Dardanelles 1915. (WSS)

Eleven

Dreadnought, a Ship whose Time had Come

1. J A Fisher, *Naval Necessities*, October 1904. MoD library.

2. Bacon, *The Life of Lord Fisher of Kilverstone*, Vol I, p229.

3. It will be argued that this view was incorrect but it was accepted at the time and was a major influence on policy.

4. While Bacon, who is not a very reliable witness, is emphatic that salvo firing was a key feature of the all-big gun ship, he, as *Dreadnought*'s first captain, used single shots to establish range throughout her working-up cruise.

5. One is reminded of the saying 'There they go, I must hurry after them for I am their leader.'

6. Note, however, that Russian ships, without telescopic sights, seem to have fired quite accurately at about 12,000yds on 10 August 1904.

7. Bacon actually refers specifically to trials against the *Surcouf* but since these took place on 15 May 1902 they cannot be the spur to the RN's 1900 trials. French ships fired 340 rounds at *Surcouf* at ranges between 4300 and 2400 yards, scoring 41 hits. The heavy guns fired at the rate of one round every 3 minutes (*Brassey's Naval Annual* 1903).

8. Harding published under a pseudonym – 'Radian', 'The Tactical Employment of Naval Artillery', *Engineering* (London 1903).

9. E W Harding, 'Fire Control, A Summary of the Present Position of the Subject', MoD Library

EVEN AT the opening of the twentieth century, the Admiralty headquarters and the Royal Navy were large and complex organisations within which each department and specialisation was pursuing its own line of development. Quite suddenly, in 1904 all these separate developments came together, with great enthusiasm, in the concept of the *Dreadnought*, the 'all big-gun ship.' Some of these developments made such a concept desirable or even essential whilst others made it feasible at acceptable cost.

Bacon[2] lists the developments which led to *Dreadnought* as:

The torpedo menace necessitated longer ranges in action.[3]

Long-range hitting (gun) had become practicable.

The only method known of ranging at long ranges was by firing salvoes.[4]

This necessitated a uniform armament of eight or more guns.

The heaviest gun gave the greatest blow, and was the most accurate at long range.

Developments which made the concept feasible included turbine machinery, lighter and cheaper construction (despite major improvements in subdivision) and the scrapping of old ships which allowed the cost of the new ships to be contained within a budget which was politically acceptable.

Weaving across these separate developments strode the demonic figure of 'Jacky' Fisher who, as First Sea Lord, was to provide the drive which brought the *Dreadnought* into being. His consistent theme for much of his career can be seen in his introduction to the *Dreadnought* design committee: 'The battleship is the embodiment of concentration of force.' The other quotation at the head of the chapter shows that he at least tried to work from a role to a design instead of merely trying to produce a 'better' ship than those of the potential enemy. However, Fisher took a long while to decide on how best to achieve his concentration of force; he was almost the last of the key players to support the 'all big-gun' concept which he then pushed through with the usual enthusiasm of a new convert.[5] Even as the design commenced, he still did not seem to understand how her heavy armament was to be used. The separate developments will be described before seeing how they came together.

The Need for the *Dreadnought*

Gunnery – 'Hit first, hit hard and go on hitting!' (Fisher)

Percy Scott's earlier work, in which he introduced telescopic sights, dramatically increased the rate of fire by his loader training and the rate of hitting at short range by practising 'continuous aim' with the dotter has been described in Chapter 9. There was a growing realisation in the Navy that rate of hitting was what mattered and that this was not necessarily directly dependent on rate of fire; a point which armchair critics were slow to appreciate. At the end of the nineteenth century target practice was carried out at about 1500yds and in a lecture given by Fisher as C-in-C, Mediterranean, he said that, at that time, the effective range of heavy guns with telescopic sights was then about 3-4000yds and about 2000yds without telescopic sights.[6]

Bacon suggests that the firing trials by the French[7] were the spur to longer-range trials in the RN and by 1898 Sir John Hopkins had initiated such trials in the Mediterranean fleet at the then unprecedented range of 6000yds. These trials were continued by Fisher when he took over the Mediterranean Fleet. These showed that the only effective way of obtaining range was by spotting the fall of shot and, for this to be effective, a salvo of about four rounds had to be fired together so that one or more would be short and others over. Against a moving ship, salvoes had to be fired at reasonably short intervals to correct for changes in range and hence at least eight guns were needed.

In 1901 Captain E W Harding, RMA, who had taken part in the Mediterranean trials wrote a series of articles in the United Services Journal on fire control followed by a second series in *Engineering* which were combined in a book published in 1903.[8] Percy Scott gave an important lecture at the gunnery school in 1904 called 'Remarks on long-range hitting'. Further, very careful, trials using the *Victorious* and *Vengeance* were carried out over a period of three months in 1903 using Harding's articles as the basis of planning. Harding's report on the trials was issued by the Gunnery Branch.[9]

The findings of the earlier trials were confirmed and it was also realised that the splashes from the 6in secondary armament merely obscured the more important splashes from the 12in. The need to spot the fall of shot and apply corrections before the next salvo meant that the effective rate of fire of a 6in at 6000yds was much less than that achieved in short-range target practice; in fact, as range increased, the rate of hitting by the 12in exceeded that from the 6 inch. The effect of a 12in hit was vastly greater than that from a 6in. There was also hope that the 12in BVIII mounting (1904-05 programme ships) could be elevated sufficiently quickly for 'continuous aim' as in smaller mountings.

As Director of the War College[10] within the RN College at Greenwich, Captain May carried out a series of 'war game' studies in 1902 which had a considerable influence on thinking about the future battleship. His reports on some of these exercises have survived in the PRO;[11] in one such study he investigated the value of speed, concluding that it was of little value compared with guns and armour. Another study showed the value of the big gun (see below).

Prior to the design of the *Lord Nelson*, the then Controller, Sir William H May, initiated an inquiry into the gun power and protection of battleships[12] and in conjunction with this, the new DNC, Phillip Watts, prepared a wide range of battleship designs of different characteristics. Diagrams were prepared which showed the areas of the ships side which were armoured or unprotected as a base. On this, ordinates were set up showing the thickness of the armour (allowing for curvature, *eg* barbettes). On a separate, parallel base another set of ordinates were plotted showing the projectile weight which could be delivered from each size of gun in the attacking ship in a given time. Horizontal lines showed the weight of each projectile and areas which could resist the given attack were coloured blue whilst areas which could be destroyed were shown in red.

These diagrams showed very clearly that the extent of damage and rate of damage from the secondary (6in) battery was much less than that due to the main armament and that the damage caused by the big guns was so severe that the secondary armament would be swept away before it could get into effective range. Heavier armour was required over a much larger area than had previously been customary. It was also concluded that the secondary armament of 6in guns was of little value. In consequence, the *Lord Nelson* was given thicker and more extensive armour and the 6in battery was done away with in favour of a heavy 9.2in secondary armament. A proposal by the battleship section for an all-12in armament was not accepted.

The increasing distance at which fire was opened led to the requirement to measure range and estimate its future changes so that projectile and target should meet.[13] Fully integrated fire control systems lie just outside the time scale of this book but *Dreadnought* had many more mechanical aids to gunnery than is generally realised, all part of the drive to 'hit first, hit hard and go on hitting' as Fisher put it. Accurate sights were the first requirement and *Dreadnought* had the first direct action sights, attached directly to the trunnion, eliminating the backlash in the linkages which had caused many problems.

Rangefinders, devised by Professor Barr, had been introduced in 1892. These instruments had a length of 4ft 6in and had a 1 per cent accuracy at 3000yds. A 9ft rangefinder was introduced in 1906 which had the same 1 per cent accuracy at 7000yds and *Dreadnought* was amongst the first ships to receive these longer rangefinders.

With opposing fleets moving at different courses and speeds, perhaps manoeuvring as well, range and bearing would be altering continually, even during the time of flight of the shell (up to 30 seconds). The Dumaresq was a mechanical computer which could estimate the range rate and deflection when fed with the ship's own speed and estimates of the enemy course, speed and bearing. Spotting the fall of shot allowed corrections to be made first for deflection, then for range and, once hitting, for rate.[14] The information from the Dumaresq was used to update another instrument, the Vickers' clock which gave a continuous indication of the estimated range of the target. *Dreadnought*'s embryonic fire control system had both these instruments. As completed there were two transmitting stations on the middle deck, in the lower conning tower and the lower signal tower. These were very vulnerable and the forward one was moved below the protective deck in 1909.

Dreadnought's fire control equipment was adequate when neither the range nor its rate was changing rapidly. Once the training and elevation gear was improved, it became both possible and, indeed, essential to examine the far more difficult problem of rapid changes. Fisher was still talking of the need for firing single shots (rather than salvoes) at long range and while *Dreadnought* was given a big fire control top supported on a rigid tripod, Jellicoe ensured that it was in the hot smoke plume from the fore funnel.

The establishment of a 'central nervous system' connecting control top, transmitting station (TS) and guns made it possible to destroy the capability of the ship by damage to the connecting wires. This problem was appreciated by her designers who tried to reduce the vulnerability of the system by protecting as much as possible and by duplicating both cable runs and their power sources.[15] It was a general requirement that cables should be behind armour 'as far as possible' though in *Dreadnought* herself the TS were unprotected initially.[16] Cables were led into the turrets along the hydraulic walking pipes and up the central trunk. The main cables were not duplicated but were fed from two switchboards, fore and aft, and below the protective deck, each of which was fed from two motor generators supplied from different sections of the main electrical supply, itself below the protective deck.[17] An armoured tube carried communications to the conning tower; those to the foretop were not duplicated initially (probably later) and were run down inside the tripod legs which gave them some protection against splinters, though not against a direct hit as experienced by *Invincible* at the Falklands.

Sir Phillip Watts, responsible for the *Dreadnought*. (RCNC Archives)

10. The author attended the War College in 1973-74.

11. ADM 1/7597 'Exercises carried out at the RN College Greenwich' No 653 May 1902.

12. J H Narbeth, 'Three Steps in Naval Construction', *Trans INA* (London 1922). (The complete May paper has not been found: it is not in the May papers at the NMM.)

13. This section is largely based on a lecture at King's College by John Brooks, February 1994, 'Dreadnoughts and fire control', later published in *War Studies Journal*. I am indebted to John Brooks and to John Roberts for many helpful contributions to this section. See also Sumida, *In Defence of Naval Supremacy*.

14. Spotting for rate was not used at least until 1909 and probably later.

15. This paragraph is based on a note by John Roberts. Complete details of the *Dreadnought* arrangement are not available and the note is based, in part, on that fitted in later 12in ships.

16. The after TS seems to have been seen as a reserve as several contemporary documents imply a single TS, forward and later under armour.

17. J Roberts, *The Battleship Dreadnought* (London 1992).

On her experimental cruise to the West Indies the communications from the foretop to the forward TS consisted of four voice pipes and two navyphones so that range, range rate, spotting corrections and deflection from the Dumaresq had to be passed verbally. As a result of the recommendations from that cruise, *Dreadnought* was one of the first eighteen ships to receive 'step by step' transmitters to pass range from the finder to the transmitting station and hence to the gun. These required less wiring than earlier communications. The earliest such transmitters were troublesome and *Dreadnought* had the Vickers Mark II which was generally satisfactory.

The torpedo menace

It is interesting that Bacon (and others) gives the increasing range of torpedoes as one reason for increasing the range at which the gunnery action was to be fought. The latest RGF 'cold' compressed air torpedo in service at the time *Dreadnought* was designed had an extreme range of about 3000yds at slow speed but were normally used at shorter range (1500yds) and higher speed though the introduction of the gyroscope from about 1895 had much increased its accuracy. In 1905 Armstrong demonstrated the first heater torpedo in which fuel was burnt in the air to increase the energy available. Though this prototype was not really practicable, the potential was clear and heater systems were introduced by Whitehead (largely a subsidiary of Armstrong) from 1907.

The Factory, *Vernon* and all concerned with torpedoes were convinced by 1905 that long range (6000yds or more) torpedoes would soon be available. In turn, this led gunnery experts to see the torpedo as a reason

for increasing gun range. The fear of the torpedo was a major factor in forcing the Navy to longer battle ranges though experience in the First World War showed that the torpedo was much less effective than anticipated.[18] At 6000yds, the running time would be at least 6 minutes during which the speed or course of the target was only too likely to change. It was also found much more difficult to launch a co-ordinated attack than had been expected, something which should have been recognised from the Russo-Japanese war.

Other pressures

Fisher and, independently, the DNC battleship section saw standardisation with a single-calibre armament as leading to worthwhile savings in ammunition supply, spares and in training. Narbeth[19] gives a fascinating account of the development of battleship design from *Majestic* to *Dreadnought*. In particular, he says that the increased power of secondary batteries in foreign ships led the design section to propose four twin 7.5in turrets be added to the *King Edward VII* class, changed by White to four single 9.2in. While White was absent sick, his deputy, H E Deadman, proposed a very large battleship. In the next class, the *Lord Nelson*, the design section proposed an all-12in armament, which was not agreed. It would seem that the design team saw the all big-gun ship as the logical end point of a more powerful secondary armament. It is worth pointing out that prior to *Dreadnought* the fighting range was about 3000yds at which both the 6in and 12in could hit frequently. The generally-accepted view was that the enemy should be disabled by a hail of 6in fire, using HE shells and then sunk by AP shells from the 12in. The 6in 'secondary' armament was an important (to some the most important) weapon in fighting enemy battleships. Lesser guns, 12pdr and below, were provided to deal with torpedo boats.

There were a number of other influences, mainly writers of books and press articles, which may have affected the general climate of opinion. The most important of these was Cuniberti, the distinguished Italian naval constructor, who wrote an article for the 1903 *Jane's* advocating the fast, all big-gun ship. Cuniberti seems to have been thinking of fairly close range fighting but he did bring out the destructive power of the 12in gun. His proposal was quite impractical; he envisaged twelve 12in guns in eight turrets, a complete 12in belt and a speed of 24kts, which would require double the power needed for 21kts, much more powerful machinery of heavier, reciprocating design, more guns and armour than *Dreadnought*, and all on a smaller ship of 17,000 tons!

At the period when naval thinking was moving to the *Dreadnought* concept, most naval journalists were still preaching the 'hail of fire' from 6in guns as the decisive weapon. They misread – or were unaware of – the lessons of long-range firing and saw only that few hits

18. D K Brown, 'Torpedoes at Jutland', *Warship World* Vol 5/2 (Liskeard 1995).

19. J H Narbeth, 'Three Steps in Naval Construction', *Trans INA* 1922. It is remarkable that Narbeth's account has been accepted so uncritically by most writers. He is often described as an Assistant Director of Naval Construction (his rank in 1922) but at the time *Dreadnought* was designed his rank was Assistant Constructor, three ranks less. His story was contradicted during the discussion in important aspects by Deadman, an exceptionally able and well-liked officer who acted as DNC whilst White was sick (I don't think Deadman's remarks were simply a senior putting a junior in his place. Also contradicted by Sir W E Smith, possibly less reliable, with a chip on his shoulder following his own dismissal). There are also some errors of fact, eg *Amethyst*, discussed later. None of this is intended to denigrate Narbeth who, at the time of the *Dreadnought* design was 38 years old, just entering the age group at which

engineers are usually most innovative and productive. He was highly respected by both his senior officers and by his juniors. Goodall, much his junior and who would become one of the greatest warship designers of all time, wrote very favourably of his ability. His account of ideas which he produced are almost certainly correct and at least partially confirmed by his papers in the Ship's Cover but the hierarchical organisation of the day would ensure that his ideas were put to his own senior officers and not directly to Controller. Narbeth's later paper of 1941 was also demonstrated to be inaccurate in detail. Narbeth is an important eyewitness but, as such, his evidence must be examined critically.

20. Engineer Rear-Admiral Sir R W Skelton, 'Progress in Marine Engineering', *Trans Inst Mech Eng* (London 1930). This reference is not entirely clear and needs reading in the context of White's discussion to H E Deadman 'On the Application of Electricity in the Royal Dockyards and Navy', *Trans Inst Mech Eng* (London 1892). Dr I L

Buxton has discovered that the Parsons 12kW unit No 13 was fitted in 1885 and returned and replaced by No 25 in 1886. It is uncertain whether this machine remained on board when the *Victoria* went to sea though there is no record of it being used elsewhere.

21. Sir S V Goodall, 'Sir Charles Parsons and the RN', *Trans INA* (London 1942). *Turbinia's* form is still one of the best for very high speeds. This paper was Goodall's almost only 'relaxation' during the Second World War.

22. The design of multiple propellers on one shaft is very difficult. The forward propeller accelerates the flow so that the second (and any subsequent) propeller works in a different velocity, needing different geometry. I think Parsons was lucky!

23. It is probable that this demonstration was encouraged by Durston.

24. It was unheard-of for a contract to be placed with a company other than the shipbuilder.

were scored, failing to realise that those few could be decisive and that properly equipped and trained ships could score many more hits. Attention will now be directed to the technical developments which made *Dreadnought* feasible.

Turbine machinery

The idea of the steam turbine occurred to several people at about the same time but the first to patent a workable design was the Honourable Charles Parsons in 1884 and, as all early RN turbines were of his design, the others need not be mentioned. His early turbines were intended to drive dynamos where their high rotational speed was valuable and one such unit was fitted in *Victoria* to provide lighting while she was building in 1885.[20]

In 1894 Parsons set up the Marine Steam Turbine Company at Wallsend and, after some very careful model experiments,[21] he built an experimental steam yacht, *Turbinia*, now preserved at Newcastle. Her steel hull is 100ft long with a beam of 9ft giving a displacement of 44.5 tons. Steam was supplied by a water tube boiler at 210lbs/sq in and, initially, passed to a single, radial-flow turbine developing 960shp at 2400rpm. Despite many trials and modifications she was unable to exceed 19.75kts due to cavitation on the single screw.

In 1896 she was re-engined with three turbines – HP, intermediate, LP – each driving one shaft with three widely-spaced propellers on each shaft.[22] She reached 34.5kts on trials which were attended by White and the Engineer-in-Chief, Sir John Durston, who had done much to encourage Parsons. The following year she gave a demonstration at the Diamond Jubilee Review,[23] steaming up and down the lines some 4kts faster than any warship.

Again, the Admiralty reacted quickly and in March 1898 they ordered the destroyer *Viper* from Parsons (hull sub-contracted to Hawthorn Leslie[24]) of 370 tons and generally similar to the '30-knotters' but with a contract speed of 31kts. Her hull cost £19,800 and the machinery £32,000 with a further £1200 for auxiliary machinery. On trial she reached 33.38kts at design load and, running light, made a one hour run at 36.5kts. *Viper* had four shafts each carrying two 20in diameter propellers, the HP turbines driving the wings and the LP, the inner shafts. At 31kts the specific coal consumption was 2.38, as good as the 30-knotters, but at lower speeds her consumption was very high.

Coal consumption – in lbs/hp/hr

Speed (kts)	Viper	Average 30-knotter TBD
15	2.5	1.2
20	4	2.5
22	5	3.3

Engineer Vice-Admiral Sir A J Durston, Engineer-in-Chief 1889-1905. *(Jnl of Naval Engineering)*

In service, *Viper* could make 26kts with half her stokers at work and, using them all, 31.5kts for a very short time, 30.5kts for half an hour. There was little or no vibration (by the standards of the day), steering ahead was good but, going astern, she could not be kept straight and would circle though there was plenty of astern power. The following year (1901) she was wrecked on rocks off the Channel Islands.

Armstrong built a somewhat similar destroyer for 'stock' and she was surveyed by Mr Ball, Assistant Constructor. In his report he noted many structural details which needed improvement to bring her up to Admiralty standards but thought her generally satisfactory. A later report by Mr Pine, Constructor, was less satisfactory, drawing attention to lack of girder strength, particularly aft and this was noted by the very experi-

Cobra, 1899, one of the first turbine TBDs, broke in half on her delivery voyage, initiating an enquiry into the strength of all TBDs. (WSS)

enced Henry Deadman in a note of 12 February 1900. Despite this and the very high price of £70,000 compared with £53,000 for *Viper,* she was purchased for the RN in 1900 as *Cobra,* subject to stiffening. Her four shafts each carried three propellers – twelve in all, a record. It was decided that she needed forty-eight stokers and a complement of eighty but there was cramped accommodation for only seventy. On trials, in June 1900, with numerous stokers, she reached 35kts. In September 1901 she broke in half on her delivery voyage, discussed later. The loss of both *Viper* and *Cobra* delayed the gathering of experience on turbines.[25]

Velox had been laid down by Parsons at Hawthorn Leslie as a private venture but was purchased by the Admiralty in 1901. She, too, had four shafts (eight propellers), the outers being driven by HP turbines while the inners had both LP turbines and small triple-expansion engines for cruising. She was intended for 27kts at design displacement which she achieved on trial (she made 34.5kts light). Fuel consumption was very heavy, even at full speed, and the reciprocating engines which could give 10kts were not very economical either. The real problem was that turbines are efficient only at high rpm whilst propellers function best at low rpm; only the introduction of the geared turbine could resolve this dilemma.

Also in 1901 the Admiralty ordered *Eden* of the *River* class to be fitted with turbines. She had three shafts with two propellers on each, running at much higher rpm than her near sisters, which had two shafts, each with one propeller. She had special cruising turbines with the HP on the port shaft and the LP to starboard. At speeds below 14kts steam passed through both cruising turbines and then into the main turbines. Between 14 and 19kts, the HP cruising unit was cut out and above 19kts the main turbines only were used.

With this complicated arrangement she could steam 3.39nm/ton at full speed and 17.33nm/ton at 13.5kts (12-hour trial), the latter figure comparing badly with the reciprocating boats which achieved 24-31nm/ton under similar conditions. Later there was a comparative trial with *Derwent,* also built by Hawthorn Leslie.

Excess coal by *Eden* over *Derwent* in 4 hours at 20.5kts

Total over 4 hours	4 tons
First hour	1.5 tons
Last hour	0.15 tons

This must have been seen as encouraging as it was the last trial before turbines were selected for *Dreadnought.*

The next naval trial of the turbine was in the cruiser *Amethyst* but she had not gone to sea[26] when the decision was taken to use turbines for *Dreadnought;* indeed, she had shed the blading and broken the casing of one of her turbines during a basin trial.[27] In addition to turbine trials in warships there were a number of installations in merchant ships whose success contributed to the decision to use turbines in *Dreadnought.* Perhaps the most influential was that of the Clyde passenger steamer *King Edward,* 3500shp and 20.5kts, in 1901. Other important applications were the Cunard *Carmania* (1901) and the Allen liner *Virginia* (1902) and in 1903 Cunard, on Admiralty advice, decided on turbines for *Lusitania* and *Mauritania.*

The *Wolf* trial

Following the loss of the *Cobra,* the Admiralty set up in 1901 the 'Torpedo Boat Destroyer Committee' to look

25. It was widely believed at the time that turbines were the 'cause' of the losses. Others, equally credibly, blamed them on unlucky 'Snake' names.

26. *Pace* Narbeth.

27. Bacon, *The Life of Lord Fisher of Kilverstone.*

28. Lyon, *The First Destroyers.*

29. Though these two were experienced in light, fast craft, they were not building destroyers and hence could be seen as independent.

30. The full report of the Committee is held in the MoD Library and is summarised in D K Brown, 'The Torpedo Boat Committee 1903', *Warship Technology* 2 (London 1987) and 3 (London 1988).

Amethyst, 1903, the first cruiser with turbines. She completed after it had been decided to fit turbines in *Dreadnought.* (WSS)

into all aspects of the strength of *Cobra* and all destroyers in service. It was a very well-qualified committee with Professor Biles from Glasgow University, H E Deadman RCNC who had so much to do with the design of early destroyers,[28] two shipbuilders,[29] J Inglis and A Denny, together with Vice-Admiral Sir H Rawson as chairman. Their study on seakeeping and loading in a seaway has been quoted at length in Chapter 8; they then went into a detailed study of the strength of steels and joints[30] before the most important part of their work, full-scale measurements of the loading and stress in the destroyer *Wolf*.

They began by a re-examination of Reed's standard strength calculation and varied some of the assumptions to see if there was a worse condition. the only change which they proposed was that the assumed wave height should be ½0th length for all ships. Stresses calculated in this way are shown for *Cobra*, *Wolf* and other destroyers.

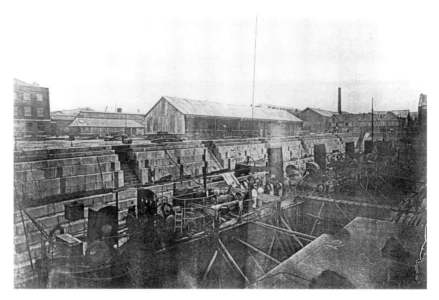

Standard calculated stresses for destroyers

Maximum stress	Sagging condition		Hogging condition	
(Tons/sq in)	Deck	Keel	Deck	Keel
Cobra	11.4	7.3	4.8	4.65
Wolf	7.95	6.0	4.5	4.7
Vulture	10.35	7.7	6.6	6.5
Daring	5.55	5.3	4.4	3.8
Swordfish	8.5	5.4	Not given	
Stag	8.4	7.5	Not given	

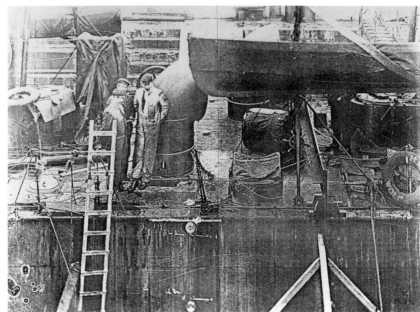

Though these calculated stresses involve many assumptions, the figures are not unrealistic and are certainly comparative between similar ships. *Wolf* was then docked at Portsmouth and supported on two cradles 26ft apart. The water was gradually lowered until the ship was exposed to a very severe hogging load. The experiment was then repeated with the cradles 120ft apart, generating a sagging load. The strain in the deck and keel (extension per unit length) was measured using sixteen pairs of strain gauges, increased to thirty pairs for the sagging trial. The stresses corresponding to the measured strains were 6.98tons/sq in in the deck and 6.4tons/sq in in the keel.

Wolf was then taken to sea to look for bad weather, with the strain gauges in place. In the worst conditions experienced, off the Lizard on 8 May 1903 the measurements corresponded to stresses of 5.38 tons/sq in in the deck and 2.68 tons/sq in in the keel. The captain of *Wolf* said that he had no concern for the safety of his ship in these conditions; he thought that, even allowing for her weaker structure, *Cobra* would have been safe though he made the important point that her dinghy, which carried her few survivors, could not have lived in such a sea. The Committee then interviewed leading builders on

the calculations which they carried out and on their building procedures. This was a most thorough and searching investigation, completely justifying Admiralty design methods and inspection procedures. Only the chairman dissented, seeing its report as critical of the court martial on the loss of *Cobra*.

This court martial reached the simple conclusion that *Cobra* broke because she was not strong enough. The Committee's work showed that she was weaker than destroyers built to Admiralty specification but not by very much and the survival of her dinghy shows that the sea she encountered was not extreme. There were 140 very similar destroyers in the RN and some 230 in foreign navies, none of which broke up, even in much more severe seas. Sir Phillip Watts suggested that *Cobra* hit

A stern view of *Wolf* in dock during strength trials by the Torpedo Boat Destroyer Committee (*top*), and a close-up view of the strain gauges (*above*). (Author's collection)

some semi-submerged wreckage which buckled the keel and caused flooding which could have increased the loading. This suggestion has been developed by K C Barnaby,[31] grandson of Sir Nathaniel, though the court martial pointed out that there was no evidence to support it. This author believes that the evidence is insufficient to reach any firm conclusion though Watts' suggestion fits quite well.

Hull weight

The success of White and his battleship section in reducing hull weight from *Majestic* onwards has been described in Chapter 9 where *Dreadnought* has been included for comparison. Because of the different layout, it is not possible to make a very good comparison with White's ships but it is quite clear that further savings in hull weight had been made. Scantlings had been more carefully matched to the expected loads and excessively heavy fittings had been replaced by lighter versions.[32]

Underwater protection

This reduction in weight had been accompanied by an increase of safety. Following the loss of *Victoria*, there had been a continuing effort to reduce the number of holes in bulkheads such as doors, ventilation trunks and penetrations for pipes and wires. By the *Lord Nelson*, the main transverse bulkheads were virtually unpierced. Lifts were fitted in the machinery spaces to reduce the effort needed by engineers[33] to get from one space to another. The need for such unpierced bulkheads was perceived as a lesson of the Russo-Japanese War but action had already been taken.

The Russo-Japanese War had shown the need for improved protection against mines and torpedoes and it was thought, probably incorrectly, that the heavy internal bulkhead of *Tsessarevitch* had saved her.[34] This was discussed in August 1904 during a visit of the Admiralty Explosives Committee to the Armstrong test sites at Silloth and Ridsdale during which Noble suggested a 4½in bulkhead and proposed secret tests at Ridsdale with a mock-up of a battleship.[35] Tests were carried out during 1905-06 with a thick longitudinal bulkhead built into a merchant ship named *Ridsdale* which was able to withstand a 230lb charge.[36] These trials were carried out in great secrecy and no further details have been found. Their importance is shown by a note on the First Lord's briefing paper for his Parliamentary statement on *Dreadnought* which said 'Do not tell House of Commons about special measures to protect magazines and shell rooms as these are the result of very secret experiments carried out at great cost before she was laid down to test the experience of the Russo-Japanese war in submarine explosions.' There is also a reference in the Ship's Cover to changes as a result of the *Ridsdale* tests.

Fisher's contribution[37]

Fisher is rightly seen as the father of the *Dreadnought*, supplying the drive and enthusiasm; while others debated, he decided. In detail, his lightning-swift brain was also unstable and his vision changed frequently; only in November 1904 did he settle on the all-12in ship. Fisher's obsession with the 'super battleship' goes back at least to the time in 1881 when, as captain of the *Inflexible*, he discussed with the young Phillip Watts the design of an improved version with four twin 16in MLR. Much later, in 1900 as C-in-C, Mediterranean, he persuaded the chief constructor of Malta Dockyard, W H Gard, to prepare studies for powerful battleships. Though some of these had a uniform calibre armament, probably 10in, Fisher's letter to the Admiralty in June 1901 proposed a mixed armament of 10in and 7.5in.[38] Whilst C-in-C Mediterranean, Fisher was still writing that, at the 'longer' range of 3-4000 yards, the 6in was superior to the 12in because its higher rate of fire enabled the range to be found more quickly.[39]

Fisher and Gard came together again in 1902 when the former was C-in-C Portsmouth, and the latter manager of the Dockyard. Gard prepared two more studies, one with sixteen 10in[40] and the other with twelve 12in. At that date Fisher favoured the 10in version, still under the influence of Armstrong (who died in 1900) who suggested a new gun with a high rate of fire. Gard was a highly respected officer but his career had mainly been in Dockyards and he lacked recent design experience.[41] While it is easy to sketch a ship with sixteen big guns, it is less easy to produce a realistic design, particularly when the effects of blast are considered. In favour of the 12in was the more extensive damage caused by the bigger shell.[42]

During 1904 Fisher created an unofficial think-tank (Captains H B Jackson, J R Jellicoe, R H Bacon and C E Madden, Commander W Henderson together with Gard and A Gracie, managing director of Fairfields, later joined by an accountant named Boar). Initially they seem to have considered several options for the armament:

Mixed 12in and 9.2in[43]
All 10in or all 9.2in
All 12in

It would seem that Bacon was the leading supporter of the all-12in armament, influenced by the papers of the two Mays,[44] and by November, Fisher had decided on this fit though his papers make it clear that he was still thinking of firing one gun at a time at about 6000yds. So far, this account has concentrated on factors which led to the *Dreadnought* battleship concept but many of the developments involved were also applicable to big cruisers and, by 1904, Fisher was beginning to suggest that the submarine would soon make the battleship

31. Barnaby, *Some Ship Disasters and their Causes*. An excellent book.

32. W H Whiting, 'The effect of modern accessories on the size and cost of warships', *Trans INA* (London 1903).

33. Said to have been reserved for the use of officers only – but they were probably the only people who needed to get from one space to another frequently.

34. It is most likely that the torpedo hit abaft the protection.

35. Fisher, *Naval Necessities*.

36. D K Brown, 'Attack and Defence, Part 3', *Warship 24* (London 1982). No full account of this trial has been located nor has *Ridsdale* been identified.

37. Consideration of Fisher's contribution is made difficult because he changed his views frequently and because he wrote for effect, suiting his approach to the people he was trying to influence. His views on 'facts' can be seen in the following extract from *Naval Necessities* – 'I had an excellent secretary. Whenever I asked him for facts, he always asked me what I wanted to prove. There is no doubt that facts are most misleading.'

38. Sumida, quoting 'Lecture and Discussion' ADM 1/7521.

39. Sumida, *In Defence of Naval Supremacy*, p41.

40. It is unclear where this scheme originated; it may have been with Armstrong.

41. His last real design had been the torpedo cruiser *Vulcan* in 1888 and the *Edgars* in 1889. Since then he had worked in Dockyard management. (See Lambert, New DNB.) In defence, it must be remembered that the highly experienced battleship section forgot the effect of blast when adding 9.2in to the *King Edward VIIs*. He was a very well-liked senior officer.

42. Fisher wrote that damage depended on the cube of shell weight. Though this is theoretically correct, the experience of two World Wars, suggests that damage is more likely to vary with the square of the weight, still giving a considerable advantage to the big gun.

43. It should be remembered that armoured cruisers as well as battleships had a mixed armament (9.2in and 7.5in or 6in).

44. Bacon was a student at the War College under H J May whom he greatly admired.

obsolete and that the fast armoured cruiser was the surface ship of the future.[45] The concept of the battlecruiser, as it was to become, is discussed later but, to Fisher, they were interacting ideas though his heart lay with the cruiser. In *Naval Necessities*, he floated the idea of doing without battleships but Lord Selborne quoted Mahan in rejecting such a radical proposal saying the time was not ripe until other navies did so.[46]

Prior to taking office as First Sea Lord in 1904 Fisher produced a manifesto which he titled 'Naval Necessities'. There were several versions of this paper but the first and most influential is dated October 1904 and sent to the First Lord, Lord Selborne, and the help of the think tank was acknowledged. It was a complete plan for the re-organisation of the Navy. The new ships were to be paid for by savings from the scrapping of old, ineffective units which would also supply the manpower. There were already problems with the 1904-05 Estimates due partly to the unscheduled purchase of *Swiftsure* and *Triumph* the previous year and to outstanding payments on Navy Works. There was emphasis on the need to keep both the battleship and the cruiser under 15,900 tons, presumably a magic figure to keep politicians happy.

An argument often advanced against the introduction of the *Dreadnought* is that it rendered obsolete the older ships in which the RN had such superiority. All navies would start equal with the new type. The counter argument seems valid, that the all-big gun ship was coming anyway and the RN should get in first. As will be seen later, the USN was far advanced with such ships and there were indications that Japan and Italy were thinking on similar lines. Fisher also made the point that 1905-06 was a particularly favourable time to make this inevitable change since the powerful Russian navy had been largely destroyed.[47] A further point which could have been made, but was not, was that the power and speed of *Dreadnought* depended on turbine machinery and it would be a few years before other navies caught up.

This version of the paper still sees a choice between 10in and 12in (9.2in or 10in for the cruiser; the 12in is ruled out as too heavy) and says that the choice is between sixteen 10in or eight 12in. He claimed that the layouts would permit ten 10in to fire on any bearing[48] but only six 12in. He expected three to four rounds per minute from the smaller gun and 'nearly two' from the 12in with about 50 per cent hits at 6000yds. The torpedo threat made it essential to keep outside 3000yds which, with an allowance for manoeuvring meant a mean action range of 5000yds. In a somewhat confusing passage he says that the action will be fought at a range chosen by the faster fleet but accuracy depends on peacetime practice – no mention of fire control – and the important factors are hitting with a low trajectory (suggesting fairly short range) and deliberate fire for spotting. The damage per hit will depend on remaining energy and charge weight whilst rapidity depends on time to

load and number of guns limited by spotting time. An all-12in armament is right for a battleship but unnecessarily heavy for a cruiser.

Fisher quotes Noble on the need for 4in anti-torpedo boat guns; the 12pdr was to small to disable the target quickly. The 12pdr dated back to the 1894-95 shore trial, discussed in the previous chapter. The Russo-Japanese War suggested that a 4.7in was the smallest suitable gun which was followed up in the firings against *Skate* leading to the 4in gun but with the heavier 31lb shell replacing the 25lb.[49]

All Fisher's concepts were high-speed ships, generally some 3-4kts faster[50] than contemporary designs. He offered no analysis to support this choice of speed – but analysis was not common in those days – nor did he appreciate that the advantage would be lost when other navies built faster ships.[51] When C-in-C Mediterranean in *Renown* he though that ship fast enough to roll up enemy cruiser lines.[52] He insisted that the speed must be 'real', achievable at sea and required a high forecastle to this end. He was still envisaging triple-expansion engines but made no comment on the inability of such machinery to sustain high speed.

Fisher's paper contains an interesting section on 'Unsinkability' which, surprisingly, is rarely quoted. He suggests unpierced bulkheads with no doors, pipes or wires except the steam pipes which were to be high up. Each machinery compartment was to be self-contained with lifts for access and an increase in engineering staff would be accepted. Ventilation and drains would be separate for each compartment. The magazines were to be clear of the outer bottom and protected by a thick longitudinal bulkhead. The 10in design was to have a 9in belt and 12in in the ship with 12in guns. There would be a 7in upper belt but no armour above the 2in protected deck.[53] Any hatches in this deck which had to be opened in action should have a coffer dam to 5ft above the waterline. The unprotected deck above would provide light and airy mess decks; he wanted square ports. Examination of the plans[54] suggest that there were no vital spaces on this deck once the transmitting station had been moved down.

Bunker doors were a hazard in action and he proposed the use of oil fuel when in action though retaining coal for cruising. No wooden decks were to incorporated, corticene being used on the upper deck and bridge. He wanted the foremast taken down to the armour deck as a communication tube, 6in thick. Boats were to be worked by crane as in *Vulcan*. Fisher does not seem aware that most of these ideas were already incorporated in the *Lord Nelson* design.

The 'All-Big Gun' ship in the USN[55]

USN thinking evolved in very much the same way and to much the same time scale as that of the RN. In that navy Commander W S Sims had initiated a gunnery

45. Prof J T Sumida, 'Sir John Fisher and the *Dreadnought*; The Sources of Naval Mythology'. *Jnl of Military History*, Oct 1995.

46. Quoted more fully by Sumida, ref 38, p52.

47. Mackay, *The Life of Lord Fisher of Kilverstone*, p321.

48. This claim seems dubious in the light of blast effects.

49. The Germans do not seem to have realised that RN destroyers carried the heavier 4in and long thought their 22pdr to be adequate.

50. It is interesting that the 3-4kt advantage cropped up a few years later in the concept of the *Queen Elizabeth* class as a fast squadron whilst in the mid-1930s the staff were prepared to consider designs 3kts slower – but no more – than foreign ships.

51. He should have formally countered H J May's paper – May was a Fisher protege.

52. Mackay, *The Life of Lord Fisher of Kilverstone*, p268.

53. He recommends two thicknesses of 1in 'special' steel – why two thicknesses?

54. Roberts as note 17.

55. This passage is based entirely on N Friedman, *US Battleships* (Annapolis 1985). Friedman gives a much fuller account than is possible in the limited space available here.

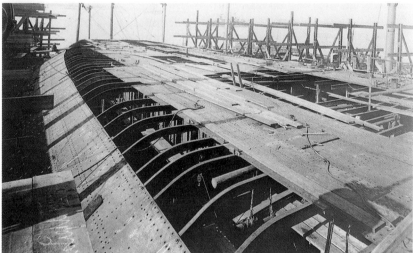

Building *Dreadnought*

Top left: Two days after the formal keel-laying on 2 October 1905, the bottom framing is largely complete and the first deck beams are in place. Note the few small derricks which had to lift everything into place.

Middle left: By 14 October the beams are complete, the protective decks are in place and the first deck plates are to be seen on the slopes. All this material had been cut and drilled before laying-down.

Bottom left: Most of the shell plating is in place by 30 December and she is almost ready for launch on 10 February 1906. The scaffolding in the Royal Dockyards was much more elaborate than that used in commercial yards of that date (or even after the Second World War), but would fail modern safety rules – there are no handrails to the walkways. It was accepted that there would be one death per year on each ship being worked on. (John Roberts)

revolution in much the same way as his friend, Percy Scott. The increasing ability to hit at longer range, c6000yds, combined with the threat from torpedoes with a range in excess of 3000yds led to studies of the capability of big and small guns at such ranges. A proposal by a Lieutenant Signal in the May 1902 US Naval Institute *Proceedings* led to an interesting discussion with Professor Alger, a leading gunnery expert, eventually favouring a ship with eight 12in guns. Later studies revealed the limited armour penetration of intermediate guns, 8in, 9in and even 10in.

The General Board war games of 1903 and 1904 came out strongly in favour of the 12in. They also seem to have concluded that a speed advantage of 3kts or less was of little value. The US designers in the Bureau of Construction and Repair were handicapped by a Congressional limit of 16,000 tons[56] and the chief constructor, W L Crapp, suggested four twin turrets, with B and X turrets superfiring, as a weight-saving measure. Blast effects were studied in a trial using the old monitor *Florida* in March 1907 and found to be negligible. By this time *South Carolina* and *Michigan* had been ordered (March 1906). Turbines were considered but thought insufficiently proved. One may see Fisher's true merit in getting *Dreadnought* to sea quickly in comparison with the more leisurely US progress.

In a memo to the President, Sims[57] criticised the *South Carolina*s as too small, limited by Congress. Compared with *Dreadnought* the bow fire was less, freeboard 10-18ft instead of 35ft. (These are Sims' figures, probably referring to an early study. As built, freeboard forward was about 22ft 9in and the speed 2-3kts less.) Sims referred to the difficulty caused by Congressional limits on size in several other papers to the President.

Sims was concerned that his USNI article[58] rebutting Mahan's views on the Russo-Japanese War had attracted little attention in the USA. In a letter to his wife[59] from London he describes a meeting with the DNI (Captain Cettle) he describes a scheme to generate correspondence in London on the opposing views. It was clear that the majority of serving RN officers supported Sims and, as a result, a 'secret' visit to *Dreadnought* was arranged for him. There was an extensive correspondence between Sims and both Scott and Fisher on gunnery methods but it does not seem that new ship designs were discussed.

The *Dreadnought* Committee

Very soon after taking up his post as First Sea Lord, Fisher set up a Committee on Designs to consider the new battleship, cruiser, destroyer and submarine designs. The membership[60] was very similar to that of his earlier, informal group. The terms of reference made it clear that the committee was an advisory body and that '. . . it is no part of the function or purpose of the committee to relieve the Director of Naval Construction of his official responsibility.' It had already been decided that the armament was to be of 12in guns only, the speed was to be 21kts and armour 'adequate'.

The first meeting was held on 3 January 1905 and the chairman, Fisher, read a statement in which he said that previous design committees had largely been concerned with safety and stability but naval architecture had advanced to a position where discussion of this subject was unnecessary. The object was to bring the naval officer, the 'user', into discussion with technical and scientific experts both inside and outside the Admiralty.

Fisher set the scene: 'The battleship is the embodiment of concentration of gun power', *ie* to bring an overwhelming fire on part of the enemy line. The first task was to decide on the number and disposition of the 12in turrets. Fisher directed that consideration be given first to designs E and F, attributed to Wilson.[61] These had superfiring turrets and were objected to on the basis that blocks of turrets made too good a target. More seriously, Jellicoe (DNO) maintained that the blast[62] from the upper turrets would make the lower turrets untenable over an arc of about 30° either side of the fore-and-aft line. The problem was that sighting hoods were arranged on the roofs of the turrets and blast could enter through these openings. The alternative of sighting on the side or the use of periscopes was not considered until much later. Sims pointed out that open sighting hoods had been abolished in US battleships, mainly to keep splinters out, but blast was also excluded.

A little later, Jellicoe, advised by Watts, was to write[63] '. . . while considerations of weight alone might allow more guns, those of space forbid any large increase in numbers, if they are to be used with effect, unless the ship is lengthened abnormally, so as to space them well apart.' Naval architects are usually taught that the battleship was the prime example of a weight-dominated design, a view which this passage shows was incorrect.

Overnight, the DNC (mainly Gard[64]) was asked to prepare Design G with turrets side by side at each end.

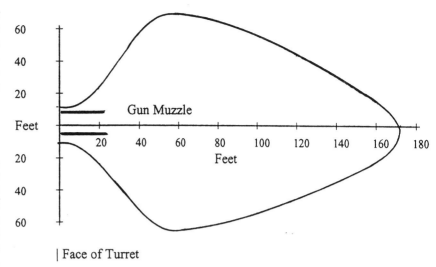

| Face of Turret

This, too, was thought to have too close a grouping of turrets and the low freeboard at the bow was criticised. Design D, based on Narbeth's study for a *Lord Nelson* with the 9.2in replaced by 12in was then considered. The forecastle, with A turret, was raised for seakeeping and the distance between the wing turrets was increased, again from blast considerations. Finally, it was realised that replacing the two after, sided turrets by a single one on the centre-line would reduce the size and cost of the ship and alleviate the blast problems without reducing the number of guns which could fire on most bearings. With a few minor changes, this became Design H from which *Dreadnought* was developed.

The DNC (Watts) thought that boat handling would be difficult and a subcommittee of Captains Madden, Jellicoe and Jackson was set up to consider the problem. They came up with a layout in which the mast was abaft the fore funnel ensuring that at most speeds the control top would be in the hot, black funnel smoke.[65] Though there was a small mast aft to carry the aerials, it was not very satisfactory and the secondary fire control on the signalling platform even less so. It is strange that such a highly skilled group of naval officers and engineers

This drawing of the blast from a 12in gun is based on a stiff paper cut-out in the *Dreadnought* Ship's Cover labelled 'Model used in determining dangerous areas of gun blast in battleships and armoured cruisers', signed by J H Narbeth, February 1905. It appears to represent a pressure of 30lbs/sq ft.

56. This was a much more severe limit than it seems as US practice included a larger percentage of fuel than did British.

57. W S Sims, *The Inherent Tactical Qualities of All-Big-Gun, one calibre Battleships of High Speed, Large Displacement and Gunpower.* Sept 1906. Memo to the President.

58. This is a slightly censored version of the above reference with the same title.

59. From the Savoy Hotel, London, 16 December 1906. Sims Papers, Library of Congress.

60. Rear-Admiral Prince Louis of

Battenberg (DNI), Engineer Rear-Admiral Sir John Durston (E-in-C), Rear-Admiral A L Winslow (CO Torpedo and Submarine flotillas), Captain H B Jackson (Controller), Captain J R Jellicoe (DNO), Captain C E Madden (NA to Controller), Capt R H S Bacon (NA to 1SL), Sir Phillip Watts (DNC), Lord Kelvin, Professor J H Biles (Naval Architecture, Glasgow), Sir John Thornycroft, Alexander Gracie, R E Froude (AEW), W H Gard (ADNC), Cdr W Henderson (Secretary), E H Mitchell RCNC (Asst Sec).

61. They were probably due to Fisher, who often attached other

people's names to controversial proposals

62. It was thought that men could stand up to 30lbs/sq ft.

63. Jellicoe.

64. Examination of the sections of *Dreadnought* through the end turrets and through the side by side turrets amidships. J Roberts, *The Battleship Dreadnought*, pp76-77, suggests that this arrangement was totally impracticable.

65. J Brooks, 'The Mast and Funnel Question; Fire Control Positions in British Dreadnoughts 1905-1915', *Warship 1995* (London 1995).

should come up with a configuration which was so unsatisfactory.[66]

The committee then directed its attention to the machinery. Durston, the E-in-C, pressed strongly for the use of turbines which would give a direct saving of 300 tons in weight and, with consequential reductions elsewhere, an overall saving of about 1000 tons. There was little consideration of the high fuel consumption of turbines in the destroyers, described earlier and it may be that a paper by Parsons, in the Ship's Cover, which gave estimated fuel consumption based on recent designs of turbine was influential. These figures are more favourable than those from earlier warship trials and probably derive from later merchant ship experience.

Coal consumption in lbs/ihp/hr

Power	Reciprocating	Turbine
Battleship, 27,000hp		
Full	2.2	1.8
$\frac{3}{5}$	2.2	1.8
10kts	3.35	3.4
Battlecruiser, 41,000hp		
Full	2.2	1.8
$\frac{3}{5}$	2.2	1.8
10kts	4.5	4.6

There was concern over the ability of the fairly small, high-revving propellers to produce sufficient astern thrust. Froude was able to re-assure the committee on this point and Durston was strongly backed by Watts who said 'If you fit reciprocating engines, this ship will be out of date in five years.' It was a very brave decision which few modern engineers would have taken on the evidence then available.

The detail design was then commenced and the one major change was the introduction of longitudinal bulkheads to protect the magazines from underwater explosions, discussed above.[67] In order to avoid increasing the displacement of the ship, the thickness of the belt was reduced by 1in. It is often suggested that the omission of the upper belt was an economy measure but this is denied by Narbeth and Fisher, in *Naval Necessities*, specifically calls for its omission to improve ventilation and natural lighting on the mess decks.

The hull form had to be very different from earlier ships as the increased speed put her in a zone where bow and stern wave systems combine, giving a maximum resistance.[68] Up to about 18kts there was little difference in the resistance of *Dreadnought*, *Lord Nelson* or *King Edward VII* but, at higher speeds, the *Dreadnought* was much superior. The form was developed from Narbeth's proposal by Froude, with extensive model tests at Haslar.[69] In *Naval Necessities*, Fisher had said that a ram was no longer required but, when he saw the proposed straight bow for *Dreadnought*, he asked for the appearance of the old style. When a model was tested, it went slightly faster than the straight bow model as the 'ram' acted as a bulbous bow and for some years, British ships retained the old profile.[70]

Fisher wanted his new ship in service as quickly as possible to increase the problems of other navies in catching up. To the greatest possible extent, plate and section sizes were standardised and much material was ordered in advance. Portsmouth was still by far the fastest building yard in the country[71] and they were given the task of building *Dreadnought*.[72] Work began in May 1905 and by the date of her official laying down in October, £12,217 had been spent on labour and £29,078 on material, representing some 6000 man-weeks of work, with 1100 men engaged by October.

After the official laying down the assembly of this pre-fabricated material was very rapid with the main deck beams in place at the end of the first week. Long hours were worked; from 6am to 6pm, six days a week, with only 30 minutes for lunch. These hours were not popular[73] but many men in the Dockyard were being made redundant and pressure was put on to accept the hours.

Dreadnought went on preliminary trials on 2 October 1906, 12 months after laying down, a spectacular feat, but there was another 3 months work to complete her. The claim that she was built in 12 months was to backfire a few years later when the Government saw no urgency in catching up with the German building programme since we could build so fast. Her true building time was at least 18 months but this was still far faster than battleships had been built before.[74]

Dreadnought commissioned on 11 December 1906 under Captain Bacon who had contributed so much to

66. Perhaps they were too senior and out of touch.

67. Based on the *Ridsdale* trials, discussed earlier. This feature was considered most secret.

68. This is known to naval architects as the prismatic hump and occurs when the speed V (kts) is numerically equal to the square root of the length (ft). For this condition, a form is needed with buoyancy concentrated amidships and fine ends – another unrecognised problem with design G. See J H Narbeth, 'A Naval Architect's Practical Experience in the Behaviour of Ships', *Trans INA* (London 1941). (Note, however, the discussion which cast doubt on some parts of Narbeth's paper.)

69. There was a measles epidemic at Gosport and the men carrying out these tests were in quarantine!

70. The ram shape had only a marginal effect on speed but it

contributed significantly to making such ships wet.

71. See Chapter 8.

72. The Constructive Manager, Thomas Mitchell, received a knighthood for his work, unusual at his rank. E J Maginess was the constructor in direct charge of building while J R Bond planned the work in the mould loft.

73. F Yearling, 'Construction of HMS *Dreadnought* at Portsmouth 1905/06', Internal paper, now in RCNC Collection, NMM. Modern thinking suggests that such long hours may not have been productive either.

74. It is interesting that Portsmouth built the generally similar *Bellerophon* in 26 months and followed with *St Vincent* in 17 months.

75. It would have been higher on the return but the added drag from a

damaged rudder slowed her.

76. Prof J T Sumida, 'Sir John Fisher and the *Dreadnought*; The Sources of Naval Mythology', *Jnl Military History*, Oct 1995.

77. The old term 'armoured cruiser' continued in use and *Invincible* was described as such when ordered. In the Report of the Navy Estimates Committee of November 1905 the battleship and cruiser were lumped together as 'large armoured ships' and in October 1906 the term 'capital ship' was used for both.

78. Fisher thought that oil fuel would eliminate the need for funnels.

79. Parkes, *British Battleships*, p487.

80. I once inherited a big destroyer design in which my predecessor had arranged four gas turbines side by side – once a section had been drawn it was clear that the outer ones lay outside the ship!

her concept and early in January 1907 went to Port of Spain, Trinidad, to work up. Bacon may have been biased in his enthusiastic report but it seems that everything worked well and six more ships were built of generally similar design. She averaged 17kts[75] on both crossings of the Atlantic and when she returned, and her engines were inspected, there was no wear or other problems, something which would have been impossible with reciprocating engines. Durston's advocacy of the turbine was justified as was Parsons' work.

The battlecruiser – *Invincible*[76]

The big armoured cruisers designed by White and Watts were nearly as costly as contemporary battleships and, like them, had a mixed armament, in their case with 9.2in backed by either 6in or 7.5in. The same pressure from gunnery development was leading to a uniform armament whilst developments in machinery and hull design made possible a more capable ship.

The clarity of thought which led to *Dreadnought* was lacking, as Fisher included opposing points of view even within the same paper. In one of his Mediterranean lectures, *c*1900, he said 'It is a cardinal mistake to assume that Battleships and armoured cruisers have not each of them a distinct mission'. However, in the same paper he also said '. . . the armoured cruiser of the first class is a battleship in disguise. It has been asked that the difference between a battleship and an armoured cruiser may be defined. It might as well be asked to define when a kitten becomes a cat.' White's paper on the *Cressys* in quoted in Chapter 8 shows that the idea of using the armoured cruiser[77] to support the battle line was not novel.

In early 1902 Fisher wrote a number of letters and papers which were consolidated into a proposal 'Fast Armoured Cruisers' sent to Lord Selborne on 26 March. He envisaged a ship with a margin of speed over any foreign cruiser, which was taken as 25kts, and an armament of four 10in (soon changed to 9.2in) and twelve 7.5in. Armour was the 6in belt normally fitted in armoured cruisers with a 2in deck. There were many Fisher 'dreams'; funnels were to abolished if possible, telescopic if not,[78] and bridges were to be abolished as were masts except for one wireless pole. Magazines were to be below the guns, eliminating ammunition passages and reducing the number of men needed to pass ammunition.

Sketch designs were prepared by Gard who was asked to give the maximum possible end-on fire; if possible the same number of guns should bear in every direction. This led Gard to arrange two 7.5in turrets, side by side, both forward and aft.[79] It is very doubtful if there was space below for the supports and magazines.[80] This proposal was roughly contemporary with the design of the *Duke of Edinburgh* of 23kts, with the same number of 9.2in but fewer 6in in place of the 7.5in and similar armour.

By 1903 Fisher was deeply impressed with the growing potential of the submarine and was seeing the end of the battleship with the armoured cruiser as the capital ship. In *Naval Necessities* (October 1904) he suggested, rather tentatively, that 'There is good ground for

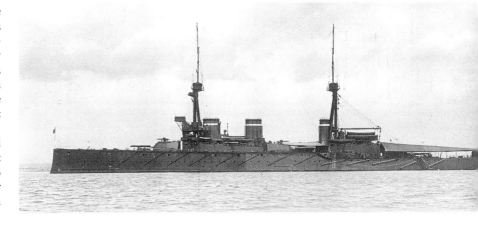

Invincible 1907. The low fore funnel was unsatisfactory and had to be raised. (Author's collection)

Indomitable and her sister-ship *Inflexible* at sea during the First World War. (Author's collection)

81. See Sumida, *In Defence of Naval Supremacy* for longer extracts.

82. Bacon, *The Life of Lord Fisher of Kilverstone*.

83. Examine the section on pages 18-20 of John Campbell's *Invincible Class* (London 1972). Watts seems to have backed this scheme (Ship's Cover).

84. It appears likely that there were deliberate leaks to give the impression that they were 'all 9.2in' ships which could be the origin of the German *Blucher* with all 8.2in.

85. It seems possible that the last-minute decision to fit 12in guns was so hurried that the armour was not considered.

86. There is considerable debate over the liability of cordite to explode rather than burn when exposed to flash, a subject which will be considered in a later volume. Some Second World War studies suggest that contemporary propellants were far more likely to explode from the effect of hot splinters rather than flash. It may be that splinters were involved in some of the Jutland explosions though there is no direct evidence.

enquiry whether the naval supremacy of a country can any longer be assessed by its battleships. To build battleships merely to fight an enemy's battleships, so long as cheaper craft can destroy them, and prevent them of themselves protecting sea operations, is merely to breed Kilkenny cats unable to catch rats or mice.'[81] Selborne rejected this approach, believing that the battleship was still essential. In this paper of October 1904 Fisher was proposing sixteen 9.2in for the armoured cruiser. Shortly afterwards his think-tank convinced him that the cruiser, too, should have 12in guns. Bacon wrote 'that ships of the size and tonnage necessary . . . should have an additional use in being able to form a fast light squadron to supplement the battleships in action, and worry the ships in van or rear of the enemy's line. They were never intended to *engage battleships single handed*; but they were designed to assist in a general action by engaging some of the enemy's ships which were already fighting our battleships'[82] (Bacon's italics). Bacon also points out that a requirement was that they should be fast enough to hunt down and destroy any armed merchant ship afloat.

The battlecruiser concept may also have been influenced by the Italian fast battleships of the *Regina Elena* class, laid down from 1901, with a speed of 21kts and mounting two 12in and twelve 8in guns. In 1904 the Admiralty learnt of the two Japanese *Ikoma* class with four 12in and twelve 6in and a speed of 21kts.

The design committee turned to the cruiser once the particulars of *Dreadnought* had been fixed and on 12 January 1905 considered a Gard proposal with two twin 12in turrets side by side forward[83] and two turrets, superfiring, aft. Some variants were considered but all were rejected. Plan D from the design section under Whiting, including Narbeth, with one turret at each end and two sided amidships was preferred, leading to alter-

natives labelled E with the midship turrets *en echelon*. This was intended to permit the further turret to fire across the deck should the closer turret be disabled. At the Falklands battle, *Invincible* fired from both turrets, though the sightsetter of the exposed turret had to be relieved frequently. The first two ships, then named *Invincible* and *Immortalite*, were to have hydraulically-worked turrets whilst the third ship, *Raleigh*, was to have electric working.

Surprisingly, the early studies all had reciprocating engines but E was further modified to have turbines and her forecastle was extended aft to improve her seaworthiness, raising the midship turrets. A comparison in the cover of turbines with triple-expansion gives the following figures for a 41,000hp plant. In fast ships the weight saving would have been particularly important.

Comparison of reciprocating and turbine powerplants

	Reciprocating	Turbine
rpm	110	275
Stroke (ft)	4	–
Wt of engines (tons)	1490	1080
Propulsion and auxiliaries (tons)	335	320
Boilers (tons)	1875	1600
Total Wt (tons)	3700	3000

All these studies had four funnels but the forward two were combined during the detail design. Fisher's wish to abolish funnels probably led to the class completing with short funnels; the forward one was raised later.[84]

There does not seem to have been very much discussion on the armour for these ships and the traditional

6in belt was unchanged. In proposing a 6in belt for the *Canopus* class, White had said that it would keep out any 6in shell at battle range (he probably meant 3000yds), most 9.2in at most ranges and all HE shells. At the turn of the century and later the Admiralty was rightly concerned over the effect of large-calibre HE shell on the extensive, unarmoured parts of the ship.[85] Sumida draws attention to the improved AP shell introduced about 1903 and the imminent introduction of the capped projectile which would penetrate even *Dreadnought*'s belt at 6000yds but it is not clear that projectile development was discussed at the time. Fisher, himself, was turning towards his aphorism 'Speed is armour'. A view with hindsight is given later.

When the three *Invincible*s entered service in 1909 they did all that Fisher had dreamt of and were thought very satisfactory. It is interesting that, whilst no battleship studies have come to light with other than an all-12in armament (or larger), there were several later studies for 9.2in cruisers. One of the last, E2, a beautiful, mini-*Queen Elizabeth* of 1913, is compared in the table below.

Comparison of armoured cruiser designs

	Warrior	*Invincible*	E2
Date, Estimates	1903	1905	1913
Displacement (tons)	13,350	17,300	17,850
Cost (£m)	1.2	1.75	1.5
Armament	6-9.2in,	8-12in	8-9.2in,
	4-7.5in		8-6in
Speed (kts)	23	25	28
Belt thickness, (max) (ins)	6	6	6
Weights (tons) -Hull	5190	6120	6000
Armament	1585	2500	1900
Armour	2845	3370	5070
Machinery	2270	3140	3000

Unless E2 was exceptionally lucky with early hits, one feels confident in an early victory for *Invincible*.

Hindsight

In 1905 it was generally thought that major warships should have belt armour which would keep out shells similar to those which they themselves fired at battle ranges. Today's designers are accustomed to weapons against which there can be no practical protection and ships are designed to limit the consequence of such hits. Ships are intended to retain some mobility and fighting capability after at least one such hit.

When *Invincible* was designed, it was not appreciated that British cordite charges would explode rather than burn if exposed to enemy fire.[86] Tests had been carried out on charges but only on small quantities and the effect of a rapid build-up of both temperature and pres-

sure when a large mass was ignited was not recognised. Hindsight suggests a very thick box round the magazine and supply trunks – as well as better propellants. Ammunition passages were a serious hazard, as Fisher seems to have recognised.

Without increasing the size of the ship, there would have been little more weight to spare and the waterline could only have had splinter protection. Experience in the war showed that the 3in belt of light cruisers would keep out 4.1in and 6in HE shells and this might have been sufficient for *Invincible*. The need to subdivide machinery spaces had been recognised but not the need for a true unit system, alternating boiler and engine-rooms which would have been essential if protected only by 3in plates. This concept of a thick magazine box and splinter protection elsewhere was finally adopted for the *Kent* class of post Washington cruisers.

Justification

It is fashionable to decry the whole concept of the battle-cruiser but consideration of *Invincible*'s brief but glorious operational life suggests strongly that Fisher was right. She began by participating in the battle of Heligoland Bight, helping to sink the *Koln*, before dashing off to the Falklands where she sank the *Scharnhorst*. She received some twenty-two hits, mainly from 8.2in, without serious damage. At Jutland she disabled the *Wiesbaden* and *Pillau*, inflicted much of the fatal damage to *Lutzow* and hit *Derflinger* before blowing up. In these actions she was used very much as Fisher intended and the trade-off was favourable. Campbell's schoolmasterly summing up is fair; a good start but could do better.

Later destroyers

It was soon realised that the 30kt trial speed of early destroyers was unrealistic as the power could not be sustained. This was due mainly to lack of stokers and they also soon lost speed in a seaway, mostly due to their low freeboard. Finally, there was concern over

Mohawk 1907. 'Tribal' class destroyers were designed by their builders to a loose specification. *Mohawk*'s vestigal turtledeck was not a success. (Vicary)

Surly 1894, later used for early oil fuel trials. (Author's collection)

The loss of *Cobra* emphasised the need for strength; high tensile steel was used for the upper deck and shell. Though this material is stronger, it is also more likely to crack and the specification called for rivet holes to be drilled since punching can initiate cracking. There were a number of minor improvements to habitability.

The table below compares the destroyers discussed in this section with a typical torpedo gunboat (*Alarm*). The *Rivers* were well liked in service and their general style was adopted in most following classes. They cost £70-80,000 compared with about £60,000 for earlier destroyers.

Comparison of early and later destroyers

	Alarm	*River: Ribble*	*Tribal: Mohawk*	*Swift*
Date (ld)	1890	1902	1907	1907
No in class	13	34	12[a]	1
Disp (tons)	810	660	864	2390
Length pp (ft)	230	225	270	353
Freeboard (F) ft approx	14.5	16	16.2	20
F/sq rt L	0.96	1.07	0.98	1.06
Bridge abaft bow/L	0.27	0.26	0.16[b]	0.19
ihp/kts	3500/ 18.7[c]	7500/ 25.5	14,000/ 33	30,000/ 35
Armament	2-4.7in, 5TT	1-12pdr, 5-6pdr	3-12pdr, 2TT	4-4in, 2TT

Notes
a. The bow of *Zulu* and the stern of *Nubian* were joined to form *Zubian* in 1917.
b. *Mohawk* had a turtleback forecastle. Freeboard for those with a forecastle c17ft, F/sq rt L = 1.03.
c. About 21kts when re-boilered.

their strength following the *Cobra* disaster. This was emphasised by the performance of the German *S90* class seen on a visit of British destroyers to Wilhelmshaven in 1901. This led to a radical reconsideration of the requirements for destroyers and their configuration.

The *River* class contract called for 25.5kts on a 4-hour trial with the ship fully equipped and with 90 tons of coal. They were given a high forecastle, much improving their performance in head seas and giving better mess decks. In service, they were little, if at all, slower than the so-called '30-knotters', even in calm water. The bridge was further aft and built over a small chart house. The perceived motion on the bridge was reduced quite rapidly as it moved aft as was the amount of spray reaching it. A modern designer would put the bridge at least 30 per cent of the length abaft the bow.[87] The armament was the same as in earlier ships – one 12pdr, five 6pdrs and two 18in torpedo tubes. Following the Russo-Japanese War, the 6pdrs were replaced by three additional 12pdrs in 1906. The forecastle 12pdr was on a bandstand to keep it dry.

When Fisher became First Sea Lord, he thought that

Viking 1909, seen here on trials, was the only six-funnelled ship in the RN. (Author's collection)

there was no need for warships between the battlecruiser and big destroyers. His original idea required 33kts for 8 hours in a 'moderate sea', oil fuel, an armament of two 12pdrs and five 3pdrs and stores for 7 days. This proved wrong or impossible in almost every respect. It is impossible to write a contract for speed in a moderate sea[88] and calm water trial had to be accepted. The armament was inadequate and had to be increased; the first five completed with three 12pdrs (increased to five in 1909) and the remainder had two 4in, probably as a result of experience in the Russo-Japanese War. Fisher was right in wanting oil but he was too far in advance and there were real difficulties in obtaining oil in some ports.

The ships were designed by their builders and differed considerably,[89] one from the other. *Mohawk*, *Tartar* and *Viking* were built with turtleback forecastles which proved very wet. *Mohawk* was rebuilt with a conventional forecastle in 1911 and, following damage, *Tartar* was similarly rebuilt in 1917.[90]

Trials, penalties and shallow water

When destroyers were designed by their builders, it was normal to include in the contract a clause which imposed a penalty if the design speed was not reached. For the first destroyers the penalty was £1000 per knot or 2.4 per cent of the total cost. A more serious failure could mean that the ship was not accepted and, occasionally, there was a bonus for exceeding the required speed. This penalty was not excessive as a rough calculation suggests that the cost of increasing the speed by one knot was about 3 per cent of the total cost. For the *Tribal*s, the penalty was increased to £1200 per 0.1kt, rejection at 2kts below design and a bonus of the same amount offered for 34kts. The large penalty, nearly 9 per cent of the cost per knot, led to much acrimony, some famous model tests and trials and to a major legal action.

It had been known for some time that shallow water could greatly affect the speed of a ship for better or for worse. The pressure distribution round the hull is altered if the water is constrained by the bottom and this affects the waves which the ship makes. The diverging waves flowing from bow and stern make an increasing angle with the fore-and-aft line until above the critical speed it is no longer possible to make transverse waves. The critical speed is given by $\sqrt{(g.depth)}$, about 22kts for the *Tribal*s on the Maplin mile.[91] A ship at this critical speed will be slowed considerably whilst, well above that speed, it will go faster than in deep water. On trials, *Tartar* made 35.6kts on the Maplin 'without pressing'. *Cossack* made only 33kts in deep water at Skelmorley but reached 34.3kts on the Maplin mile.

There were claims and counter-claims for bonus or penalty, further confused by penalties for late delivery. The Admiralty sought to establish the facts of the matter by running *Cossack* over three measured miles with differing depths:

Skelmorley	40 fathoms
Chesil Beach	16
Maplin	7

The deep water, Skelmorley, mile may be seen as correct and there is a slight loss of speed at all powers on the moderate Chesil Beach mile but there are more dramatic effects on the Maplin. At 33kts the ship receives a bonus of at least one knot whilst at 22kts there is a penalty of about 3kts with a very large stern trim. The power hardly alters between 22 and 26kts. At least one case reached the House of Lords and Stanley Goodall, then an assistant constructor at Haslar, was selected to appear as a witness, describing the *Cossack* trial. He was not called as the firm's counsel pointed out that the contract did not specify any particular mile or depth and they even had an Admiralty letter recording 'no objection' to the Maplin mile.[92] Since then, Admiralty contracts have specified the mile to be used.

Most nineteenth-century trials were run on the Stokes Bay mile which became increasingly inadequate as ships got bigger and faster.

Ship	Loss of speed at Stokes Bay (kts)
Edgar	0.75
Latona	0.4

It was also said that a torpedo gunboat made 17.8kts at high tide and 17.2kts at low tide.[93] Much later, the Polish destroyer *Blyscawica* was to gain half a knot from this effect on the Talland mile.[94]

Swift

In October 1904, Fisher asked for a destroyer similar to the *Rivers* but with a speed of 36kts. After many attempts both within the DNC's department a design by Laird's was accepted in December 1905. By this time the displacement was 2390 tons (deep) and the trial speed was only 35kts. She was expensive, rather fragile in service and was not repeated.

Coastal destroyers

By 1905, Fisher was coming to think that submarines, torpedo boats and mines might make it impossible to operate a battlefleet in narrow waters such as the English Channel.[95] He believed that the narrow seas should be dominated by numerous small craft and, since money was scarce, they had to be cheap. This led to a class of thirty-six coastal destroyers of 225-255 tons, 175ft long, with two 12pdrs and three 18in torpedo tubes. They were structurally weak and had low freeboard with a turtle deck. They cost about £41,000 instead of the £75,000 of a *River* but, since they were of little value, it was false economy. Even when the quantity versus quality balance tilts in favour of numbers, the chosen design must still be capable.

87. D K Brown, 'Sustained Speed at Sea in the RN', NEC100, Newcastle 1984.

88. It is now possible to write a contract in terms of speed in rough weather demonstrated by a specified computer programme but I do not think this has been tried.

89. *Viking* was distinguished as the only ship built for the RN with six funnels.

90. The turtle deck re-appeared in Baker's design for the Canadian *St Laurent* class and, though these were seen as excellent sea boats, the turtle deck was not used in later classes. It is expensive to built and reduces the all-important freeboard at the side.

91. D K Brown, 'Speed on Trial', *Warship 3* (London 1977).

92. Brown, *A Century of Naval Construction*.

93. Many Thornycroft destroyers of the First World War were tried on the St Catherine's mile which gave them a 1-1½kt advantage. This was not dishonest, the was no financial bonus, both the company an the Admiralty were aware of the effect and it saved time.

94. D K Brown, A & A *Blyscawica*, *Warship 12* (London, October 1979).

95. Dr N A Lambert. 'Admiral Sir John Fisher and the concept of Flotilla Defence 1904', *Journal of Military History*, (London October 1995.

Swift 1907, a 'super destroyer'
inspired by Fisher, was
expensive and not very
successful. (Author's collection)

Captain H J May and the War College Studies

As Director of the War College[96] within the RN College
at Greenwich, Captain May carried out a series of 'war
game' studies which had a considerable influence on
thinking about the future battleship. His reports on
some of this exercises have survived in the PRO.[97] In
one such game[98] forces comprised of heavily-armed battleships (A) were matched against ships which were 4kts
faster but more lightly armed and protected.

96. The author attended the War
College in 1973-74.

97. PRO ADM 1/7597.

98. Tactical value of speed as
compared with extra armour and
guns.

99. Notes by Captain H J May of
Tactical Exercises and Problems.

100. Admiral Sir R H Bacon, *From
1900 Onward* (London 1940).

A coastal destroyer, No 4,
formerly Sandfly. (Author's
collection)

	A	B
Displacement (tons)	17,604	15,959
Armament	4-12in, 8-8in,	4-10in, 16-6in
	12-7in	
Main belt (ins)	10	6
Speed (kts)	18	22

Games were played with small and moderate-sized
squadrons and fleets of the two types and with mixed
forces. There were no circumstances other than running
away in which the Type B – battlecruiser – proved superior or was able to improve the capability of a mixed
force. It was assumed that fire would be opened at long
range; 6000yds when the bigger guns of Type A would
penetrate the thinner armour of B. The dangers of split-
ting the fleet into divisions are brought out.

In another paper[99] May describes the way in which
the games were played. These bring out the need to consider rate of hitting rather than rate of fire showing that
even at 6000yds the 12in was scoring a higher percentage of hits than the smaller guns. This advantage was
then increased by the much heavier bursting charge of
the 12in shell and by the fact that hits on medium and
thick armour by the smaller shells were useless. This
conclusion strongly favours the 'All-Big Gun Ship'
though in the papers so far located May does not draw
that specific conclusion.

Ramming is considered (in 1902!) and thought possible whilst torpedoes are particularly useful fired from
aft submerged tubes by a ship being pursued. The size
and disposition of guns in cruisers is considered in some
detail and British inferiority in HE common shell is
lamented.

These studies were among the first to quantify the
value of aspects such as speed, rate of hitting etc and at
once showed the value of the big gun. Bacon was a student at the college and has written[100] of the value of such
studies and of their contribution to *Dreadnought*. The
approach is quite similar to that of the 1906 papers by
Jellicoe and Sims discussed earlier.

The Achievement | *Twelve*

THE TACT and ability of Baldwin Walker and the professionalism of Isaac Watts had largely healed the feuds between naval officers and naval architects which had been initiated by Symonds and Graham. Under Spencer Robinson and Edward Reed a true partnership developed between naval requirements and ship design and, although there was a temporary interruption due to political interference over the *Captain*, this partnership would endure with only occasional lapses. Although the Board, through the

Dreadnought as completed 1906. Among the signatures are: *Designers*: Sir Philip Watts, J H Narbeth, Sir T Mitchell (Manager Portsmouth Dockyard), E J Maginnes (in charge of building). *Engineers*: Sir Charles Parsons, Sir H J Oram, Eng Rear-Admiral J T Corner. *Controller of the Navy*: Captain H B Jackson. *Captain*: R H S Bacon. (Courtesy Mr Smith, great-great-grandson of Sir Phillip Watts)

Controller, would lay down the requirement and the Director would design to fulfil this requirement, these roles were not seen as exclusive and both were the subject of debate. As another great designer was to say much later, 'The requirement is to the design as the chicken is to the egg'.[1]

Some idea of how White would interpret a requirement and direct his staff is given in Chapter 9 under the *Drake* class. Though the Director was an autocrat, an independently-minded head of section – and most of them were – would still have considerable autonomy. Even in such details as the makeup of the hull weight group there would be differences between the battleship and the cruiser section and such differences would alter as the heads of section changed. For this reason, the long-term trends shown in following sections are broad-brush indications only and it would be wrong to attempt to extract too much detail from them.

The design process[2]

Perhaps the biggest and most important change was in the design process itself. *Warrior* was largely designed by one man, on a basis of experience, with very few, simple calculations. Her success is a great tribute to Watts and Large but it was almost impossible to introduce any major, novel features as the consequences could not be foretold. There was no formal statement of design methods and stages from the early years and they probably varied from time to time. The changes initiated by Reed meant that, by the White era, there was considerable consistency.[3] One may recognise three main phases of the process:

Phase	Approx. modern title	
	British	*USA*
Design Study	Concept	Feasibility
Sketch Design	Feasibility	Concept
Design	Detailed Design	Full Design

Each of these phases will be considered in turn, outlining the work and how it was carried out in White's day.

A Design Study was a very quick study, taking perhaps a day, in which a number of alternatives were generated for discussion with Controller and the Board. The main parameters were scaled from a similar ship usually referred to as the type ship[4] (sometimes called PSS – Previous Successful Ship). It was recognised that the same type ship should be used for all aspects since if one weight group was scaled from a different ship, the differences in definition could be important. It was believed that scaling up from a smaller type ship was more accurate than scaling down from a larger one.[5]

The starting point would be the weight of the armament which could be added up provided that the num-

ber and type were decided and the weapons etc, actually existed. It would often be assumed that the armament weight would be the same percentage of the displacement as in the earlier ship. The design of ships like Barnaby's *Inflexible* whose armament was in flux throughout the design was thus very difficult. This would lead to a first shot at the displacement. The next step is more difficult; as White wrote[6]:

At the outset the dimensions, form and displacement are undetermined and yet upon them depend the power which the engines must develop to give the required speed, the weight of the hull and the weight of certain items of equipment. In the finished ship the sum of the weights of the hull, machinery, equipment, coals and load must equal the displacement of the designed waterline, a problem with so many unknown but related quantities which can be solved only by experience. On the basis of experience, recorded data and model experiments it is dealt with readily.

A truly vicious circle.

A quick estimate of power and speed could be obtained using the Admiralty Coefficient but in more difficult cases, the Froude Iso-K data would be used, once it became available.

The centre of gravity would be assumed to be at the same percentage of the depth as in the type ship with a simple correction for any known major changes. This would enable the beam to be adjusted to give a metacentric height which was suitable, based on experience. A profile and plan of the upper deck would be prepared together with a short note emphasising important or difficult aspects of the design.

Once the Board had agreed on the preferred design study, usually giving more detail on the requirements, the Sketch Design would begin. The study stage would be referred today as divergent thinking but, once the decision is made, the next stage converges rapidly. This would take a few weeks at most and would involve sufficient calculations to justify or correct the chosen study.

One of the first steps would be to select a suitable form using the Iso-K books, something possessed by no other navy. Once the form was chosen, stability data could be prepared. Weights would be estimated in a number of ways; the armament weight would be rechecked, adding up known components and making a generous guess where these were uncertain.[7] Stores and provisions etc, depended on the size of the crew and the intended endurance. The weight of structure could be obtained with fair accuracy by calculating directly at a few sections and interpolating the rest but there were many other items which the naval architect referred to as 'judgement items'. These included pipes, wiring, hatches, brackets and many others and it was easy to go wrong. It was usually possible to decide that some var-

1. D K Brown, 'Sir Rowland Baker', *Warship 1995* (London 1995).

2. This is discussed in much more detail in D K Brown, 'British Warship Design Methods', *Warship International* 1/95 (Toledo 1995).

3. This account is built up from hints in the Ships' Covers, from submission papers and from the RN College notes.

4. Modern computer-aided design systems do not differ greatly in approach except that they usually work from a trend curve representing several modern ships rather than from a single type ship.

5. It is not clear why this should be but there is a fair amount of evidence in support.

6. Sir W H White, *Manual of Naval Architecture*.

7. Changes in the armament or other requirements would cause the ship to sink deeper in the water, possibly submerging the belt. White was to establish the authority to control such changes, designing in a margin of weight to allow for a few essential changes.

8. This approach was little changed when the author started work in 1953, though we had far more data.

9. Scaling the weight of hull structure from a similar ship implied that the strength would be of the same standard.

10. This Statement remains in use today, little changed. It was last reviewed after the Falklands War (by the author) and the only major change was to add an expiry date.

ied as the displacement and others as the length but a crystal ball was – and still is – useful.[8]

Strength was sometimes checked during the sketch design using a bending moment (Appendix 6) based on the type ship but if the new ship was fairly similar, strength might be taken for granted during the sketch design.[9] The layout would be drawn in more detail and, in later days, consideration given to blast damage from the muzzles of the more powerful guns. The sketch design was intended to prove and refine the accepted study and it would be most unusual for any major new features to be introduced at this stage.

The final design would start with the selected main features and use analytical methods to verify and further develop the earlier estimates of strength, stability, powering etc. These methods of calculation have been outlined in earlier chapters and the Appendices and the passages which follow demonstrate the value of such design methods. In parallel with the detail design calculations, the general arrangement would be developed in detail with complete deck plans, profile and sketch of rig. These drawings, together with a few structural sections, a specification and a summary of the calculations formed the design package. Discussion with other departments of the Admiralty had been a continuous process during the design but, at the end, the package would be laid out for a final inspection by senior officers who would sign to confirm their agreement. Once all had agreed, the Director of Naval Construction would sign the drawings, taking personal responsibility for the design which, after Board approval, could then be sent to shipyards invited to tender for the building.

The whole design process depended on accurate weight estimates. In the early phases of the design, much of the weight was scaled from previous ships and this can be very accurate if the general style of the ship is similar. In the detail design phase, much more of the weight is built up from direct calculation, for example, the weight of the deck beams is known in terms of weight per foot run and it is simple, if tedious, to measure the total length of such beams. This information is also used to calculate the vertical and horizontal position of the centre of gravity for stability and trim whilst the distribution of weight is needed for the strength calculation. The early weight estimates seem to have been quite accurate but during the eighties ships tended to complete overweight, floating deep. Most of this weight increase was due to additions to the design during building which was controlled as White won authority and added a margin for essential, approved changes.

Reed had been successful in reducing the weight of the hull and this was continued by his successors (see Chapter 9). The diagram below shows how hull weight was reduced between *Warrior* and *Dreadnought*. Since much of this saving in cheap steel was used to increase expensive armament and armour, the cost per ton of the ship rose.

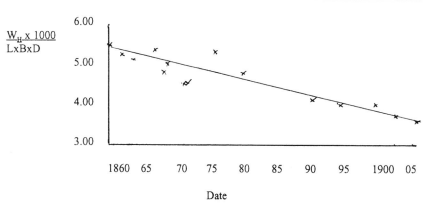

$$\frac{W_H \times 1000}{L \times B \times D}$$

Stability

The understanding of stability had advanced considerably; first, there was Barnes' simple plot of stability data – the Metacentric Diagram – which could be used by ships' officers to see how metacentric height varied with loading. After the loss of the *Captain*, a stability statement was introduced setting out key parameters over the operating range of displacements with any limitations on the use of fuel. This statement was signed by the Director and without it, no ship should go to sea.[10] Since *Captain* no undamaged British warship has capsized; this is no idle boast, as in the decade 1935-1945 the USN lost four destroyers, the Italian Navy two, and the Russian and Japanese navies one each from capsize in bad weather. As discussed in Appendix 5, it was not advisable to 'play safe' with an excessive metacentric height since this would lead to violent rolling. Metacentric height had to be just right, neither too low nor too high. The loss of the *Captain* showed what was unacceptable whilst the lengthy investigations into the damaged stability of the *Inflexible* further contributed to the setting of safe criteria. Once the form was decided, stability curves (GZ) were prepared, based on an accurate estimate of the centre of gravity. In 1893 Amsler's mechanical integrator was introduced greatly reducing the work required.

White frequently drew attention to the problems caused as more guns, such as quick-firers and machine-guns, were added, which were mounted high up while machinery weight reduced, raising the centre of gravity, a particular problem for stability after damage. Additional equipment added in service would cause the displacement to increase, usually implying a lowering of the metacentre whilst the centre of gravity would rise further. These reductions in stability would be monitored by inclining experiments and, if necessary, weights would be removed or ballast added.

Form, power and propellers

The Froudes' development of model testing methods meant that a bank of data on the way in which resistance varied with hull form was soon built up, enabling a good

This diagram shows how hull weight in relation to the product of the dimensions reduced over the period. As discussed in the text, changes in definition of hull group and the uncertainty of the depth dimension mean that individual spots may be suspect but the overall trend is clear. It was due mainly to improved understanding of the loading and of structural design.

This diagram shows how the resistance of individual battleships (expressed in Froude's non-dimensional notation) fell in relation to the standard series models (suffix S) between 1870 and 1905.

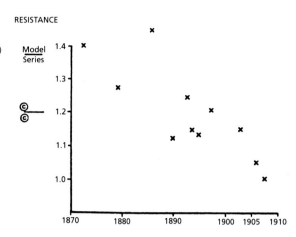

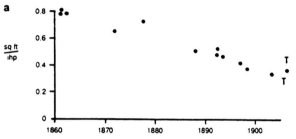

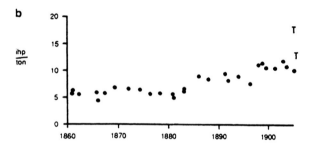

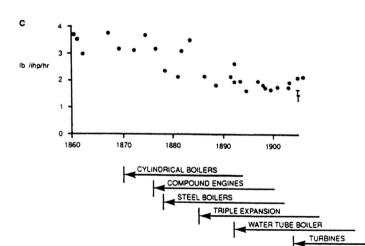

form to be selected at an early stage with an accurate estimate of power at both full and cruising speed. A model would be made of this preliminary form which, since it was made of wax, could easily be altered to obtain further improvement. Typically, one might expect a saving in power and fuel of some 3-5 per cent from such testing and that was starting from a hull form which was based on earlier tests and hence already good.

The Royal Navy was far ahead of other navies in the use of model testing, giving it a small but important advantage. The graph below compares the actual resistance of battleship forms with an idealised series of forms,[11] showing that the ratio steadily fell as experience was gained. Testing of model propellers followed quickly and the old, expensive and lengthy process of matching a propeller to the ship and machinery by trial and error was almost a thing of the past, although during the period covered by this book, the problem of designing propellers for fast ships such as destroyers, with high rotational speeds, was not solved. Parsons recognised the problem as 'cavitation', water being vaporised in the low-pressure areas on the back of the propeller. He and Edmund Froude soon realised that these suction peaks could be reduced by increasing the total area of the propeller blades, which led to the fitting of several propellers on each shaft – a total of twelve propellers on four shafts in *Viper*. The problem was greatly reduced by the later introduction of geared turbines with larger, slower-running propellers.

Strength

The method of structural design proposed by Reed proved very satisfactory and is little changed in principle today. The only catastrophic failure was that of the purchased destroyer *Cobra*[12] which was not built to Admiralty standards. The careful enquiry which followed justified Reed's work with a few, minor improvements. The Admiralty can, again, boast that there were no serious structural failures; the Japanese had several major failures whilst the French *Branlebas* broke in half off Dartmouth in 1940 and several German ships had their sterns fall off.

Machinery development

Though the Admiralty constructors designed the ships and built most of them in the Royal Dockyards, the

These graphs show the trends with date of:
a. Machinery space floor area with power
b. Indicated horsepower per ton (wet)
c. Coal consumption per ihp per hour
Key dates are shown for major machinery developments which indicate that improvements were not continuous but depended, to a large extent, on design changes.
T denotes turbine ships.

machinery was usually designed and manufactured by commercial firms, working to Admiralty specification. It is not clear why this difference arose. The Admiralty engineers, both civilian and naval, were highly skilled. Indeed, many of the outside engineers were Admiralty-trained. The Dockyards had the capability to build engines[13] and occasionally did so. The Engineer-in-Chief was usually amongst the leaders in adopting new types of machinery though not often the very first.

The graphs below show how weight of machinery, fuel consumption and, perhaps most important, the floor area occupied dropped as simple expansion engines gave way to compound, triple-expansion and finally turbines. Boiler design led to further advances as did auxiliary machinery. Reduction in weight of machinery posed increasing problems for the naval architect as the centre of gravity rose. This could be partially offset by increase of beam, whose penalty on power was minimised by the work of the Froudes.[14] Many of these advances depended on improved materials, the introduction of steel and of seamless tubes being particularly significant. Reliable lubricants and lubrication systems contributed to the use of machinery rotating at higher speed. The Navy was fortunate in a succession of great Engineers-in-Chief; Lloyd, Wright, Sennett and Durston.

Guns and gunnery

The most obvious gains in fighting capability came from improvements in gunnery. The first graph shows how penetration of armour increased over the years. In turn, this improvement depended on better propellants, used in guns made from improved materials, used more effectively. The Royal Navy was, perhaps, a little slow in turning from muzzle-loaders to breech-loaders but this was of little importance until slow-burning propellants became available, particularly with the very efficient hydraulic loading systems devised by Armstrong and Rendel. The introduction of steel for guns was also a little slow.

More important, late delivery of guns was a major cause of the long building times in the 1880s and there seems little doubt that the Ordnance Department, controlled by the War Office, was not very progressive. In defence, it should be recognised that the big gun incorporated the most advanced technology of the day, stretching knowledge to the limit and beyond.

The introduction of the quick-firer led to an enormous increase in the rate of fire with demands for much greater ammunition stowage. It was insufficiently recognised that the ammunition supply to these numerous and widely-distributed guns, protected by armour of only moderate thickness, posed a hazard to the ship (*eg Kent* at the Falklands, *Malaya* at Jutland). Percy Scott and his numerous supporters showed how a high rate of fire could be translated into a high rate of hitting

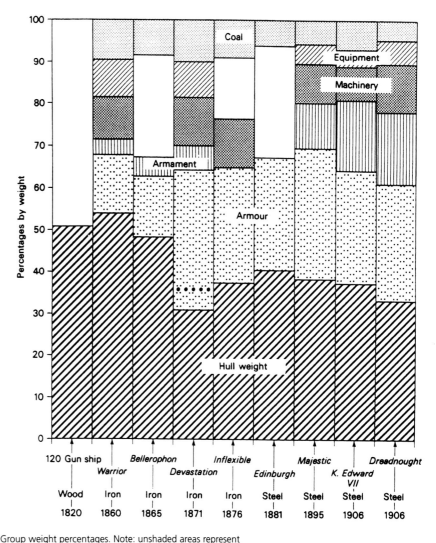

Group weight percentages. Note: unshaded areas represent weights where allocation between two or more hull groups is uncertain. The hull weight for *Devastation* (column 4).is almost certainly too low and a more credible figure is indicated by the dotted line.

aided in the last years of the period by embryonic fire control systems.

The worst problem of the later half of the era was in the shells themselves. The first effective steel armour-piercing shells were bought from France, the principal, potential enemy. The problem of designing a shell and fuse which would penetrate thick armour and burst inside was not solved, indeed, the extent of the problem was not fully appreciated even in the light of the evidence of the Russo-Japanese War.

Steel hulls

The use of steel in the hulls and machinery of British warships steadily increased during the 1860s and 1870s but, while the only source of steel in quantity was from

11. D K Brown, 'R E Froude and the Shape of Warships', *Journal of Naval Science* Vol 13/3 London 1987. The series of forms tried by Edmund Froude was based on that of the *Vulcan*.

12. There remains some doubt as the cause of *Cobra's* collapse. Though she was weaker than Admiralty designs, the difference was not great and fairly similar boats survived much worse seas. The author is inclined to support the view of K C Barnaby that she hit some semi-submerged wreckage, initiating structural failure.

13. There were twenty sets of machinery built in the Dockyards; Devonport nine, Sheerness five, Portsmouth three, Chatham two and Malta one.

14. Increasingly, the object of testing a model in a tank was to minimise penalties from a form dominated by non-hydrodynamic considerations rather than to seek an optimum.

the inconsistent Bessemer process, it was not possible to use steel in the most vital areas. Barnaby and White were strong advocates of steel construction and were further impressed by French advances in the *Redoutable.* Once the Landore works demonstrated their capability of making reliable steel by the Siemens-Martin open-hearth process, steel hull construction rapidly became universal and parallel advances in machinery construction were achieved. The British stayed with compound armour longer than other major navies, apparently justified by trials.

The lead which the French had obtained was due to advances in their steel industry and was not in any way due to reactionary ideas in the British Admiralty. It was, however, the first occasion in which British industry had fallen behind their rivals. It would seem that it took longer for British manufacturers of guns and shells to use the later, improved steels to advantage.

Armour

Initially, the only material for armour was wrought iron and, as guns increased in power, they could only be matched by thicker iron plates. The weight of such protection meant that only a very small area could be covered, reaching a climax in the *Inflexible* which had an armour citadel only just capable of floating the ship if the ends were riddled. Even so her 24in of armour (1100lbs/sq ft, with backing) was confined to a narrow strip with thinner protection to the rest of the citadel.

The ends of *Inflexible* were protected by a combination of a thick deck and close subdivision of the spaces above it, these spaces being filled with coal and other stores which would limit the loss of buoyancy and stability. This idea, probably first suggested by Reed, was improved and extended in later battleships and was the sole protection for many cruisers. The use of the protective deck system was often criticised and, since there was no clear proof of its value in action, these criticisms have remained unanswered. At the time, many believed that any ship without an armour belt was ineffective but today's warships face far more powerful weapons without any armour and it is possible to understand the protective deck system more rationally – and favourably.

The use of deck protection for the ends of battleships

is easy to defend. The ends of these ships were narrow, particularly after Froude's improvements to hull forms, and if flooded, the loss of buoyancy was small. The ends make little contribution to stability and if well subdivided and coal-filled, there was little risk. The extensive damage to the Chinese battleships at the Yalu gives some support to these views. To have provided an end-to-end belt would have been possible only if either its thickness or its depth was reduced. There was justification for thin protection, particularly at the bow, to prevent flooding from splinter damage and this was provided in White's later ships.

Most of the arguments above apply to cruisers in which the deck and subdivision formed the only protection. A belt of compound armour thick enough to resist all cruiser shells would cover only a very small area and the deck system was a more effective use of weight. The Spanish cruisers at Havana were disabled by fire but their machinery was functioning, suggesting that the deck system was effective. Protection for the gun crews was necessary but was insufficient on many foreign ships. White's casemates, tested in the *Resistance* trial, were heavy but generally effective when at a reasonable height above the water, though as mentioned above, the ammunition supply to these dispersed mountings was at risk.

Cemented armour

Cemented armour, first Harvey then soon superseded by Krupp, was so much more effective than earlier armour that it led to major changes both of projectiles and ships. It is usual to compare the effectiveness of armour on the basis of an equivalent thickness of wrought iron, but this conceals the fact that many projectiles, such as Palliser shot, could not penetrate cemented armour at all.

The Royal Navy was alerted to the danger from large, high-explosive shells from trials and used the new armour to protect a larger area of the ship. Six inches of Krupp would keep out HE-filled shell of any size and, under battle conditions, would probably protect against any shell up to 9.2in. The effectiveness of 6in armour made it possible to re-introduce the armoured cruiser, leading to the battlecruiser. It should be noted that the Harvey process came from the USA and the Krupp from Germany. Once the Industrial Revolution had spread, it would be foolish to expect British industry to lead every time but the performance of the British iron and steel industry seems consistently disappointing.

Underwater protection

Though there were a number of trials using mines and torpedoes against ships fitted with some degree of protection, it was only with the *Ridsdale* trial of protection for the *Dreadnought* that real success was achieved. As underwater weapons got bigger, it was inevitable that there would be extensive flooding and there were two failures of imagination amongst designers of all navies.

The solid lines show the actual thickness of armour fitted to ships at the date shown together with the material used. The upper, dotted line shows the equivalent thickness of iron usually quoted.

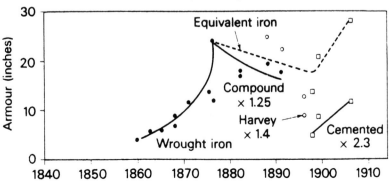

There was some excuse; calculations on the effect of major, asymmetric flooding was almost impossible until computers were available but Reed in his evidence to the 1871 Committee showed that he clearly recognised the problem. He pointed out the danger of centreline bulkheads in big compartments which would cause very large heel if flooded – the number of pre-Dreadnoughts which capsized (Chapter 10) shows how right he was.[15] There was also a failure to recognise the risk[16] of being hit on a transverse bulkhead, flooding at least two main compartments – and if these had centreline bulkheads capsize was almost inevitable. The effect of trim following severe damage could not be calculated with any accuracy and it was not fully realised that there would be a severe loss of stability if the decks at the ends went under – a powerful argument against low-freeboard ships.

The *Victoria* collision showed how flooding could spread through open doors and ventilation ducts and considerable efforts were made to reduce the number of openings in main bulkheads leading to unpierced machinery bulkheads in *Lord Nelson*. Though this was a major advance, the sinking of *Audacious* in the First World War showed that not enough had been done.

Seakeeping

The majority of the battleships described in this book had much less freeboard than would be adopted by a modern designer. Such ships were very wet and lost speed rapidly in head seas. Turrets of the Coles or Ericsson type were very heavy and it was desirable to keep them low in the ship, whilst low freeboard meant that there was less ship's side to be armoured. Only in the *Royal Sovereign* and later classes was the freeboard even adequate.[17] This problem was compounded by numerous projections and recesses in the hull side – gun ports, torpedo nets, external anchor stowages etc, which threw up vast sheets of spray. French ships had higher freeboard but with even more obstructions and openings etc, and they often had excessive tumblehome giving very poor righting moments at large angles of heel.

The early destroyers were worse; to obtain a small silhouette and to save weight they had about half the freeboard ratio of a Second World War destroyer and hence were extremely handicapped in even moderate weather.[18] Even today, freeboard is selected more on a basis of experience than from theoretical considerations and Victorian designers had plenty of experience. There seems to have been an almost masochistic view that life at sea should be unpleasant.

William Froude explained the nature of rolling in waves and showed how it could be controlled using bilge keels, sized by an empirical procedure which he set out. Despite this, bilge keels were usually too small – even omitted by White, who should have known better, in the *Royal Sovereigns* – leading to heavy rolling and hence to poor gunnery.

Costs

Over the years weight was saved in cheap items such as the hull and in replacing simple engines and boilers by more complicated types and hence the cost per ton rose. The ships also got bigger and, from the Naval Defence Act, more numerous, and hence the cost of the Navy rose rapidly. Fisher, in his *Naval Necessities*, not only realised the need to keep the Navy affordable as well as effective but, in scrapping obsolescent ships, made a big step in achieving this aim.

Parliament often tried to find out if Dockyard-built ships were cheaper or dearer than those from commercial builders but there was never a clear answer. In the earlier years, the accounting methods were too different but even after White's reforms the answer was unclear. Elgar tried hard in the context of the Naval Defence Act ships and his report is summarised in Appendix 9. There is no doubt that from *Royal Sovereign* onwards, the Dockyards were by far the fastest builders and economy is usually associated with fast building.

Between 1860 and 1905 the size of battleships nearly doubled whilst the cost increased by a factor of four; the cost per ton doubled. Comparison of costs is very difficult; as explained in the Introduction, the treatment of overheads differed between commercial yards and the Dockyards whilst the rate was changed for the latter more than once. Some costs are quoted without armament. In an attempt to get some consistency, the figures in the table below are all taken from White[19] though some of his figures are suspect.

The rising cost of warships 1860-1902

	Cost £1000	Date (ld)	Disp (tons)	£/Disp
Battleships				
Warrior	380	1859	9137	4.2
Minotaur	500	1861	10,600	4.7
Bellerophon	356	1863	7557	4.7
Hercules	380	1866	8677	4.4
Monarch	370	1866	8322	4.5
Devastation	360	1869	9330	3.9
Inflexible	812	1874	11,880	6.8
Anson	662	1883	10,600	6.2
Royal Sovereign	760	1889	14,150	5.4
Implacable	1100	1898	14,500	7.6
King Edward VII	1337	1902	15,585	8.6
Cruisers				
Inconstant	230	1866	5780	4.0
Iris	225	1875	3730	6.0
Comus	190	1876	2380	8.0
Cressy	750	1898	12,000	6.3
Drake	1000	1899	14,150	7.1

15. It is possible to investigate the effect of flooding using floating models with the correct subdivision. Such tests are surprisingly difficult and expensive, but even one such test would have shown the seriousness of the problem and given guidance on a general solution.

16. One is tempted to attribute this to a failure to understand probability theory, often badly taught even today.

17. D K Brown. 'Sustained Speed at Sea', NEC 100 Conference, NECI, (Newcastle 1984).

18. TBD Committee.

19. W H White, 'Presidential Address', Inst Civil Engineers 1903.

Though individual figures may be suspect, the overall trend is clear. There is a big jump around *Inflexible* which one may associate with the rapid increase in auxiliary machinery. The later growth may show the extra cost of quick-firing guns and of cemented armour.

Distribution of the Fleet 1906

By 1906, Fisher's concentration had begun to take effect and the fighting ships of the Navy were moving towards home waters; compare the distribution below with that given in the introduction.

Area	Battleships	Cruisers			Others
		Armoured	1st class	2nd class	
Mediterranean	8	4		3	17
Channel	16	6		2	42
Atlantic	8	6		1	3
N Atlantic		3		3	
China		3	1	2	23
E Indies				2	5
Australia			1	3	6
Cape			1	2	1
Pacific					1
Special Service					67
Totals	32	22	3	18	165
Tenders etc	1		3	2	2
Reserve	14	6	14	15	133
Grand total	47	28	20	35	300

The number of days spent at sea had also increased considerably and, in the Mediterranean, was some 121-133 days per year while even reserve ships were at sea for 10-14 days per quarter.

Innovation or reaction?

The nineteenth-century Navy, and to some extent the Admiralty as a whole, is often accused of being reactionary but in the numerous advances described in this book, the Admiralty was usually the leader and in the few cases when it was not the leader there were usually good reasons and it was not far behind. The two main accusations centre on retention of sails and on muzzle-loading and while these have been discussed in earlier chapters, some re-consideration is desirable.

The fuel consumption of simple-expansion engines was too great for prolonged operation under steam. *Devastation* was intended to be able to cross the Atlantic but there was barely enough coal with no margin to fight. Most of those who gave evidence to the 1871 Committee saw that the compound engine would reduce the need for sail to no more than jury rig. However, in the more distant areas of the British Empire, coaling stations were few and there remained a good case for sail in cruising ships. The triple-expansion engine changed the situation in two ways; directly because its much-reduced fuel consumption made possible longer passages under steam, and indirectly because its efficiency led to more commercial steamship routes to be opened with many more coaling stations. There was, indeed, a mystical view of the moral virtue of sail training (even today there are misguided people who believe in it) and this was combined with a penny-pinching view of the cost of burning coal. There was no opposition to the innovations which made possible the abolition of sail and if, as is likely, the Navy was a little slow in giving up sail, it was by a few years only.

This is not a history of gunnery but though there was some reluctance to adopt new ideas in gun construction there was little advantage in the more expensive and less reliable breech-loader until slow-burning powder came into use.

To the author, as a naval constructor, the conventional image of elderly admirals – seadogs – opposing change is incorrect. The real problem was that many did not understand new technologies and sought for 'wonder-weapons' which would give them victory at low cost. One may see this in the battle over the design of *Captain*, linked with a political view that industry knew better than their own staff. There was also a reluctance to think numerically, to put figures to a claimed advantage – and to its cost. One can also see the monster guns of *Inflexible*, *Benbow* and *Victoria* in the light of the 'wonder-weapon'. Incidentally, Spenser Robinson demonstrated that a seaman officer can understand technical problems sufficiently for rational decision making.

Conclusion

From 1860 to 1905 British warships, with a few minor exceptions, were the best in the world. Budgets were small for most of the period and British ships, thanks to the efficiency of the Royal Dockyards were built more quickly and at lower cost than those of other navies. Watts, Reed, Barnaby, White, Watts, their staff and the Engineers-in-Chief from Lloyd to Durston deserve every credit for their work.

Appendices

Appendix 1
Naval Estimates – New Construction

The figures quoted in the table below are taken from the statements on the Navy Estimates recorded in Parliamentary Papers. The figures are those voted and may differ from actual expenditure by a few hundred thousand pounds.[1] The table shows:

1. The year presented.

2. The total of Vote 6 and Vote 10 (Vote 8 from 1888) which covers expenditure on new construction (excluding guns), maintenance and repairs.

3. The Total Navy Estimate. Expenditure is in millions of pounds (£M)

Navy Estimates

Year	Vote 6/10 £M	Total £M	Year	Vote 6/10 £M Vote 8 from 1888	Total £M
1859	3.0	11.8	1883	3.9	11.4
1860	3.4	12.8	1884	4.0	11.6
1861	3.7	11.8	1885	5.3	11.6
1862	3.4	11.8	1886	4.9	13.0
1863	2.4	10.7	1887**	4.0	12.5
1864	2.0	10.4	1888	4.7	13.1
1865	1.9/3.0*	10.4	1889	4.6	13.7
1866	2.6	10.4	1890	4.9	13.8
1867	3.1	10.9	1891	4.8	14.2
1868	3.2	11.2	1892	4.8	14.2
1869	2.7	10.0	1893	4.7	14.2
1870	2.1	9.3	1894	7.0	17.4
1871	2.5	9.8	1895	7.9	18.7
1872	2.4	9.4	1896	9.7	21.8
1873	2.8	9.9	1897	9.2	21.8
1874	3.0	10.2	1898	10.8	23.8
1875	3.5	10.8	1899	12.8	26.6
1876	3.9	11.3	1900	13.0	27.5
1877	3.6	11.0	1901	15.3	30.9
1878	3.6	11.1	1902	19.2	31.0
1879	3.3	10.4	1903	18.8	35.7
1880	3.1	10.4	1904	16.0	35.9
1881	3.3	10.7	1905		33.2
1882	3.5	11.0			

* The definition of Vote 6 was altered and earlier figures are not directly comparable with the later ones.

** Vote 6 and 10 were combined into Vote 8 (3 Parts) Armament was introduced as Vote 9. (Previously War Office.) Figures above are total vote 8.

It is surprising that significantly different figures are quoted in different 'official' documents.

1. Note that the Estimates cover a financial year from 1 April, spreading over two calendar years, *eg* the 1877-78 Estimates were presented to Parliament in 1877 and are shown as 1877 in the table.

Appendix 2

Law of the Sea

At the outbreak of the War with Russia in 1854 the governments of the United Kingdom and France voluntarily imposed limits on themselves with respect to traditional, but ill-defined, belligerent rights affecting war at sea. These were formalised after the war in the Declaration of Paris, 1856, signed by Great Britain, France, Austria, Germany, Russia, Italy and Turkey. The rules were only to apply to wars between signatories. The main clauses were:

1. Privateering is and remains abolished.

2. The neutral flag covers enemy's goods with the exception of contraband of war.

3. Neutral goods, with the exception of contraband of war, are not liable to capture under enemy's flag.

4. Blockades, in order to be binding, must be effective, that is to say, maintained by a force sufficient really to prevent access to the coast of the enemy.

An attempt was made to persuade the USA to sign but was unsuccessful as they wanted almost unlimited freedom for a neutral to trade with belligerents. During the Civil War the Union claimed an 'effective' blockade of the whole of the Confederate coast line with only about twenty ships!

A strict interpretation of the Declaration of Paris would make a war on trade almost impossible, which was possibly a factor in the lack of attention given to trade protection by the Admiralty – and also a factor in American opposition. On the other hand, some of the terms were capable of very broad interpretation – what is contraband and what is an effective blockade, for example? The question of ultimate destination was also important and difficult. What was clear was that belligerent warships could not sink merchant ships but only send them to a formal Prize Court.

In 1899 further negotiations began in the Hague, culminating in the Declaration of London, 1909, but this was not ratified by any country.

Appendix 3

The Use of the Admiralty Coefficient (Ad Cft)

The Admiralty Coefficient was introduced in the 1840s, possibly by Thomas Lloyd,[1] and was a rational way of comparing the power required by ships which were similar in form, had a similar design of engine and were not too fast. It became increasingly inaccurate as the speed/length ratio (V, kts/sq rtL, ft) approached unity. The Admiralty coefficient is defined as: Ad Cft = $ihp/c.V^3$ where c is either midship section area, A_o, or displacement raised to the power 2/3 ($\Delta^{2/3}$).

There is a note in the Ship's Cover for *Temeraire* which shows how the Admiralty coefficient was used in design. The writer begins by setting out the two forms of the Ad Cft for *Swiftsure*; by midsection area (A_o) and by displacement ($\Delta^{2/3}$), deducing a speed of 13.7kts, 0.3kts less than required. He then looks at some other ships, noting their coefficient of fineness which he defines as: Δ /A_o x L, ie prismatic coefficient divided by 35.

Admiralty cft based on Cft fineness C_P

	Area	Dispt	C ft fineness	C_P
Swiftsure	603	185	.0205	.718
Hercules	488	157	.0205	.718
Monarch	513	171	.0203	.711
Bellerophon	518.9	163.5	.02035	.712
Sultan	439	138.5	.02033	.711

The assistant notes that *Swiftsure* is slightly fuller than the others (except *Hercules*) and is copper-sheathed and that one should not expect the new ship to be as good as if sheathed. He decides to use a value of Ad Cft as mean of *Hercules*, *Monarch* and *Bellerophon* giving, by area, 506.8 and, by displacement, 163.8.[2] Using these figures he deduces 6060ihp for 14kts and decides to take 6100ihp. The weight of machinery is then proportional to the power for similar, compound engines. Coal is estimated for 3 days at full power.

The *Iris* Cover gives the Ad Cfts for *Inconstant* as 550 and 186.6 which would give 17.28kts for the *Iris* and for *Volage* as 489 and 162.9 which would give 18kts. The writer (Dunn) points out that both these ships are single-screw and hence the use of their coefficients for *Iris*, twin screw, is dubious. He thinks that twin screws will give better results but is not sure. He then compares the prismatic coefficients C_P *Inconstant* (.646), *Volage* (.662) and *Iris* (.619 – later much reduced, see *Iris* note on model testing).

The scatter and uncertainty of these estimates show the unreliability of the Admiralty Coefficient, even for ships of moderate speed, and the true value of the Froude model testing procedure.

1. Brown, *Before the Ironclad*.

2. It is amazing that he quotes these very approximate figures to four-figure accuracy.

Appendix 4
Stability and Capsize

For much of the second half of the nineteenth century, the design of warships was dominated by problems of stability, which must be explained if the reader is to follow the great and angry debates of the time. The principles of ship stability are simple but the calculations needed to quantify the values for a real ship are so long and difficult that complicated mathematical methods were soon introduced to reduce the amount of arithmetic involved. Though these methods eased the work of calculation, they also obscured the basic simplicity of the subject. The subject of stability advanced very rapidly during the 1860s, due to Reed and his brilliant assistants, though many, including some well-qualified naval architects, failed to understand the implications of this new work.

Even the word 'Stability' is used with at least three meanings which differ one from the other. Stability is used to describe the force needed to heel a ship through a small angle; the ship being described as stable if a fairly large force is needed to heel it. A ship is also said to be stable if it can be heeled to a large angle without capsizing and, although this is a proper meaning of the word, it is not the same as the first case. A ship can require a large force to heel to a small angle and yet capsize at an angle little greater. Finally, the word stability is often used to describe a ship which does not roll violently. As shown in Appendix 5, this usage is incorrect as it is almost the opposite of the first two meanings of stability.

Forces in balance

When a ship is floating stationary in still water, there are just two forces acting on it, weight and buoyancy. The weight is constant – equal to the displacement – and will act vertically downwards through the centre of gravity[1] which, with some exceptions discussed later, is a fixed point. Buoyancy must equal weight for a floating object by Archimedes' principle and will act vertically upwards through the centre of buoyancy which is not fixed. The centre of buoyancy is the centre of the underwater volume of the ship and, since this volume changes shape radically as the ship heels, the centre will move. With the ship upright these two forces will be equal and opposite and work in the same line, balancing completely (the first, uppermost small sketch).

As the ship heels, the underwater volume will increase on the immersed side and reduce on the emerged side so that the centre of buoyancy moves to the immersed side (the next three small sketches). One may envisage a 'wedge' of volume being transferred from the emerged to the immersed side. The forces of weight and buoyancy, though still equal, no longer act in the same line but are separated by the distance GZ. This length is referred to as the righting lever and the

product Weight or Displacement (W) times GZ is the righting moment. For small angles of heel the buoyancy force is outboard of the weight and the righting moment will try to bring the ship upright.

For normal ships the righting moment and lever (GZ) will increase quite rapidly at first as the ship heels more and more but as the bilge comes out on one side and the deck edge goes under on the other, the GZ will increase more slowly and finally begin to reduce. The angle at which the maximum GZ occurs is critical; if there is a steady force heeling the ship and the heel passes the maximum, the righting moment will decrease and capsize will follow very quickly. Eventually, the righting moment falls to zero (the angle of vanishing stability, 82° in the fourth and lower sketch) and will become negative, the buoyancy force increasing the heel (the fifth small sketch).

The curve of righting levers (GZ curve)

The features described in the previous section can be shown on a graph where the value of the righting lever is shown on the vertical axis for each angle of heel (the curve below the sketches). As well as the angle and value of maximum GZ and the angle of vanishing stability (the angle at which it occurs is sometimes called the 'range of stability'), the so-called down-flooding angle is important. This is the heel at which water will begin to pour down gun ports, hatches, funnels, ventilators etc, and is the practical limit beyond which survival is unlikely.[2] In the early years undue importance was

1. The centre of gravity is the centre of all the individual weights which go to make up a ship. The force of gravity acting on each and every component may be represented by a force equal to the total mass acting through the centre of gravity.

2. It is so difficult to walk or work on a ship which has a steady angle of heel greater than about 20° that this angle may be said to be the limiting one for survival in all ships.

Curve of stability.

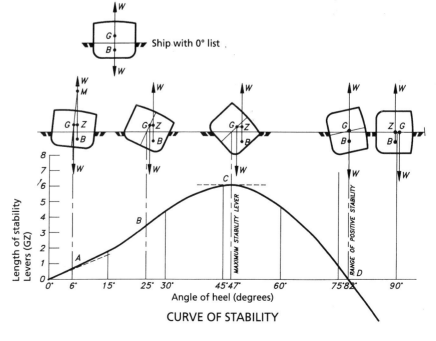

CURVE OF STABILITY

attached to the range of stability instead of the down-flooding angle. The key factors are the maximum value of GZ and the angle at which it occurs and tables in the text for individual ships will usually be limited to these figures (when available).

The adequacy of a GZ curve can only be judged in relation to the heeling moment to which the ship may be exposed. The heeling moment will include some or all of the following; the effect of wind pressure on superstructure, masts and rigging, wave forces, shifting cargo or other loads, crowding of people to one side and flooding. An all too common build-up to disaster sees a ship broadside on to wind and sea. The ship heels over to leeward to a considerable angle due to wind pressure and on this is superimposed large roll angles due to the waves. There will then be slow flooding through intakes, leaking hatches and doors etc. Such flooding can lead to loss of electric power (in modern ships) and hence to steering; followed by more flooding and capsize. Between 1935 and 1945 the USN lost four destroyers in much this way,[3] the Italian lost two,[4] Japan one, Russia one – and the RN none.[5]

The resistance to short-duration forces, such as a gust of wind, is measured by the area under the curve so the naval architect will refer to a GZ curve as 'good' if it rises quickly at first, reaches a satisfactory maximum at a fair angle and has plenty of area beneath it. These subjective values have now been quantified.

Approximations and justification

It was realised from its introduction that the GZ curve was only an approximation to the behaviour of a ship in a severe storm. The GZ curve implies the ship at rest in a flat sea, very different from moving through giant waves. The justification is that it works, at least in a comparative sense. In the century or so after the introduction of the GZ curve it was clear that ships with a 'good' curve, as described above, would survive a storm which would cause less well-endowed ships to founder. The loss of three USN destroyers in the great typhoon of December 1944[6] showed first that the GZ curve was correct in identifying the ships most at risk and also led to an investigation which suggested a way of arriving at numerical values for the good GZ curve. The values derived by Sarchin and Goldberg[7] form the basis for the safety standards of most navies today.

Stability at small angles – the metacentric theory

It was long believed that the direct calculation of the movement of the centre of buoyancy was so difficult as to be practically impossible and from the seventeenth century onwards an approximation, known as the metacentric theory was developed. This was based on the assumption that the line of action of the force of buoyancy crossed the centre line of the ship (the upright vertical) at a fixed point known as the metacentre (M). The separation of the centre of gravity (G) and the metacentre is called the metacentric height, GM.

The righting lever GZ at an angle of heel θ is then given by the simple expression GM x Sin θ. This expression is valid up to heels of about 10° for normal ships with a decent freeboard and is useful for estimating heel from shift of weights and moderate winds but is little guide to safety at large angles when capsize is likely. In the early design phase it is often assumed that if the GM of the new ship is the same as that of an existing ship of the same general configuration, then the GZ curves will be similar. Provided that the ships really are similar and the designer is experienced, this assumption is a reasonable starting point.

It is not too difficult to calculate the position of the metacentre but the calculation of the position of the centre of gravity (G), though simple, is very lengthy and needs some experience. The height of the metacentre above the centre of buoyancy is given by I/V where I is the second moment of area of the waterplane[8] and V the immersed volume. The height of the metacentre is dominated by the broader part of the hull and hence flooding of the fine ends was not important, often not appreciated by contemporary critics of warship design. The first direct calculation of the position of the centre of gravity (G) was probably by William Bell for the *Great Eastern* in 1859 but in 1865 Barnaby was to tell the INA that it was so difficult as to be practically impossible. However, more assistant constructors were appointed and very quickly the position of G was calculated for all ships. This position will, of course, vary with loading, G normally being highest in the light condition.

The metacentric height, GM, is the slope of the GZ curve at zero angle of heel. In sailing days the metacentric height was linked to 'the power to carry sail', defined as:

W x GM/ (A x h)

Where A is the sail area and h the height of the centre of pressure on the sails.

The inclining experiment

The metacentric theory can be used to measure the separation of G and M directly by experiment. A known weight (w) is moved a measured distance (d) across the deck giving a known heeling moment, w x d. The angle of heel (θ) produced is measured using long pendulums and then

w x d = W x GM x Sinθ

Since W, w, d and θ are all known, GM can be found. The inclining experiment is simple in principle but there are a considerable number of precautions needed to ensure that the answer is accurate beginning with – 'Ensure the

Note in this case GZ = GM Sin Ø (Buoyancy force passes through metacentre).
W = Displacement
G = Centre of gravity
M = Metacentre
B₀ = Centre of buoyancy (upright)
B = Centre of buoyancy (heeled)
GZ = Righting lever
GM = Metacentric height
Ø = Angle of heel

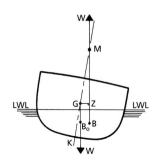

ship is afloat', *ie* not resting on the bottom! The value of GM obtained is that for the loading condition of the experiment and considerable care is needed to record what variable weights such as fuel, stores, ammunition etc, are on board and what is still to go on. This work takes time and it must be doubted if Barnes' inclining of the *Captain* in less than a day was very accurate.

The theory of the inclining experiment was known by about 1750 and a few RN ship were inclined about 1790.[9] There were a few more experimental inclinings in the 1830s but it did not become regular practise till after the capsize of *Perseverance* in 1855. The French Navy was a little ahead of the RN in experimental inclinings but seems to have been even slower in using the experiment regularly. At first, the inclining experiment was seen as a direct check on the stability on the day of the experiment but, since the position of the metacentre is fairly easy to calculate accurately, the inclining experiment was soon seen as an experimental determination of the position of the centre of gravity.

In isolation, knowledge of the value of GM is of little value. It has to be judged against values found safe in similar ships and should also be considered together with the character of the GZ curve. The tables at the end of this Appendix show that the values for the GZ curve are very similar for different classes of battleship but, to obtain these values, quite large changes in GM are needed.

Calculation of the GZ curve

The basic theory was published by Atwood at the end of the eighteenth century but the arithmetical solution for even one condition and one angle of heel was so difficult that it was not used in practice. In 1861 Barnes presented a paper to the INA in which he used radial integration to solve Atwood's equations and in 1867 W John read a paper which introduced the GZ curve in its present form. The work required was still very lengthy but it could be done.[10]

In 1893 a mechanical device, Amsler's Integrator, was introduced which greatly eased the task. Using a specially prepared body plan it was possible to obtain one spot in 20 minutes – and six spots were needed for each of 5-6 angles.[11] This machine arrived just in time for the numerous calculations on the sinking of the *Victoria*.

Liquids

It has been assumed in earlier sections that the centre of gravity is fixed but this is not entirely correct. Liquids will move downhill as the ship heels and this shift of weight will move the centre of gravity. In all cases such movement will reduce the stability of a ship and it is important to reduce such movement to a minimum. Water (or oil) tanks should be full or empty as far as is possible with only the one in use being part full.

The calculations for shift of liquid, referred to as 'free surface', are again tedious and an approximation, based on the metacentric theory, was used. A higher, virtual centre of gravity was calculated through which the weight would act for small heels.[12] The movement of liquid was not a serious problem until the introduction of oil fuel.

Coal bunkers

In a full coal bunker the coal will occupy ⅝ths of the volume so that if it is flooded, the sea water will only fill ⅜ths of the volume, limiting the loss of buoyancy. More important, the coal would preserve ⅝ths of the second moment of area so maintaining much of the stability. This was well known to designers[13] but ignored by critics of the protective deck system.

A sense of proportion

The relationship between the form and proportions of a ship and the stability parameters is hard to set out as it is almost impossible in a real design to alter one characteristic of the form alone. The generalisations which follow should be read with great caution.

An increase of beam will increase the metacentric height but the scope for this is limited as high values of GM cause violent rolling (Appendix 5). Such an increase of beam will have little effect on GZ at larger angles of heel. The benefits of an increase of beam are much less effective in maintaining stability after damage causing flooding. For a time, after the Second World War, the proportions were decided on the basis of stability in a nominal, serious case of flooding.

An increase in freeboard will lead to bigger values of the maximum GZ at larger angle of heel but in a real ship the centre of gravity will also rise negating some of the improvement. The diagrams below are based on a paper by Barnaby of 1871 and show that increase of freeboard will considerably increase both the maximum GZ and the angle at which it occurs. Practical changes of beam have much less effect on the value of the maximum and none on the angle at which it occurs. The diagram, based on work by Barnaby, indicates the effect of changes to freeboard and beam on GZ for a typical battleship. It is assumed that the centre of gravity does not move.

One can see a change of freeboard leading to poorer stability for small heel angles and an improvement at larger angles. This was a common feature of late nineteenth-century passenger liners which were designed with a small GM to give an easy roll but relied on their high sides to get an acceptable GZ curve. In warships, the effective freeboard was the height to gun ports, low in the side. Unarmoured sides could not be relied on to be effective after battle damage unless very well subdivided.

A box-shaped form will usually have a GZ curve which rises rapidly whilst a very fine form will have only a slowly rising curve. Tumblehome, as used in

3. C R Calhoun, *Typhoon: the other enemy* (Annapolis 1981). See also D K Brown, 'The Great Pacific Typhoon', *The Naval Architect*, September 1985 (London 1985).

4. Amiraglio di Squadra G Pollastri and D K Brown, 'The Loss of the Destroyer *Lanciere*', *Warship 1994* (London 1994), p195.

5. D K Brown, 'Stability of RN destroyers during World War II', *Warship Technology* 4/1989 (London 1989).

6. Calhoun, *Typhoon: the other enemy*. See also D K Brown, 'The Great Pacific Typhoon'.

7. T H Sarchin and L L Goldberg, 'Stability and Buoyancy Criteria for US Naval Surface Ships', *Trans SNAME* (New York 1962).

8. Second moment of area=∫y³ dx

9. It seems that Bouguer inclined the French frigate *Gazelle* about 1746. Early British inclinings, c1790, are described in 'Remarks on the forms and properties of ships.' *Collection of papers on naval architecture*, London, 1800.

10. About 1948 the author was required to calculate one value using Barnes' method. I think it took about 6-8 hours.

11. There was a tradition that once an assistant was launched on a 20-minute run he should not be interrupted for any reason whatsoever. I was once interrupted by the Director himself but – unusually – he was very apologetic over the extreme urgency which had forced him to this break with tradition.

12. Misunderstanding of this approximation leads to ridiculous claims that a few millimetres of water on the car deck can capsize a Ro-Ro ship. Such a shallow layer will destroy the metacentric stability but a heel of a very few degrees would cause the water to collect in a corner where it would cause little trouble. If there is a leak and more water is entering here will soon be a serious problem.

13. Attwood, *Warships, a Textbook*, p214.

Effect of Varying Beam and Freeboard on GZ.

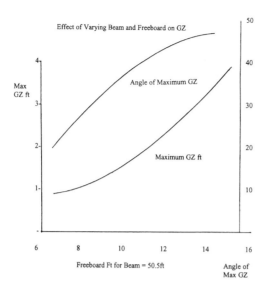

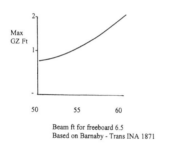

Beam ft for freeboard 6.5
Based on Barnaby - Trans INA 1871

many French and Russian ships reduces stability at large angles very considerably.[14]

Damage

All the tedious and difficult calculations discussed above become very much more difficult once the ship is holed and flooded. The ship will sink deeper in the water and will both heel and trim – and even to calculate the position of the new waterline is a lengthy task – whilst the hydrostatic parameters which govern the height of the metacentre and the characteristics of the GZ curve will change. A full treatment of damaged stability was not possible until the introduction of the computer, well after the Second World War.[15]

In the early days the effect of flooding a single large compartment was considered by taking the flood water as an added weight, at the virtual centre of gravity. The GM was modified by this and the effect of heel and trim[16] considered. It was implicit that the effect of flooding two compartments could be obtained by adding the effects of each compartment taken in isolation. A position for the metacentre in the intact state was obtained, by varying the beam, which, it was hoped, would allow for the losses following serious flooding.

There was a reasonable subjective understanding of the effects of damage but the magnitude of the effects of

flooding was under estimated, particularly the effect of off centre loading when stability was reduced at the same time. Until at least the *Victoria-Camperdown* collision the hazards were not appreciated of flooding spreading through doors and ventilation valves which though nominally watertight had either been left open or leaked due to distortion.

Some typical values of GM[17]

Classes of ship	Metacentric Ht (GM)(ft)
Prince Consort, Gloire (Fr)	6-7
Warrior, Minotaur, Flandre (Fr)	4-4¾
Bellerophon, Hercules, Alexandra, Alma (Fr)	2½-3½
Ocean (Fr)	1¾-2½
Devastation, Dreadnought, Trafalgar	3½-4½
Admirals and *Imperieuse*	4¾-6
Barbette Ships (Latest 1900), British and French	2¾-3¾
Inflexible, Ajax	5½-8¼
Glatton, Belier (Fr)	6-8
USS *Monitor*	c14
Wooden Screw Battleships	4½-6½
Wooden Screw Frigates and Corvettes	4-5
Wood and Composite Gunvessels and Gunboats	2¼-3
Inconstant, Active, Tourville and *Seignelay* (Fr)	2½-3
Iris	2¾-3
Small Cruisers: *Mersey, Medea, Apollo, Archer*	1¾-2½
Sloops, Torpedo Gunboats, Small Cruisers	2-2½
Coastal and River Gunboats	7-12
Torpedo Boats, 1st class, early	0.8-1¼
later	1¼-2
2nd class, early	0.4-0.8
later	0.8-1.0

Later Battleships	GM (Load)	Angle max GZ(°)	Vanishing angle(°)
Camperdown	4.4	36	67
Victoria	5.05	35	68
*R Sovereign**	3.6	37	63
Hood	4.1	34	57
Barfleur	4.35	42	78
Renown	3.65	42	70
Majestic	3.4	38	62
Glory	3.84	39	65.5
Implacable	4.1	37	65
Russell	4.1	38	65
K Edward VII	5.2	39	68
Swiftsure	3.44		
Lord Nelson	3.43	32	58
Dreadnought	5.0	38	63

* Note how the high freeboard of the *R Sovereign* enables good GZ to be obtained with a lower GM (Also *cf Hood* with a greater GM but poorer GZ).

14. P J Sims and J S Webster, 'Tumblehome Warships'. To be published, *SNAME* 1996.

15. The author did carry out these sums by hand for the *Tribal* class frigates c1955. These were simple ships with no longitudinal subdivision but, even so, it took three months of boring arithmetic. It did show that some of the simple assumptions used previously were wrong and an additional bulkhead was fitted and the freeboard aft increased.

16. Since large compartments were amidships, the effect of trim was small. This simple approach fails completely if the ship trims sufficiently to bring the upper deck at either end under water.

17. W H White, *Manual of Naval Architecture.*

Appendix 5

Rolling

Human senses are not very good at measuring roll angles. On the deck of a rolling ship the balance organs in the ear are upset and the brain is deceived into accepting a false direction for the vertical. The size of the error depends on the lateral – sideways – acceleration and hence it is difficult, by observation alone, to separate the angle of roll from the associated lateral acceleration. The same errors affect an ordinary pendulum which may indicate roll angles very much greater than the true angle. In consequence, a number of rules of thumb have grown up which are either wrong or half-truths and some of these are discussed later.

The main effect of rolling in ships of this era was on the performance of manual tasks such as loading a gun and then training and elevating the barrel. Performance of such tasks is governed by lateral acceleration, which causes sideways forces, more than on the angle of roll. The speed at which the ship rolls will be greatest as the deck moves through the horizontal and firing the guns in this position is likely to lead to the largest errors in elevation. For guns at high elevation, firing near the fore-and-aft axis, the angle of roll will alter the training angle as well as the elevation but this only became a serious problem when long-range firing was adopted. Contrary to popular belief, roll has little direct effect on seasickness which is due to vertical acceleration, the combination of pitch and heave.[1] However, a tired man is more susceptible to seasickness and rolling can be very tiring.

Period

A ship floating in the sea behaves like a pendulum having a natural period, the time it takes to roll out to out and back.[2] Some typical roll periods are given below.

Typical roll periods[3]

Ship	Period (seconds)	Notes
Inflexible	10½	High GM, 8ft
Royal Sovereign	16	Moderate GM, 3½ft, high inertia due to armour
Majestic	16	
Powerful	14	Protected cruisers with no side armour
Arrogant	12	
Pelorus	11	
Destroyers	4–8	

The roll period of a ship is given by $2\pi.k/\sqrt{(g.GM)}$ where k is the radius of gyration,[4] a measure of the 'average' distance of the weights from the axis about the roll axis and GM is the metacentric height. An approximation for modern ships is period = 0.42. Beam/$\sqrt{GM}$ (ft) and, to the author's surprise, this seems to work quite well for the ships in the table above. Heavy side armour much increases the moment of inertia and hence leads to longer, slower roll periods. The longer the period, the more gentle will be the roll giving less lateral acceleration.

Theory

The theory of rolling was first explained in a paper by William Froude in 1861, amplified by many more over the following decade. Though his work was correct, it was almost impossible to use until the computer age. Froude realised this and developed an empirical method based on data from model tests but it was time consuming (and not very easy to understand) and was rarely used. Froude was to complain to a Parliamentary committee in 1872 that his work had not been fully utilised in warship designs of that period.

He showed that ships with the same natural period will roll in the same way in a similar sea state and that the worst rolling will occur when waves are met at time intervals equal to the natural roll period. He also showed that ships with the longest roll period, that is least metacentric height, will generally roll the least. Though correct, this last statement needs a lot of qualification, supplied in a later paragraph. (The need to ballast the *Audacious* – Chapter 2 – derived from Reed's excessive attention to this point!)

Froude's work was proved in full scale trials with two sloops and later with tests and trials with both *Inflexible* and the *Devastation* (*qv*). One of the sloops was fitted with bilge keels and rolled 6° whilst the sister ship, identical except for lacking bilge keels, rolled 11°.

Resonance

The worst rolling will occur when a wave hits the side at the same point in the roll, *ie* the period of encountering the waves is the same as the natural roll period of the ship. This condition is known as resonance and, since the natural periods of ships differ, it is quite possible for one ship of a squadron to be rolling heavily in a sea state which the others hardly notice, making nonsense of the many comparative table of roll angles collected during the nineteenth century.

A subcommittee of the 1871 Design Committee considered the danger of resonant rolling to low-freeboard ironclads such as *Devastation*. They pointed out the heavy rolling would occur when the ship was beam on to regular waves of the same period as the ship.

1. On a very wide ship, roll can give high vertical accelerations at the side.

2. In the nineteenth century it was customary to use period to mean the time from out to out only. Hence it is necessary to double the values quoted in contemporary books to relate to modern usage.

3. E L Attwood, *Warships* (London 1904).

4. The moment of inertia is obtained by multiplying the mass of every item – including the weight of water set in motion by the ship – by the square of its distance from the axis. The radius of gyration is then found by taking the square root of the moment of inertia divided by the total mass.

However, the period of the ship would change as soon as the deck edge went under and hence rolling would no longer be resonant.

Measurement of roll

In some cases, reported roll angles were measured by pendulum which is deceived by lateral acceleration in much the same way as the human mind, described earlier (a pendulum on the bridge can indicate roll angles up to double the true value). Accurate figures can be obtained by sighting on the horizon – if you can see the horizon in bad weather. Froude devised a special, very long period pendulum which gave accurate roll angles but it was big and heavy and needed much maintenance so was rarely used.[5]

Big waves can force ships, particularly smaller ships, to roll in the period of wave encounter rather than their natural period though such forced rolling is not usually so severe. Real sea states contain a mixture of waves of different periods and the ship will mostly respond to those of its own frequency. Since these are often the longest waves which are the least obvious one can get the upsetting sight of a ship apparently rolling in opposition to the most conspicuous waves.

The changing pressures in the sea below a wave and the different shape of the waterline affect the basic stability. In general, a ship will have much less stability on the crest of a wave. This particularly affects faster ships and it appears that the early destroyers had problems in consequence (as did modern fast patrol boats).

Metacentric height

As William Froude showed in 1861, a small metacentric height will usually reduce the severity of rolling but the effect is complicated.[6] A large value of metacentric height (GM) will not usually lead to much greater roll angles but the motion will be more rapid with higher accelerations and forces. Both calculation and trials show that rolling will be heaviest in quartering seas for ships with a small GM and in seas approaching from ahead of the beam for those with a high GM. A low value of GM leads to a long roll period and, since long waves are less steep and less common, resonance with its heavy rolling is less likely and less severe when it occurs. It is often not possible to adopt low values of GM in small craft and resonance can be avoided by going to the opposite extreme of a very high GM.

The designer's selection of a value for metacentric height which is sufficient to resist capsize, even after severe damage, and yet not so high as to lead to excessive roll accelerations is never easy and may be impossible. Many liners of the late nineteenth century were built with very small values of GM, relying on their high freeboard to give sufficient righting moment at large angles of heel. This can be quite satisfactory for undamaged ships but may be dangerous when damage reduces stability and, possibly, makes the high sides non-watertight.

Reduction of roll

The resistance to roll of a bare hull is quite small but can be increased dramatically by fitting bilge keels. The value of bilge keels was demonstrated by Froude though small keels had been fitted in some ships before his work. Froude also showed that the added drag of bilge keels was small with a negligible effect on speed and endurance. However, there was – and remains – some reluctance to fitting large bilge keels; over the last century or so, all too many ships have had to be docked for bigger keels to be fitted.[7] It is generally inadvisable for bilge keels to project beyond the line of the side or of the bottom as bigger keels would make docking difficult.

Inflexible and her diminutives were fitted with antirolling tanks devised by the young Phillip Watts, assisted by the Froudes. Water would rush from side to side with a speed depending on the depth of water. This would be tuned so that the forces generated would oppose the roll. The idea was sound and has been used with some success in modern ships but the tanks fitted to the battleships were far too small to have much effect – and the sloshing water was very noisy – and they were soon abandoned.

Miscellaneous

As guns got longer, there was a serious risk of low-mounted broadside guns rolling their muzzles under water.

For a more detailed study of rolling read Dr A R J M Lloyd, *Seakeeping, Ship Behaviour in Rough Weather* (Chichester 1989) – but only if your maths is pretty good! Most of the author's knowledge of the behaviour of a ship in the sea came from Dr Lloyd and my thanks are due to him for correcting this Appendix.

5. Now displayed in the Science Museum, South Kensington.

6. For boats and small ships it may be better to avoid resonance by adopting a large value of GM.

7. K A Monk, 'Warship Roll Criterion', *Trans RINA* (London 1987).

Appendix 6
The Loading and Strength of Ships

The concept that the loading on a ship's hull depends on the difference between the longitudinal weight distribution and the varying distribution of buoyancy in still water and in waves goes back at least as far as Bouger (1746) and Euler (1759) though their analysis was flawed. Seppings gave a correct description of the loading which led him to add diagonal stiffening to his designs. In 1866 Rankine put together a book *Shipbuilding – Theoretical and Practical*, with contributions from Isaac Watts, Barnes and Napier in which he showed how a graphical representation of weight and buoyancy could be integrated to give correct numerical values for forces in the sides of the ship and could also give the overall bending moment on the hull. Rankine also correctly distinguished between stress and strain[1] which could be used with the bending moment in designing the structure. Reed and his new assistant, White, developed this into a formal design process which Reed described to the Royal Society in 1871.[2]

Loading

Even in still water the weight of any section along the length may not be equal to the buoyancy of that section (see Chapter 2 for White's description and for the relevant diagrams). Hence at any section along the length there will be a vertical force due to this difference. This force is known as the shearing force. A diagram can be prepared showing how the load, the difference between weight and buoyancy, varies along the length. Summing up the area under this curve ('Integrating') gives the variation of shearing force along the length. In turn, the shearing force curve can be integrated to give the bending moment which leads to stresses in the deck and keel.

In waves the distribution of buoyancy will change, the worst loadings occurring when the ship is supported on a wave of its own length. Two cases are considered; one with a wave crest amidships and the ends relatively unsupported in the troughs (Hogging) and the other with a trough amidships and a crest at each end (Sagging).[3] For each case, loading, shearing force and bending moment curves are prepared as illustrated in Chapter 2.

Calculation

Reed's paper described a standard procedure for loading and strength calculations which had already been introduced into the Admiralty design office. The longitudinal distribution of weight would first be estimated, a boring task but not difficult. The ship would then be 'balanced', floating in equilibrium, head-on to a wave of its own length; first with a wave crest amidships, reducing the support to the ends and then with crests at bow and stern and the trough amidships reducing support, a long and tedious calculation though some mechanical aids were available by the end of the century. Initially, the height of the wave was selected as the most severe likely for waves of that length but gradually a standard height ratio of ¹⁄₂₀th length was adopted and this was formalised after the *Wolf* experiments (Chapter 11).[4] Some detail refinements were added; the variable loads, fuel, stores etc, were adjusted for both conditions to give the most severe loading and attempts were made to allow for the varying pressure under an actual wave.

It was always recognised that this calculation is comparative and was not intended correctly to represent the extreme load on real ships in a confused sea – though it is not far out. Very long waves with a height of ¹⁄₂₀th their length are rare indeed and it was customary to accept a higher nominal stress in very long ships.

In resisting the load, a ship will act as a box girder with deck and bottom forming the flanges and the sides as the webs. The effectiveness of such a girder is measured by the second moment of area of the section (often called the moment of inertia though this is not strictly correct). The second moment of area (I) is obtained by multiplying the cross sectional area of every item of structure which contributes to longitudinal strength by the square of its distance from the neutral axis. There are two problems in this simple approach; the first is that the position of the neutral axis about which the ship bends is not known. This is easily overcome by assuming a position and calculating moments about that axis which leads to the true position of the axis and hence a small correction to the second moment. This was not a difficult calculation – half a day – but needed some careful thought.

The second problem is more difficult; that of deciding which items contribute effectively to longitudinal strength. Short stiffeners such as those between hatches are not effective. Rivet holes weakened the plate and, to allow for this, it was usual to deduct ¹⁄₇th of the area of the section in tension from the strength calculation[5]. The actual design of a heavily loaded, riveted joint was complicated[6] in order to minimise the weakening of the plate by the holes. Wood decking and sheathing contributed to the strength and their contribution was taken as ¹⁄₁₆th of that of the corresponding cross sectional area of steel. Armour was usually considered as effective in compression but not in tension due to lack of fixity at the butts though protective decks were often worked structurally and included.

There is then a simple relationship between the bending moment (M), the moment of inertia (I) and the stress (p) at a distance y from the axis.

$$p = \frac{M.y}{I}$$

1. Stress – the load per unit cross sectional area of structure. Strain – the extension per unit length of a piece of structure under load.

2. E J Reed, 'On the unequal distribution of weight and support in ships and its effects in still water, waves and exceptional positions', *Phil Trans, Royal Society* (London 1871).

3. Occasionally, checks have been made to see if waves of a different length or position can make things worse but the conditions described above are the worst for all normal ships.

4. The procedure is very similar today though now with a uniform wave height of 8 metres for all lengths.

5. Biles' analysis of the *Wolf* trials showed this correction for rivet holes was unnecessary but it remained in use for the sake of consistency.

6. E L Attwood, *Warships – A Textbook*.

In the early stages of design it was sufficient to use approximations for the bending moment based on previous ships. The bending moment was taken as W (Displacement) x L (length)/(Constant) and some typical values are given below.

Bending moments for typical ships[7]

| | | | Maximum bending moment = W.L divided by | | |
| | | Wave | | | |
Ship	LxHt ft	L/H	Still water	Wave crest amid-ships	Wave trough amid-ships
Royal Sovereign	380 x 24	16	297	39	51
Bellerophon	300 x 20	15	176	49	53
Invincible	280 x 18	16	227	70	38
Minotaur			88	28	38
Rupert	256 x 17	15	263	43	41
Shannon	270 x 18	15	121	33	67
Ajax	300 x 18	17	79	146	30
Blake	375 x 24	16	109	32	65
Iris	300 x 15	20	58	29	-
Torpedo Gunboat	230 x 11.5	20	87	23	34
Destroyer	180 x 9.5	19	166	30	21

Stresses

There are two key figures measuring the strength of materials in tension; the ultimate tensile strength at which it will snap and the elastic limit or yield strength beyond which it will not recover when the load is removed. The elongation before fracture is also important and is expressed as a percentage. Some typical values follow:

Material	Yield (Tons/sq in)	Ultimate Elongation%	
Wrought iron*	12	20	10 along, 3 across grain
Mild Steel	15.5	26-30	20
High tensile steel (Cruisers)	20	34-38	20
High tensile steel (Destroyers)	37-43		'Less'

*Wrought iron was a very variable material and these figures are typical only.

Stresses are always increased locally at sharp corners and other discontinuities and it was appreciated that the acceptable stress in a ship's structure should be much less than the yield point; typically, the design stress would be about one third of yield. It was not fully realised until after the Second World War that metals become brittle at low temperatures, permitting cracks to spread rapidly. SS *Great Britain*'s wrought iron becomes brittle at about 50°C, *Warrior*'s at about 20° C, *Titanic*'s steel at about 28° C and her wrought iron rivets at 20°C.

Steel permitted thinner plates and angle bars than iron with an increased risk of failure by buckling. Calculations on buckling were introduced for the first time in the design of the *Edinburgh* and *Colossus*.

Local strength

There were many items whose strength was dependent on local loads rather than on the bending of the hull as a whole. Examples include structure exposed to gun blast, rams, the supports to armour, masts, machinery, turrets etc. This explains why the weight of hull structure cannot be expressed as a simple function of longitudinal loading.

7. W H White, *Manual of Naval Architecture.*

Appendix 7
Freeboard

Increasing the freeboard will help to keep the ship dry when steaming into head seas but will raise everything on deck such as turrets and increase the area of side which needs armour protection. There are other aspects, too, dealt with later, but it was the balance between seakeeping and extent of armour which caused most of the arguments in the latter half of the nineteenth century. As with other aspects of design, 'Enough is enough'.

Minimum freeboard

At the time the *Captain* was designed, even Reed saw the selection of freeboard as a matter for seamen rather than naval architects. A rule recommended by the Institution of Naval Architects for merchant ships was that freeboard should equal Beam/5 (for L/B <5, see Appendix 8). Much of the evidence to the 1871 Design Committee was to the effect that only sufficient freeboard was needed at the ends to work the anchors at rest in an exposed anchorage. It was realised that this would limit speed in bad weather though the magnitude of such a limitation was not recognised. In 1870 it was still hoped by many that the whole side could be armoured and, for a given size of ship, the greater the area of the side, the thinner would be the armour.

It was even believed that water washing over the low ends would reduce pitching whilst water on the low sides outboard of Reed's breastwork would similarly reduce rolling. There is some truth in these views but the price paid for small reductions in motions was high. Riveted seams will always leak and these low ends made life unpleasant for the sailors. Ventilation, too, was difficult and ducts into the ends could form dangerous leak paths, low down, in a damaged ship.

Stability

It was shown in Appendix 4 that increase in freeboard would lead to a higher maximum righting lever (GZ) at a greater angle, slightly offset by a rise in the position of the centre of gravity. It must be understood that, in this context, freeboard means watertight freeboard. Splashtight covers over gun ports might (or might not) be enough to keep the ship dry but, if the ship had a steady heel, they would leak, making the heel worse. The low gunports of so many late nineteenth century ships were a bad feature. High, unprotected sides would be riddled in action and fail to contribute to stability after such damage. Good subdivision above the protective deck which was such a feature of British ships limited such loss of stability.

Protection etc

The weight of a Coles or Ericsson turret was so great that it had to be mounted low in the ship, leading to a low freeboard. (Even the freeboard to the top of a Reed breastwork was still low.) Barbettes were lighter and hence the gun could be higher but the early barbettes were vulnerable to shells penetrating the almost unprotected side and bursting below the thin barbette floor. Rendel provided a thick floor for his barbettes in the Admirals while in the *Royal Sovereign*, White carried the barbette armour down to the protective deck.

The introduction of the quick-firing gun increased the value of the secondary armament whilst making it more difficult to protect from similar enemy batteries. White's casemates were an effective protection but it was still thought necessary to separate the casemates as much as possible, both vertically and horizontally. In many ships, the main deck casemates were very close to the waterline which meant that the muzzle could dip into the sea for quite a small roll angle, visibility was poor and leaks through the gunport could increase heel.

Height of main deck guns above still water[1]

Ship	(ft)
Edgar	10
Terrible	15.5
Drake	11
Monmouth	12
Duke of Edinburgh	10.5

A guideline

Towards the end of the Second World War a survey was carried out to find out what was a suitable freeboard. It was found that there were few complaints from ships whose freeboard forward was equal to $1.1\sqrt{L}$(ft). This relationship is not a natural law but a crude indication of what was then seen as acceptable and this figure has been used as a basis of comparison throughout the book. The need to maintain higher speeds in rough weather has led to a higher standard today with a freeboard forward of about $1.3\sqrt{L}$(ft).

A Second World War ship, 200ft long, meeting the criterion above would be able to make nearly 20kts in 10ft waves and 10kts in 20ft waves. An early destroyer would only be able to reach 10kts in 10ft waves and steerage way, if that, in 20ft waves.

Early destroyers

The early destroyers had a very low freeboard ($c0.5\sqrt{L}$(ft)) which made them very wet and impossible to drive into head seas. The main reason for the low freeboard was to make them more difficult to see, particularly at night, but the reduction in weight helped them to reach the very high trial speeds, in calm water, called for in the contracts. Even as late as the Second World War reduction in silhouette was seen as desirable in destroyers.

These early destroyers were given a 'turtledeck' forecastle on the argument that since water was bound to come on the deck, the turtledeck would throw it off quickly. Baker used the same argument in his very successful Canadian *St Laurent* class after the Second World War but it was not repeated in later classes. A turtledeck is very expensive to build, it is difficult to use the space inside and effectively reduces the freeboard at the side. One or two of the early *Tribal* class were rebuilt with conventional forecastles.

The River class of 1901-03 programmes had a conventional forecastle and more or less met the $1.1\sqrt{L}$(ft) criterion. They were able to maintain speed in head seas to a far greater extent than the earlier boats with a trial speed some 5kts greater.

Bow shape

The shape of the bow can affect the amount of water coming on deck but this is very much a second order effect. The most important feature is rake of the stem and none of the ships described in this volume had any significant rake – indeed the battleships mainly had negative rake to their ram. Flare can help but it is easy to overdo it. Again, ships of this era had far less flare than most modern designers would incorporate.[2]

1. I would see 12ft as the absolute minimum height if I were forced to such an arrangement today though there are reports that 15ft on *Terrible* was insufficient.

2. Flare and the related topics of knuckles and spray deflectors are topics which will cause heated arguments among naval architects today – heated because evidence is scanty and somewhat contradictory. The author's views are visible in the extreme flare and knuckle of today's 'Castle' class OPV – though I probably overdid it slightly.

Appendix 8
Subdivision and Bulkheads in Merchant Ships

The early iron-hulled merchant steamships were generally small; they had a collision bulkhead and another at the stern to hold any leakage from the stern gland.[1] In addition, by Act of Parliament, they had a bulkhead fore and aft of the machinery space. These latter bulkheads effectively divided the ship into three equal parts which was not an unreasonable subdivision of small ships.[2] As iron ships developed and their length increased, while at the same time improved machinery led to shorter engine-rooms, such an arrangement of bulkheads became unsafe with two holds, each about twice the length of the machinery space.

The Merchant Shipping Act gave Board of Trade surveyors an ill-defined authority to require additional watertight bulkheads to be fitted but this section was repealed in 1862 since it was believed that industry could set its own standards. The better ship owners did set their own standards as high or higher than those laid down by the government and resented what they saw as interference. Alfred Holt, in his classic paper of 1877,[3] suggests, in a lengthy diatribe, 'Any interference is justifiable which provides for safety.' Holt, and other good owners, failed to realise how bad were the standards of others.

The losses of merchant ships were horrifying and one of the first actions of the newly formed Institution of Naval Architects (INA) on it formation in 1860 was to direct its Council to consider the requirement for the safety of merchant ships. They recommended that passenger ships, at least, should float with two compartments flooded and all ships with one compartment flooded; recommendations which were finally implemented in 1990.

In 1870, Rundell of the Liverpool Underwriter's Association addressed the INA on the various rules of thumb used to evaluate safe freeboard. His Association used 3in freeboard per foot depth of hold, the INA had suggested 1/8th beam whilst another used that equivalent to a reserve of buoyancy of 30 per cent of the displacement. Surprisingly, in the light of the Council report discussed above, there was strong opposition to any rule for freeboard. Naval architects, shipbuilders and shipowners each thought this was a matter for them alone, on an individual basis.

In 1875, the Admiralty reviewed the use of merchant ships as auxiliary cruisers. The Admiralty list of suitable vessels comprised ships which would float if one compartment were flooded. In 1875 there were only 30 British ships which met even this minimum, one-compartment standard and 4000 ships of 100 tons and over which failed – any hole between the collision bulkhead and the stern gland would sink them. Dunn[4] shows that there was a real difference in safety between those on the Admiralty list and the others. In the 6 years up to 1882 there was a 1 in 86 chance of a ship on the list being

lost from all causes in each year whilst the rate for those not listed was 1 in 25. Dunn's paper did not get the usual hostile reception, indeed William Denny said 'The Admiralty and especially Mr Barnaby may claim for themselves that in the watertight subdivision of hulls they have revolutionised the merchant service.'

What is a bulkhead?

Many of the bulkheads fitted in ships were of little value; indeed, Dunn shows examples of bulkheads which were worse than useless, accelerating the sinking of a damaged ship. The main failing was to stop the bulkhead at a deck close to the undamaged waterline so that the sinkage caused by flooding a single compartment would immerse the top of the bulkhead, allowing water to flow into the adjoining space.

Some bulkheads which were adequate in extent were simply not strong enough. The bulkhead should withstand the static pressure of water on one side up to the maximum height which flooding can reach without the ship sinking. It is very difficult to test a completed bulkhead, installed in the ship, under such loads and there were too many failures even as late as the Second World War. Gradually, classification societies such as Lloyd's and later the British Corporation set out rules for bulkhead construction which much reduced the number of failures. Corrosion at the bottom of the bulkhead, to which access was difficult, accentuated structural problems whilst distortion of the shell in collision or grounding could cause failure of the boundary.

Samuel Plimsoll

Losses of merchant ships in the middle years of the century were frequent and the cause of concern to many people; designers, owners and those representing the developing social conscience of the country. In 1866 James Hall, a northern shipowner, began to press for laws on design and operation to improve the safety of merchant ships, an idea picked up by Samuel Plimsoll, MP for Derby. The agitation for reform became very bitter as responsible owners were tarred with the same brush as the irresponsible owners of overloaded coffin ships. Some of the proposals put forward were impractical and others valueless.

Eventually, a Royal Commission on Unseaworthy Ships was set up which reported in 1874 and, the following year, a Merchant Shipping Act was passed, based on their recommendations. This required each ship to have a mark – the Plimsoll Mark – on the side showing the maximum draught to which it could safely be loaded. In 1875 there was no agreed, straightforward way of carrying out flooding calculations and the original Act left it

1. D K Brown, 'The Development of Subdivision in Merchant Ships', RINA Symposium on Watertight Integrity, London 1996.

2. J Dunn, 'Bulkheads', *Trans INA* (London 1883).

3. A Holt, Review of the Progress of Steam Shipping during the last Quarter-Century', *TICE* (London 1877).

4. J Dunn, 'Bulkheads'.

to the owner to decide where this mark should be placed.

By 1882, Lloyd's Register had established rules for estimating permissible freeboard and within a year some 2000 ships had been certified on a voluntary basis. With experience, Lloyd's modified their rules reaching a definitive form in 1885. A Board of Trade Load Line Committee considered these rules which formed the basis for legislation in 1890 by which ships had to have a load line assigned by one of a small number of classification societies or to satisfy the Board of Trade that they had attained a similar standard. In the 21 months 1881-83 there were lost, from various causes, 120 iron steamships. Not one of these could survive the flooding of a single compartment.

In 1887 a Select Committee was set up under the chairmanship of Lord Charles Beresford to enquire into existing legislation on lifesaving boats and gear on merchant ships. It was a strong committee containing many shipowners and made two main recommendations. The first was that an advisory committee be set up to frame new rules for lifesaving gear and, secondly – clearly outside their terms of reference – that the spacing of bulkheads is vital to lifesaving and that the efficiency of lifesaving gear depended on subdivision.

The advisory committee was set up under Sir Thomas Ismay of the White Star Line with other shipowners. Their report, in 1889, recommended a very large increase in the provision of boats etc and, despite opposition, their recommendations became law in 1890. It is ironic that the weakness in these new rules became apparent with the loss of Ismay's liner *Titanic*.

Another committee was set up under Sir Edward Harland (*Titanic*'s builder!) to examine bulkhead spacing and construction. They, too, came up with much improved recommendations. Virtually all passenger ships were required to float with two compartments flooded and cargo ships were to float with one compartment flooded. They also allowed a reduction in life saving gear and boats to passenger vessels which met the full subdivision proposals, a clause which was not involved in the *Titanic* whose lifeboat capacity much exceeded the legal requirement.

Appendix 9
Costs of Naval Defence Act Ships

The Auditor General reported[1] in March 1894 on the costs of Dockyard and contract built ships of the Naval Defence Act and this report was summarised and reviewed by Elgar, late Director of Dockyards.[2] Elgar's paper forms the best attempt to compare Dockyard and commercial costs and was made possible by White's reform of the accounting system.

Summary of costs

Costs are given in the tables in £x1000; the upper figure is the average cost for dockyard built ships, the lower for commercial build.

Even these carefully recorded and analysed figures are not easy to compare. There is a considerable scatter of the data;[3] for example, there is no reason why the cost of machinery for sheathed cruisers should be 3 per cent greater than for unsheathed. The most useful figure is the direct hull cost and it is clear that the Dockyards were significantly cheaper in building battleships as they were well equipped and experienced in building such ships. (Elgar notes that preliminary figures for the *Majestics* showed that the gap had narrowed.) Conversely, the commercial yards did better with the smaller craft. Elgar explains some apparent anomalies; such as the two Dockyard built Second Class, sheathed cruisers, one at Devonport, which was ill-equipped at the time, and one at Sheerness which had never built such a big ship before.

Elgar says that the price paid for materials differed little, if at all, between the builders. There does seem to be a trend for the machinery cost to be higher in Dockyard built ships. He says that wages were higher in the private yards but this was in proportion to productivity and there should be no significant difference in overall labour costs.

The different accounting methods make comparison with ships of an earlier era almost impossible. Elgar gives some interesting figures for the labour cost per ton of the hull (excluding armour), warning that even these are approximate (see overleaf).

Despite the scatter in the data, it is clear that there was a very significant reduction in cost per ton as time passed. The main reasons were that, in the early years, the design was not settled when building started, even the main armament might change. Linked with this, little effort was made to build ships quickly. A fixed design and quick building reduced costs. Further improvement came with the changes in Dockyard management initiated by White[4] and with improved equipment at about the same time.

It is of interest that though the cost of the hull (excluding armour) and of machinery was reducing, that of armour was increasing amounting to nearly half the hull cost in the *Royal Sovereign*. Elgar concludes with a brief discussion of incidental charges – overheads – and points out that this expenditure in the Dockyards would be incurred even if no ships were built. The intention of Parliament was that the incidental charges

1. *Report of the Comptroller and Auditor General* (Sir Charles L Ryan), 31 March 1894.

2. F Elgar, 'The Cost of Warships', *Trans INA* (London 1895).

3. Elgar records each ship individually.

4. Note that White and Elgar were not on good terms and 'The Cost of Warships' does not mention White's major contribution.

applied to Dockyard building should be equivalent to the overheads of a private yard but it was never really possible to achieve this result.

Various inquiries at the time failed to give a clear answer as to whether Dockyards were cheaper than commercial yards or vice versa but there is no doubt that the Dockyards were quicker and this is usually associated with lower cost.

Summary of costs

Type		No Ships	Hull	M/C	Guns etc[a]	Direct[b]	Total[c]
Battleships		5	593	102	86	783	844
		5	683	97	84	873	883
Cruisers, 1st Class,	Sheathed	2	232	97	35	363	397
		2	234	97	34	369	374
	Unsheathed	2	224	103	37	364	402
		3	224	95	34	356	361
Cruisers, 2nd Class,	Sheathed	2	118	60	12	190	214
		8	107	66	10	184	187
	Unsheathed	2	98	67	10	175	190
		9	97	65	10	173	175
Cruisers, 3rd Class		4	77	55	8	140	157
		5	64	46	11	123	123
Torpedo Gunboats		5	28	24	6	58	66
		5	26	20	5	52	52

(a) This column is the sum of 'guns and torpedo tubes' and the small figure for 'steam boats'.

(b) There is a small charge for Admiralty inspection added to commercial costs so this figure differs slightly from the sum of the previous columns.

(c) The total is direct charges plus Dockyard incidental charges *ie* overheads. These are large for Dockyard-built ships (battleships £61,000) and smaller for the commercial ships (£10,000).

Labour Cost per ton, Hull

Battleships	Date	£/ton	Cruisers	Date	£/ton
Ajax	1876-85	46.5	Iris	1875-79	44.2
Agamemnon	1876-85	46.2	Canada	1879-83	44.0
Edinburgh	1879-85	53.9	Warspite	1881-88	48.0
Colossus	1879-86	57.4	Mersey	1883-87	41.9
Collingwood	1880-87	49.7	Medea	1887-90	31.4
Anson	1883-89	42.8	Blanche	1888-91	38.5
Hero	1884-88	44.4	Pallas	1888-91	32.1
Trafalgar	1886-90	36.3	R Arthur	1890-93	36.7
R Sovereign	1889-92	32.0			

Review of Principal Sources

A book like this relies on many sources of varying completeness and accuracy. Here I try to give my personal assessment of the major sources. Minor documents dealing with only one topic are covered in the footnotes, where full references are given.

Oscar Parkes, *British Battleships* (London 1956)
The starting-point for any study of this period should be Parkes' great work. However, this book poses many problems. Most official documents were unavailable to the public, and although Parkes was allowed to see some (mainly Ships' Covers), his study was far from complete. Furthermore, the book is not referenced and hence it is not possible to check all his stories. Finally, his technical understanding was very limited and some parts of his book, particularly those concerning the design and loss of *Captain*, are misleading.

Parliamentary Papers
These are an invaluable source for many aspects of design history. The reports and the evidence of the great Design Committees, such as that of 1871, are to be found in full. The evidence to that Committee is most impressive: that of the serving officers is thoughtful and often the answer to a question was to the effect that 'we've tried it'. The covering paper to each year's Naval Estimates will usually describe the previous year's manoeuvres and even the lessons learnt from them. The Estimates themselves are essential factual material. However, like any official document, the content is what ministers and their officers, civilian and naval, wished to be seen by Parliament, so whilst they are usually 'the truth and nothing but the truth', they are rarely 'the whole truth'.

PRO Documents
Many of these, particularly from the White era, are invaluable but it is likely that there are many gaps. Those used are individually referenced in the footnotes. Manning's *Life of Sir William White* quotes many documents which cannot now be found and it must be concluded that White's papers were destroyed after the book was finished.

Ships' Covers
Most of those of this period are disappointing, with little background to the design and many gaps. I have inspected the vast majority of Covers from the period and only a few appear as references. Those few, however, are often very important.

Published Sources

Transactions of the Institution of Naval Architects (Trans INA)
There are many papers by warship designers of the day, and also by admirals, who joined the Institution as Associates. The obituaries are helpful on personalities. It is surprising that these papers have not been used more.

E J Reed, *Our Ironclad Ships* (London 1868)
A fine, non-technical description of ships from *Warrior* to *Monarch* and *Captain*. Although written to justify his own views and work, it is accurate and fairly impartial.

E J Reed, *Shipbuilding in Iron and Steel* (London 1868)
This is a much more technical book but very helpful in explaining why certain features were adopted. It has been used as a background source even when not specifically referenced and the diagrams are most useful.

N Barnaby, *Naval Development of the Century* (London 1904)
Written from memory long after his retirement, it is a jumble of extracts from his earlier papers with often inaccurate additions. The first chapter on ethics is amazing to modern readers.

K C Barnaby, *Some Ship Disasters and their Causes* (London 1868)
An account of famous disasters to merchant ships and naval vessels. Barnaby gives his own views, often different from those generally accepted, as to their causes and how to prevent similar tragedies in the future.

W H White, *A Manual of Naval Architecture* (1900 edition, considerably revised by W E Smith)
This is an elementary textbook written for the use of naval officers. It is, however, surprisingly readable and contains many tables giving information on stability and strength.

F Manning, *The Life of Sir William White* (London 1923)
Commissioned by Lady White after her husband's death, it draws heavily on his official papers, many of which no longer exist. It is slightly biased but not unduly so. There are some surprising gaps: for example, White's visit to *Redoutable* is hardly mentioned.

E L Attwood, *Warships, a Text-Book* (London 1910)
A clear and well-illustrated textbook on the design methods and building technology of his day. He is particularly good at explaining why things were done as they were.

G A Ballard, *The Black Battle Fleet* (London 1980)
Originally published as a series of articles in *The Mariner's Mirror*, they were republished as a book in 1980. Admiral Ballard had served in several of the ships he described and had seen many others. His descriptions of seamanship are fascinating.

J Sumida, *In Defence of Naval Supremacy* (Boston, Mass. 1989)
The first chapter gives a very clear picture of the financial background to the Naval Defence Act of 1889.

W Hovgaard, *Modern History of Warships* (London 1920, reprinted London 1971)
Very good technical descriptions of warships of all navies but weak on the reasons for decisions.

R A Burt, *British Battleships 1889-1905* (London 1989)
A careful and detailed account of the design and service lives of battleships. There are excellent diagrams of machinery and gun turrets.

R Gardiner (ed), *Conway's All the World's Fighting Ships 1860-1905* (London 1979)
Complete tabulated data on all ships of the era.

Glossary and Abbreviations

Ad Cft: Admiralty Coefficient (Appendix 3)

AEW: Admiralty Experiment Works, the ship model test tank, originally at Torquay, later Haslar

AP: armour-piercing

APC: armour-piercing, capped (shell)

BL: breech-loader

BLR: breech-loading rifle

bm: tonnage, builder's measurement

c: circa

°C: degrees Celsius

C-in-C: Commander-in-Chief

circ: Froude's circular notation

cmpd: compound engine

cu: cubic (*ie* cu rt = cube root)

Cupola: Coles' original turret design with sloping sides

Cyl: cylinder

Deg: degree

dia: diameter

disp: displacement in Imperial tons (2240lbs)

DNC: Director of Naval Construction

DNO: Director of Naval Ordinance

drt: draught

E-in-C: Engineer-in-Chief

EC: Electro contact

F: freeboard

Fr: French

ft: feet/foot

G: Centre of gravity

GM: Metacentric Height (Appendix 4)

GNP: Gross National Product

GZ: Righting lever (Appendix 4)

Harvey: Type of hardened armour

HE: high explosive

HP: high pressure

hp: horsepower

hr: hour

ihp: indicated horsepower

in: inches

INA: Institution of Naval Architects (Royal since 1960)

KC: Krupp Cemented (armour)

kt(s): knot(s)

lb(s): pound(s)

ld: laid down

LP: low pressure

min: minute

MLR: muzzle-loading rifle

mv: muzzle velocity

nm: nautical mile (knot)

no.: number

oa: overall

Palliser: chilled iron shot or shell

pdr(s): pounder(s) – weight of shot from gun

pp: between perpendiculars (length)

QF: quick-firing gun, *ie* firing ammunition where shell and propellant are combined

RCNC: Royal Corps of Naval Construction (formed 1883)

rev: revolution

rpm: revolutions per minute

RMA: Royal Marine Artillery

RML: Rifled muzzle-loader

RN: Royal Navy

RNEC: ?

rpg: rounds per gun

rt: root

SB: smoothbore

SBC: Slow Burning Cocoa (gunpowder)

sq: square (as in square root)

T: Draught

T Exp: Triple-expansion engine

TB: Torpedo Boat

TBD: Torpedo Boat Destroyer

Ton: Size of gun in tons weight of barrel excluding carriage etc, *ie* 80-ton gun

TT: torpedo tubes

USN: United States Navy

wl: waterline (length)

wt: weight

yds: yards

Abbreviations used in footnotes

Inst CE: Institute of Civil Engineers

Proc ICE: Proceedings of the Institute of Civil Engineers

JNE: Journal of Naval Engineering

Trans (R)INA: Transactions of the (Royal) Institution of Naval Architects

Index